TRADITION AND TRANSITION
IN EAST AFRICA

Contributors:

P. H. GULLIVER

W. J. ARGYLE

GEORGE BENNETT

TOM J. MBOYA

W. H. WHITELEY

EUGENE COTRAN

J. W. TYLER

J. S. LA FONTAINE

MICHAEL TWADDLE

KATHLEEN M. STAHL

KIRSTEN ALNAES

DAVID J. PARKIN

R. D. GRILLO

H. F. MORRIS

I. M. LEWIS

TRADITION AND TRANSITION IN EAST AFRICA

*Studies of the Tribal Element
in the Modern Era*

Edited by
P. H. Gulliver

UNIVERSITY OF CALIFORNIA PRESS
Berkeley and Los Angeles
1969

Published 1969
in the United States by
University of California Press
Berkeley and Los Angeles
California

© *P. H. Gulliver 1969*

Library of Congress Catalog Card No. 78-84787

Printed in Great Britain

CONTENTS

CONTENTS

EDITORIAL PREFACE

THE idea of this symposium was originally developed in the inter-departmental African Seminar held during the academic year 1966–7 at the School of Oriental and African Studies, University of London. That Seminar was attended by staff and postgraduate students from the School and from other colleges in the University. In this volume are included redrafted versions of some of the papers given to the Seminar; and to these have been added a number of others which widen the scope of treatment of the general topic. It is no longer useful to distinguish between these, however.

This symposium is not intended to be, and could not be, an exhaustive and definitive treatment of the nature and problems of the tribal factor in East Africa and of the interplay of factors and forces, institutions and values, interests and emotions, realities and phantasy, deriving from 'tradition' and from the continued 'transition' involved in modernization. Such exhaustive treatment is not possible. It would require consideration of virtually every aspect of human activity in a highly variegated region of Africa; and in any case there are large areas and important topics on which reliable information and understanding are still unavailable. Moreover, we are not dealing with a period in history, over and done with, but with the recent past flowing into the present and on into the future. Instead, therefore, we have sought to examine some of the more important aspects and themes, and to illustrate the general discussion with particular, selected examples.

The symposium is therefore broadly divided into two main parts. In the first of these, contributors examine the significance of the tribal factor in certain general contexts and discuss some of the particular backgrounds to contemporary transition in East Africa. This part contains essays on politics, economic

I

development, language, law and education, together with a comparative look at European nationalism. In the second part, contributors consider the grass-roots basis and development of the concept of tribe and its operation in social life in certain rural areas. The significance of the tribal factor in modern urban life is examined separately, as are the two special cases of Somalia and Buganda. There is also an account of one of the few instances of open, violent conflict between tribes—the revolt of the Konzo against the Toro in western Uganda.

Both in the original seminar and in their present essays the contributors have been free to organize their accounts and express their views as they thought best. I have not sought to restrict them editorially nor to obtain conformity of viewpoint, nor to prevent a modest degree of overlap. We are dealing with what must necessarily be a broadly defined topic—of great importance nevertheless—and approaches over the same ground have operated at different levels. The contributors are specialists in the disciplines of anthropology, history, law, linguistics, and sociology, and one is an active politician. It is hoped that their differing experience and expertise will provide a range both of factual information and analysis and interpretation.

I make no apology for our continued use of the word 'tribe', although we are all aware that it has become unpopular in some ways, and perhaps especially in the discourse between Africans and Europeans in the public arena. We do not continue to use it in any spirit of defiance, let alone of derogation and disparagement. We use it simply because it continues to be widely used in East Africa itself when English is spoken (and sometimes when it is not) among the citizens of the countries there. I note that statesmen and politicians, administrators and officials, university students and their teachers, clerks and artisans, farmers and shopkeepers, all use the word. I note also that a euphemism such as 'ethnic group' is scarcely used at all (except by visiting intellectuals), whilst other substitutes, such as 'people', 'cultural group, 'community', and so on, are neither common nor necessarily helpful to profitable communication. I do not think that we should avoid discussion of a most important feature of the contemporary scene; and I do not think that we should avoid the word itself, for that would seem to be an aspersion on the readiness and ability of East Africans to examine their own problems. We are concerned with the contextual meanings attached to 'tribe', and with using the term as a tool of analysis. Our 'spade' may, it is true, sometimes be a 'bloody shovel'; but does it really help to call it an 'agricultural implement'? I think not; and I hope that our actual treatment of the whole subject will absolve us from any suggestion that we perpetuate the use of the word 'tribe' in a pejorative sense. All the contributors to this volume are experienced in East Africa and have considerable personal involvements there.

The concentration in this symposium on 'the tribal factor' in no way implies that it is necessarily the most important problem confronting East Africans in the contemporary world. The ongoing transition to modernization raises all kinds of difficulties and affords all kinds of opportunities. Nevertheless it is abundantly clear from the repeated references in the speeches and writings of East African leaders that the building of unity and the dangers of disunity are major preoccupations. Another persistent problem, similarly demonstrated, is that of introducing innovations and persuading people to accept and utilize them, whilst retaining the value of 'tradition' where that is desirable. And there is the vital matter of individual, local, and national identity in a changing world. In these matters and others the ideas and the facts of 'tribe' are quite crucial, along with other ideas and facts.

P. H. Gulliver
S.O.A.S.

INTRODUCTION*

P. H. Gulliver

THE East African countries share with the rest of tropical Africa, and other under-developed regions of the world, those much-discussed evils and limitations which have been summarized as poverty, ignorance, and disease. Along with these, and all they imply in the contemporary era of political independence and of efforts towards modernization, there are two other crucial problems in each East African country—the problems of unity and of identity. And these problems exist irrespective of the particular form and character of the political and economic systems of these countries. A critical factor at the core of these two problems is that of 'tribe'. To some extent this factor represents real divisions of the people on the ground; to some extent it is a mental concept, strongly coloured by emotion, made use of to 'explain' or to justify divisions which have their sources elsewhere. It has some basis in traditional and persisting cultural differences, and it has been given new forms and had attached to it new interests and loyalties. 'Tribe' means many things to many individuals—not the same thing to everyone, nor even the same thing to particular persons or groups at different times. It is sometimes denied to exist at all; and it is often used as a facile explanation of enormously complex social, political, and economic crises.

In the past, and still sometimes in the late 1960s, there has been a tendency on the part of African leaders to deny or ignore the existence of tribes within their own countries, or at least to minimize their importance and persistence. Tribes were often

---

* In this Introduction, citations of authors without reference date (e.g. Smith; but not Smith, 1968) refer to the essays of those authors in this present symposium.

5

discussed as a pernicious product of colonialism, and one that would disappear or be reduced to readily manageable proportions with the full achievement of freedom and political independence. The whole matter was exacerbated for many educated Africans by the assumption that the very concept of 'tribe' connoted primitiveness and backwardness both in their own minds and in the ideas and attitudes of the Western world. There was resentment that the term, with such implications, should be used; and, of course, it was and sometimes still is used in that pejorative sense by Westerners unsympathetic to African aspirations and abilities, or merely in thoughtless ignorance.

Later, with the harsh, practical realities of power and responsibility, but also with growing self-confidence among the leaders, there has come to be a fairly general and open recognition both of the persistence of tribes and of their critical role in the processes of nation-building, stabilization, and economic development. Thus, for example, in a speech in 1964 President Nyerere could say: 'The conflicts resulting from contact between members of different tribes have not completely stopped, but the sovereign authority which had previously been transferred from the individual to the tribal unit has now been transferred to the larger group—the nation' (Nyerere, 1967, p. 270). In his book published in 1963, Tom Mboya discussed what he called the 'positive' and 'negative' contributions of tribalism in Kenya with some frankness (Mboya, 1963, p. 67ff.).

Nevertheless, this subject of 'tribe' remains a highly sensitive one to all African leaders, apprehensive that the violence of the Congo or Nigeria might erupt in their own countries. There remains a disinclination to discuss it thoroughly in public and a tendency to sweep it under the carpet. There are endless references in speeches and writings to the paramount need for national unity, couched in general terms but with rather little examination of the facts fostering disunity. This is entirely understandable in the political arena. Yet clearly, at an objective level, a principal threat to the unity of the modern nation-state is the existence and strength of the tribes, of tribal particularism, loyalties and alignments, and of discrimination on the basis of tribe. I must add, however, that tribes and tribalism are not wholly and irreconcilably detrimental to national

6

unity and stability, nor are they the only threat to success.

The question of the meanings consciously and unconsciously attached to the term 'tribe' and its derivatives is a complex one, and can only briefly be considered here. 'Tribe' has long been used in English, with specific reference to the biblical people of Israel and to certain divisions of ancient Rome (Latin: *tribus*); but since its appearance in Middle English it has acquired both the vagueness of everyday speech and a plurality of meanings which often are contradictory, dogmatic, pejorative and emotive, and both specialized and general. Its widening usage in Africa, concomitant with the European invasion and colonization, added to its meanings and implications. The difficulties are not made easier by the tendency for dogmatic assertions to be made as to what a tribe 'really is', or by ill-considered assumptions and subjective discriminations. For example, one seminar participant denied that a certain African group is a tribe, and asserted it to be 'a people'. This was elucidated to refer to the contemporary modernization of the group which had 'outgrown traditional loyalties and assumed new ones'. But no satisfactory determination could be attained as to the degree of modernization required before the tribe becomes a people. Another person will allow 'tribe' to be applied to small groups but not to the larger ones, or to those traditionally without centralized government but not to those with it. The diversity of usage continues and misunderstandings occur. Yet the term continues to be used in informal conversation, historical research, political debate, philosophical discussion, and almost everywhere. Furthermore, it is used extensively by East Africans when speaking English, and even as an adopted term in some African languages. It is impossible to ignore the word and almost impossible not to use it.

Partly because of the lack of an agreed definition, partly because of certain derogatory implications attached to it in some contexts by some people (i.e. primitive, uncivilized, conservative, inferior), and partly because in contemporary conditions certain new elements, ascriptions and alignments have become attached to it, there have been strong and well-intended demands to replace the term by some other word. Instead of 'tribe' we might use 'people', 'cultural group',

7

'community', etc. These alternatives are even more vague and more confusing. The sociological alternative is 'ethnic group', with its convenient 'ethnic' and 'ethnicity'. Unfortunately perhaps, this usage seems to be largely confined to intellectuals—mainly non-African ones too, and sometimes with an almost desperate air of self-righteousness in refusing to use the allegedly out-of-date and pejorative term, 'tribe'. Yet the advocates of this newer term mean, and refer to, precisely the same set of confused facts and elastically defined units of people as are encompassed by the older word. Moreover, this usage of a newer, seemingly scientific term wrongly suggests that the whole complex problem has somehow already been cleared up. But of course it has not been cleared up at all. Admittedly, there may be some value in avoiding some of the unfortunate associations of 'tribe', etc., by taking up the euphemism. Nevertheless I prefer to use the older term: partly because it is still the term used by East Africans themselves,[1] but also because it may be valuable to eschew the somewhat spurious scientific certitude carried by the term 'ethnic'.

More important, it is essential that we fully recognize the varied meanings and implications attached to the term 'tribe' and its derivatives, and that we bear constantly in mind that the units of people designated by it (or by 'ethnic group') vary over time and, according to context, even in the same era. This will help us towards an understanding of the social situations and processes that are involved. Whatever term we may use, it is but a tool to the elucidation of these situations and processes in the actualities of East Africa.

The nineteenth-century explorers, missionaries, military officers, and early administrators used 'tribe' in a general way to apply to such separate groups of people as they considered they found identified by name, culture, and, where relevant, political autonomy.[2] Thereafter, anthropologists, the first serious scholars to concern themselves with Africa and Africans, used the term in no less general a way to indicate the major cultural units, and being much influenced in this by colonial stereotypes. Gradually, however, some social anthropologists narrowed down the application of the term and gave it, somewhat arbitrarily, a specifically political connotation. Evans-Pritchard was the influential figure in this. For him, the tribe

8

is the largest group of people 'who, besides recognizing themselves as a distinct local community, affirm their obligations to
combine in warfare against outsiders and acknowledge the
rights of their members to compensation for injuries' (Evans-
Pritchard, 1940, p. 5). That is, morally at least, the rule of
law holds within the tribe, and resort to warfare beyond
it.[3]

Not all anthropologists accepted this kind of definition. For
many it referred too much to reconstructions of the pre-colonial
past and had little or no applicability to contemporary conditions in Africa. For many the term could be left deliberately
vague whilst research and analysis concentrated on particular
social systems (a village or a sub-chiefdom, say, or the structure
of economic organization or of religious beliefs, etc.). Nadel
suggested a 'tautological definition . . . a tribe or people is a
group the members of which claim unity on the grounds of
their conception of a specific common culture' (Nadel, 1942, p.
17). That is, the emphasis is put on what the people themselves
think, or perhaps feel; though there is also the element of objective criterion in the 'common culture'. This kind of definition
refers to 'traditional' patterns of culture and forms of social
organization, and tends to be associated with both conservatism
and the rural areas. Certainly, whatever kind of definition is
employed, the concept of 'tribe' must have some reference to
tradition, to the pre-colonial past, as that has persisted in
some degree and with whatever transformations into the
present.

One anthropological definition of 'tribe' (deriving from L. H.
Morgan and H. S. Maine), current in the later nineteenth
century, asserted that it was a group of people held together
and given a social structure through their kinship relationships
with one another (and the absence of kinship links with outsiders). Often this was taken to the point of assuming that the
people were all descended necessarily from a common ancestor,
so that the tribe was an expanded form of the family. Coupled
with this was the idea that the tribe represented an early stage
in the lineal evolution of human societies, coming later in the
scale than small bands but preceding the development of
peasant and modern societies, and coming before the growth
of the nation. Such intellectual inventions might be dismissed

out of hand in the second half of the twentieth century, but they have an unfortunate habit of persisting and further complicating an understanding of the contemporary world. Some Marxist theorists still openly hold to this sort of theory,[4] but so do some others also. One modern social anthropologist at least seeks to limit 'tribe' to 'people both tracing common descent and socially organized on bases of descent and age' (Lloyd, 1967, p. 27). Such a definition would, if applied to East Africa, effectively rule out virtually all of the units of people to whom the term 'tribe' is conventionally applied. It would also make the term apply to kin-groups which, presumably, have a residential basis (e.g. a localized lineage, as among the Luo, Lugbara, or Gusii). The genealogical link, and rights and obligations, co-operation and loyalties, based on kinship beyond the immediate family, are most usually of great importance among East Africans—and the particular pattern of these are a significant part of a people's culture. Nevertheless, kin-groups and categories are not only parts of larger wholes, but they are themselves often intermingled with each other and are, therefore, distinctive in only certain kinds of social activity.

Another anthropological definition of a similar kind is put forward by Gluckman, who seeks to distinguish 'tribe' as a particular kind of unit by socio-economic criteria. In this formulation a 'tribal society' is one in which there are very simple tools and a consequent low level of production and consumption. It is a society with basically an egalitarian standard of living, without significant socio-economic classes; and it is a society dominated by kinship statuses and by relationships of a markedly multiplex type (Gluckman, 1965, p. 4ff.). This is a restricted kind of definition of a specialized technical character which excludes not merely almost all contemporary groups but also many pre-colonial ones. It seems reasonable and useful, sociologically, to distinguish this kind of society, but less justified to monopolize the term 'tribe' for it.

The parade of suggested definitions could be extended further, but with diminishing returns. Before seeking to provide some general definition it may be useful, however, to consider first some further features of relevance.

We may note the interesting fact that the common derivatives of 'tribe' have to some extent acquired their own distinctive overtones of meaning. However 'tribe' is used by a particular person in a particular context, and with attempt at precision or with conscious or unconscious vagueness, it tends, in East Africa, to be more or less neutral emotionally. It refers to certain more or less accepted divisions of a country's population. Only in connection with the implied contrast with the Western world does it carry the overtone of 'primitive', etc. 'Tribal', however, carries the clearer imputation of reference to tradition, and hence to conservatism. This is not inevitably the case, but it is quite commonly so.

'Tribalism' tends to be more evocative, carrying with it both the reference to tradition and the element of contemporary divisiveness, unscrupulous partisanship, and lack of modernity. To belong to a tribe is a fact of life, but to engage in tribalism is reprehensible in others and to be denied in oneself. Grillo brings out this point in his study of conflict in a modern trade union: he shows how members of each faction accused members of the opposing faction of engaging in tribalism to gain their ends, whilst protesting their own innocence of such pernicious tactics. It is an ideological weapon to be used in political conflict and economic competition. Parkin, writing on the current urban situation, suggests that tribalism, both in name and in effect, is used also as a 'blame-pinning device' · it is other people's tribalism which is partly responsible for one's own difficulties, perplexities, and failures. This point was well illustrated in a debate in the Kenya National Assembly in April 1968. Opposition (K.P.U.) members accused the Government of tribalism, by which they seem to have meant 'tribal imbalances' in the allocation of posts and privileges in the government service and commerce. Three ministers denied the charge; but neither they nor any of their supporters attempted to deny the existence of tribes as such. This was not a matter in dispute, for both sides took their existence for granted. Tribalism, however, was agreed by all sides to be iniquitous, and each side accused the other of practising and supporting it.[5]

A 'tribalist' is, if anything, even more condemnatory. The implication is that such a person does not merely use tribal particularism for certain purposes, but that he is devoted to such particularism against the wider, more approved, aims of unity, modernization, and justice.

These overtones of meaning are, of course, somewhat variable. But they illustrate the emotional concomitants of the concept in the contemporary reality, and the variations of meaning and evaluation according to context. This, then, is an important aspect of the tribal factor in East Africa which must be held in mind.

Some writers have sought to separate two elements inherent in the concept of tribe. On the one hand, there is the commitment to traditional culture—'the persistence of, or continued attachment to, tribal custom' (Epstein, 1958, p. 231). This is a conservative, backward-looking element. On the other hand there are loyalties and identification with particularist groups within the wider framework of the modern state[6]—an element born of the new nation-states, urbanization, and industrialization. Although analytically this distinction is justifiable and helpful, the degree of separation of these two elements must be limited, for they do not represent two distinct modes of thought, feeling, and action. They are too intimately interconnected. As many writers have shown, tribal loyalties and identification are closely linked with appeals, both emotional and practical, to traditional culture even where the concrete basis for tribalism, for inter-tribal conflict or allegations of unfair partisanship, is firmly established in contemporary competition for power and economic advantage. From the outside, tribalism may appear to be either conservative adherence to tradition, or the loyalties and identification of people engaged in conflict. Yet people do not simply adhere to tradition in a vacuum, but only in the contemporary context of the struggle for interests and rights and privileges, and in defence of those they already have.

It is, of course, quite false to assume that traditional cultures and traditional groupings of people on the basis of them were clearly determinate and stable in pre-colonial times. It is true that some names of tribes have been reported by travellers over a long period—Nyamwezi is a notable example; and other names have long existed in connection with a kingdom, such as Buganda. But this is no reason for assuming that the land area, or the group of people and their direct descendants, or the culture and social organization, have been more or less unchanging over that period. We know that there was a great deal of movement in past centuries, causing earlier groups to split up or formerly disparate groups to coalesce. In Tanzania, for example, large numbers of twentieth-century tribes were formed and added to by people (individuals, families, larger groups) moving into new areas from surrounding ones (e.g. Arusha, Chagga, Gogo, Ngoni, *et al.*). We know a little, and can logically assume a great deal more, of the changes in membership, institutions, and values in East African societies as the result of movements of people, changes in population density, the introduction of innovations, the fortunes of war and of climate, internal evolution, etc. Anthropologists have too often sought to describe *the* traditional system of a tribe, or to eliminate twentieth-century innovations from their analyses; and they have therefore tended in effect to give support to facile lay views which conceive of immutable patterns of culture and of tribal alignments that 'have not changed for generations'. Whereas in reality there must have been great fluidity throughout East Africa as far back as we can see.

It has often been said that the early colonial authorities froze the pattern of tribal groups as they found it at the time of imposing their alien government, and without appreciation that the particular pattern was merely the one that happened to exist at the arbitrary time of colonization. As a first approximation this is a fair statement perhaps; but it becomes increasingly inadequate as account is taken of all the factors involved. It is true that colonial governments, for their own convenience, rigidified and over-simplified the situation; but at the same time they necessarily introduced new elements into it—chiefly, their own imposition of overarching authority. Thus they were able to stimulate tribal identity and distinctiveness by coupling tribe with administrative area and with so-called native authorities; quite often the name of an administrative area, even of the 'boma' or town, was tribal. Tax books and receipts, forms of all kinds, court records, labour rolls, and similar bureaucratic instruments, demanded specific tribal identification by Africans. Tribal councils, courts, treasuries, and the like were commonly introduced. In addition, in the colonial era linguists, anthropologists, and historians (whether professionals or local missionaries and administrators) recorded and published tribe-oriented accounts; whilst certain traits, artefacts, dances, stereotyped expectations, and characterizations, were given prominence by Europeans. It is well known how some missionaries and administrators became fervent admirers and protagonists of particular tribes. Tribal history began to be taught in schools, some of the schools at least being effectively monotribal and providing a new symbol for the tribe. Not all of these factors occurred together everywhere in East Africa, but no local area was free of some of them.

Much of this was put into practice with the best of intentions, to foster and use local loyalties and institutions for administrative and development purposes. There was very often a genuine desire to preserve and encourage African tribal cultures—when it was not too inconvenient or repugnant to do so—even if this was more or less motivated by paternalistic romanticism or downright assumptions of African inferiority. It was often considered to be more convenient, and cheaper, to use tribal territories and tribal authorities, even sometimes where greater efficiency was seen to be possible by radical changes. A personal experience may illustrate this. On one occasion in Tanganyika, in company with the local District Commissioner and his District Officer, I watched the formal procession of a chief and his subordinates (all hereditary office-holders) *en route* to a meeting. It was a small, poorly dressed line of men who were notable for conservatism and inefficiency as 'The Native Authority'. The young D.O. laughingly commented on what seemed to him a pathetic display of outworn authority, but he was sharply reprimanded by his D.C. on the grounds that respect should be shown to this piece of indigenous culture. The D.O. deferred to this, learned his lesson, and thereafter supported the chiefly institutions. Yet in fact the people of the chiefdom were resentful of the chief's inefficiency and extortions and would most probably have supported removal or limitation of his authority in favour of a more enlightened local administration on lines they knew were operative in another area of the same District. The D.C. too favoured that kind of change, but at least one major reason for his continued support of the existing chiefly system was its indigenous, traditional character. And this was only partly his political rationalization.

Critics have often accused the colonial governments of a deliberate policy of 'divide and rule', and of suppressing wider African loyalties and individual and group development. That this was commonly the effect of colonial rule is evident, but there is limited evidence to demonstrate that such policy was deliberately thought out and put into practice. The process was more subtle and complex than that. But probably most administrators, of both high and low rank, merely took it for granted that the tribe was a readily identifiable, time-honoured unit, indigenous to African perceptions and activities. They were not absolutely wrong in this assumption, though the situation was far less simple than they thought. Certainly they gradually made the divisions between tribe and tribe more rigid, more distinctive, and more associated with vested interests, rights and privileges. As much by unconsidered reaction as by positive policy, this emphasis on tribe was strengthened in the later opposition of colonial officials to growing nationalism. Thus these officials so often supported federalism rather than centralism in the last years of their era, and in the formulation of independence constitutions.

Nevertheless, colonial régimes did not in fact altogether preserve the indigenous cultural units. This they could scarcely have accomplished where such units were vague, even in some areas almost unrecognizable. Nor did they wish to do so where it was highly inconvenient for their own purposes. New tribes were sometimes created, though typically where there was already some degree of cultural connection. These were given new forms of integration, new symbols, and new interests to defend and propagate: for example, the Teso in Uganda, the Pare, Nyakyusa and Nyasa in Tanganyika. Further amalgamations were encouraged as the result of administrative action: creating original unity among previously divided, acephalous societies such as the Gisu (see La Fontaine) or the Lugbara of Uganda. Missionaries often stimulated this kind of process in their desires and efforts to establish standard languages from out of a number of related dialects, as among the Luhya of western Kenya. Reaction against the colonial power and common defence against it, and against other new threats (e.g. European settlement, or the growth of pressures from neighbouring African people) also encouraged and sustained new tribal consciousness and alignment. The Kikuyu, never united before, fairly quickly developed a growing sense and reality of unity, as Bennett points out. The creation of the Luhya tribe was partly a common reaction among the constituent groups against Luo and Nandi to south and south-east, and European farmers to the east and north-east. The Gisu found common cause against the Ganda. New interests and new activities developed which made new and larger unities possible, valuable, and even essential. Africans were able to manipulate their colonial overlords to gain and consolidate these new ends: the case of the Chagga is an excellent example of this. Moreover, the development of these new interests and activities, particularly of an economic kind, and the rights and privileges involved, have served to deepen the divisions within the tribal framework. These interests have very often become vested in the tribal divisions, rather than cutting across and weakening them. Land rights in particular became jealously defended as the better land became scarcer under population pressure, as the demand grew for more land for new agricultural enterprise, and as land became more productively valuable under cash crops. Land rights, so vital to a predominantly rural, agricultural population, became very strongly tribalized as the result of the general process of the emphasis on tribal distinctiveness.

Thus, for the kinds of reasons briefly mentioned, the net effect of the colonial era was a marked heightening of tribal consciousness and a deepening of tribal differences. The distribution of power and of economic interests and opportunities was closely tied to this enhanced tribalism, and both new and old symbols gave powerful support and rationalization. One may say this despite certain trends in the opposite direction. To a large extent, the common opposition to and struggle with the colonial governments, and the preferential position of Europeans, produced a pan-tribal or in part a non-tribal nationalism. But this was not altogether the case, for nationalist movements and independent national governments have been motivated by tribal interests and affected by tribal divisiveness. How could it have been otherwise, in the short run at least? Indeed, it has been suggested with a good deal of truth that the very creation of the independent states has stimulated divisive particularism, because 'it introduces into society a valuable new prize over which to fight and a frightening new force with which to contend. The doctrine of the nationalist propagandists notwithstanding . . . [particularism is, in its] political dimensions, not

16

so much the heritage of colonial divide-and-rule policies as . . . [the] products of the replacement of a colonial régime' (Geertz, 1963, pp. 120–1). The valuable new prize is, of course, political power and the uses that can be made of it. Nevertheless, the actual particularist units of conflict and competition—tribes, in one form or another—derive from tradition, transformed during the colonial era, and vested with interests and privileges to defend and to develop.

An extreme view has been expressed by Colson. 'The African tribal groupings are not survivals from the pre-colonial political world, though they may seek to acquire legitimacy through a myth of ancient unity. . . . They are not grassroots movements springing from the genius of a people. . . . They are largely the conscious creations of intellectuals and other active leaders who have had the greatest opportunity to participate in the larger political and social world' (Colson, 1968, pp. 202–3). This seems to overstate the case, for although the active leaders have certainly encouraged tribal distinctiveness for their own purposes, they have done this for the concomitant purposes (however ill-defined) of the members of their tribal groups and with their willing support. Nor have the leaders 'created' the tribes: rather they have made use of them and, for the most part, developed what is for themselves the political and economic advantages of the tribe. It has frequently been remarked that African politicians necessarily require a firm base for their operations in the still unstable, inchoate national arena. What better, in the short run, to ensure support, electoral and other, and to wield a powerful political weapon, than to stand as the representative and spokesman of the tribe—looking to its interests and benefiting from its emotive symbols? As Bennett points out, this development is more marked in Kenya than in Tanzania. In Kenya one large tribe tended to dominate the anti-colonial movement, the successful nationalist party, and consequently the direction of government; but its influence is opposed (logically, one might say) by the two or three other large tribes who have major interests and major claims, and are strong enough to engage in effective competition. On the other hand, in Tanzania there are very few large tribes, none dominating the centre of political action, and none able to afford powerful strength to its spokesmen in the national arena.

Economic developments, which might seem superficially to be producing modern farmers with common interests and problems, tend rather to exacerbate divisiveness through competition for the allocation of resources, for land, over marketing and price policies, etc. An illustration of this relates to the allocation of former European lands in Kenya. 'Given the tendency of major tribes or groups of tribes to regard certain areas as their zone of influence or settlement, it has proved impossible to use European farm land solely for the relief of the most overpopulated areas. For example, Kikuyu [and Kamba] could not be settled on farms in the Rift Valley region' (de Wilde, 1967, p. 189). Similarly, competition for jobs in towns is at least coloured, and also rationalized, by tribal divisions and by tribal nepotism—though the situation is, as Parkin shows, more complex than that. It might be suggested that less rapid economic development and the lower potential for it in Tanzania has tended therefore to be a factor in limiting tribalism there in political life.

A common, Western-type, expanding educational system has often been considered to be a prime antidote for tribalism: partly in the dissemination of new ideas and values, but more importantly perhaps in bringing common ideas and values, a common language (or at least a lingua franca), and a common experience in the formative years of individuals. Tyler examines this question, but it is a fair summary to say that the evidence is inconclusive at the moment. Unfortunately for the idealist and the true nationalist, education can and does stimulate tribalism. Argyle quotes Dr Dike, who described the educated Nigerian as 'the worst pedlar of tribalism'. In East Africa, as in Europe, particularism is led by the educated, stimulated by their knowledge, and disseminated by their example and active proselytisation. The educated man tends to turn from a more passive, taking-for-granted, particularism to become an active and positive factionalist, seeking power and advantage. National élites in Africa may find common standards, aspirations, tastes, and values, but they are much inclined to become divided in competition as the activist members of the new states. Education (formal and informal) can probably only be a broadening, unifying influence when particularist division, founded on other factors, begins to diminish.

The development and, in many ways, intensification of tribal divisions and inter-tribal oppositions and conflicts have not ceased with the end of the colonial domination. All of the essays in this symposium demonstrate this in one way or another. Political leaders can seldom afford to neglect the particularist divisions of their country, the power and support that they derive from one or another of these, and the necessity to satisfy demands of a local or regional kind. The phenomenon of so-called 'ethnic arithmetic' has frequently been noted in the composition of cabinets, committees, boards, secretariats, etc., as particularist interests and loyalties are recognized and catered for.

It is obvious that, in examining the nature of tribe and tribalism in East Africa, we are concerned with a wide range of variables in a wide range of social contexts. We are concerned with a form of particularism in these new states which involves groups of people distinguished from each other both territorially and culturally. Except in the towns (which special case is mentioned later) there are very few areas whose residents are tribally mixed—the joint heritage of pre-colonial and colonial periods. And invariably these territorial groups have, and see themselves as having, distinguishing cultural characteristics. These characteristics refer in large part to traditional cultures —language, institutions, customs, values, history, and myths, etc. New institutions and new values and symbols have been developed in the colonial and independence periods, but these are attached to and receive strength and validity from the persisting or revived parts of the older cultures. Parts of the older cultures have disappeared or been transformed. Old symbols and old institutions and values are put to new uses and they gain new and different significance to deal with and to express new interests (as, for example, La Fontaine describes for the Gisu). Tribes, tribal territories, and tribal cultures are not the same as they were at some previous period in time, and, as already noted, they are unlikely ever to have been stable and unchanging. The cultural differences may well have been stimulated, even to the point of almost artificial creation or re-creation, by entirely modern circumstances, interests and goals, and by leaders making use of these for political ends. Nevertheless, these cultural differences in their territorial context are the essence of tribe. That is to say, tribalism in East Africa is more than regionalism: it is regionalism inherently characterized by emphasized cultural distinctions. In many cases, though not all, these distinctions are quite radical, concerning essential and basic matters of, for example, language, family life, religious beliefs, fundamental values, and dispositions. Linguistic differences provide a good example, as well as a much-used symbol, of these differences. The large number of mutually unintelligible languages regularly spoken in an East African country needs no emphasis. But where the cultural differences are, objectively, rather slight, they can if necessary (and indeed, are) subjectively magnified to represent and to 'explain' the concrete differences between group and group. And conversely, quite considerable differences in culture can be played down or accommodated tolerantly when necessary. The criterion of cultural distinction is very highly flexible, and therein lies its major significance.

In making a definition of 'tribe' in terms of cultural-regional distinctions, I am not suggesting that this is all that is important in the phenomenon. The distinctions are entirely real and concrete, in one sense; but they are also stimulated, maintained, and contrived as they are intimately associated with practical interests (say, land rights) and with competition for power, privileges, and resources. These cultural-regional distinctions operate directly within the context of contemporary conditions, even though the appeal is partly to tradition. And that context changes, sometimes slowly, sometimes radically.

It is then, of course, wrong to suggest that the empirical distinction between tribe and tribe is clear and unequivocal. There can be no implication that, if we really look hard enough and carefully enough, we shall be able to determine the precise limits of each tribe, culturally and territorially. Neither now in the present, nor in some discoverable time in the past, have tribes and the tribal pattern crystallized. Cultural differences change both in their actuality and in the degree of emphasis and importance given to them. Geographical boundaries are indistinct, and they change as interests and activities develop, and as populations shift, expand and contract. I do not say that real cultural differences are unimportant—say, in customs, beliefs, or organization; but these differences can be ignored

or consolidated, minimized or emphasized, as overriding interests demand. Cultural differences are in part the ideology and
the symbolism of group distinction, and in part the concrete
reality of it. Both can and do change; both have varying
referents according to context.

Thus the groups of people so distinguished are in no sense
absolute. The lists of tribes established by late colonial times
(see Appendix) are in many ways arbitrary. They had been
moulded by European preconceptions and political requirements, and by the development of the African peoples' interests
and activities. But it is essential to recognize that cultural-
regional distinctions have continued to operate at both smaller
scale and wider-scale levels. The concept of the so-called 'supertribes' is well known (Rouch, 1956). We may take it to refer to
the larger-scale amalgamation of tribes (usually for political
purposes) which in other circumstances operate separately and
are conceived of as being separate. The same principle can,
however, be applied in reverse: it can refer to the fragmentation
of such groups at certain times and for certain purposes. The
error of Rouch and others lies in the assumption that there is
one level of grouping, to be called 'tribe', which is not only
unambiguously identifiable, but is in some sense real and right.
Colonial practice, of course, and a good deal of anthropology
too, strongly encouraged this conception.

We should observe, on the contrary, that there is a range of
levels of groupings with differing kinds of relevance and reality.
Thus at any one level the groupings are, on the one hand,
amalgamations of those at a smaller-scale level and, on the
other hand, they are constituents of the larger groupings at a
wider-scale level. The level of conceptualization and/or of
actual operation in social life depends on the kinds of interests
and activities concerned. Social anthropologists will be familiar
with this general principle of fission and fusion in a segmentary
system. The number of levels to be identified varies, and particular emphasis can be given at a certain time to a particular
level—e.g. for political purposes, or in solidary defence against
outside interference or threat—both by the people themselves
and by outsiders who impose upon them—e.g. a colonial authority or a neighbouring group. Stated here in brief, the principle
may seem to have a clarity and neatness which in actuality

is often far less apparent. The emphasis on the grouping at a particular level may be so great that both narrower- and wider-scale cultural-regional differentiations are overlooked both by protagonists and their observers. It may then seem that a particular tribe is clearly delineated and culturally distinct, such that in its case there can be no doubt of its single unity.

Let me take an example of the contextual relativity of tribal definition. The 'Kikuyu' have become conventionally identified as one tribe. But these people had no unity in pre-colonial times, not even in their own subjective conceptions. There were a large number of overlapping, more or less autonomous communities distinguished in varying degrees by residence and ecological factors, separate organization, variation in customs and institutions, and in dialect. It would be straining the facts unduly to say that these communities could have been clearly demarcated on a map—but that is a European way of conceptualizing politico-economic systems and groups. The situation was less well-defined than that; but the differentiation existed and operated, nevertheless. These communities, for certain purposes, amalgamated into larger groupings—the 'sub-tribes' as they were later called and as they were formalized and rigidified by colonial administration—based on geographical contiguity, socio-cultural similarities, practical co-operation, and the needs to cope with problems of inter-community conflict. Under the pressures of colonial conditions, and the better to defend and develop old and new interests, these larger groupings, for some purposes, amalgamated into the 'tribe' known as 'Kikuyu'. Old interests, values, and symbols were given novel emphasis and new ones were added, whilst old differences, cultural variations, and distinctions tended to be played down or partly forgotten.[7] Although Kikuyu unity found its supreme emphasis in the Mau Mau revolt it is quite clear that even among the active freedom-fighters the smaller-scale unities and loyalties remained, with their cultural-regional bases. Indeed, they tended to emerge more clearly as the external forces began to become overwhelming.

For wider political purposes, however, these Kikuyu could on occasion join with their north-eastern neighbours—the Embu and Meru, themselves amalgamations of variously disparate groups—to form the grouping of largest scale, sometimes also known as 'the Kikuyu'. There have from time to time been suggestions of an even wider grouping—a north-eastern Bantu bloc, taking in the Kamba. This would have represented, *inter alia*, common opposition to the European in a single, continuous region, the recognition of common problems of land shortage, a degree of common distinction from other Kenya tribes, and, if successful, a most powerful political force.

The modern emergence of the Luhya in western Kenya has been structurally and operationally similar, and largely politically inspired, in creating the tribe of largest scale in the cultural-regional basis. But here, too, the constituent segments remain active in idea and in practice: the so-called sub-tribes (about twenty in number) and their own constituent parts, and also combinations of some of these 'sub-tribes' (such as the Western Luhya—*Abaluhya be mumbo*). Each constituent part at whatever level is marked by the tribal characteristic of cultural-regional identification. The emergence of the Kalenjin, and the re-emergence of the Mijikenda, are further examples of the larger-scale extension of the tribal continuum. The so-called 'Northerners' (sometimes the Lwoo) in Uganda provides another case in the modern political arena. The Gisu and the Masai described in this symposium provide other examples in different contexts. But virtually every culturally distinguishable, territorial group—i.e. tribe—exists within a similar range, and is operative and conceived of according to context and the interests involved. The exceptions to this might seem to be those tribes which, historically, gained an added intensity of unity and of marked specificity through strong political centralization: the interlacustrine tribes of western Uganda, and one or two others. Even here, however, it would be a mistake not to recognize either the internal segmentation or the larger amalgamations, both actual and potential. Fairly recent circumstances in Uganda caused the peoples of the Bantu kingdoms to see themselves in some sense, to be seen by others, and to operate (or at least to be accused of operating) as a single unit for common purposes. This kind of development was effectively limited, but that was the result of political weakness rather than of cultural criteria.

A most interesting observation is made by Parkin, with reference to circumstances in Kampala, which throws light on

23

the fluidity of tribal definition and identification. In the competition for jobs and influence in Kampala the alignment of townspeople was sometimes directly 'tribal' (e.g. Luo as against Ganda, etc.), and at other times, as circumstances seemed to dictate, alignment was 'national' (e.g. Kenyans against Ugandans). That is to say, in a particular context at a particular time, 'Kenyan' became tantamount to a tribal designation for all practical purposes. In this connection, Mitchell has pointed out that in the Zambian Copper Belt towns, the large number of different tribes represented there tend, in individuals' perceptions, to be 'reduced to three or four categories bearing the labels of those tribes who, at the coming of the Europeans, were the most powerful and dominant in the region' (Mitchell, 1956, p. 28). Something similar existed among the sisal estate workers in the Tanga region: 'Ngoni', for example, was the tribal name for men from all over southern Tanganyika. Thus is the scale of levels of definition of tribe put at its most extensive.

In brief, then, the term 'tribe' can be taken to apply to *any group of people which is distinguished, by its members and by others, on the basis of cultural-regional criteria*. It is and must be an essentially dynamic concept to meet the fluidity of contextual conditions within which such groups emerge and operate. This variable character gives no reason at all for dismissing it as an inadequate concept. In fact it is this very character which gives it analytical value. And because of this character it plays so significant a role in changing East Africa, and it allows East Africans themselves to use and manipulate the concept and the allusion, consciously and unconsciously, in differing and sometimes contradictory ways. It is necessary to get away from the notion that somehow tribes are real and absolute groups of people, whether in an historical or contemporary context. The cultural-regional criteria on which tribe is based, and the underlying realities of the actual world, are both too diffuse and too variable for that.

One further distinction must be noted: that is between what some writers have called rural and urban tribalism (e.g. Southall, 1961; Mitchell, 1965; Parkin). What has been said so far refers principally, though not entirely, to the rural populations. These populations continue to comprise the large majority in each of the East African countries and to set the basic patterns and requirements. But in the modern towns of

East Africa the populations are of mixed origins, operating within an urban-industrial complex as townsmen and wage-earners. For them, tribe is largely a matter of the persistence of loyalties and values stemming from the rural (cultural-regional) background. As Parkin shows (following Mitchell, 1956 & 1965), tribe is a category of interaction among urban people, a means of dividing up the heterogeneous population into some manageable proportions. These categories are used to give some kind of standard of expectations of attitudes and behaviour. Parkin indicates that tribal standards and practices are dominant at the level of domestic relations among all strata of urban people; but the incidence of tribe-based interaction amongst friends and neighbours is higher for lower-income than for higher-income strata. Political and economic conflicts, and problems and difficulties of novel urban life, are 'explained' more readily by lower-income people in terms of tribe and tribal differences and loyalties. Higher-income people, usually the better-educated, more experienced people with wider responsibilities, tend to perceive more easily the non-tribal factors. Yet at times of crisis leaders tend to look for and to encourage 'tribal solidarity' in order to gain and consolidate support. This urban aspect of tribalism is, of course, directly related to its rural sources—sources which are still close to the townspeople. The differences between rural and urban conceptions and uses of tribe relate to two important factors. First, urban people live in tribally heterogeneous groups, partly divorced from the cultural-regional bases of the rural areas; and second, they are affected by the purely urban environment and its commitments. Here, then, the significance of tribe, and the processes of tribalism, take on rather different forms and significance as a result of the different social context in which they are used. But we should emphasize that still virtually all urban dwellers in East Africa continue to maintain close links with the rural, tribal areas. Very many are but temporarily in town; and those whose urban careers are more prolonged, even to the expectation of permanence, are still caught up in the pervasive tribal categories, being influenced by them and taking advantage of them when necessary and useful.

One matter which demands attention is the relationship between and comparison of tribe and tribalism, and nation and nationalism. This question has been much discussed, sometimes in emotional and political terms which have clouded the issue. There is a variety of opinion, deliberate or implied. It has been suggested, asserted no less, that the smaller groups in Africa may be referred to as tribes, whilst the relatively few larger ones should be called nations. This is an attempt to distinguish by scale, and seems unhelpful; but there is also sometimes the implication that the larger units—the 'nations', such as Ibo or Hausa, Kikuyu, Sukuma or Ganda—by virtue of their size have claims and the strength to support claims to sovereignty, or at least to some special autonomy within a larger state. Some people wish to distinguish between the new nations which are the African successors to the former colonial territories, and the constituent parts of these, which are tribes. Such a view rightly takes note of the fact that the three East African countries are not yet nations in the old European sense, for although they are sovereign states they lack the basis of established common culture, or even stable institutions and a common language. There are also some people who wish to apply the epithet of 'tribe' to indicate what seems to them to be a social unit of less complex, even more primitive, kind than the accepted European nations.

We are compelled to go to the concepts of nation and nationalism which were historically developed in nineteenth-century Europe, for here inevitably is the locus of comparison. We might do worse than adopt the definition of the Serbs in 1848: a nation is a group (the Serbs appear to have said 'a race') 'which possesses its own language, customs and culture, and enough self-consciousness to preserve them' (quoted by Argyle). Independent self-government was not then held to be a necessary criterion or aspiration of nationhood. But meanings and aspirations change as the socio-political circumstances change. Later in the century and at least up to 1919, it is fair to say that the goal of sovereignty became an integral part of nationalism. The demand for some degree of autonomy within a larger state became insufficient.

Mere size as such may be rather unimportant, except perhaps a larger group could exert greater strength in favour of independence. It has often been pointed out that several European nations were, and are, smaller than some of the larger African groups. On the other hand, a large majority of African tribes are small—less than a quarter of a million people, and many have fewer than 100,000 people. Many writers assert that size is irrelevant. They hold that African tribe and European nation are the same—sociologically, politically, and culturally. On this view both tribe and nation are seen to be based on cultural identity and powerfully supported, emotive appeals to that identity. Both tribe and nation have the territorial basis on which to seek independence. The development of particular nations as political forces in Europe (e.g. in the old Austro-Hungarian and Ottoman Empires) is held to be paralleled by the modern development of tribes, or at least of some of them, in Africa. The calculated appeal to culture, tradition, and language, the increased interest in the group's history, the revival of old customs and especially of old culture-heroes (their near-invention in some cases). Much of this, in Africa as in Europe, has been led by the educated minority, the group's leaders, many of whom sought political advantage and who resented their exclusion from the power system controlled by the overruling authority. There has also often been an aggressive opposition to neighbouring groups, even amounting to an intolerance of their similar claims and aspirations. Argyle summarizes the many similarities later in this book. They are undeniable; and they have their sources in comparable imperial contexts. The argument leads, therefore, to the desire to drop altogether the term 'tribe'. This conclusion is further reinforced by the contention that a major connotation of tribe and tribalism is 'a negatively valued equivalent of what in Europe has been called "nationalism"' (van den Berghe, 1968, p. 210).

Despite the obvious similarities, there are nevertheless some arguments against this conclusion. Perhaps a minor one is that in Africa the word 'nation' has been pre-empted for the new states in expression of their aspirations and efforts to build and consolidate new unity and common culture. Again, we may note that value-judgements (approved or disapproved) are likely to become associated with almost any term used in the political arena. Careful description and analysis can take account of this.

More important, however, is the matter of scale and the

political context within which these social groups operate. It seems to me that, with one or two notable exceptions, African tribalism is concerned with aspirations and efforts for local or regional (i.e. tribal) autonomy in some degree, but within the structure of a larger political unit: i.e. under the accepted superior authority of the wider state. Mainly because of their smallness in size, tribes seek to govern their own local affairs without seeking full sovereignty. Most significantly, from the sociological point of view, they become actively prominent in their structural opposition to each other within the larger unit, as each seeks to preserve its interests and to obtain its maximum share of resources and attention. Tribe and tribalism is primarily a product of the interaction of cultural-regional groups *within* the state: their competition with each other, their apprehensions of each other, fears of deprivation of interests and rights, attempts to dominate, stimulated awareness of differences, and so on. That is to say, unlike European nations, tribes are mainly in opposition to one another, rather than to the overarching authority of the encompassing state.

The Somali, Rwanda, Rundi, Sotho, and Tswana, have indubitably translated any notion of tribe into the accomplished fact of nation. These are, however, exceptions in the generality of African conditions. The issues are even more befogged if the focus of reference is allowed to be monopolized by the dramatic, violent, much publicized and exceptional cases of the Ibo or the Ganda. In these latter cases we are dealing with a different sociological phenomenon. Nothing of this kind has occurred in either Kenya or Tanzania, and is perhaps unlikely to do so. Tribes and tribalism there concern local autonomy, local rights and interests, and local bases for political and other action within the national arena. In Uganda the case of the Ganda is of course different, and one may endorse the cogent argument by Morris that Buganda is a nation. Yet even there the tribes of Uganda do not seek separate sovereignty against the authority of the existing state. The recent defeat of Ganda nationalist aspirations—at least for the moment—and current government plans to put the Ganda on a par with the tribes of the rest of the country, would seem to reduce their nationalism to tribalism by *force majeure*. In the rebellion of the Konzo, described by Alnaes, the prime focus of opposition was the neighbouring Toro, and the aim was explicitly for local autonomy within the framework of Uganda. Indeed, the later declaration of an independent Konzo state (Rwenzururu) can be construed as a final act of desperation inspired by an over-wrought, failing leader, and scarcely supported by the mass of the people.

If we follow the 1848 Serbs in denying the necessity for nationhood of sovereign self-government—or at least aspirations and efforts to that end—this kind of argument may seem less important. But the significant feature is the structural relation of the tribe to central authority and to other tribes. There is some danger of merely playing with words, and of seeming to deny the many similarities between tribe and nation. But the discrimination is not, I think, merely a minor one, for it concerns fundamental criteria in analysis. There seems to be importance in the distinction between tribe and nation because it relates to differences in the pattern and distribution of authority and political power, as well as in human aspirations and ideas. On this view, African tribes have the political status of the semi-autonomous segments of any state, particularly of a federal state such as Australia—although the marked cultural character of the tribe gives a considerably different dimension otherwise. This involves the whole structure of socio-political organization, not only in terms of power and authority, but also in terms of the institutions and the roles of members of tribes. The Kikuyu in Kenya, the Sukuma in Tanzania, or the Teso in Uganda, do not seek, and have not sought, sovereign independence; neither do they have or seek to develop the institutions and roles, nor the subjective orientations, of that kind of endeavour. As Bennett points out, the Kikuyu may well have sought a Kenyan independence in which they themselves would be dominant, to their own advantage; but always it has been, in intention as well as in fact, the desire for a Kikuyu local autonomy within the state of Kenya.

I note also the tribalism exemplified in this symposium by the Arusha and Masai in northern Tanzania which, in the commitment to tradition, is concerned with the problems of identity and with self-defence against what are perceived of as threats to established interests. Gisu tribalism, and that of the Chagga, is concerned with the protection and development of new interests in the changing contexts of their respective countries. These are examples (included in this symposium for that purpose) of the grass-roots of tribalism. They are in certain fundamentals (though not all) quite different from the nationalism of the former parts of the eastern European empires, or of once-fragmented Italy and Germany.

If this argument is reasonable, it would then be useful to perceive of tribe and tribalism in East Africa not as a form of nationalism in the old European sense, but as one form of a different and general sociological category—*particularism*. Particularism is a component of any sovereign state—and of other larger human groups also—taking different forms, clothed with different details and externalities, according to the circumstances. Thus tribalism can be most fruitfully compared with other kinds of particularism: regionalism, sectionalism, communalism, casteism, etc. Lewis makes the point that within the Somali nation-state there is an important particularism based on traditional, genealogically-defined segments—another example of the same general phenomenon. This Somali particularism has sometimes been referred to in Somalia as 'tribalism' —by direct comparison with other African countries, though doubtless inspired by earlier colonial perceptions.

Thus a state or a country may have within it both nationalism and particularism. The United Kingdom contains the overt nationalist movements of the Scots, the Welsh, and even the Cornish, and the particularist sections of variable importance—for example, the North-east, the West Country, East Anglia. Similarly, Uganda—but not Kenya or Tanzania—has, or at least had, both.

This kind of analytical comparison must not be pushed to extremes or its usefulness will be lost. Certainly the similarities between African tribalism and European nationalism cannot be ignored. Yet too strong an insistence on equating the two leads to a neglect of certain important characteristics of tribe and the tribal factor in modern East Africa. The subjective rejection of the term 'tribe' could lead to that unfortunate neglect. The notorious lack of unity, or threat to unity, in the independent African states is not primarily because these constituent segments wish to secede, but because they operate in terms of opposition to each other. Indeed, part of the opposition between tribes specifically operates in competition to influence or even to control that authority for particular purposes. And, finally, the operative fact of the structural and contextual variability of tribe—the range of levels at which it emerges—is a characteristic peculiar to particularism and not one inherent in nationalism.

The opposition between these particularist segments—tribes —is invariably represented and expressed by a wide variety of symbols. These have a most powerful evocative force among the participants, but also among their observers, so much so that there is some danger that symbols come to be taken in themselves as the real factors of differentiation. As I have suggested already, the cultural factor is an integral element of tribalism. But the cultural factor comprises, at least from one point of view, a set of symbols of varying kinds ranging from language to ritual, from culture-heroes to material objects. It is often said that tribe is distinguished from tribe by virtue of these symbols. Another aspect of culture comprises forms of social organization and of social roles, and the patterned interrelation of these. Tribal boundaries are then perceived to be drawn by the range within which these cultural items hold good. Thus, for example, the Gisu of Uganda can claim to distinguish themselves from all others by reference to their particular, interconnected set of initiation rituals, peculiar to them alone (La Fontaine); and the Arusha can exclude outsiders who do not have established status within their clan and age-set systems (Gulliver). There are the true, or 'pure', Kikuyu (*karinga*) taking the continuation of clitoridectomy as a major demonstration of essential Kikuyu-ness. That these and a multitude of comparable features help to mark off the adherents of one tribe from those of another is abundantly clear. What is less obvious, and not always properly considered, is the extent to which they are the real differentiating factors or only the highly effective representations of the real factors.

Sociologists on the whole seek to look beneath the evocative symbols and cultural forms to the concrete interests which are represented and explained by them. These interests arise out of ecological, economic, and political considerations: such matters of basic concern as land rights, communications, and access to markets, the distribution of political power and participation in decision-making, the allocation of resources (finance, materials, manpower), and the planning of development. Groups of people adhere together in order to generate and control these interests, and rights and privileges associated with them, for mutual benefit. Groups also adhere in common protection of these interests, to seek to prevent their erosion or transformation by others. These particularist groups emerge most powerfully in contradistinction, opposition, to other groups with which they are in competition and which seem to threaten them. Both Twaddle and La Fontaine note this occurrence among the tribes in eastern Uganda, but every other tribe can demonstrate the same sort of phenomena.

Put in an extreme form, the argument runs that it is the concrete politico-economic interests that are the basis of tribe and tribalism—the defence of these against external encroachment and their development according to local preference and advantage. In this argument, it is held that common values, symbols, and social forms emerge, and are caused to emerge, where and as they will give support to the essential interests of the people. According to the kinds of interests and the extent of their distribution, so this or that cultural feature is emphasized (and others minimized). Potentially usable cultural forms are neglected, even denied in the circumstances, where they do not reinforce the basic interests concerned. Where interests change, and therefore the range of people affected and concerned, so will the cultural forms of tribalism. But, on the contrary, the cultural forms themselves do not dictate the interests which are important.

This is, of course, to state the argument in crude and extreme form, partly for emphasis, and partly as an antidote to somewhat facile or unthinking assumptions of the primacy of common cultural forms, symbols, and expressed values, in determining and differentiating tribes and creating tribalism. But it would be a mistake to perceive of the cultural factors as purely subsidiary, as only providing an ideology and a set of weapons in intertribal oppositions. Symbols of whatever kind though 'merely representational' of more concrete interests, have an autonomy and a force of their own. People can become so affected by them that they will act even against their interests in furtherance of the symbols. Leaders, who may have a more or less conscious perception of the economic and political interests involved, use these symbols not only in expressive, emotive manner, but to gain the support of followers who may not all see clearly what the interests are. Leaders' interests may in any case differ from those of followers—e.g. where leaders are an educated élite minority, and their followers are semi-literate peasant farmers—but the same set of symbols may serve a common purpose. Threats from the outside can be exaggerated, even fabricated, for the leaders' advantage, by appeals to cultural identity. Moreover, the extent of the interests involved may be widened or narrowed as a result of cultural difference. Two adjacent tribes may, for instance, have virtually common interests to defend and to generate (say, security of land or access to irrigation water) against a common external power. Yet the two tribes can remain divided from each other by their variant cultural forms and symbols which, it is passionately insisted, separate them irreparably.[8] And as a result the two tribes may be driven to increasingly intensive competition with each other at the expense of adequate protection of their interests against external threat, or of losing resources or political influence in the wider field.

One might take the line that in fact it is cultural forms, including all the symbols, which demarcate tribes and precipitate tribalism, and that concrete interests attach to these culturally determined groups. This at least must be rejected, for it is evident that cultural forms can and do change as the concrete interests and the groups they generate alter. Pan-Kikuyu-ism had not developed in this century as the result primarily of common cultural forms—language, organizational patterns, values, etc.—for they were all there beforehand. The pan-Kikuyu movement developed as a result of opposition to European colonial rule and in counter-distinction to other tribes. It developed to protect commonly threatened land interests, to obtain greater advantage from modern educational, economic and political developments, and the like. The cultural rationalization and expression of these concrete interests developed (one might almost say, were developed) as a result. But as they developed they took on an impetus of their own and to some extent cut off the Kikuyu from like groups and against their own advantages.

There is no definite conclusion to be reached in this connection, any more than in the not dissimilar, age-old controversy between 'nature' and 'nurture' in determining human personality. In neither case, however, need we assume any necessary 'either-or' dichotomy; for clearly both concrete interests and cultural forms and symbols are inherent in tribal differentiation. It remains important to note, nevertheless, the danger of assuming that the culture and its symbols are the only or even the main factors. Let me quote one of the contributors to this symposium: ' "Tribal culture" provides an ideology of unity rather than any real identity of interests, by symbolizing the moral community. The Gisu are not united by a common language and rituals, rather they are united when opposed to non-Gisu and represent this by reference to language and culture. The cultural symbols of tribalism are thus abstractions from cultural reality, not its basic elements' (La Fontaine, pp. 329–30).

This brings us back to that most important point in the understanding of the tribal factor. Both the concept and the operative groups denoted by the term 'tribe' are flexible, sometimes very highly so. The cultural forms and symbols can be, and are, manipulated to conform to and give support to differing groups (i.e. tribes) for differing purposes and interests. Thus the groups on the ground are capable of variable cultural definition according to circumstances. There are no absolute groups of people, defined and delineated once and for all, and to be labelled tribes. This is a general characteristic of particularism within the wider society.

In conclusion, I believe that the tribal factor in East Africa has been both overrated and underrated in its importance. It has been overrated by those commentators who see it as a catch-all explanation for almost everything that occurs in these countries—and not only journalists are guilty of that superficiality. Complex sociological processes cannot be explained and understood by such facile reference: for example, the role of Buganda in the modern state of Uganda, the development of political parties in Kenya, the problem of a national language, the development of legal institutions, urban conflicts and competition, the apparent acceptance or rejection of modernization. These and many other phenomena in East Africa involve a wide range of different kinds of factors which require careful discrimination in analysis, and of which particularism in the form of tribalism is but one. It is usually not even a factor in itself, but rather a reflection of and a combination of some of the other factors involved. To say that a (or the) cause of some development is tribalism is, in a sense, to say very little, until one begins to examine the particulars.

On the other hand, and paradoxically, particularist factors stemming from cultural-regional differentiation may be rather more important than is sometimes suggested. One reason for this is that there seems to be rather little evidence to indicate that this form of particularism is becoming less evident in recent years. If anything, it appears more strongly as the people attempt to cope with the great problems thrown up by political independence and modernization. Vested interests of all kinds are necessarily threatened, and people are simultaneously required to adjust themselves to many radical kinds of transformation. There are new prizes, new power and wealth and advantage to be competed for, and new responsibilities to be undertaken. Tribalism provides both a refuge from seemingly intolerable burdens and a base from which to engage in the competition. One great importance of tribalism lies in its intrinsic flexibility as a concept, and in its ability to represent a highly flexible social process: the tribe, variously defined according to circumstances and need, can be made the unit of reference, the banner, and the cluster of symbols, for groups of people involved in the manifold upheavals and opportunities of the contemporary world. A less flexible concept, and more rigidly-defined groups and group boundaries, would not only be less useful at the several different levels, but it would most probably be unable to withstand the powerful pressures and requirements of the second half of the twentieth century.

APPENDIX

The Conventional Tribes of East Africa

It may be useful, as an *aide-memoire*, to give lists of the larger conventional tribes of the East African countries as the named groups emerged from the colonial era, and have more or less officially been taken over in later times. In doing this there is a risk of seeming to contradict my thesis of the essential fluidity, and contextual character, of the meaning and application of the term 'tribe'. There may be a risk, too, in appearing to give credence to the supposed clarity of the tribal classification and differentiation of the colonial era. However, by 'conventional tribes' I mean here those which were designated in the last censuses to be held in the three countries, Tanganyika in 1957,[9] Uganda in 1959, and Kenya in 1962. Apart from the removal

POPULATION OF CONVENTIONAL TRIBES

	over 1 million	*½–1 million*	*100,000 to 500,000*
KENYA	Kikuyu Luhya Luo	Kamba Kisii	Elgeyo, Kipsigis, Masai, Meru, Mijikenda, Nandi, Somali, Tugen, Turkana
TANZANIA	Sukuma	—	Bena, Chagga, Gogo, Ha, Haya, Hehe, Iramba, Iraqw, Luguru, Makonde, Makua, Mwera, Nyakyusa, Nyamwezi, Nyika, Pare, Rangi, Sambaa, Turu, Yao, Zaramo, Zigua
UGANDA	Ganda	Ankole Soga Teso	Acholi, Alur, Dama, Gisu, Gwere, Karamajong, Kiga, Konjo, Lango, Lugbara, Nyoro, Toro.

of arbitrarily-used linguistic prefixes, the names as given here appear in the relevant Census Reports. Not all these names are acceptable to the peoples themselves, or to ethnographers. (Tribal maps can be consulted in Goldthorpe, 1960, and Gulliver, 1959 and 1960.)

NOTES

1 Lloyd notes that 'ethnicity' has not found its way into colloquial usage in English-speaking West Africa (Lloyd, 1967, pp. 28–9).
2 Many nineteenth-century writers—Burton, for example—seem to have used 'tribe' and 'race' interchangeably and without particular definition (Burton, 1861).
3 Evans-Pritchard was seeking to overcome the problems of analysing political processes in a large acephalous group, the Nuer of the southern Sudan (cf. also Mair, 1962, p. 15).
4 e.g. I. Potekhin: 'A tribal community is based on blood relations: it is a community of people descended from the same actual or mythical ancestor' (1958, p. 309). But Potekhin does not suggest that his evolutionary definition should be applied to most of the units called 'tribes' in modern Africa.
5 *East African Standard*, 6 April 1968.
6 On this distinction, see for example Epstein, 1958; Edel, 1965; La Fontaine.
7 Colonial administrations tended to impose a common pattern. They suppressed certain important differentiating features, e.g. the age-groups, elders' grades, and the *kiama* system. The marked socio-cultural differences and variations among the Kikuyu are well brought out by Lambert, 1956.
8 I have in mind the case of the Arusha and the Meru, adjacent to each other on the slopes of Mt Meru in northern Tanzania. But the same kind of situation can be seen on virtually every tribal boundary.
9 In the 1967 Census in Tanzania tribal enumeration was expressly omitted.

REFERENCES

BURTON, R. F. 1860, *The Lake Regions of Central Africa*, London.
COLSON, E. 1968, 'Contemporary Tribes and the Development of Nationalism', *Proceedings of the 1967 Annual Spring Meeting of the American Ethnological Society*, University of Washington Press.
DE WILDE, J. C. 1967, *Experiences with Agricultural Development in Tropical Africa*, vol. 2, The Johns Hopkins Press, Baltimore.
EDEL, M. 1965, 'African Tribalism: some Reflection on Uganda', *Political Science Quarterly*, 80.
EPSTEIN, A. L. 1958, *Politics in an African Urban Community*, Manchester University Press.
EVANS-PRITCHARD, E. E. 1940, *The Nuer*, Clarendon Press, Oxford.

37

GEERTZ, C. 1963, 'Primordial Sentiments and Civil Politics in the New States', in Geertz, C. (ed.), *Old Societies and New States*, Free Press, Glencoe.

GLUCKMAN, M. 1965, *The Ideas of Barotse Jurisprudence*, Yale University Press, New Haven.

GOLDTHORPE, J. E. and WILSON, F. B. 1960, *Tribal Maps of East Africa and Zanzibar*, E. African Institute of Social Research, Kampala.

GULLIVER, P. H. 1959/60, 'A Tribal Map of Tanganyika', *Tanganyika Notes and Records*, 52 & 54.

LAMBERT, H. E. 1956, *Kikuyu Social and Political Institutions*, Oxford University Press.

LLOYD, P. C. 1967, *Africa in Social Change*, Penguin.

MAIR, L. P. 1962, *Primitive Government*, Penguin.

MBOYA, T. J. 1963, *Freedom and After*, Deutsch.

MITCHELL, J. C. 1956, *The Kalela Dance* (Rhodes-Livingston Paper No. 27), Manchester University Press.

1965, 'Theoretical Orientations in African Urban Studies', in *The Social Anthropology of Complex Societies* (A.S.A. Monographs, No. 4), Tavistock.

NADEL, S. F. 1942, *A Black Byzantium*, Oxford University Press.

NYERERE, J. 1967, *Freedom and Unity*, Oxford University Press.

POTEKHIN, I. 1958, 'The Formation of Nations in Africa', *Marxism Today*, 2. 10.

ROUCH, J. 1956, 'Migrations au Ghana', *Jo. de la Société des Africanistes*, 19.

SOUTHALL, A. W. 1961, *Social Change in Modern Africa*, Oxford University Press.

VAN DEN BERGHE, P. 1968, Review of Lloyd 1967, *Africa*, 38, 2.

Part One

GENERAL STUDIES

EUROPEAN NATIONALISM AND
AFRICAN TRIBALISM

W. J. Argyle

I N April 1848 Louis Kossuth met a delegation of Hungarian
Serbs who told him that their nation demanded the recognition of its language.

'What do you understand by "nation"?' inquired Kossuth.

'A race which possesses its own language, customs and culture',
was the Serb reply, 'and enough self-consciousness to preserve
them.'

'A nation must also have its own government', objected
Kossuth.

'We do not go so far,' Kostić explained; 'one nation can live
under several different governments, and again several nations
can form a single state.' (Seton-Watson, 1911, p. 46).

Kossuth, then, would probably recognize only two or three
nations in modern Africa south of the Sahara—Botswana,
Lesotho, Somalia. The Serbs would recognize hundreds: the
'tribes' that are contained within, or that sometimes overlap,
the boundaries of the new states. In this paper I adopt the Serb
definition, and try to show that African tribes and their tribalism can indeed be equated with European nations and their
nationalism.

One initial manifestation of nationalism, sometimes appearing in the eighteenth century or even earlier, but especially
common in the nineteenth, was a quickening interest in
'national' cultures. Among the Slavs of the Habsburg and
Russian Empires at this period 'the young generation set out
to write grammars and compile dictionaries of their native

tongues, to translate foreign works, to collect folksongs, to explore national antiquities, to do research in historical chronicles and archives' (Kohn, 1955, pp. 46–7).

Rather later, 'among the Scandinavian peoples the study of folk-lore, history and philology, made each more conscious of its distinctness from the others' (Bury, 1960, pp. 218–19). Later still in Spain, 'the Catalan language, customs, and artistic traditions were feverishly revived' (Thomas, 1965, p. 34).

To promote such studies (which often had barely-concealed political implications) learned societies were established. The Magyar Academy of Sciences had its beginnings at the Diet of 1825 which, among other things, demanded the recognition of Magyar as an official language of the Empire. The Slovak Literary Society was founded even earlier and was a major centre of resistance to Magyar onslaughts against the languages of the Hungarian minorities. By 1869 eight of the Slav groups in the Empire had their own literary societies in addition to the various academies (Petrovich, 1956, p. 148). In the Russian Empire some of the non-Slav peoples took up the example: 'the Riga Latvian Society, founded in 1868, was the centre from which Latvian nationalism spread among the educated classes' (Seton-Watson, 1952, p. 36).

Cultural movements on quite this scale are understandably lacking in Africa. Yet from very small beginnings, mostly inspired by the missions, the production of vernacular literature, dealing often with tribal history, folk-lore and custom, grew rapidly in all parts of the continent. Although the initiative to write it came ordinarily from individuals, there were tribal associations which devoted part of their energies to encouraging such work. One of the largest and best-known of the Congo associations, A.B.A.K.O., was officially founded in 1952 to work expressly for the unification, preservation, purification, and expansion of the Kongo language (Verhaegen, 1962, p. 13). The Kikuyu Central Association, an openly political body from the beginning, 'decided in 1928 to start a monthly journal, published in the Kikuyu language . . . [and] its riddles, proverbs, and stories encouraged its readers to think of themselves still as Kikuyu' (Rosberg and Nottingham, 1966, pp. 100–1). In South Africa the Zulu Society listed one of its aims as being 'to encourage the production of literary works, comprehending subjects relating to us in correct Isintu [Zulu]' (Zulu Society). The assistance of the Society is acknowledged by the compilers of the major Zulu-English dictionary (Doke and Vilakazi, 1953, p. xii). West Africa is well-known for its innumerable tribal associations, some of which included similar 'cultural' projects in their elaborate programmes.

It was, though, clearly no use writing literary and scholarly works unless there were someone to read them. The European nationalists worked ceaselessly to promote literacy. 'The loudest demands made on the Austrian government by the earliest exponents of Czech nationalism were on behalf of national schools in which the Czech language and Czech history should be taught' (Hayes, 1926, p. 85). The same demands for the same privileges were voiced just as loudly by all the other nationalities. They could be heard too, if in more muffled tones, from the Russian Empire, where, for example, the Esthonian Students' Society formed a committee 'to collect funds for the foundation of a secondary school in which teaching was to be in the Esthonian language' (Seton-Watson, 1952, p. 36).

Inevitably the vernaculars in African schools had to take second place to European languages, but even so there was some agitation on their behalf. The Luo Union in Kampala ran seven nursery and primary schools there for Luo children, 'because our children do not speak Luganda and cannot benefit from local schools' (Dahya, 1963, p. 6). In Lusaka a confederation of tribal organizations, which included representatives of the Lenje, 'supported the claim for the use of the Lenje vernacular in schools' (*African Affairs*, 1955, p. 48). One of the many complaints of baKongo was that their children who attended school in Leopoldville were instructed in a bastard language (liNgala) to the detriment of their own (Verhaegen, 1962, p. 11). In West Africa the twentieth-century Ibo State Union outdid the nineteenth-century Esthonians by trying to raise funds for the building of six 'National Colleges' in Ibo country (Aloba, 1954, p. 634). It did, in fact, help to build a number of secondary schools.

Once such movements had begun in Europe there was no reason why they should stop at schools. European nationalists usually moved on to agitate for universities, and in many cases they got them. Even now the distribution of universities between different nationalities is a live political issue in countries like Belgium, Canada, and South Africa. It was obviously not practical for most African tribes to sustain universities of their own. Yet in Nigeria the University of Nsukka was thought of as an 'Ibo' institution,[1] and the new university at Ife was even more clearly a 'Yoruba' foundation. Where these two tribes (and others, of course) shared a university, as at Ibadan, it was by 1966 split from top to bottom by disputes between them[2] in a way strongly reminiscent of the endless squabbles between, say, Czechs and Germans in Prague before (and after) they were given separate universities there. We have Dr Dike's word for it, given at the Ibadan graduation ceremony in 1966, that the educated Nigerian was 'the worst pedlar of tribalism' (*West Africa*, 9 July 1966, p. 783). It is common knowledge that in Europe the most rabid nationalists were often university professors, schoolteachers, lawyers, and priests.

So passionate a concern for the culture and education of the tribe or nation is not likely to be completely disinterested, even among intellectuals. In fact it was often directly related, in both Europe and Africa, to competition for those salaried jobs which the literati commonly regard as their right. In Austro-Hungary the main employer was the government, which never showed much enthusiasm for laissez-faire doctrines, and therefore maintained a vast bureaucracy through which it constantly interfered in every aspect of economic and political life. Consequently 'the appointment of every schoolteacher, of every railway porter, of every hospital doctor, of every tax-collector was a signal for national struggle (Taylor, 1964, p. 187). One aspect of the struggle was that each group sought to ensure that only its own nationals were employed within its homeland. For example, the 1908 programme of the Rumanian National Party included a clause that only Rumanian officials were to be employed in the districts inhabited by Rumanians (Seton-Watson, 1908, p. 471).

Most of the colonial régimes in Africa were also the main employers of labour even before the Second World War. After 1945, at least in the British territories, they were increasingly affected by welfare state notions, and were expected to do something about promoting economic growth and providing amenities. So they created jobs under both local and central government at a rate which accelerated immediately before the colonies were given independence. Many of the Africans who came to power after independence held left-wing ideas of some sort about the role of the state, and were in any case committed to a further expansion of its activities by the often lavish promises they had made to their followers. One unintended consequence of all this state bounty was a sharpening of tribal feeling. In 1962 some of the Padhola leaders from West Budama county in Uganda wanted a separate Budama District to be carved out of the Bukedi District because 'most of the administrative posts in the district administration are filled by the Bagwere and the Banyuli' (Burke, 1964, p. 215). Similarly, a motion was introduced at a meeting of the Soli Tribal Council in Northern Rhodesia (as it was then) that 'Soli Native Authority employees should be Soli by birth' (*Soli Native Authority*, 22–5 July 1958).[3]

These two examples may seem rather trivial, but I believe they differ only in degree and not in kind from other manifestations of the same feeling which have had very serious consequences. The Commissioners appointed to enquire into the fears of Nigerian minorities before independence frequently encountered allegations that, for example, 'all public boards in the Western Region . . . were Yoruba in composition and discriminatory in operation', or, in the Eastern Region, that 'it was the deliberate object of the Ibo majority . . . to fill every post with Ibos' (Willink, 1958, pp. 13, 39). In the Congo a common complaint in Luluabourg and elsewhere was that 'all the top jobs were held by Baluba' (Young, 1965, p. 264), which provided an excuse for the later massacre or expulsion of thousands of them. It was not, of course, only the Luba who were after the best jobs they could get. In Elizabethville the leaders of some tribal associations actively sought, for themselves or for their fellow tribesmen, jobs at all levels of the local and central administration (Caprasse, 1959, p. 34).

The two last examples introduce another important theme: tribal struggles often began in the towns where the most jobs were and where, at the same time, competition for them was most intense. A further instance from the Congo was the baKongo claim to Leopoldville as 'their' city against all those

45

other tribes who were lumped together as 'Ngala' (Young, 1965, p. 255). This claim was no different from that of a Kenya politician who could say, 'Nairobi is Kikuyu. Therefore it is right that the local administrators be Kikuyu. Kisumu and the Nyanza region on the other hand, are for the Luo, and no Kikuyu would have a chance there' (Werlin, 1965–6, p. 190). Nobody could be quite as confident, perhaps, about the status of Mbale Township in Uganda which was hotly disputed between the tribes of Bukedi District on the one hand and the Gisu on the other (Burke, 1964, p. 206; see also p. 325 and p. 341 in this volume).

Many towns of Central and Eastern Europe witnessed conflicts of the same kind. Places like Vilna and Bratislava were situated at border points between different nationalities, each of which claimed the town as its own and wished to dominate or even exclude the others (Kolarz, 1946, pp. 15–16). The struggles between Czechs and Germans for the towns of Bohemia and Moravia were especially prolonged and were carried to extraordinary lengths (Wiskemann, 1938, pp. 97–113).

Yet if these movements often began and flourished in the towns, they eventually reached out to the country. The involvement of the peasantry with nationalism in the Habsburg Empire was an important, though usually late, stage in its development. It is true, of course, that many of those who invented cultural nationalism were peasant-bred intellectuals, but although they admired and studied peasant art, dress, dance, and song, their political allies were rather the bourgeoisie and aristocracy who were their patrons and audience. Still, they had defined the nation in terms of a distinct language, culture, territory, and these were as much the property of the rural masses as they were of the relatively small urban populations. It was inevitable that the peasants, or some of them, should eventually claim their share of the nation. Quite often they ended by taking as well the share of those who had founded it (Taylor, 1964, p. 34).

The same development can be traced in parts of Africa where it was encouraged by the system of migrant labour. One Nigerian writer on tribal unions remarked that nearly all of them were started 'outside their own villages, and sometimes outside their own tribal territories. . . . It is when the union has been solidly founded abroad that efforts are made to establish a branch at home' (Offodile, 1947, p. 941). Young (1965, p. 251) makes a similar general assertion that the urban tribal associations of the Congo also had an appeal in the rural areas. In Northern Rhodesia the Soli Tribal Association, based in Lusaka, made several attempts to gain representation on the rural Tribal Council. Their efforts were supported by some of the Council's elected members, but were thwarted by the District Officers. In a few cases it seems that the associations originated in the rural areas rather than in the major towns. The Kikuyu Central Association, the Abaluhyia Central Association, the Ukamba Members Association, and the Taite Hills Association, were all responses to rural problems in Kenya between the wars (Rosberg and Nottingham, 1960, pp. 161, 170, 174). They were therefore organized primarily to resist the Europeans rather than to compete with other tribes. Still, they were founded by educated men who had often held clerical jobs in Nairobi or other East African towns, where tribal associations of the more usual kind were to be found at a somewhat later date (Rosberg and Nottingham, 1960, p. 210; Dahya, 1963).

In general, then, both national and tribal organizations did commonly recognize the backwardness of the rural areas and their need for the enlightenment and development which the organizations tried to foster initially amongst their own members. Thus they raised money to found scholarships and schools or, sometimes, to provide roads, water supplies and other amenities in the rural homelands. The scale of their voluntary activities, especially in education, was often impressive in both Africa and Europe. Yet they could not possibly meet, by their own efforts, the demand for all the modern opportunities and amenities which they had themselves helped to stimulate. They therefore looked once more to the state for assistance, and thus contributed again to the growth of competition between nationalities and tribes.

It was bound to be the case, for accidental reasons, that some areas and peoples were more advanced and prosperous than others. Such differences in the multi-national states of Europe were easily attributed (sometimes with reason) to the dominant

47

position held in these states by the more favoured peoples. The remedy was then for the less-favoured to try and upset the existing distribution of power and amenities, while those who benefited from it fought to maintain it. Certainly in the Habsburg Empire, 'the struggle for position between the different nationalities was unceasing, precisely because of the historic inequalities which existed between them' (Macartney, 1934, p. 143). The contemporary situation in Nigeria seems to be essentially the same, for 'in many parts of the country, economic and ethnic differences coincide. Whenever this happened, economic competition took on racial overtones and charges of tribalism were invoked by the contending parties' (*Nigerian Daily Times*, 21 June 1966). Such inequalities contributed in Kenya to the formation of K.A.D.U. with its policy of 'democratic regionalism' which included 'protection against deliberate measures by a central government to starve any particular area of money for development and recurrent services' (*The Reporter*, 14 October 1961).

K.A.D.U. was, of course, a political party and it represented one form of the process by which tribalism changed from being primarily a 'cultural' or 'educational' movement into a political force. A major reason for the coalition of tribes it represented was implied in a remark made by its Chairman, Daniel arap Moi, at a public meeting in 1961: 'Today K.A.N.U. doesn't stand for "Kenya African National Union" it stands for "Kikuyu and Nilotic Union".' (*The Reporter*, 14 October 1961). The importance of this tribal factor in party politics was clearly demonstrated by the results of the 1963 elections in Kenya (Gulliver, 1964). It is ironical that one of the most prominent members of the original Kikuyu-Luo alliance (and therefore opponent of K.A.D.U. and *its* tribalism) Mr Oginga Odinga, was himself later responsible for the formation of an opposition party, the Kenya People's Union, which found its main support amongst the Luo of Central Nyanza and Kisumu[4] (the *Observer*, 12 June 1966).

The relation between tribes and political parties in the Congo was much more complex, but it is clear that one reason for the formation of Lumumba's party, the *Mouvement National Congolais*, was the fear felt by some smaller tribes that they would be dominated by the larger ones, either at the local level or in the country as a whole. Such fears were natural enough, in the face of well-organized bodies like A.B.A.K.O. which had changed itself into a political party by 1958. Other tribal organizations followed its example to such an extent that Young remarks, 'Congolese parties are the only significant ones in Africa to adopt specifically ethnic names; there are no important parallels for the Abako, Unimo, and Balubakat' (1965, p. 305).

Perhaps there were no parallels for the names; there were certainly other examples of parties based on single tribes. Morris (*infra*, p. 308) says of the Kabaka Yekka that it was 'in fact, though not in name, a Buganda national political party'. It was equally easy, and not very misleading, to equate Nigerian political parties with tribes or coalitions of tribes: Action Group for the Yoruba; N.C.N.C. for the Ibo; N.P.C. for the Hausa-Fulani; United Middle Belt Congress for the Tiv and Birom. Certainly any reading of the Nigerian English-language press before and after the 1964 elections shows that such equations were made almost daily. One can safely guess that they were made as frequently—and perhaps more violently—in the vernacular press.

There are so many and such well-known examples of European national movements forming themselves into political parties that I will confine myself to one.

Until the end of the nineteenth century, the Ukrainians had no political parties of their own. In the Ukraine . . . there were numerous provincial organizations of a cultural character, the so-called *Hromady* (Communities), devoted to the study of Ukrainian life, but they had no part in political activity. It was only in 1900 that a society of young Ukrainians founded the first political organization, the Revolutionary Ukrainian Party . . . The R.U.P. utilized the local *Hromady* to spread its influence to the provincial towns and villages (Pipes, 1954, pp. 10–11).

This organization of nationalities and of tribes into political parties was not, however, achieved overnight. After all, the majority of their members were originally unconscious that they had any national or tribal identity. They thought of themselves as members of villages, communes, regions, or of clans and lineages. They had to be *taught* that they belonged also to a nation or tribe. One way of teaching them, in Europe, was by inventing national flags, national dress, national anthems, national days, national mottoes, and by reviving the memories of national saints and kings, more or less authentic. The Magyars invoked the 'crown of St. Stephen'; the Czechs, the 'Bohemian Crown' or the 'crown of St. Wenceslaus'; the Croats, the 'Triune Kingdom'. 'Serbian children were taught to look back to the glories of Dušan, Bulgarians to the Empire of Simeon, Roumanians to the wars of Stephen the Great and Michael the Brave' (Seton-Watson, 1946, p. 141). They, and all the others, learned to attach such importance to national emblems that they were often prepared to risk imprisonment and even, sometimes, death for the right to them. It is another of the many ironies attending this whole subject that this consciousness of a distinct political identity was often stimulated by foreigners:

> Historical awe for the Austrian provinces and their Diets was the invention of Metternich, a Rhinelander, and of Gentz, a Prussian . . . this political antiquarianism made a deep mark in Austria's history. . . . Manufactured traditions were the ruin of Austria; and Metternich was the founder of the trade (Taylor, 1964, p. 48).

There was a very brisk trade in the same sort of manufactures among African tribes. A.B.A.K.O. in 1953 had as its emblem the head of a leopard on a shield, and used the Congo flag with a leopard added in the middle and bordered by the Belgian colours. Its founders appealed to the memory of the alleged eponymous ancestor of the whole Kongo people and to the traditions of the old Kongo kingdom (Verhaegen, 1962, pp. 17, 20). Similar symbols and traditions were used by other Congo tribal organizations (Caprasse, 1959, pp. 33–4, 37).

A popular and presumably effective one in East and Central Africa was the demand for a Paramount Chief or King. As early as 1926 the Kikuyu Central Association was petitioning for the recognition of a Kikuyu Paramount (Corfield, 1960, p. 40). The North Kavirondo (Abaluhyia) Central Association actually proclaimed a Paramount for themselves in 1935, though he was not recognized by the British administration and was indeed suspended by it (Rosberg and Nottingham,

1960, p. 163). There is evidence that such demands in Kenya were partly inspired by the example of the large kingdoms of Uganda. It is therefore not surprising that the same example should have influenced the Alur and Lugbara:

> Agofe/Obimo was the new title concocted at the time [1955], half from the Lugbara and half from the Alur language, for the post which somewhat uneasily combines the roles of ceremonial head of the District and chief executive officer of the Council, of which he was also chairman. It was intended to echo, emulate and approximate the titles of the Kabaka, Bakama, and other prestigeful hereditary rulers in Uganda, and to gain for West Nile District the dignity, attention and advantages which they were held to have won for their respective areas (Southall, 1963, p. 5).

Elsewhere similar demands were made, with varying success, by the Chagga of Tanganyika; the Lenje and the Lala of Northern Rhodesia; the Fang of Gabon (Liebenow, 1958, p. 78; *African Affairs*, 1951, p. 38; 1958, p. 36; Balandier, 1955, p. 200). No doubt there are other examples, but it is perhaps significant that nearly all those I have cited are of tribes that were originally segmentary states or even acephalous. It may be that they particularly felt the need of some political symbol to encourage that cohesion necessary for meeting the competition of other tribes in the modern situation. Another way of doing it was to insist on the value of those traditional practices that had transcended political divisions, such as circumcision amongst the Kikuyu or the Gisu (*infra*, p. 328). Yet another was to revive or invent legends of a common ancestor, as amongst the Yoruba (Coleman, 1958, p. 344), or of a common migration to their present home, as amongst the Fang (Fernandez, 1962).

Such deliberate attempts to foster the sense of group identity were often encouraged, directly or indirectly, by outsiders, as they were in the Habsburg Empire. It is common knowledge that the definition of 'tribal' units; the formation of 'tribal' councils; the use of 'tribal' names in censuses and on official forms—all helped (especially in the British territories) to promote a tribal consciousness which had not previously existed.[5] So, too, did the personal attachment of some European missionaries, administrators, and anthropologists to 'their' tribes. One of the most extraordinary examples of this familiar theme (and it is one which supports my general argument) comes from the Congo where . . .

> it was the task of four major writers, three missionaries and an administrator, to accredit the thesis of a single Mongo people. These four . . . became dedicated advocates of Mongohood; Vanderkerken urged the unification of the Mongo in a single province, Boelaert after independence called for the creation of a Mongo state, and all urged the fusion of Mongo dialects into a single Lomongo, to be used both in education and administration. It is no mere coincidence that all four were Flemish; the parallels are striking between what was advocated for the Mongo and demands then formulated by the growing Flemish nationalist movement for the unification and development of their language and people (Young, 1965, pp. 248–9).[6]

It was perhaps easy for Europeans to endorse such claims when they were made for relatively large groups like the Mongo, which could readily be equated with European nations. Some Europeans (and some Africans, too) apparently found it difficult to concede the same 'national' status to smaller groups. For example, Coleman, trying to define his terms in the Nigerian context, included as one criterion of nationhood, 'largeness in scale, which, although imprecise, at least excludes city-states, principalities, and small tribal societies'. Again he wrote: 'whereas several nationalities are both potential and incipient nations (for example, the Hausa, the Yoruba, and the Ibo), others are too small or awkwardly situated to become nations' (1958, pp. 422, 423). A decade later, the *Observer* apparently held to the same criterion when it commented that Nigeria 'is not a country of hundreds of tribes, but one in which three major nations (Ibos, Yorubas, and Fulani-Hausas) coexist among 250 or so tribal groups' (4 June 1967, p. 8). The status of 'nation' has been similarly allowed from time to time to other large groups, such as the Ashanti, the Ewe, the Ganda, the Zulu, and denied, explicitly or implicitly, to smaller tribes.

It is, of course, true that size has usually influenced a group's chances of winning and maintaining independence, that ultimate test of nationhood, and it is also true that the most conspicuous attempts to seize independence have been made by large tribes like the Ibo, the Kongo, the Luba, the Lunda, the Ganda. Yet similar bids have been made by much smaller groups. The Konjo and the Amba of Uganda cannot number together more than about 150,000, but in 1962 some of them began a rebellion, followed by the declaration of an independent state and an appeal to U Thant for United Nations' protection against the forces of the Uganda government (Stacey, 1965, p. 81; and *infra*, p. 252ff.).

No doubt many of those who took part in this rebellion saw it merely as a chance to free themselves from the domination of the hated Toro. For its leader, Mukirane, and for his closest followers, it meant something more which would have been recognizable to European nationalists. Its origin went back to a 'Bakonjo Life History Research Society' (partly inspired by an outsider, Mr Stacey) which Mukirane later turned into a political movement and renamed the 'Rwenzururu Secessionist Movement'. After the rebellion had begun, Mukirane set up a rudimentary administration in the mountains with himself as self-proclaimed 'President' of the new state of Rwenzururu, which had its own national flag and anthem. A statement justifying the secession included many of the classical nationalist complaints and demands: too few schools and scholarships for Konjo and Amba children; hardly any Konjo or Amba teachers and priests; an unfair allocation of land and of the products derived from it; discrimination against Konjo and Amba in appointments to the bureaucracy.

Such pretensions on behalf of so small a people seem bizarre enough, and it is not surprising that Mr Stacey came, reluctantly, to the conclusion that Mukirane was mad. Yet was he any madder than, say, the leaders of the Basque nationalists? There are only about three times as many Basques as there are Konjo and Amba,[7] but numbers did not prevent them demanding and obtaining from the Spanish government in 1932 the same degree of local autonomy as had previously been given to the Catalans, a much larger group. During the Civil War, Basques took the next step and set up the Republic of Euzkadi with a provisional government headed by a President (Thomas, 1965, pp. 81, 83, 370). The Republic was, of course, suppressed by General Franco's armies, but Basque nationalism and separatism still survive today, and Basques are still being imprisoned for advocating them. Nor are the Basques a unique case in Europe. The populations of Albania and Esthonia were probably both under a million when they achieved national independence, and that was one argument which their larger neighbours used against their national aspirations. Unless we wish to identify ourselves with Russians, or Serbs, or Greeks, or Italians, we surely have no reason to accept the argument. By the same token we cannot, on the grounds of size alone, deny the nationalism of many small groups all over Africa today.

In fact, it has already been implicitly conceded by a few authorities. Not long ago Post (1964, p. 67) pointed out that 'if a nation is conceived as having a common culture, language, and historical experience, as the eighteenth- and nineteenth-century European writers held, then the closest approximation to national sentiment in West Africa must be the "tribalism" so often denounced by the nationalists'. What I have done in this paper is to extend the scope of Post's generalization to cover other parts of Africa and to document it by apt illustrations.

It could, I believe, be extended even further. To take only one example, the movements known in India as 'casteism', 'regionalism', or 'communalism', seem to bear a close resemblance to African tribalism. The resemblance is not surprising, for all of them are expressions of that intensified competition for wealth and power which has become a fundamental characteristic of the modern world. In that world the Industrial Revolution greatly increased the resources available, but there were still not enough to go round. At the same time, democratic and, later, socialist theories spread the belief that everyone was entitled to a share of them. In the general scramble that followed, there emerged numerous, mutually exclusive groups whose members had, or believed that they had, certain characteristics in common which enabled them to combine and thus compete more effectively against others who were similarly organized. Since the economic and political revolutions began in Europe, the new groupings appeared there first. As those revolutions spread to other parts of the world they generated similar responses. It is, therefore, essential for us to reflect on our own experiences if we wish to understand those of others. Out of Africa never anything new.

54

NOTES

1 Major-General Gowon has very recently claimed that the breakaway of Biafra was plotted by Ibo academics at Nsukka, formerly at Ibadan (*The Times*, 20 November 1967). I have myself witnessed tribal fighting between Nigerian students in London at a meeting called to discuss the Nigerian crisis in March 1967, before the Ibo secession.

2 Some details of the splits, involving academic, administrative, and labouring staff, as well as the Students' Union, are reported in the *Nigerian Daily Times*, 30 May 1966.

3 The occasional references to the Soli in this paper arise out of my own field research among them, as a Research Officer of the Rhodes-Livingstone Institute, 1957–60.

4 Not, of course, amongst *all* Luo. There are frequent examples of factional splits within the modern tribes and their organizations, just as there were within the nationalist parties of Europe. Even the external threat from other tribes and nations has not always been sufficient to prevent or delay these internal conflicts.

5 During my own fieldwork, I was told emphatically by one old chief that he and his people had not been Soli and had not thought of themselves as such, until the District Commissioner said they were in 1937.

6 The parallel, seen from the other side, is also drawn in an ironical passage by a Kongo writer: 'We do not want to meddle in the internal affairs of our Belgian friends, but we cannot help saying that if this union between Flemings and Walloons were conceived on a federal basis, the almost interminable quarrels which have often broken forth between these two tribes would have been avoided' (Young, 1965, pp. 267–8).

7 If the French Basques are included, there are about 600,000 all together. But the main inspiration and support for the nationalist movement has come from the Spanish Basques who comprise about two-thirds of that number.

REFERENCES

AFRICAN AFFAIRS, 1951; 1958, *Northern Rhodesia: African Affairs. Annual Reports*. Government Printer, Lusaka.

ALOBA, A. 1954, 'Tribal Unions in Party Politics', *West Africa*, 10 July.

BALANDIER, G. 1955, *Sociologie actuelle de l'Afrique noire*, Presses universitaires, Paris.

BIEBUYCK, D. & DOUGLAS, M. 1961, *Congo Tribes and Parties*, Royal Anthropological Institute, London.

BURKE, F. G. 1964, *Local Government and Politics in Uganda*, Syracuse University Press, Syracuse, N.Y.

BURY, J. P. T. 1960, 'Nationalities and Nationalism', *The New Cambridge Modern History*, vol. 10, Cambridge University Press.

CAPRASSE, P. 1959, *Leaders Africaine en milieu urbain (Elizabethville)*, Centre d'Étude des problèmes sociaux indigènes, Collection des mémoires, No. 5.

COLEMAN, J. S. 1958, *Nigeria: Background to Nationalism*, University of California Press, Berkeley & Los Angeles.

CORFIELD, F. D. 1960, *Historical Survey of the Origins and Growth of Mau Mau*, H.M.S.O., London, Cmd. 1030.

DAHYA, B. W. 1963, 'Some Characteristics of Tribal Associations in Kampala', *Proceedings of the East African Institute for Social Research Conference, Jan. 1963*, Part C, Kampala, E.A.I.S.R. Mimeograph.

DOKE, C. M. & VILAKAZI, B. W. 1953, *Zulu-English Dictionary*, Witwatersrand University Press, Johannesburg.

FERNANDEZ, J. W. 1962, 'Folklore as an Agent of Nationalism', *African Studies Bulletin*, 5, 2.

GULLIVER, P. H. 1964, 'Tribes and Political Parties in Kenya', *Institute of Race Relations Newsletter*, February.

HAYES, J. H. C. 1926, *Essays on Nationalism*, Macmillan, New York.

KOHN, H. 1955, *Nationalism: its Meaning and History*, Van Nostrand, New York.

KOLARZ, W. 1946, *Myths and Realities in Eastern Europe*, Lindsay Drummond, London.

LIEBENOW, J. G. 1958, 'Tribalism, Traditionalism and Modernism in Chagga Local Government', *Journal of African Administration*, 8, 2.

MACARTNEY, C. A. 1934, *National States and National Minorities*, Oxford University Press, London.

MIDDLETON, J. 1965, 'Kenya: Changes in African Life', in Harlow, V. & S. Chilver (eds.), *History of East Africa*, vol. 2. Clarendon, Oxford.

OFFODILE, E. P. O. 1947, 'Growth and Influence of Tribal Unions', *The West African Review*, 18.

PETROVICH, M. B. 1956, *The Emergence of Russian Panslavism, 1856–1870*, Columbia University Press, New York.

PIPES, R. 1954, *The Formation of the Soviet Union*, Harvard U.P., Cambridge, Mass.

POST, K. 1964, *The New States of West Africa*, Penguin.

ROSBERG, C. G. & NOTTINGHAM, J. 1966, *The Myth of Mau Mau: Nationalism in Kenya*, Praeger, New York.

SETON-WATSON, H. 1946, *Eastern Europe Between the Wars, 1918–1941*, 2nd ed., Cambridge U.P.

1952, *The Decline of Imperial Russia, 1855–1914*, Methuen.

SETON-WATSON, R. W. 1908, *Racial Problems in Hungary*, Constable, London.

1911, *The Southern Slav Question and the Habsburg Monarchy*, Constable, London.

SOLI NATIVE AUTHORITY. 1958, *Minutes of a Meeting of the Soli Native Authority held . . . between 22nd July and 25th July*, Lusaka, mimeographed (copy in possession of W. J. Argyle).

SOUTHALL, A. W. 1963, 'Micropolitics in Uganda: Traditional and Modern Politics', *Proceedings of the East African Institute of Social Research Conference, Jan. 1963*, Kampala, E.A.I.S.R., mimeographed.

STACEY, T. 1965, *Summons to Ruwenzori*, Secker & Warburg, London.

TAYLOR, A. J. P. 1964, *The Habsburg Monarchy, 1809–1918*, Penguin.

THOMAS, H. 1965, *The Spanish Civil War*, Penguin.

VERHAEGEN, B. 1962, *A.B.A.K.O. 1950–1960*, Les dossiers du C.R.I.S.P., Brussels.

WERLIN, H. H. 1965, 'The Nairobi City Council: a Study in Comparative Local Government', *Comparative Studies in Society and History*, 8.

WILLINK, H. 1958, *Nigeria: Report of the Commission Appointed to Enquire into the Fears of Minorities and the Means of Allaying Them*, H.M.S.O., Cmd. 505.

WISKEMANN, E. 1938, *Czechs and Germans*, Royal Institute of International Affairs, London.

YOUNG, C. 1965, *Politics in the Congo*, Princeton University Press.

ZULU SOCIETY, 1939, *The Charter of the Zulu Society*, 2nd impression, Pietermaritzburg (copy in possession of W. J. Argyle).

TRIBALISM IN POLITICS

George Bennett

THE very names of the three East African states indicate the contrast of tribal influences. While Tanzania and the two names it incapsulates—Tanganyika and Zanzibar— have no tribal connotation, Uganda provides the complete antithesis. There the locative form in Swahili of the name of one tribe became the title of the British Protectorate and thence of the independent state. In Kenya's case this is the European shortening of the name of the mountain sacred to the country's largest and central tribe, the Kikuyu. Each tribe, the Kikuyu and the Ganda, forms nearly one-fifth of its country's population and is, moreover, positioned in such a way as to dominate the life of the country's capital. Kampala, containing the traditional capital of Buganda, is now the capital of Uganda, while the immediate proximity of the Kikuyu country to Nairobi ensures that its population is predominantly Kikuyu. The contrast in Tanzania is notable, for there no tribe of any size or significance abuts on the capital, Dar es Salaam. Indeed, the old name Tanganyika suggests rather a mass of undifferentiated bush people.[1]

Yet the division between the tribal politics of the two northern countries and the lesser emphasis on tribalism in Tanzania does not exactly follow the frontiers. In Tanzania more tribal feeling is apparent in the north of the country. Might this have something to do with the 'Nilotic' and, even more, the 'Nilo-Hamitic' thrust from the north which means that the Bantu line dips down almost to central Tanzania? Recent political phraseology in Uganda, stressing a dichotomy between 'Bantu' and 'Nilotic', might suggest the validity of such an idea; but one needs to look deeper. In Uganda, 'the Bantu' find it difficult to maintain a solid front—there has long been rivalry between, for example, Buganda and Bunyoro—while in Kenya the 'Nilo-Hamitic' Masai have provided cultural patterns which have been adopted by their Bantu neighbours. The linguists' categories, 'Bantu', 'Nilo-Hamitic', and 'Nilotic', are not concepts which arise naturally among the people themselves. In so far as the expressions 'Bantu' and 'Nilotic' are being used today, they are the weapons of political warfare only because the politicians and the newsmen have made them so.

This artificiality is no less true of tribal feeling itself, as elsewhere it has been, and remains so, with nationalistic feeling. Nationalism and tribalism are political attitudes, the result of the activity of political leaders seeking to bind their followers together. The forms that nationalism takes throughout the world, and the forms that tribalism takes in Africa, are essentially the products of the nineteenth and twentieth centuries. Outside Africa the hammering of imperial rule may have produced nations, whether in reaction to the domination of the Habsburgs, the Ottomans, or the British; but within Africa the reply to colonial rule was until very recently expressed mainly at the tribal level. In East Africa the forms of British rule caused tribal sentiment to cohere.

Indeed, it is questionable whether some groups, thought of today as tribes, had much sense of tribal cohesion, or even of tribal identity a hundred years ago. Even at the end of the last century Kikuyu groups were warring among themselves and thus offering the opportunity for Europeans to play on their internecine rivalries. The divisions of the Kikuyu were such that, in 1922, a Scottish missionary who knew them well could comment on their first modern-style political activity under the leadership of Harry Thuku: 'It has been a revelation to me that the Kikuyu have been able to combine in this way'.[2] While the Kikuyu may have, through the pressures of the twentieth century, come to feel increasingly one, they may have lost some whom they, at least, once considered to be Kikuyu (Kenyatta, 1938, p. xv)—for certainly the Embu and the Meru are now generally regarded as separate though closely related tribes. Further south the Chagga have shown an increasing coherence and unity in the period since the Europeans first knew them (Stahl, 1964). A recent study of the Nyamwezi suggests how in the past disparate groups under different chiefs have come together so that today they are regarded as an entity, a tribe (Abrahams, 1967). These are but instances. The list might be extended in a tour around East Africa to produce the conclusion that the tribe is a developing and changing organism.

Uganda

While the tribe may be a sociological, cultural, and linguistic entity, its unity increases most under political forms and pressures. In traditional Africa this was the work of powerful chiefs and war leaders. Among the inter-lacustrine kingdoms of Uganda the almost legendary Chwezi may be taken as the counterparts of such leaders as Arthur or even Alfred, but Ganda tradition insists on the primacy of Kintu in the long line of Kabakas. The Kabaka may have been 'head of the clans', the *ssabataka*, as he was greeted in the politics of the late 1950s; nevertheless, while the clan organization may have been the more ancient, the strength of Buganda lay rather in the hierarchical structure of its *bakungu* chiefs. Certainly these administrative figures displayed a remarkable capacity to adapt to a new position in relation to the British. Their shrewdness both impressed Lugard in 1890 and made possible that Uganda Agreement of 1900 with Sir Harry Johnston which laid the basis for the preservation of the Ganda state through the colonial period.

However, the *bakungu* chiefs were not the only Ganda who saw that they could profit from co-operation with the British. More adventurous spirits went forth. There were Ganda agents of both church and state—of the Christian missionaries expanding from their base in Buganda and of the colonial authorities similarly spreading outwards. The effective alliance between the Ganda and the British was well-typified in the name Uganda for the Protectorate proclaimed in 1894, but whose area was still being brought under control in the next two decades. Buganda's expansion in these years was, it has been well said, 'consonant . . . with her own history . . . in a sense, informal succeeded to formal empire' (Roberts, 1962, p. 448).

But imperialists are never loved. From the moment the Ganda received in 1894 the spoils of war in a large area taken from Bunyoro—'the lost counties' as they were soon called—the seeds of dissension were sown. However, there was more to come. Developing hostility to the Ganda agents led to the Protectorate authorities deciding on their withdrawal. To the Ganda this was regarded as a mark of rejection, a sign that their alliance with the British was breaking up. They had seen themselves as partners in the work of civilizing the Bakedi, 'the naked people', as they contemptuously referred to the people around them. Then after 1935, with the growth of indirect-rule ideas, the British went so far as even to seek to resuscitate the heads of family groups who had been so long eclipsed, first under Ganda agents and then through the continuing patterns of Ganda administration.

Nevertheless, the prestige of the Ganda and their Kabaka remained high. While 'tribal separatism' may have been a factor in generating the steady opposition of the Ganda to European attempts at East African federation in the 1920s (Low & Pratt, 1960, pp. 254–8), Africans took note that theirs was the only African country able to speak out in this way. As far away as South Africa the leading Jabavu family could believe that the Ganda, at least, had maintained a position of security for themselves and their land in the colonial situation by their Agreement of 1900 (Jabavu, 1960). It was thus natural for others in Uganda and elsewhere in East Africa to seek the same symbolic position of having a paramount chief. In 1933 the ancient rival kingdom of Bunyoro at last attained the status of an Agreement with Britain. In 1939 one of the saza chiefs of the Soga, the people to the east of Buganda, was allowed to assume the title of Kyabazinga ('the leader') (Hailey, n.d., pp. 194–5; Nabwiso-Bulima, 1967), but in Kenya all such aspirations for the recognition of a paramount, whether in Nyanza Province or among the Kikuyu, were rejected by the colonial authorities. In Uganda, a Commissioner on Local Government found, in 1953, that the local governments of the various districts of Uganda were . . .

> bent upon reaching the status of a native state. Their object is to achieve a constitution as like that of Buganda as possible, and they believe that they will eventually supplant the Protectorate

Government as the Government of their areas in nearly all affairs. In short they aim at Home Rule and think that this was the Protectorate Government's intention in handing over, as they say, the power to govern their areas.

Moreover, it seems to them that this is the logical development of past administrative policy. Clan barriers have been broken down, sections have been amalgamated, a tribal organization has been created and a tribal loyalty has been developed. In their own estimation they have arrived and they cannot understand why the Protectorate Government, having granted them the name of Governments, still withholds the realities of power and still resists the appointment of rulers or paramount chiefs, and the officers appropriate to a native state (Wallis, 1953, pp. 13–14).

These words were written in the questioning atmosphere of a Uganda under a new and dynamic Governor, Sir Andrew Cohen. He had arrived from the Colonial Office in January 1952 with a mission to prepare Uganda for independence as a nation-state. His necessarily centralizing policies provoked an inevitable clash with Buganda. Her young Kabaka saw his duty as the protection of her institutions. After remarks, in June 1953, by the British Colonial Secretary, Oliver Lyttelton (later Lord Chandos), concerning the possibility of federation in East Africa, Buganda replied by asking that a date be set for her separate independence and that she should in the meanwhile come once again under the Foreign Office (Kabaka, 1967, pp. 114–21). When in the ensuing crisis the Kabaka was deported, his people rallied to his support in defence of their state and against the overweening power of the colonial ruler. Elsewhere hostility to colonialism might lead to nationalism, but for the Ganda the focus of their thought was on their still lively institutions represented in the person of their Kabaka.

The tragedy of the incident was that it turned the Ganda in upon themselves and prevented any possibility of their acting as effective leaders in the new and coming era of nationalism. Yet the year before, in 1952, some among them had, in forming the Uganda National Congress (U.N.C.), shown signs of seeking to do just that. The leader of this new organization was Ignatius K. Musazi, a man long active in the politics of Buganda, who had been chief organizer and secretary of 'the Sons of Kintu' in 1938. This body, voicing the complaints of farmers and merchants, was, however, limited to Buganda, as its name indicated (Apter, 1961, pp. 203–6). When Musazi sought later to organize a wider mass following he found little support. In 1948 and subsequently he formed organizations with the word 'Uganda' in their titles; but in the disturbances of 1949 the battle-cry was 'B.U.' (Bataka Union, pronounced Boo). The Ganda were not looking forward to nationalism, but back to the Bataka agitation of the 1920s and the strong, popular, but tribally-orientated, feelings then expressed over land (Low and Pratt, 1960, p. 274). The Kabaka crisis of 1953 provided the U.N.C. with an insoluble dilemma: to develop in Buganda it had to support the Kabaka, but elsewhere in Uganda that issue was irrelevant. Tribal division, the lack of sympathy between the Ganda and the rest as a result of Buganda's accretion of strength through allying with the colonial rulers, prevented common action of a nationalist pattern.

Musazi's Congress did obtain some support outside Buganda, and it could boast an original organizing committee with members from Teso, Toro, and Lango (Apter, 1961, pp. 311–315). Nevertheless it ceased in the mid-fifties to be an effective organization outside Buganda. For two years, from 1953 to 1955, Uganda was dominated by a tribal, not a national concern. Then, as political parties began to be formed, the new activity occurred first in Buganda. As the Ganda had been the dominant creative force in the early colonial period, so it appeared they might now be again in the new stage of nationalism. However, these parties were so related to the position within Buganda that they found it difficult, if not impossible, to make any impression outside. To this there was only one exception: the Democratic Party (D.P.), whose moving force was the Catholic protest against 'the Protestant ascendancy' in Buganda and elsewhere. When the first direct elections to the Legislative Council were held in 1958 the D.P.'s president, Benedicto Kiwanuka, could say with some justice that the electors' choice had been made mainly on tribal grounds.[3] Indeed, a pattern was beginning whereby the members elected to the Legislative Council appeared as tribal spokesmen or 'ambassadors'.

In this situation, and with the continuing attempts at the building of a national political party, the reaction of the Ganda was of first importance. By the settlement of 1955 which brought about the Kabaka's return, the chiefly hierarchy was established in full control of Buganda. They were determined to maintain their authority against the nascent political parties. In 1956 they found pretexts for expelling E. M. K. Mulira, the leader of the Progressive Party, and Mutayo Mugwanya, the D.P.'s first president, from the Lukiko, Buganda's Parliament.[4] Then events in Ghana, with the developing tension between Nkrumah's government and the chiefs, particularly in the clash with the central kingdom of Ashanti, made the Buganda establishment the more determined to squash any form of nationalism. A declaration was obtained from the clan leaders that political parties were 'in conflict with our good customs and traditions'; and the threat of expulsion from his clan was levied against any Ganda who associated with a party. Finally, after a debate in the Lukiko, the Buganda government issued a statement that political parties were not recognized in Buganda.[5]

At the other end of the political scale in East Africa, Ghana's independence and the Pan-African planning of its Prime Minister, Nkrumah, stimulated the formation, in September 1958, of the Pan-African Freedom Movement of East and Central Africa (P.A.F.M.E.C.A.). The only Ugandan present at the initial meeting in Mwanza with the leaders from Kenya, Nyasaland, Tanganyika, and Zanzibar, was E. M. K. Mulira. The fact that the proceedings were conducted in Swahili led him to decide that the Ganda would have to learn the language[6]—a remarkable conclusion for a leading member of the tribe which, proud of its own Luganda, had opposed the introduction of Swahili into administrative usage in the inter-war years (*infra*, p. 811). The P.A.F.M.E.C.A. leaders, on their side, 'attempted as their first task to bring unity' (Mboya, 1963, p. 210) to the East African countries that were divided. Thus Kampala received first, in November, a visit from Julius Nyerere and Tom Mboya. While they succeeded in arranging meetings between the leaders of Uganda's political parties, they could not bridge the gulfs between them, especially between the Ganda and the rest. Then, in December, seven of the ten African elected members of the new Legislative Council formed a new body, the Uganda People's Union (U.P.U.). Despite the smallness of the numbers involved, the action was

65

doubly significant: as an attempt to counter Buganda's political dominance, and as the first political initiative of non-Ganda. The leader, B. K. Magezi of Bunyoro, explained that the U.P.U. had developed from a study of 'the various districts where the political movement has not yet penetrated deeply'. In fact, the men concerned comprised four from the three western kingdoms of Bunyoro, Toro, and Ankole, two from Busoga, and one from Bugishu.[7]

On their side the Ganda developed the tactic of the boycott which they had first applied to the Legislative Council in 1958. They refused to appear before the Wild Committee which was set up in February 1959 to make recommendations for constitutional development. To express their complete opposition to all such ideas they decided to form their own political organization: the Uganda National Movement, the title of which could only be justified by reading 'Buganda' for 'Uganda'. In this Movement the Ganda masses were organized, with the U.N.M.'s large meetings in Kampala culminating in the singing of 'the Buganda anthem' and the crowd facing towards the Kabaka's palace at Mengo. Ganda suggestions of similar meetings elsewhere in Uganda facing 'tribal centres of administration' with the singing of tribal anthems[8] met only contemptuous rejection. The Ganda chiefs had to learn, then as later, that there was no future for them in building on a system of tribal alliances.

Inside Buganda, the U.N.M. became an increasing force, a 'Congress-movement', which united the Ganda in a common front. It declared itself against political parties and nearly all the Ganda political leaders were drawn in, with Mulira and Musazi playing prominent parts (Pratt, 1961, p. 168). However, the main lead was taken by the less Westernized members of Buganda's society, men who expressed the popular feeling of Katwe, the African trading centre of Kampala. Of these, Augustine Kamya, a building contractor, made the boycott really effective by developing it beyond the original narrow constitutional questions and by applying it to the Asians.[9] Thus the U.N.M. soon developed into 'the most powerful [party] which the country had so far seen', and was 'singularly successful in ejecting the Asian traders from the Buganda countryside' (Low, 1964, p. 442). With its intimidatory methods including arson, the Protectorate authorities had to take action against it; though they were scarcely supported in this by the Kabaka's government, which found it 'extremely difficult' to make a 'complete' condemnation of the Movement.[10] The Ganda establishment had in effect constructed an alliance with the masses so that they remained inoculated against the virus of nationalism.

On their side, the African members in the Uganda Legislative Council spoke against the U.N.M.'s boycott and even called for a suspension of grants to the Buganda government.[11] However, there was one politician with the shrewdness to see that it was necessary to come to terms with this consolidated Ganda power. This was Milton Obote, who from June 1959 turned from outright condemnation of the boycott to a criticism of its handling by the Protectorate government (Rothchild and Rogin, 1966, p. 356). The rise of Obote was to turn the whole tribal structure of Uganda's politics upside down. Having learned his politics outside Uganda, in the hard school of Nairobi during the Mau Mau period, he had returned in 1957 to his home district of Lango in northern Uganda. There he quickly built up a solid base in trade union and local political activity. He was elected to the Legislative Council in 1958 as a member of the U.N.C. and was soon caught up in the divisions of that organization. Such strength as it still had in Buganda was sapped by the rise of the U.N.M. With the breakaway also of the U.P.U., men from the north now became predominant in the U.N.C. In August 1959 delegates from Acholi and Lango, meeting at Gulu, passed a motion of no confidence in the party chairman, J. W. Kiwanuka, a long-established Ganda figure and something of a stormy petrel. While the grounds of their attack were many and various, Kiwanuka retorted by accusing his opponents of 'tribalism'. In the upshot the U.N.C. split. The majority of the 'Obote wing' of the U.N.C. were northerners and Obote had to confess that it had 'very little strength in Buganda',[12] although one of its leaders was Abu Mayanja, a Ganda who had been while a student a founder member of the U.N.C. When Mayanja became Minister of Education in the Kabaka's government in January 1960, some thought that he might be a link to bring together Obote's U.N.C. and Buganda.[13]

Meanwhile the U.P.U. was growing mainly in western Uganda. One report, in August 1959, indicated that a third of its members then were in Kigezi. In October, students at Makerere College organized a meeting of the leaders of the political parties, at which Obote was chairman and Magezi secretary. This foreshadowed the coming together of the two parties in March 1960 after they had jointly protested against the Governor's refusal to accept the Wild Committee's recommendation of responsible government under a chief minister. Thus the Uganda People's Congress (U.P.C.) emerged with Obote as its president-general: a party the more effective as it commanded the strength of the Obote wing of the U.N.C. in northern Uganda with that of the U.P.U. in the western and eastern provinces.[14] Its first administrative secretary, and subsequently secretary-general, John Kakonge, has acknowledged that 'the basic forces in the formation of the U.P.C. were tribal and personal, and its structure was based on a conglomeration of tribes'.[15] However, the U.P.C. did not then overcome the main tribal cleavage, for at its formation only one of its seventeen officers was a Ganda. While it could claim strength throughout the rest of Uganda, 'it had no support in Buganda' (Rothchild and Rogin, 1966, p. 357).

The reaction of the Buganda authorities to the Wild Report was to demand once more separate independence for their kingdom. Faced with two national parties, the U.P.C. and the D.P., some Ganda decided to reply with a party in which the Ganda would again predominate: the so-called Uganda National Party (U.N.P.). Much speculation ensued as to whether it was supported by the Kabaka and his ministers: certainly it was spoken of in the vernacular press as 'the party of the Buganda magnates'. It made a point of seeking to guarantee the traditional rulers, while negotiations did go on between the Kabaka and his fellow kings. Then a merger of the U.N.P. with the U.P.C. was mooted, but this came to nothing when one U.N.P. condition appeared to mean the debarring of Obote from holding office in such a party.[16] Some at least among the Ganda had understood his potentiality. Moreover, fears were being expressed lest he might become Uganda's first prime minister: certainly the prospect of being governed by a non-Ganda filled the Ganda with dismay. Kamya, imprisoned for his activities in connection with the U.N.M., celebrated his release by saying that the Kabaka must rule the country. There were further attacks in Buganda on the political parties, culminating in a mob obtaining the ejection from the Lukiko of all who belonged to a party.[17]

As tension increased in Buganda, the Protectorate government told the leaders of P.A.F.M.E.C.A. that they could not hold their annual meeting in Kampala. After the Lukiko had passed a resolution for separate independence for Buganda (set for 1 January 1961) the P.A.F.M.E.C.A. meeting at Mbale in October 1960 was left only to condemn tribalism, with special reference to Buganda.[18] At this time the Buganda establishment was able to demonstrate its power by preventing more than 3·5 per cent of potential Ganda voters registering as electors for the forthcoming Legislative Council election (Welbourn, 1965, p. 22).

In 1961, however, they found that they could not make their declaration of independence effective. By abstaining from the elections they allowed the D.P. to win all but one of the seats in Buganda, so that the Kabaka was affronted by having a Ganda *mukopi* (a peasant), Benedicto Kiwanuka, as Prime Minister above him. After Kiwanuka had tactlessly celebrated his victory with slighting remarks about the Kabaka, the Ganda turned again to organization. They capitalized on their cry of support for their monarch by establishing 'the Kabaka Yekka' (K.Y.: 'the Kabaka alone'). While its leaders denied that it had any connection with the banned U.N.M., it was noted that in many places the K.Y. simply built on that old organization. Most of the K.Y.'s leaders were land-owners of some standing, and it was soon openly supported by Buganda officials. Once more opinion in Buganda had solidified.

Since the D.P. and its leaders were regarded as 'traitors' in Buganda, the only national party that could negotiate with this new power was the U.P.C. Its leader, Obote, ever shrewd and holding to his aim of power in an independent Uganda, took up the challenge. The suggestion was made for an 'alliance between Buganda and U.P.C.' The Kabaka accepted, despite the opposition of his Katikiro (prime minister) who recalled an Obote speech 'that he meant to crush the Baganda' (Kabaka, 1967, p. 160). While this alliance between the most nationalist

69

party, the U.P.C., and the traditional leaders of Buganda appeared to outside observers as incongruous, some in the U.P.C. could regard it as the final stage of Uganda's 'tribal conglomeration' (Kakonge, 1966, p. 3). It was sufficient for new elections to be held in both Uganda and Buganda, and these resulted in a U.P.C.-K.Y. government which took Uganda to independence in 1962.

While the Kabaka kept his part of the bargain in accepting Obote as Prime Minister, there was some concern whether Obote would be able to persuade his northern followers in the U.P.C., men of non-monarchical tribes, that the Kabaka should become Head of State. In fact, Obote was more than loyal in bringing this about in October 1963, since the Kabaka had by then thrown down the gauntlet on the most acute tribal issue possible, that of Bunyoro's lost counties. Ian Macleod, then British Colonial Secretary, had laid it down, with Obote's agreement, that the fate of two of the counties should be decided by a referendum two years after independence. By going to a 'hunting lodge' in the area in March 1963, followed by some 8,000 ex-servicemen for a resettlement scheme, the Kabaka appeared to be introducing possible voters to swing the plebiscite. However, the courts ruled that they were ineligible to vote. Then in September 1964, the Kabaka failed to sign the Bill providing for the referendum, thus suggesting that he considered his loyalty to Buganda was more important than his duty as Head of State.[19]

In November the announcement of the referendum result— 13,602 for Bunyoro, 3,542 for Buganda—provoked rioting among the Ganda in Kampala and the fall of Kintu, the Katikiro, after a stormy debate in the Lukiko (Bennett, 1965, p. 107). The pretensions of the Ganda had been exposed. Already in August Obote had felt himself strong enough to break the alliance by dismissing the K.Y. members of his Cabinet. The Ganda had yet to learn, however, that after the breaking of this alliance they would be treated more firmly than they had been by the British after the disappearance of the earlier alliance. When mutual trust between Obote and the Kabaka finally disappeared in early 1966, Obote simply but effectively announced that he was assuming the functions of the President, on the grounds that the latter had committed a series of 'unconstitutional acts'. The Lukiko might protest, and even appeal to the United Nations; but when this was followed by widespread disturbances in Buganda, Obote replied by ordering in the army with its large northern constituent. They mounted a full-scale attack on the Kabaka's palace. The Kabaka and his Katikiro escaped but the palace was ransacked and the royal drums, the sacred symbols of Buganda, destroyed. In June President Obote announced the end of the Kabaka's government, and that henceforth the central government would deal not with Buganda as a unit but with each of its four separate districts which would be organized in a way similar to that of the other districts of Uganda.

If any members of the other traditional kingdoms chuckled at Buganda's discomfiture, their turn was to come. A new Constitution introduced in the National Assembly in July 1967 provided for the ending of the monarchies, the pensioning of their rulers, and the reduction of these ancient states to the status of ordinary districts. Obote was determined to build a nation. He had set out his objective quite clearly in a speech in 1963: 'the problems of people putting the tribe above national consciousness is a problem that we must face, and an issue we must destroy'.[20] The only question that remained was whether he would be successful through the strong methods he had employed.

Kenya

In Kenya the contrast of the roots of tribalism is complete: here there was no dominant kingdom, nor ancient monarchies, but a pattern of interlocking acephalous tribes and clans. Here tribal unity has been produced, not by powerful chiefs acting from within, but rather by the interplay of events and the pressures of external forces. It is the twentieth century, with the coming of European colonial power in its political and economic aspects, that has given the people an awareness of themselves as being members of 'tribes'.

In Kenya the important factor has been not alliance but resistance. Those who put up the stoutest opposition to the incoming British were the Nandi, who paid the penalty when their ritual leader (*orkoiyot*), Koitalel, was shot by a British officer in

71

the Nandi rebellion of 1905. His effective successor, Parserion arap Samwei, was violently anti-British and was deported to Meru after plotting a rebellion in 1923. Others of the Nandi *orkoiyots* were called in by the closely related Kipsigis. They caused such trouble in cattle-raiding against neighbouring tribes and European farms that the colonial administration decided in 1934 to remove the whole *orkoiyot* clan from the Kipsigis reserve (Middleton, 1965, pp. 381–2). However, such activity was never more than an expression of resistance, of a desire to maintain the old ways. Not from this or from the action of others, like the Gusii and the Taita who provoked colonial 'punitive expeditions' in the years before the First World War, nor even from the larger-scale Giriama rising of 1913 to 1914, was anything constructive for the future to develop. Africans may today find heroes in this period; but these men were operating within the tribal framework and may hardly be considered as forerunners of nationalism, even though Waiyaki of the Kikuyu, dying 'it is said by his own hand, at Kibwezi on the way to his exile', is now regarded as 'the first Kikuyu martyr, and this incident is still a turning-point in Kikuyu nationalist mythology' (Rosberg and Nottingham, 1966, p. 14).

This last phrase, in a recent study of 'nationalism in Kenya', illustrates in an acute form the problem of the relationship between 'tribalism' and 'nationalism'. By which of these terms is the activity of the Kikuyu to be designated? May one say that so far as it looks forward to a constructive future it is 'nationalist', whereas if the focus of thought and action is essentially local it is 'tribal'. Can the judgment of non-Kikuyu Africans in Kenya be accepted if they designate Kikuyu activity 'tribalist'? These questions are pointed up through the contrast with Buganda. Whereas its leaders did not look to the creation of a Ugandan nation, the problem with the Kikuyu has been rather whether they, in putting forward the wider objective of the building of Kenya, were not doing so in the expectation that they, through attaining education and positions of responsibility before other peoples in Kenya, might be able to control the larger unit.

The double focus of Kikuyu activity may be illustrated from the actions of the first major African political figure in Kenya's history, Harry Thuku. The Europeans referred to the attraction he exerted in his exile, after his arrest in 1922, as 'Thukuism'; but they conveniently avoided, thereby, the problem of definition, whether he was mainly a tribal figure or could be designated a nationalist leader. Particular attention has recently been paid to Thuku's activity in the East African Association (E.A.A.), with the claim that he 'boldly precipitated a crisis' in the rural areas of central Kenya between this Association and the recently formed Kikuyu Association (K.A.) (Rosberg and Nottingham, 1966, p. 47). While there was undoubtedly a rivalry, it would seem that the members of the latter body, chiefs and headmen, regarded Thuku's challenge as coming rather through his Young Kikuyu Association (Y.K.A.). At Kahuhia, the very centre of Thuku's activity in the Kikuyu countryside, was stationed a missionary, the Rev. Handley D. Hooper, who had two long conversations with Thuku early in 1922. He considered that Thuku had modelled his Y.K.A. on the Young Baganda Association (Kyle, 1966, p. 18)—the Ganda were thus providing an example for Africans at the populist level, as elsewhere at the monarchical. In Nairobi Thuku might operate with his 'cosmopolitan' (Hooper, n.d.) friends in the E.A.A. and concentrate on those common grievances which bound workers of all tribes together, thus leading one observer to comment: 'A polyglot *nation* was beginning to emerge from among certain of the highland and lake tribes' (Ross, 1927, p. 228). However, in Kikuyuland there were other questions to stir people. Thuku wrote to the Senior Commissioner, Nyeri, in the name of 'the Gathirimu Community' to protest about the dismissal of one chief, Waweru, and his replacement by another, Waruhiyu [sic].[21] Hooper noted that Thuku's 'detractors' considered his intention was to exalt his Gathirimu community 'into a royal clan'. Hooper knew that by his attacks on unpopular chiefs Thuku had attained a far wider support than had the K.A. After Thuku's arrest in March 1922, young Kikuyu women were heard bewailing, in a dance-song, '*Gicukia*', that they had 'taken away the chief of the girls', for Thuku was being looked on 'as the only one who stood up for the Kikuyu against the Government', since no chief or missionary would have done what he did.[22]

The Thuku agitation of 1920–2 set a long continuing pattern

for Kikuyu politics, in the relationship between the urban activity of Nairobi, where the largest African group was Kikuyu, and the central area of Kikuyuland, Fort Hall (now Muranga), which was at this time the mainspring of Kikuyu radicalism. It was men from Fort Hall who formed the Kikuyu Central Association (K.C.A.) in Nairobi. In a petition to the Governor at the end of 1925 they were asking for the release of Thuku, for the publication of the laws of the country in Kikuyu, and for the appointment of a Kikuyu paramount chief, an idea which was to be repeated but which showed again the strong influence of the Ganda model (Rosberg and Nottingham, 1966, pp. 92–9).

In 1928 the K.C.A. obtained as its general secretary Johnstone (later Jomo) Kenyatta, who began to edit for the Association a monthly paper, *Muigwithania* ('the reconciler'). While one colonial administrator welcomed it as 'energetic, virile and enterprising . . . deserving of much commendation',[23] the Chief Native Commissioner later commented on its enigmatic articles and parables,[24] in that use of the Kikuyu language which was, in Kenyatta's case, so to trouble the colonial authorities around 1950. As an English-speaker, Kenyatta was chosen by the K.C.A. leaders to represent them in a visit to Britain in 1929. There he was concerned both with constitutional matters, asking for African representatives to be elected to the Kenya Legislative Council,[25] and with a major issue then developing in Kenya: the quarrel between the Kikuyu and the missionaries of the Church of Scotland over female circumcision (Beck, 1966; Atholl, 1958, pp. 176–8). It was Kenyatta's defence of Kikuyu custom that created the impression in London that he was 'uninterested in widening his views beyond the narrow perspective of his tribe'.[26] In his second and longer stay in Britain, from 1931, Kenyatta produced a full-scale study of his Kikuyu people under the title *Facing Mount Kenya* (1938), a book which is a fascinating mixture of anthropology and political tract, casting an aura over practices which might otherwise seem barbarous and repulsive. In all this Kenyatta has appeared as the African leader who has most stressed, and even gloried in, his tribal roots.[27] Yet in London he became the most 'sophisticated and Westernized' (Abrahams, 1960, pp. 55–9) of the Pan-African group of leaders, so that on returning to Kenya in

1946 he faced an enormous, and possibly insoluble, problem in his relationships with his old Kikuyu associates. Kenyatta was given a hero's welcome and elected president of the Kenya African Union (K.A.U.) in 1947. He wished to operate as the nationalist leader of Kenya; but the Kikuyu were planning in tribal terms, binding the people together through the taking of 'an oath of unity'—they were concerned with the defence of their land. In the symbols used they were appealing to the original ancestors of the tribe, Gikuyu and Mumbi, and to the early age-set of Ndemi and Mathathi who represented 'the golden age of tribal unity and prosperity'. There were prayers to Ngai, the Kikuyu high god who dwelt on the sacred Mount Kenya to which the Kikuyu faced in prayer. The traditional Kikuyu oaths, *muma*[28] and the more serious ones taken on a goat (*thenge*) and a stone (*gethathi*), were used and developed.[29]

Such methods were, however, no less divisive than they were unifying. The female circumcision issue of 1929 had added other divisions within the tribe. When the Kikuyu opposed their educators, the missionaries of the Church of Scotland, they expressed their dominant desire for education in establishing their own independent schools, one group of which were designated *karinga* ('the pure'). They were thus separated from the *kirore*, the fingerprinters, those, that is, who signed the mission declaration against clitoridectomy.[30] The latter were the convinced Christians whose successors, after 1946, refused the oath with its pagan tribal background. Moreover, how could such symbols appeal to others beside the Kikuyu? In the 1920s the Kikuyu, James Beuttah, had been in touch with the Young Kavirondo Association of western Kenya; while in the 1930s the significantly named North Kavirondo Central Association came into being through Nairobi contacts, and was further stimulated in 1938 by a visit from a leading K.C.A. figure, Jesse Kariuki. Thus there was 'a marked increase in Kikuyu-style political activity in Nyanza' (Lonsdale, 1964, pp. 314 and 324–5). With the Mau Mau oath, such interconnected action was less possible. Nevertheless, some Kamba were oathed, and the colonial government was concerned about happenings among the Masai and the Kipsigis, the latter having a Kipsigis Central Association formed in 1947. Finally, the government heard of a 'secret society in South Nyanza, known

GEORGE BENNETT

as *Meru Meru*, with aims and objects identical with those of
Mau Mau, but its existence proved brief' (Corfield, 1960, pp.
212–14 and 216). In general, however, 'the oathing accelerated
the isolation of the Kikuyu from other African peoples in
Kenya' (Rosberg and Nottingham, 1966, p. 261). For the
future there was to be yet another problem, noted by four men
who were Ministers in Kenyatta's government at Kenya's
independence in 1963: 'The symbols of the revolt . . . were
traditional symbols. The educated young man of today either
does not understand these symbols at all or is taught to look
down upon them. They represent a way of life from which he
has become increasingly isolated.'[31] The whole movement was
then a blind-alley. In fact, there is a danger of it becoming 'a
myth' in the new Kenya, for it did not lead to independence.
Instead, it deepened the divisions both among the Kikuyu and
among Kenya Africans.

Since Mau Mau was defeated by the mid-1950s, independence came rather from the activities of the new political leaders
who became prominent during the Mau Mau Emergency.
While the colonial government's Emergency regulations banned
political organizations above the district level (Bennett and
Rosberg, 1961, pp. 32–7), there may have been other, and
deeper, factors in the difficulty of developing national politics.
The new men were the first Westernized, educated English-
speakers, sent to represent their tribal groups as 'ambassadors'
in the Legislative Council in Nairobi; they became, in effect,
tribal 'boss-men'.[32] While the Emergency regulations may have
compelled the network of personal alliances that was the pattern
of Kenya politics in the late 1950s, this might have happened
in any case, for something similar was happening in Uganda.
The new men had to begin afresh, but the older organization
of K.A.U. had become increasingly 'Kikuyu-dominated' (Ogot,
1963, pp. 269–70); with the growing Mau Mau intimidation
in Nairobi around 1950 some non-Kikuyu leaders left the
capital in disgust.

During the Emergency, which temporarily barred the
Kikuyu from politics, others built up positions on tribal bases.
One such was Oginga Odinga. While he did seek to maintain
an apostolic tradition with Kenyatta and K.A.U., yet his
effective work was in the Luo Thrift and Trading Corporation

and in the Luo Union of which he became *Ker* (chief or president). His autobiography indicates the need he felt to build among his own Luo people a sense of pride in themselves (Odinga, 1967, pp. 79–81 and 87). Being always respectful to Luo customs and the Luo elders, Odinga soon established himself as the leader of traditional and conservative opinion. Then, for the first African elections to the Legislative Council in March 1957, he found support in the African District Association (Central Nyanza), making it a centre of his appeal to the more radical sentiments of the intelligentsia and the townsmen of Kisumu (Ogot, 1963, p. 274). Thus Odinga built up in Kisumu and the surrounding district of Central Nyanza a power structure in which he harnessed together in a remarkable fashion both the conservative and the radical forces among the Luo. Odinga became, as he remains to the present, the supreme example of Kenya's 'boss-men'. A no less significant achievement was that of Daniel arap Moi of the Tugen, and Taita Towett of the Kipsigis, in constructing a unity among those 'Nilo-Hamitic' semi-pastoralists known to anthropologists in the past as 'the Nandi-group'. In the late 1940s Towett, while a pupil at the Alliance High School, formed a tribally-focused society with 'Kalenjin' in its title. This word was taken for the Kalenjin Political Alliance, formed in April 1960 of the Independent Parties that Moi and he had established by districts among these closely related tribes with common customs and mutually comprehensible languages[33] (Bennett, 1963a, p. 125). While Towett has subsequently fallen in the political game, Moi has, on the foundation of this activity, attained an importance in the national arena so that today he is Kenya's Vice-President.

The effect of the Emergency regulations, and the way in which these new men came up, meant that the political parties —formed in 1960 when national parties were again allowed —appeared, in both the Kenya African National Union (K.A.N.U.) and the Kenya African Democratic Union (K.A.D.U.), as agglomerations of the district associations. The main K.A.N.U. tribes, Kikuyu, Luo, and Kamba, were those whose members had been most drawn as workers into the European economy; while K.A.D.U. was composed of pastoral tribes and of smaller agricultural tribes who had been

77

much less affected by the colonial impact. In both parties tribal strains were considerable. In 1962 the Kamba members of the Legislative Council, K.A.N.U. by party, made plain to the Regional Boundary Commissioners the Kamba desire to be in a region separate from 'either the Kikuyu or the Masai who look down upon them'; and in the end the Kamba broke away from K.A.N.U. to form the African People's Party. It was unable to justify its title as anything more than a Kamba affair (Bennett, 1963b, pp. 297–9), and a year later the Kamba returned to K.A.N.U. By then in the 1963 election campaign, tribal stresses had appeared in K.A.D.U. between the Kalenjin and the Luhya over the siting of Kitale in either the Rift Valley or the Western Region (Sanger and Nottingham, 1964).

Against this pattern and these developments it is, perhaps, remarkable how much unity has been achieved in Kenya. Indeed, for some fifteen months from November 1964 there was a single-party situation in K.A.N.U. While the political party, the Kenya People's Union (K.P.U.), which broke from K.A.N.U. in March 1966, may stress its ideological differences, its localized, and therefore tribal, support is clear. In the 'little general election' of 1966, Odinga held unshaken his position of control in Central Nyanza, while the continuing discontents of the Kamba of Machakos were evidenced by their giving their seats to K.P.U. men.

When the K.P.U. was formed, its leaders made plain their distress at the break with Kenyatta, Kenya's President since December 1964 (Bennett, 1966, p. 341). While Kenyatta may earlier have failed to be an effective national leader, between his return to Kenya in 1946 and his arrest, in October 1952, for alleged complicity in Mau Mau, he did triumph after his release in August 1961. Built up since early 1958 by the new leaders as 'the father of nationalism in Kenya', he proved an effective 'reconciler' of the country's divisions. The fact that his real relationship with Mau Mau is problematic may have helped him in this, since it is possible both for the old forest fighters to continue to accept him as their hero,[34] and for others to believe that the connection with the brutalities of Mau Mau was only something pinned on him by the old European power-structure in Kenya.[35] Kenyatta is thus both the true (*karinga*) Kikuyu and the veritable Kenyan; for in Kenya, in contrast with Uganda, the major tribe has not stood over against the nation.

Tanzania

Tanganyika, in contrast, was not dominated by a single tribe. The largest group, the Sukuma, is situated so far from the capital, on the southern shores of Lake Victoria, that it could not play such a role. From a small tribe to their north, the Zanaki, has come President Nyerere, 'the father of the nation' as he is called today. As a student of history, he considers that the early and widespread resistance to the Germans provided for his followers in the Tanganyika African National Union (T.A.N.U.) in the 1950s 'a *mystique* in their struggle for our independence'.[36] Indeed, he has written: 'Unlike Kenya, Uganda and Zanzibar, we were a conquered people, conquered by the Germans. Unlike them too, our own people had tried to rise against their domination as early as 1905–7. During those years nearly one-quarter of our country was involved in the Maji Maji rebellion. . . '. In its failure, he believes a lesson was learned: 'that a call for unity for the purpose of achieving independence could be understood by the masses, especially by those tribes which had been involved in the Maji Maji rebellion.'[37] Certainly this transtribal action was remarkable, and it may be that the severity with which the Germans conquered, and suppressed rebellions, their 'destruction of tribal military power, and frequently of tribal chiefs themselves, had considerable consequences for later political development' (Bates, 1966, p. 400). While in the Maji Maji rebellion the African peoples may have been bound together in common peasant grievances against the Germans, yet a recent student of the movement has acknowledged that within it were reflections of 'the cultural and political divisions of the past' (Iliffe, 1967, p. 512). There is, then, a danger in seeking to build a national 'myth' on the initial resistances to the incoming Europeans, whether on the tribal basis as in Kenya or even on the transtribal basis as in Maji Maji. Moreover, in finding nationalism there, an injustice may be done to the true creators of the nation, the political thinkers and activists who bound the people together in the national movement of the 1950s.

Yet in Tanganyika the whole period of German rule, 'strict but just',[38] the devastation of the First World War in which the country was fought over, then the influenza epidemic of 1918, and the worst recorded famine, that of 1919, may together have produced a sense of common experience in suffering.

As Tanganyika recovered during the 1920s, the first African local associations, some occupational and some tribal in framework, began to appear in the more prosperous northern half of the territory. As early as 1924 there was, at Bukoba in the north-east, a Bahaya Union formed by 'the most progressive members of the Haya community' (Hailey, 1950, p. 227). This took up grievances against the chiefs and over land. In changing its name in 1927 to the African Association, and in its subsequent co-operation with the Tanganyika African Association (T.A.A.), of which it even became a branch, it served as a bridge between local and wider concerns, as in its opposition to East African federation. Nevertheless, its focus was 'almost exclusively on Buhaya'. It was repeatedly concerned with the problem of Haya women who went out across East Africa and became renowned as prostitutes (Hyden, 1968, pp. 107–11). In 1937 it protested against the coffee cultivation rules then being imposed by the colonial government, and rioting broke out in different parts of the district (Hailey, n.d., p. 241). Common interests arising from the greater prosperity engendered by the production of a cash-crop were increasing the sense of tribal identity, especially as the marketing co-operatives practically became 'part of the tribal structure' (Bates, 1966, p. 439).

As it was with the Haya, so also with the Chagga. In their case such developments began from the creation in 1924 of the Kilimanjaro Native Planters' Association. By 1928 it was being regarded as a focus of opinion against Europeans, the Chagga chiefs, and the colonial government (Ingham, 1965, pp. 556 and 582). It developed into the Kilimanjaro Native Co-operative Union, and, after the Second World War, with imposing buildings in Moshi, it came to symbolize the very spirit of Chagga progressiveness. The Chagga desire for education resulted in their being able in the 1950s to obtain positions in the civil service, in teaching and in other ways out of all proportion to their numbers. Colonial administrators might speak of the Chagga as 'the Kikuyu of Tanganyika' but they were too small a people and too far from the capital to play any similar role. Moreover, in the 1950s the Chagga became so deeply involved in their own internal affairs, being concerned again with having a paramount chief, that wider developments on the national scene largely passed them by.

In this there was a marked contrast with the Sukuma, the largest of Tanzania's tribes, comprising about one-ninth of the country's population. From 1946 the colonial government followed a policy of bringing the Sukuma chiefs together in the 'Sukumaland Federation'. With 'considerable expenditure . . . being incurred on the construction of a Council Hall', and the belief of the colonial rulers that the Federation would 'minister to the tribal pride of the Sukuma people' (Hailey, 1950, p. 232), some African political leaders began to fear lest the Sukuma be led to think of following the Ganda into the creation of 'a native state'. However, younger men in the tribe had wider perspectives. By the late 1940s they were playing such a large part in T.A.A. that the suggestion was put that its headquarters should be moved to Mwanza.[39] The Lake Province had become by 1954, through the activity of the Haya and the Sukuma, Tanganyika's most politically conscious region. Prominent in this among the Sukuma were the Bomani family, particularly Paul who in 1952 was T.A.A.'s provincial chairman. In the same year he organized and became first president of the Lake Province Cotton Growers' Association, which developed in 1955 into the Victoria Federation of Co-operative Unions (V.F.C.U.), the largest marketing co-operative in Africa. While undoubtedly its strength drew upon Sukuma tribal feeling, its various societies did also act as centres for the development of a wider nationalism. In the Lake Province, as the United Nations Visiting Mission noted in 1954, the co-operative and political movements were 'inter-mixed'; thus when, in 1954, branches of the newly formed Tanganyika African National Union (T.A.N.U.) were proscribed in Sukumuland, its life could continue through the channels of the V.F.C.U. (Bennett, 1963c, p. 19). Thus tribalism became subsumed in nationalism.

Such a development was the more possible in Tanganyika

in these years since the tribes became united in common grievances against the policies of the colonial administration. Indeed, the resistance of one tribal organization, the Meru Citizens Union (M.C.U.) provided a spark for the whole development of the national movement.[40] From the slopes of Mount Meru, Kirilo Japhet, the leader of the M.C.U. took his opposition to the alienation of Meru lands to the United Nations, and then, on his return from New York, in wide touring of the territory under the auspices of T.A.A. The Meru Land Case aroused widespread suspicion of the colonial government and hence an interest in united political action. Equally this was so in respect of the government's agricultural policies, as in compulsory communal labour for soil conservation and compulsory cattle-culling, and its 'multi-racial' policy. In Tanganyika a national party could grow on common opposition to policies operating throughout the whole territory. The situation was, indeed, different from Uganda, where one tribe had been affected by the Kabaka's deportation, and from Kenya, where the colonial government was acting against the rebellion of one particular tribe.

Another contrast is underlined in a remark by President Nyerere that in Tanzania 'no one tribal group dominated all others in size, wealth and education'. For Nyerere this was but the culminating fact in a list of 'historical circumstances' which favoured Tanganyika's rapid progress to independence after the birth of T.A.N.U. in July 1954. Before this, Nyerere noted, 'the groundwork of political organization existed in the form of a multitude of very small welfare and tribal organizations' (Nyerere, 1967, p. 1). In saying this he was being less touchy about 'tribalism' than are some of his followers who now find it necessary to provide 'operative myths' for T.A.N.U. They would distort T.A.N.U.'s past by 'denying a share in its parentage to the tribal unions', seeking instead to trace its roots 'to the T.A.A. and to co-operative societies' (Bienen, 1967, p. 25). In this they overlook the consociational spirit of T.A.N.U.'s formation which in its original constitution made specific provision for tribal associations to join (Bennett, 1963c, p. 17).

However, T.A.N.U.'s initial growth was largely through the interconnections of 'the old centres of African Muslims dotted throughout the country' (Stahl, 1964, p. 359) and through the use of Swahili as a lingua franca. Possibly Nyerere is over-stating the case when he claims that 'Swahili was understood by the majority of the people—especially the men—almost throughout the territory' (Nyerere, 1967). Nevertheless, it did make possible the posting, after 1958, of T.A.N.U. secretaries around the country—something which would have been in-conceivable in the political parties of Kenya and Uganda with the greater tribal feelings there. In 1965 Nyerere was able to go further and ban the use of tribal languages at electoral meetings, allowing only Swahili. As in the ban on candidates raising tribal, racial, and religious issues, he was seeking to focus attention on the nation; and he has claimed that the elections showed that his people accepted 'the objective—the creation of a nation out of more than one hundred-and-twenty tribes' (Nyerere, 1967, p. 4).

Even if tribalism is less strong in Tanzania than in the other two countries of East Africa, a detailed study of Tanzania's 1965 general election reveals that the old Adam of tribalism is not dead, and that it played a significant part in a number of the constituency contests.[41] How, indeed, could it be otherwise? Tribalism represents in Africa what nationalism represents elsewhere. After over a hundred years of the existence of Canada and of Belgium there are still nationalist strains which threaten to tear those countries apart, while the even older United Kingdom has recently experienced an upsurge of nationalism at elections. While African leaders may rightly desire to eliminate tribalism, they may have to learn that this will be no easy process, for tribalism draws upon the strength of deep roots in the past.

NOTES

1 In Kenya, the form *wa-Nyika*, 'the people of the wilderness', was long used for the tribes of the Coast, and they had to assert, and claim for the record, their separate identities. The mystery of the meaning of 'Tangan-yika' has provoked further correspondence in *Tanzania Notes & Records*. In the issue of June 1967, the suggestion was made 'that the name arose from the reply given to the frequent (presumed) question asked con-cerning the people of the coastal strip. "Watu wa kabila gani wanakaa hapa?" It might have been, "Hakuna kabila moja tu; wenyeji wame-changanyika." The multiplicity of tribes is evident today, and cannot be anything new' (letter from G. Brookbank).

2 Rev. Dr J. W. Arthur, reported in *East African Standard*, 1 April 1922.
3 *Kenya Weekly News*, 7 November 1958.
4 *Uganda Argus*, 17 and 26 July and 17 December 1956.
5 *Uganda Argus*, 22 and 24 March, 15 April and 15 and 22 May 1958.
6 Personal information from Dr Nyerere and Mr Mulira, June and August 1962.
7 *Uganda Argus*, 17 December 1958.
8 *Uganda Argus*, 16 February and 2 March 1959.
9 *Uganda Argus*, 2 March 1959.
10 Letter from A. F. Mpanga in *Uganda Argus*, 9 July 1959. Mr Mpanga became Legal Officer in the Kabaka's government in August.
11 Uganda Legislative Council *Debates*, 5 May (p. 51), and 29 May (pp. 195–6 and 217).
12 *Uganda Argus*, 7 and 14 August 1959.
13 *Uganda Argus*, 12 and 13 January and 22 February 1960.
14 *Uganda Argus*, 18 August and 26 October 1959, 24 February and 11, 22 & 23 March 1960.
15 Kakonge 1966, 3. Kakonge then added that 'the party strength has always derived from the support which leaders of the different tribes enjoy in their respective tribal areas'. The party organization was 'on a tribal basis' while 'the cohesive factor' was 'the mutual satisfaction of the interests of the leaders of the different tribes'. This should be compared with the observation of that careful writer Dr C. J. Gertzel, that the U.P.C. was 'a confederation of district branches rather than a national unitary party' (*Africa Report*, October 1964, p. 7).
16 *Uganda Argus*, 21–29 June 1960.
17 *Uganda Argus*, 8 and 18 July and 30 August to 1 September 1960.
18 *Uganda Argus*, 7 September and 27 October 1960.
19 In his memoirs the Kabaka makes clear that he 'was determined to retain the land', saying, surprisingly, that it 'had been part of my kingdom as long as anyone could remember' (Kabaka, 1967, p. 168).
20 Obote's statement is quoted in Rothchild & Rogin, 1966, p. 418.
21 Letter of 14 December 1921; copy in J. H. Oldham Papers, Edinburgh House, London.
22 Rev. Dr J. W. Arthur to Chief Native Commissioner, Kenya, 17 November 1922; copy in J. H. Oldham Papers, Edinburgh House, London.
23 Native Affairs Dept., *Report for 1928*, Nairobi, p. 4.
24 G. V. Maxwell to *Joint Committee on closer union in East Africa*, Commons, 156, 1931, vol. 2, questions 4017–9.
25 *Correspondence between the Kikuyu Central Association and the Colonial Office, 1929–30*. Pamphlet issued in London, 1930.
26 R. Bridgeman, quoted in Delf, 1961, p. 70.
27 However, Thomas Hodgkin, listing the various 'types of theory' of African writers, distinguishes between Danquah as 'traditionalist', Awolowo as 'tribalist', and Kenyatta as 'Africanophil' (Hodgkin, 1956, p. 175).

28 One explanation of the term *Mau Mau* is that it originated in a European mishearing a Kikuyu who reported, 'I have been given MUMA, an oath' (Barnett & Njama, 1966, p. 53).

29 For their background see Kenyatta, 1938, pp. 224–5.

30 Information from Rev. F. B. Welbourn.

31 B. M. Kaggia, Fred Kubai, J. Murumbi, and Achieng Oneko in the Preface to Barnett and Njama, 1966.

32 Cf. Martin Shikuku, Kenya National Assembly, *Debates*, 21 July 1966, c. 2146: 'I am the boss of Butere.'

33 Mr A. T. Matson informs me that in this development the figure of Isaac Koskei should not be overlooked. While he was an important Nandi, he was unable, speaking only Nandi, to go to the Legislative Council and to represent his tribe there.

34 Itote (1967), for example.

35 While as a white Kenyan, the archaeologist, L. S. B. Leakey, has accepted the new situation, he earlier indicated that he did not consider Kenyatta responsible for 'the more advanced oaths' (Leakey, 1954, p. 85).

36 Quoted in Listowel, 1965, p. 43.

37 In his Foreword to Stahl, 1964, pp. 6–7.

38 *'Wakali lakini wenyi haki'* is an African's comment recorded by Listowel, 1965, p. 52.

39 This fact provides the reason behind the provision in T.A.N.U.'s original constitution of 1954 that its headquarters should be in Dar es Salaam.

40 Nyerere in his Foreword to Japhet & Seaton, 1967.

41 Cliffe, 1967: *passim*, and especially in the detailed studies of Arusha Rural and Rungwe West constituencies.

REFERENCES

ABRAHAMS, P. 1960, 'The Blacks', in Langston Hughes, *An African Treasury*, Pyramid Books, New York.

ABRAHAMS, R. G. 1967, *The Political Organization of Unyamwezi*, Cambridge University Press.

APTER, D. 1961, *The Political Kingdom in Uganda*, Princeton University Press.

ATHOLL, K., DUCHESS OF. 1958, *Working Partnership*, Barker, London.

BARNETT, D. L. & NJAMA, K. 1966, *Mau Mau from Within*, MacGibbon & Kee.

BATES, M. L. 1962, 'Tanganyika', in Carter, G. M., *African One-Party States*, Cornell University Press.

BECK, A. 1966, 'Some Observations on Jomo Kenyatta in Britain, 1929–30', *Cahiers d'études africaines*, 6, 22.

BENNETT, G. 1963a, 'Pre-Independence Kenya', *Civilizations*, 13, Nos. 1/2.

1963b, 'Political Realities in Kenya', *The World Today*, July.

1963c, 'An Outline History of TANU', *Makerere Journal*, 7.

1965, 'Uganda', in *The Annual Register of World Events in 1964*, Longmans.

1966, 'Kenya's "Little General Election" ', *The World Today*, August.

BENNETT, G. & ROSBERG, C. G. 1961, *The Kenyatta Election*, Oxford University Press.

BIENEN, H. 1967, *Tanzania: Party Transformation and Economic Development*, Princeton University Press.

CLIFFE, L. 1967, *One-Party Democracy*, E. A. Publishing House, Nairobi.

CORFIELD, F. D. 1960, *Historical Survey of the Origins and Growth of Mau Mau*, H.M.S.O., Cmnd. 1030.

DELF, G. 1961, *Jomo Kenyatta*, Gollancz.

HAILEY, LORD, 1950, *Native Administration in the British African Territories*, Part I. H.M.S.O.

n.d., *Native Administration and Political Development in British Tropical Africa. Report by Lord Hailey, 1940–42*, Colonial Office, London.

HODGKIN, T. 1956, *Nationalism in Colonial Africa*, Muller, London.

HOOPER, Rev. H. D. n.d., 'The Development of Political Self-consciousness in the Kikuyu Native', Unpub. MS. (see March 1922, in J. H. Oldham Papers, Edinburgh House, London).

HYDÉN, G. 1968, *TANU Yajenga Nchi : Political Development in Rural Tanzania*, Uniskol, Lund.

ILIFFE, J. 1967, 'The Organization of the Maji Maji Rebellion', *Journal of African History*, 8, 3.

INGHAM, K. 1965, 'Tanganyika: The Mandate and Cameron', in Harlow, V. & Chilver, E. M., *History of East Africa*, vol. 2, Clarendon, Oxford.

ITOTE, W. ('General China') 1967, '*Mau Mau' General*, E.A. Publishing House, Nairobi.

JABAVU, N. 1960, *Drawn in Colour*, Murray, London.

JAPHET, K. & SEATON, E. 1967, *The Meru Land Case*, E.A. Publishing House, Nairobi.

KABAKA OF BUGANDA, 1967, *Desecration of My Kingdom*, Constable.

KAKONGE, J. 1966, 'The Political Party, its Structure, Organization, and its Members', in *Challenge of Independence* (papers delivered to a seminar organized by the Milton Obote Foundation, 2 Jan.–4 Feb. 1966), Kampala.

KENYATTA, J. 1938, *Facing Mount Kenya*, Secker & Warburg, London.

KYLE, K. 1966, 'Gandhi, Harry Thuku and Early Kenya Nationalism', *Transition*, 27, 4.

LEAKEY, L. S. B. 1954, *Defeating Mau Mau*, Methuen.

LISTOWEL, J. 1965, *The Making of Tanganyika*, Chatto & Windus.

LONSDALE, J. M. 1964, 'A Political History of Nyanza, 1883–1945', Cambridge University Ph.D. thesis.

LOW, D. A. 1964, 'The Advent of Populism in Buganda,' *Comparative Studies in Society & History*, 6, 4.

LOW, D. A. & PRATT, R. C. 1960, *Buganda and British Overrule*, Oxford University Press.

MBOYA, T. J. 1963, *Freedom and After*, Deutsch.

MIDDLETON, J. 1965, 'Kenya: Administration and Changes in African Life, 1912–45', in Harlow, V. & Chilver, E. M., *History of East Africa*, vol. 2, Clarendon, Oxford.

NABWISO-BULIMA, W. F. 1967, 'The Evolution of the Kyabazingaship of Busoga', *Uganda Journal*, 3, 1.

NYERERE, J. 1967, *Freedom and Unity: Uhuru na Umoja*, Oxford University Press.

ODINGA, O. 1967, *Not Yet Uhuru*, Heinemann.

OGOT, B. A. 1963, 'British Administration in the Central Nyanza District of Kenya, 1900–60', *Journal of African History*, 4, 2.

PRATT, R. C. 1961, 'Nationalism in Uganda', *Political Studies*, 9, 2.

ROBERTS, A. D. 1962, 'The Sub-imperialism of the Baganda', *Journal of African History*, 3, 3.

ROSBERG, C. G. & NOTTINGHAM, J. 1966, *The Myth of 'Mau Mau'*, Praeger, New York.

ROSS, W. M. 1927, *Kenya from Within*, Allen & Unwin.

ROTHCHILD, D. & ROGIN, M. 1966, 'Uganda', in Carter, G. M., *National Unity and Regionalism in Eight African States*, Cornell University Press.

SANGER, C. & NOTTINGHAM, J. 1964, 'The Kenya General Election of 1963', *Journal of Modern African Studies*, 2, 1.

STAHL, K. 1961, *Sail in the Wilderness*, Mouton, The Hague.

1964, *History of the Chagga People of Mount Kilimanjaro*, Mouton, The Hague.

WALLIS, A. C. 1953, *Report of an Enquiry into African Local Government in the Protectorate of Uganda*, Govt. Printer, Entebbe.

WELBOURN, F. B. 1965, *Religion and Politics in Uganda, 1952–62*, E.A. Publishing House, Nairobi.

THE IMPACT OF
MODERN INSTITUTIONS ON
THE EAST AFRICAN

Tom J. Mboya

THE reaction of people to rapid social and economic
change has long been a concern of and a subject for
study by anthropologists, sociologists, psychologists and,
perhaps to a lesser extent, economists and historians. The
literature on this subject is, I am sure, very large indeed. Certainly the Industrial Revolution in England itself prompted
scores of such studies, and other studies have followed that
Revolution as it has spread throughout the world. Now we are
concerned, both as scientists and men of practical affairs, with
the impact of its modern counterpart on people throughout
the developing nations.

The larger, indeed worldwide, problem of which this is a
part is the creation of effective change. Effective change is in
my view the resolution of two often opposing forces—an initial
innovation and the type of social reaction which takes place,
and the way in which the two are permitted to interact.

The world of today has become adept at creating initial
innovations. Indeed, technical research which lies at the root
of so many of these innovations has itself been institutionalized.
The production of technological innovation is today a massive
industry, much of it conducted by government organizations
because of the large injections of capital required and the
uncertain nature of the outcomes. None can doubt, however,
that the large-scale organization of technical research has produced the basis for enormous and worldwide social and economic change. We are only on the verge of the new technological

revolution and it is not yet possible even to visualize its extent and implications. The splitting of the atom, computer technology, automation, space travel, communications satellites, transistors and laser beams are only the visible portions of the potential changes that are nearly upon us.

As these technological innovations are introduced, the nature of economic and social life must change. It is indeed unfortunate that the massive expenditures on technical research are not being matched in even a small way by expenditures on social research. The painful dislocations and adaptations associated with rapid change might then be reduced, the path of change smoothed, and the rate of genuine progress, which is not always synonymous with change, accelerated.

The adjustment to change is therefore a world problem and the present manifestations of it are only an indication of the scale the problem is likely to assume in the future. There is, I think, a kind of social inertia that expresses itself as a natural resistance to change. If innovations are introduced too rapidly and without an appreciation of the problem of social adaptation this resistance may solidify, the innovations may be rejected and effective change may be nil. This social resistance to change can be documented throughout the world. The difficulties the British are having in increasing productivity, the resistance of many trade unions in the United States to automation, and the problems encountered in introducing collective farming in the U.S.S.R. are well-known examples.

Social research on a large scale is necessary if means are to be found to overcome social inertia and make effective change both acceptable and desirable. The alternative of forcing change on people is not an acceptable solution. Such a procedure displays no regard for human dignity and social justice and in the extreme can lead to social and moral bankruptcy.

Certainly the social upheaval accompanying the Industrial Revolution had undesirable characteristics that might have been avoided with better social research and preparation. But this is a hypothesis that will, I think, be tested again and again, and in country after country throughout the world, over the next several decades. Suffice it to say that we in East Africa are aware of the problem and are determined that effective change and economic progress here will not entail the avoidable social costs and human suffering that have marked the history of so many of the countries of the world. How successful we in Government will be in our efforts will depend in no small measure on the advice and research of those of you who are social scientists.

The modern institutions—and by institutions I mean the methods, both formal and informal, by which social behaviour is organized—that are being created in East Africa are partly borrowed, partly indigenous, and partly original innovations. Those that are planned—and certainly all of them are not— are modern in the sense that they are based on the most recent thinking, advice, and experience, and are designed to further social progress and economic development. That institutional change is necessary in East Africa in order to achieve these ends is scarcely a matter for debate. Neither the traditional institutional arrangements indigenous to East Africa, the institutions inherited from colonialism, nor the strange amalgamation of the two that has occasionally emerged offers a sound institutional basis for future progress. The indigenous arrangements are too steeped in self-sufficiency and subsistence living to be constructive without modification in a modern specialized economy; and the colonial institutions were too often designed with the narrow view of maintaining law and order, or creating an economy supplementary or complementary to metropolitan needs, a necessary but certainly not a sufficient condition for progress. It has been, and indeed continues to be, necessary to modify existing institutions and to design and introduce new ones. Such a progress is a continuous one in any country but the urgency of the matter for East African countries upon independence has been equalled only in other newly independent nations.

The nature of the institutional changes needed is determined largely by our goals and aspirations and the type of society we are seeking.

Sessional Paper No. 10 of 1965, 'African Socialism and Its Application to Planning in Kenya', deals at length with these matters as they apply to Kenya; while the Development Plans of the three countries contain concrete evidence of the institutional arrangements which will be employed in East Africa to attain the very similar objectives of the three governments.

Institutional arrangements govern the entire range of group behaviour and can be religious, family, social, political or economic in nature. Religions of various forms and kinds have had a strong influence on the people of East Africa and will undoubtedly continue to be a major social force in the future as well. In the main, religion is expected to make a positive contribution to development by promoting the high moral standards and integrity so fundamental to the effective division of labour, specialization in production and development of an exchange economy. While separation of church and state is practised in East Africa, freedom of religion is guaranteed by the state and positive support to religious institutions is encouraged by the state. It is also true that, unlike some countries, religion has not so far been a divisive force in East Africa. Tribal or even racial identity is still stronger than the religious identity. Religion has of course had its impact on the East African. In particular we find that some traditional attitudes and customs have changed, regarding polygamy, witchcraft, and even the status of women and children.

The emergence of new political institutions has been a more complicated matter. The indigenous political arrangements in East Africa largely were systems of tribal organization and government. While these clearly differed, sometimes substantially, from one tribe to another, the systems typical of most tribes in Kenya assured every mature member of the tribe a voice, or at least an influence, depending more on age-grouping than wealth.

The appearance of colonialism in East Africa meant that another set of political institutions was superimposed on the traditional arrangements. While the new set was in many ways distinct from the old in the sense that Africans, even in the later years, had only very limited participation in the political system, the new institutional arrangement did affect the traditional system. In the first place constraints were imposed which reduced the political power and freedom of the tribe. Second, the political organization of the tribe was often utilized to administer and enforce decisions which were in fact made by colonial authorities. Finally, and as a result of the first two points, the African felt less and less a participant in the political process and naturally resented the imposition of outside authority.

The struggle for independence brought with it the birth of the nationalist movement. This movement represented the first attempt to introduce a national as against a tribal or racial outlook. The existence of a common enemy, namely the colonial powers, and agitation for freedom, helped to promote the movement. Every effort was made to play down or even eliminate tribal differences and identities. The nationalist movement represented a new force with potential for future unity even after independence. The impact could be felt and seen. Party slogans and leaders emphasized the oneness of the people; and the peasants and workers accepted this new relationship.

But it would be naïve to imagine that this process has been entirely successful. As soon as independence was won, tribal loyalties began to emerge, manifesting themselves in different forms—sometimes as a demand in the name of a tribe; sometimes as a case of alleged discrimination or favouritism in relation to this or that tribe. In some cases strong doubt has been expressed about the impartiality of leaders or even Government servants when they are dealing with people who do not come from the same tribe. And then there is the yet unresolved question of race relations. Thus we in East Africa have sovereign states with democratic constitutions guaranteeing equality for all citizens, but we have still to achieve complete nationhood. Such nationhood requires commitment, a sense of identification and the submerging of tribal as well as racial loyalties to national loyalty. It is for this reason that we must seek to ensure that our political and Government institutions create the desired response among our people, and persuade and assure them that their interests, security, and welfare lie within the nation-state instead of the tribe or race. Somehow this point has not quite been reached. While our parliamentary institutions, including elections, may have had an impact in terms of the people's right to choose their Government, our local authority system and the general administrative machinery has yet to produce the necessary results. I have a feeling that we shall have to experiment a little before we find the right formula. Here we are concerned not merely with the impact that physical institutions may have, but also the ideas and concepts implied, as well as the goals and targets that we have set for ourselves. We are especially concerned with the impact of these institutions on our primary objective as governments in a developing region, i.e. the development and progress that takes place within our new nations.

One indigenous social institution that has received the greatest attention in East Africa is the extended family. As pointed out in the Kenya Government's Sessional Paper No. 10 of 1965, the extended family system has both advantages and disadvantages with regard to successful economic development. Many of the newer social and economic institutions tend to threaten the extended family system. This therefore is an area in which resistance has occurred; and the Governments of East Africa are concerned to maintain the best elements of that system while at the same time modifying those elements that are not conducive to development. We, in Kenya, are attempting to convert the spirit of the extended family to the State and the Nation through the principle of mutual social responsibility. This concept was fully explained in our Sessional Paper No. 10 as follows:

Mutual social responsibility is an extension of the African family spirit to the nation as a whole, with the hope that ultimately the same spirit can be extended to even larger areas. It implies a mutual responsibility by society and its members to do their very best for each other with the full knowledge and understanding that if society prospers its members will share in that prosperity and that society cannot prosper without the full co-operation of its members. The State has an obligation to ensure equal opportunities to all its citizens, eliminate exploitation and discrimination, and provide needed social services such as education, medical care, and social security.

Drawing on this background, African Socialism expects the members of the modern State to contribute willingly and without stint to the development of the nation. Society, in turn, will reward these efforts and at the same time will take measures against those who refuse to participate in the nation's efforts to grow. Sending needed capital abroad, allowing land to lie idle and undeveloped, misusing the nation's limited resources, and conspicuous consumption when the nation needs savings, are examples of anti-social behaviour that African Socialism will not countenance.

While the modern economy is more complex than traditional

society, the principle remains that to be successful society and its members must each acknowledge fully and willingly its responsibility to the other. But the movement towards a modern, monetary economy changes the nature of these responsibilities and the mechanisms by which a member contributes to society and society shares benefits among its members. The people must be continually and carefully informed of what society expects of them and how these efforts will promote the welfare of all.

While the many positive features of the extended family system are recognized and efforts are being made to develop appropriate institutions for retaining them, it is also clear that the system has operated in the past and, indeed, in many cases continues to operate today in a fashion detrimental to progress, change, and development. The difficulty lies largely in the system of social security implied by the extended family and in its effects on individual motivation. The extended family customarily encompasses many distant relatives who may in some cases number into the hundreds. Within this group many activities are conducted on essentially a communal basis. Among these are the joint ownership and operation of land for subsistence purposes, and a system of social security appropriate to a subsistence society according to which the income of one is shared with others when the need arises. While appropriate in a subsistence economy, these aspects of the system can be detrimental in the context of the modern, monetary exchange economy we are now attempting to create. Growth depends on initiative, and initiative can be badly stifled if the individual who makes the effort is required to share the reward with many others whose claims can only be justified on moral grounds.

In every part of East Africa, one can witness the undesirable situation in which a member of a family whose income increases suddenly is constantly besieged by demands for support from a large number of distant relatives. This continues to be a part of our lives. It holds true of the small shopkeeper and the trained professional man. In social terms, such a man contributes to society in accordance with the patterns of an economy based on individual initiative, but his rewards are severely limited by the traditions of a collective system at family level. The conflict that arises out of this is that the individual

95

initiative essential to success in any mixed economy is scarcely encouraged by the necessity to meet obligations which are made the more imperative because they arise out of the deepest ties that an individual can experience. This is at any time a deterrent to productive effort and is especially costly at this time when East Africa needs its own indigenous entrepreneurial ingenuity. In short, the system is a drag on initiative because it provides everyone with automatic but unreliable insurance against want, thereby diminishing mobility, thrift, and entrepreneurial drive.

As the State gradually assumes increasing responsibility for social security and health and medical care, the individual will be relieved of many of his present extended family obligations. Indeed, we regard essential social services as a fundamental human right that should not be subject to the uncertain ability and generosity of distant cousins. Already the activities of governments in the welfare field and other institutional arrangements have had a noticeable impact on the extended family. More and more people are looking to government for their social needs and security, thus permitting the employed person to retain more of his income for his immediate dependants.

Another aspect of the traditional society that has been undergoing rapid change is the role of women and children. As the monetary exchange economy and education grow in importance and size, the African woman is being emancipated from many of the onerous chores that have been typical in traditional society. Women and men now work side by side in offices, and jobs of all kinds are open to both sexes. The horizon of women is extending to include national and world affairs as opposed to a narrow preoccupation with household matters. More modern methods of farm-production, increasing urbanization, and the strong and growing desire of parents, have tended to free children from many of their traditional duties and replaced these duties in most cases with formal primary education. Parents increasingly are taking a longer view and are planning the affairs of the family well into the future.

I have already noted the profound effect of religion on traditional attitudes such as those discussed above. Education has also been influential in this regard and is expected to play an even greater role as the numbers enrolled increase. Indeed, formal and informal methods of education and training form a principal means of modifying attitudes and promoting an understanding of our changing economies. By providing a standard means of communication, education is also promoting understanding among tribes and acquainting those in one part of East Africa with the problems and aspirations of others.

In creating new economic institutions in East Africa we have tried to draw as much as possible on modes of behaviour that are already acceptable, thus minimizing resistance to change. Even with all the care we can exercise, it must be granted that changes in our economic institutions will often be, and indeed already have been, quite pronounced, leading to significant problems in the social process of absorbing them. The principal economic institutions being introduced are:

1. economic planning.
2. specialization in production.
3. money as a medium of exchange and a store of value.
4. the co-operative form of organization.
5. the discipline of an increasingly industrial society.
6. modern concepts of property and land tenure.
7. the use of financial incentives as a means for promoting development.
8. the assumption by the State of the responsibility for social security and welfare measures.

I have described the last institution in connection with the extended family problem. I will comment briefly on each of the others and the impact they have had so far on our people.

To date planning in all three countries has been largely a central exercise which has yet to be appreciated by the man in the rural area. To make planning an effective institution, we must bring it to the people through local district party machinery. It is my personal experience that the people in East Africa are anxious to have this exercise carried forward. They look sympathetically on planning and indeed expect more of their governments in this regard than we have so far been able to produce. We are all searching for appropriate means to utilize existing administrative arrangements and also to supplement these by bringing in local governments and party leaders. I

believe that the people of East Africa readily accept planning;
but I am also sure that many problems will arise which we have
not yet anticipated.

Among the economic changes that planning must assist to
bring about is the conversion of the subsistence sectors of our
economies into market economies. This cannot be done without providing for specialization and also markets in which
exchanges can take place. There is, however, some natural
aversion on the part of Africans in the subsistence sector to
undertake specialization in a wholehearted fashion.

The advantage to them of a subsistence economy is that
they themselves are responsible for all aspects of their daily
needs. Specialization by definition means the dependence upon
others for many needs and the opportunity to exchange one's
own produce for the produce of others. This requires therefore,
not only a trust in others but also a trust in the economic system
itself. Governments have the responsibility here to ensure that
the needs of the people who specialize are met in the event that
some type of emergency or catastrophe should nullify their
efforts to produce for the market economy. The resistance to
specialization because of risks involved requires that Government introduces educational measures as well as new organizational arrangements. In sectors which promise large incomes,
such as growing of coffee, tea and so on, this incentive has
already proved a major force and many of our people are
already involved in specialized market production.

The use of money as a medium of exchange is closely related
to our desire to develop a market economy. Both statistics on
currency in circulation and personal observation in innumerable rural areas disclose that money has become the accepted
medium of exchange in every rural area in East Africa, and
that it is having a very apparent effect on the rural way of life.
Markets are expanding and the variety of goods being offered
is increasing. As methods of transport improve, markets are
serving wider areas and production for the market is increasing. Credit facilities are being used more extensively and every
African knows about borrowing and repaying money even if
he is not in a position to do so himself. Finally, a growing number of rural workers is demanding to be paid in money rather
than in kind. Money is clearly an established institution which

will make easier our task of introducing other economic institutions.

Money and other financial claims must also serve to a greater extent as a store of value. This is a problem to which, in my opinion, too little attention has so far been paid. The use of money and financial claims for savings purposes depends upon the existence of appropriate claims, and a knowledge and understanding on the part of Africans that such claims are both safe and useful. I think a great deal more can be done by our Governments and the commercial banks in East Africa to provide a wider variety of savings instruments designed to meet the needs of our people.

Unfortunately, some of our experience in the past with some insurance companies and building societies have led many of our people to distrust financial institutions as a medium in which to store their savings. Such unsatisfactory experience tends to discourage financial saving on the part of many of our people. Nevertheless, the Post Office Savings Bank is servicing a rapidly growing number of small accounts, and more and more Africans are becoming aware of the value of insurance and provident funds. Private security arranged in these ways will make government security programmes more effective and further reduce the burden on the extended family.

Many of the new production efforts being undertaken in East Africa are being organized through co-operatives. This institutional arrangement we regard as being deeply rooted in African traditions, and we have found that this form of organization is readily accepted, particularly in the agricultural field. Nevertheless, our modern co-operatives differ in many respects from traditional methods of co-operation—embracing a larger range of economic activities, involving a formal and permanent organization, being more complex and frequently larger in scale, and having access to credit facilities. These new features are having a considerable impact on East Africans. The co-operative is first of all a means of ensuring a wider distribution of income. Second, participation in co-operation provides training and experience in a wide range of operating and managerial skills. Finally, the co-operative is a means for turning the traditional communal spirit of the extended family into modern productive efforts. Here, as in the creation of other new economic institutions, we must guard against failure, because failure tends to generate distrust among our people.

The modern industrial society, and indeed modern agricultural methods of production, require a disciplined work force. The idea of work for wages is now part of the life of our people. This is one of the greatest impacts of modern institution on East Africa. Obviously the role of organized labour is a most significant one in this respect. Our unions started off as protest organizations with only the one objective of bettering the wages of their members. Today, however, the trade unions are beginning to initiate positive steps which should have a useful impact on our economies as well as their members. These include training for members both in the skills of their work and in the importance of their contribution to their country's development, the encouragement of thrift and savings among their members, and the initiation of housing co-operatives and the assumption of responsibility for improving the discipline of workers.

Nevertheless, our people have not yet accepted fully the need for discipline in the labour force, and have been slow to learn the intimate relationship between productivity and standards of living. There is still a hangover from the past, and worn-out or rusty slogans are still used in a totally different situation. There is also the problem of importing ideas from older countries which are not relevant to our own situation. In many cases, I fear, it will take a new generation of leaders and the considerable expansion of our educational facilities before our objectives in this regard are realized.

Discipline is not only needed to make our labour force fully effective in modern industry and agriculture, but also in relations with Government. The State cannot be regarded as a perpetual source of benefits unless the individual fully accepts his responsibility to pay taxes. This, too, is a function of education as well as a matter of discipline. There is still resistance in East Africa to the payment of taxes. This resistance can be traced to the use of taxation as a punitive measure in the colonial days when Africans had to be forced to supply labour for the early settlers and administrators at nominal wages.

The growth of the monetary economy has brought with it a rapid expansion of our urban centres. These have been growing for many years at an annual rate in excess of 6 per cent, while the East African population has been increasing by less than 3 per cent per annum. The growth of urban centres has meant that more and more Africans have divorced themselves from the land and extended family groups to take up permanent positions and residences in cities. There has also been a substantial increase in the transient population in urban areas, many being unemployed or seeking only temporary work. This development has created many of our urban problems. Our urban centres are, however, an important means for bringing together people of different tribes, thus promoting understanding of each other. The separation from traditional ties with land and family stimulates self-reliance, and the varied aspects of urban life are a constant source of enlightenment to large numbers of East Africans. Undoubtedly the shift from rural to urban living requires substantial social adjustment; but much of this is necessary if we are to progress toward modern economy.

The traditional view of property and land tenure is simply unsuited to a modern economy. The identification and registration of land titles and the consolidation of land are mandatory if farm production is to be economic and financial credits for improvements are to be secured. The reorganization of property rights and the system of land tenure is enormously complicated in East Africa by the variety of existing systems of land tenure. These range from the titled European holdings, through communal and family and tribal land, to fragmented, unregistered, individual holdings. The techniques being used to modify existing systems of land tenure including settlement schemes, villagization projects, land consolidation, and registration of titles.

I think I can safely say that our new institutional arrangements with regard to land tenure have been enthusiastically accepted by most of our people, but have naturally aroused natural resistance from some who are adversely affected. Nevertheless, the change in land tenure is crucial to all our efforts to introduce new economic social institutions. Changes in land-tenure policy are already having a profound effect in many parts of East Africa although the programmes are far from complete. It must be recognized that the shift from the communal holding of land to a system in which the individual holds an exclusive title to land is a radical one. It has meant, however, that individuals can now borrow readily through mortgages, and they can use these funds for development of the land without fear that the benefits will accrue to others. As a result, productivity is increasing and standards of living are improving in those areas where the new system is established. Other evidence that the new system is being accepted is to be found in the rapidly expanding markets in land. This itself represents a major change in the outlook of our people. In order to make these incentives fully effective we must not only succeed in modifying the extended family system, but we must also educate, train, finance, and give experience to a substantial number of Africans who will become the leading innovators and entrepreneurs of our society both in government and private commerce and industry. This is an enormous task for which we have created para-statal bodies, institutions and agencies. I should also mention here the practical and necessarily innovative experience so many Africans are now receiving in the service of their governments and the East African Common Services Organization.

Our efforts to institutionalize entrepreneurial activities have been well received. Indeed, the desire of our people to own and operate commercial, industrial and agricultural enterprises is both manifest and growing. But many of our people do not yet fully appreciate that success in business depends on more than the possession of property. Knowledge, experience, creditworthiness, integrity in business affairs, hard work, and ingenuity, all have their roles to play. This task is another example of the critical place that our formal and informal means for education and training must undertake in development.

We in East Africa do not live in isolation, nor would we want to if this were possible. This means that the institutions which affect our East African citizens are not limited to those we create or which develop within our boundaries. We are also deeply affected and often concerned by the institutional arrangements common in other countries and international bodies. In business matters there must be a mutual adjustment between ourselves and those with whom we do business; our interest in cultural affairs is influenced by our travels abroad and are affected by the institutions native to the country visited; and much of the technology employed in East Africa has had its origin elsewhere. Most of our varied relationship with other countries and international organizations, such as the U.N. and O.A.U., have had a very healthy impact on our citizens. In particular, our people are becoming internationally minded and responsive to world affairs. We are also developing in East Africa a cosmopolitan outlook that derives in part from the various countries to which we travel and in which we gain experience and education. This outlook is however always tempered by our own backgrounds, traditions, and aspirations. Our domestic institutions benefit from this varied knowledge and our judgment in world affairs is not therefore based on narrow domestic considerations.

I have attempted to assess the impact on the East African of various domestic and international institutions. This cannot obviously be a definitive assessment because we are still in a state of transition and indeed always will be. Our institutions themselves are changing and those we have are affecting our populations unevenly and in diverse ways. In such circumstances any attempt to generalize about the social impact of our institutions must be hazardous at best. Sweeping generalizations must always to some extent be a distortion of facts. The rapidity with which change is occurring in East Africa is of course a principal reason why East Africa is an especially fruitful area in which to investigate social change. We in government have need of the efforts of social scientists if we are to be successful in minimizing social maladjustment while maximizing economic growth. But whatever studies we undertake, it must be realized that East Africa is part of a changing world and that the East African is part of a changing world; and further that the East African is a child of and participant in the events of the twentieth century. If we do not bear this in mind we might arrive at false conclusions in the mistaken belief that our present-day East Africa belongs to the Africa of the nineteenth century. In fact, some of what we call modern institutions have been conceived right here in East Africa and are neither foreign nor alien to our people. The impact of such institutions would differ from those imported from abroad.

LANGUAGE
CHOICE AND LANGUAGE
PLANNING IN EAST AFRICA

W. H. Whiteley

Introduction

FEW people would deny the importance of language in the recent history of East Africa, but fewer still have probed the nature of this importance in any detail. The reasons are not difficult to discover: language has not played the dramatic and dominant role in the rise of East African nationalism of the kind that captured the attention of historians of nineteenth-century Europe; the triumphant emergence of Czech, Hungarian, or Finnish finds no parallels in East Africa.[1] Here, language plays a more elusive role, being one of a number of variables and not easily isolable as the critical variable in any given situation. For this there are again a number of reasons. In the countries of Uganda, Kenya, and the United Republic of Tanzania, with a total population of around 26 million, more than 160 languages are spoken. A majority of these are, it is true, Bantu languages, with a range of relationship to one another probably comparable to that in other language families, e.g. that of French, Portuguese, Spanish, Italian, and Roumanian to one another, but there are, additionally, important groups of quite different Nilotic and Cushitic languages, especially in Kenya and Uganda. None of these languages is spoken as a first[2] language by many more than a million speakers, and only a handful of languages (Sukuma/ Nyamwezi, Kikuyu, Luo, Kamba(?), Ganda) are spoken by even this number of speakers,[3] though a majority among the population probably 'speak' two of these languages and an increasing minority have some command of English. Swahili, on the other hand, is spoken as a second language by perhaps ten million speakers, mainly in Kenya and Tanzania, after its spread inland from the coast during the nineteenth century. Thus, while each of these countries shares the same general problems as multilingual states elsewhere on the continent and Asia,[4] there is no question here of any of these small language units being coterminous with a viable political unit. Yet, if a Biafran situation is unlikely, there are real dangers that progressively greater recognition of regional languages could lead also to progressively greater demands for forms of political decentralization of an uneconomic and impracticable nature. It happened in colonial times and it could happen again, e.g. the Rwenzururu movement among the Konzo of western Uganda (*infra*, p. 121). Not unnaturally, Governments view with suspicion any undue interest in local languages as being likely to encourage political as well as linguistic fragmentation. In such cases it matters little whether the fragments are viable or not; they constitute a threat to the effective authority of the central Government.

In any multi-lingual community people speak different languages during the course of their daily lives, the patterns of language 'shifting'[5] being shaped and modified by many factors. There may be direct Government intervention, as in the recent injunction by Tanzania's Second Vice-President to all Civil Servants, Regional and Area Commissioners, to use Swahili as much as possible in carrying out Government business and to abjure the use of English as a 'colonialist language'.[6] Educational policies also fall into this category: Uganda recognizes seven languages in primary education, but only one, Luganda, is recognized up to the Cambridge School Certificate. Economic factors, too, may be important: for example, the development of high-density urban housing estates provides a kaleidoscope of social groups; from homolingual[7] groups maintaining a high degree of 'in-group' cohesiveness and consequent use of local languages, to hetero-lingual groups, especially intertribal marriages, with consequent use of English or Swahili. Households in which English is either exclusively or largely used are by no means as rare as one might suppose, especially in Nairobi. Account must be taken of religious factors, with particular Missions insisting on a particular language being used: one recalls the deliberate creation of Luyia during the 1940s as an alternative to Swahili and the other, numerous, languages in Nyanza region. There are also what I might term 'recreational' factors: the kind of language choice that is involved in drinking together in different kinds of city bar; the fact that the high mobility of football teams seems to have been a factor in the choice of a lingua franca like Swahili as the language of football, even in non-Swahili-speaking areas like Uganda. Finally, there are always an unpredictable number of fortuitous factors, as, for example, the setting up of homolingual groups in trade or in industry and the drawing into the group of other speakers of the language. So it comes about that many children in East Africa speak language A and B at home, learn to read and write in B at school and go on to be educated in C. In their play-groups out of school hours they may use D, and use varieties of D or B or A when they go to the market. As they grow older they will learn to associate A or B with the older generation, perhaps with a spirit of reaction, while looking to C as the language of prestige. On the other hand, they may invest A or B with the 'spirit of the soil' or with their African-ness and venerate it accordingly. Such are the implications of multilingualism!

The Governments of all three East African countries have objectives which require some language choice and which have, therefore, resulted in some planning: the planning has been fairly clearly formulated in the field of education—though sensitive to changes in fashion—but much less clearly so elsewhere. In some instances, indeed, planning has involved the emphasizing of different language choices.

Efficient government requires efficient means of communication both within the State and outside it; and while all three countries recognize the indispensability of English as a means of communication with the rest of Africa and the world, there is less than unanimity with regard to the linguistic pattern of internal communication. Uganda's problem is that she is a relatively small country and has a small number of languages which are held in more or less similar esteem.[8] The linguistic choices here will centre on the maximum number of languages which can be used as media for internal communication without creating intolerable financial and educational burdens on the state, and without creating wasteful tensions between the regional groups and the centre. In Tanzania, where the number of languages is large, where none of these has pre-eminent status, and where there is a conveniently long-established lingua franca, the choice may be simple but the implementation rather more difficult, despite repeated exhortation. This is the situation now that Swahili has been chosen as the national language. In Kenya, the number of languages is relatively small, but it includes a number of large, linguistically diverse groups, and furthermore a convenient lingua franca is available. Here the choice is more complicated, for advocates of the lingua franca are usually opposed by the proponents of the powerful local languages. Under such circumstances it may well be advisable to delay the promulgation of an active language policy until social and economic factors have created a new situation in which a clear policy can be more readily accepted. In short, efficient internal communication probably requires the choice of a minimal number of languages.

However, each of the East African countries, in common with new estates elsewhere on the continent, is additionally concerned with establishing some kind of national identity. What does it mean, other than in geographical or broad political terms, to say that one is a Tanzanian as opposed to a Ugandan? In social and cultural terms these countries are still very much the sum of their regional components, whose richness and diversity can, in many cases, only be reached through language. Yet if language will serve as an entry-permit, it will not serve to make local culture accessible to the nation as a whole. The meaning of poetry, dances, tales, folk-drama, or songs lies in the particular social context and the particular language appropriate to that context. It is not enough to assert that '. . . the tunes must be preserved, but the language be made national' (Manani, 1966). With a new language a new song is created, requiring new contexts and new criteria by which to judge it. As with the Otole dance of the Acholi, the criteria by which it is judged in its social context are quite other than those by which it is acclaimed when performed at Entebbe

Airport to greet the Prime Minister (p'B'Tek, 1966). All Governments recognize the need to stimulate and enrich the 'national culture' but the processes by which regional cultures are transmuted into a national culture are imperfectly understood: alchemists abound but the precious metal is elusive. Language planners must not shrink from exploiting the linguistic and cultural diversity of their countries; it should be regarded as a source of wealth rather than a threat to unity.[9] Yet there creeps in a doubt that perhaps this talk of 'national' as opposed to 'local' culture misses the point. In the cited article, Mr Mushi refers to the fact that: 'The Government has organized a national dancing group—a full-time group of dancers chosen from different tribes in the United Republic' (Mushi, 1966, p. 15). Does this mean a dancing group which is selected on a national basis, a group of dancers performing national dances, or a dancing group which is State subsidized and organized? If the latter, then perhaps a national culture should be described as the sum of those cultural institutions for which State support, organization, and expertise is available. What, after all, is the significance of the term in institutions such as the 'National Theatre' or 'National Youth Orchestra'?

There remains a further problem for the language planners which owes something to the pre-independence situation. This is the problem of the status of English as a language of internal communication. It has been aptly pointed out[10] that during the struggle for independence mastery of English constituted not merely a status symbol, but evidence of mastery over a whole range of skills wherein, in some way, the colonialists' power and prestige was held to reside. Possession of such mastery served to unite those who possessed it, conferring on them an exclusive status not shared by their less-educated fellows: it is no accident that some of the most ardent supporters of Swahili are those who were denied the opportunity to receive higher education in the past. Not merely are certain areas of social life marked by the use of English, but such areas come to be invested with a superior status. The language is thus a mark of social stratification.[11] It may be that, all other things being equal, the danger of political fragmentation in a state is in direct proportion to the potential viability of the linguistic units as political units, whereas the likelihood of language emerging as a mark of social stratification is in inverse proportion to the political significance of the language units. While the educational process in all these countries is progressively extending the teaching of English down into the primary schools, and hence reducing its exclusiveness, other factors, such as urbanization, are liable to lead to a reinforcement of local ties and increasing specialization of language use. We know from the earlier surveys of Kampala and Dar es Salaam how strongly and over what areas these ties operated (Southall & Gutkind, 1957, Pts. II & III; Leslie, 1963, pp. 37-57), and this appears to be true also from what little we know of Nairobi.

This rather complex situation is, to a large extent, the outcome of policies pursued by the colonial administrations: these in turn were largely established in the light of the situations which obtained, or were thought to obtain, during the early period of administration. Some examination of planning and choice during the colonial period must now be made.

The colonial inheritance[12]

(a) *Tanganyika.* Administering a country in which over a hundred languages are spoken is no sinecure, and the eager adoption of Swahili, both by the Germans and their British successors, is thoroughly understandable. For the Missions, however, a different solution was, in many cases, both preferable and practicable: preferable because conversion to Christianity was more effective if carried out in a people's first language, and practicable because Missions tended to operate within a single-language area.

In the early period of German administration, at least until 1908, the administrators consisted mainly of soldiers or diplomats—there being no Colonial Office in Germany at that time—and were few in number. Much of the work of day-to-day administration was left in the hands of 'Akida' and 'Jumbe', whose powers were frequently ill-defined and not subject to supervision (Wright, 1965). These Swahili, like their predecessors on the trading and slave caravans, continued to spread their language over the country, so that by the time the British took over, they had only to continue the process. One wonders why the frequent excesses of these 'local' authorities did not come to be associated with the language they spoke, and lead to a reaction against Swahili comparable to that against Luganda in those parts of Uganda where there has been hostile reaction to Baganda agents of the administration. The answer perhaps lies in the fact that however much an 'Akida' might be disliked, he was not thought to be advancing the interests of another tribal group in the way that the Baganda—for all their acting on behalf of the British—were felt to be advancing *their* own interests. It may also be true that the main centres of unified tribal authority were being so severely crushed by the Germans that no further reaction was possible, though feeling against 'local authorities' certainly contributed to a rising like that of the 'Maji Maji'.

During the period of the mandate, the British carried on the policy of Swahili in administration and education, and there is no doubt that it carried with it certain important advantages, both for the administering power and the people themselves. For the former, it was convenient to have a single language in which high standards could be imposed on officers and maintained throughout their service. For the Education Department it meant that problems of staffing were minimized and those of text-books simplified. It also meant that the Junior Service, staffed by Tanganyikans, was not restricted to regional postings; and members could be transferred without difficulty from one part to another and be sure of finding a small community of Swahili speakers round the 'boma'. There is also some evidence that it engendered a sense of belonging to a unit larger than the tribe,[13] though the situation varied considerably across the country, according to various factors, such as the scale of administration, the size of the District headquarters, the extent of counteracting tendencies among local Missions and the attitudes of local groups to their own languages. In some areas, for example, Sukuma, Mbulu, Ha, and Nyakyusa, Swahili was not widely used until much later.

After 1945, interest in local languages increased markedly from at least three areas: Haya, Chagga, and Nyakyusa.[14] Such interest did not occur immediately but had probably developed slowly over a long period: there is certainly evidence of this in M. Wilson's study of the Nyakyusa (1951), data for which was collected well before this time. Interest in Chagga dates from the appointment of Mr T. Marealle as Paramount Chief in 1951, but proved abortive because of difficulties in deciding upon a dialect of the language which would satisfy everyone. Swahili was ultimately agreed upon as belonging equally to no one! All these areas had something in common: all were important centres of Mission activity, and Haya and Nyakyusa both had recognized orthographies in which a certain amount of published material appeared regularly; all were border areas (Nyasaland, Uganda, and Kenya) and both Haya and Nyakyusa looked across the borders to areas where local languages received a great official recognition; all were wealthy by contrast with neighbouring groups, a fact which itself possibly encouraged a sense of separatism. Yet, there were other areas in Tanganyika which did not at any time witness even mild forms of linguistic chauvinism—for example, Songea (Ngoni) and Masasi. Both of these are border areas, both had been centres of intense Missionary activity for a very long period and both were comparatively wealthy. But in neither area did either the Benedictine or the U.M.C.A. pursue language policies different from that of the Central Government. Missionaries might be encouraged to learn the local language, but this was a matter for individuals not for the Mission as a whole. Then again, there is no language in Masasi which would command undivided loyalties, while in Songea the language that the Ngoni brought with them from southern Africa had long since passed out of current use.

When T.A.N.U. was founded in 1954 it was well placed to reap the benefits of a long-established and consistent linguistic planning, and by its very success justified and reinforced a policy which had recently come under considerable criticism from educationists.[15] It is easy, in retrospect, to criticize the scale, the organization and sometimes the direction of the planning at this period, but by the mid-fifties it was certainly being more widely applied than hitherto. There were, for example, as many as forty Swahili newspapers in regular circulation, a majority being Government-run. Many were well-intended, unimaginative and uncritical hand-outs of Government policy, but as there was little else to read, they undoubtedly served to extend the Swahili-reading public, and the listening public too, for they were often read aloud. Other Government departments, notably Agriculture, were at this time producing a considerable volume of Swahili material, and work had been started on legal translation and on the compilation of technical world-lists, essential preliminaries if Swahili was to assume the status of a modern African language. Finally, the technical advances which made possible the production of cheap radios gave the Tanganyika Broadcasting Services a vastly wider audience for its Swahili programmes. The value of Swahili to T.A.N.U. was quickly demonstrated, and President Nyerere once boasted that during his many tours of the country he had had recourse to interpreters only on two occasions.[16] Not merely were the Swahili-speaking communities round the 'boma' fertile sources of recruitment, but they served as an excellent example when the Party wished to organize its own country-wide branches. It might be true that Nyerere's status as a leader was enhanced by his ability to negotiate for independence in English, on terms of linguistic equality, but in this role the fact that he represented so large a proportion of the people of Tanganyika was due in large measure to the efficacy of Swahili as a means of communications on a national scale.

(b) *Kenya*. There is a certain irony in the fact that while it is Kenya that can boast of her eighteenth- and nineteenth-century Swahili literature, it is in Tanzania where most has been done for the development of a Swahili literature in this century. Though Kenya has a long coastline along which Swahili is spoken as a first language, this coastal form has never been accepted up-country, and the various up-country varieties of Swahili that have developed (especially among Nilotes, Asians and European settlers) have never been accepted on the coast. The European settler variety of Swahili [Ki-Settla) in particular, with its limited vocabulary, highly attenuated grammatical structure, and occurrence in invidious social contexts, did a great deal to encourage the myth that Swahili was unfit to cope with the requirements of the twentieth century, and discouraged any consistent planning.[17]

As early as 1906 Sir Charles Eliot made a strong plea for the learning of the local language to increase administrative efficiency: '. . . To my mind the greatest desideratum for improving our native administration and establishing friendly relations with the tribes which are still remote and diffident, is a wider knowledge of native languages. As a rule, officers only know Swahili—the lingua franca of the Protectorate, which is more or less understood by many natives of the interior, just as many Europeans understand French. But the more important chiefs cannot, as a rule, speak any language but their own . . .' (Eliot, 1906). Shortly after this speech, the problem of whether English or Swahili should be the lingua franca of the colony was voiced for the first time at a United Missionary Conference held in Nairobi in 1909, in connection with plans for primary education. It was to be raised at frequent intervals in the years that followed, and visiting Commissions gave the protagonists on both sides ample opportunity of stating their case. Government made a number of pronouncements on policy, of which that of the Education Department for 1929 seems to be representative. 'It is the policy of the Government to establish English as the lingua franca of the Colony as soon as possible' (p. 17); and 'The vernacular will be used for the first four years of school life' (p. 18). The value of the local language was also stressed by Kenya officials giving evidence before the Select Committee on Closer Union in East Africa (H.M.S.O., 1931, *passim*).

In practice, Swahili was widely used by officials and unofficials alike to suit administrative convenience, but its relegation to the status of a basic means of communication won it few adherents and reactions were not slow in coming. In education it was used both as a medium of instruction and taught as a subject, but nowhere was it surrounded with an aura of prestige comparable to that of English. The Missions continued their practice of using local languages, and by 1936 could point with pride at the number of gospels that had been translated; but in many ways they were out of touch with local aspirations. Government officers, for their part, were always in favour of learning a local language,[18] but extenuating circumstances could always be adduced as a reason why this had not been done. Just how effective these circumstances proved was not brought out clearly until the outbreak of the Emergency in the fifties, when the shortage of competent Kikuyu speakers was dramatically revealed.

As might have been expected, Kikuyu was the first language

to be linked with a quasi-political movement, when the Central Kikuyu Association specifically enjoined the use of Kikuyu in the later twenties and thirties. The area had been a centre of Mission activity, like the Tanganyika areas already mentioned, but this and other political movements were mainly of a defensive character: products of frustration and disappointment rather than of success and consequent local pride. Though the language symbolized tribal unity, this was a unity of retrenchment rather than of progress, as was exemplified by Buganda.

Another important centre of Mission activity was Central and Northern Nyanza. Here an attempt was made, principally by the C.M.S., to establish a lingua franca other than Swahili by compounding various features from some of the closely related Bantu languages of the area into a single standard language, Luluhya (Luluyia). There may have been ample justification —on educational grounds, for example—for such an innovation, but it seems to have created, or perhaps merely aggravated, resentment among groups like the Logooli whose language differed markedly from other languages in the area. The resentment was expressed in many forms, but one of these was the demand, during the fifties, for recognition of Lulogooli, in support of which a good deal of work was done to prepare a viable orthography for the language. This in turn sparked off similar demands among other languages of the area, notably Tiriki, Wanga, Bukusu, and Tacooni.

A completely different situation obtained in South Nyanza, an area in which there had been considerable Missionary activity, and where a number of Gusii became wealthy within a broadly traditional farming pattern (maize) supplemented by coffee. Yet, though four Missions had stations in the area during the fifties, all of these were small and only two (the Seventh Day Adventists, and the Mill Hill Fathers) had been in the area before 1914. Their educational work, when compared with that of the C.M.S., the Church of Scotland, and the Consolata Fathers in Central Nyanza and Central Province, must be accounted as being on a very small scale. Though they pursued a policy of working through the local language (Gusii, Luo, or Tende (Kuria)), this had not yielded very much in the way of grammatical or lexical studies nor even of much religious material. The Gusii Highlands were free from European settlers, so that this did not form a focus for local grievances. These came mainly from intertribal competition for available jobs in local administration, and Gusii were always ready with tales of discrimination shown by Luo Junior Service staff in favour of their own tribe. As so often with such myths, the available evidence did not, in many cases, support this belief, and from earlier records it seems that twenty years previously it was the Luo who were always complaining; but the facts were not sufficiently persuasive to prevent the Gusii from striving for—and ultimately succeeding in getting—a separate unilingual District Council.

A final example of Kenya's language problems must suffice: again the case in point is an extremely trivial one, but is indicative of the way in which feelings can be roused on language matters where this is felt to be evidence of a threat to the larger cultural whole. The Nandi and Kipsikis speak mutually intelligible languages,[19] but with the post-war production of literature each group refused to accept books and papers of the other, alleging that they could not be understood. This could not be attributed to the denominational differences between the Missions who produced them since the same Mission Society operated in both areas, but rather to a form of parochialism in which each group feared cultural domination by the other. So a local Nandi-Kipsikis Language Committee was formed, the terms of which gave each language equal prominence and guaranteed unrestricted distribution of approved books in a common orthography (Tucker, 1953). This apparently worked, both groups accepted the term 'Kalenjin' as applicable to both, and the literature of each proved then to be acceptable to both.

With the approach of independence the two political parties adopted vigorous but by no means consistent language policies, which seem to me to be typical of the ambivalent attitude that has characterized all language planning in Kenya. K.A.N.U., committed politically to centralism, started off by advocating Swahili as the language for the whole country and produced their party newspaper in it. Later, however, perhaps in deference to their party membership, they favoured the three main local languages, Kikuyu, Kamba, and Luo. By contrast,

K.A.D.U., committed politically to regionalism, increasingly favoured the use of Swahili, again reflecting the bulk of their members' affiliation to the smaller tribal units.

(c) *Uganda*. Here, particularly in Buganda, the Church has enjoyed an enviable esteem. C.M.S. Missionaries arrived at Mutesa's court, on his invitation, in 1876, the year following Stanley's visit, and White Fathers followed after an interval of only a few weeks. From the beginning it was clear that the kingdom of Buganda was to occupy a central place in the affairs of the Protectorate, a matter which, from the Ganda point of view, was entirely right and proper, since, to quote from a letter submitted to the Committee on Closer Union by the Lukiko: 'It is a well-known and admitted fact that the fundamental traditions and customs of the Baganda upon which the constitution of their kingdom is based are totally different from those of any other native tribe in East Africa.'

From the first the Missions concentrated on Luganda, and it is a reflection of their industry that when Pilkington of the C.M.S. was killed in 1897–8 he had already prepared a grammar, of the language and had translated the Bible. While such studies were, perhaps, a usual feature of C.M.S. activity, there seems to be no doubt that, as time passed, such knowledge bestowed a gratifying sense of power *vis-à-vis* the newly-arrived Protectorate officials, and may well have been a contributory factor to their unwillingness to see Luganda supplanted in any way. The appointment of Ganda Administrative agents to various parts of the Protectorate contributed further to the spread of the language; but here the agents were often seen—as indeed they may have seen themselves—as extending the power and influence of Buganda, and in due course reaction against both language and people set in (*infra*, p. 119).

The position of Swahili, in this land of Christians, was jeopardized from the outset by its association with Islam, a rival and 'inferior' religion, about whose alleged vices apprehensive Christians of many denominations were prepared to unite. Whatever merits the language might have from an administrative point of view, and these were frequently voiced between 1910–20, it is clear that for the Church it was an alien tongue and for the Baganda a thinly-veiled threat to their status. In 1927 the Governor, Sir W. F. Gowers, wrote a Memorandum entitled, 'The Development of Ki-Swahili as an educational and administrative language in the Uganda Protectorate'. In it he proposed, among other things, that Swahili should be adopted as the lingua franca throughout a considerable part of the Protectorate—but *not* Buganda—for purposes of education. The part concerned included portions of Eastern Province, excluding Busoga, and portions of Northern Province and West Nile District. It was not intended that the teaching of Luganda in Buganda should in any way be discouraged, though it was suggested that Swahili might be introduced as an extra subject in Buganda as well as in Bunyoro, Toro, and Ankole. There seems to have been some opposition to these views, and the *Uganda News* of 22 February 1929 carried a Memorandum by the Kabaka, Sir Daudi Chwa, in which he made a strong protest: '. . . I feel, however, that it is my duty to add here in conclusion, that it is quite unnecessary to adopt the Ki-Swahili language as the Official Native Language in Buganda, and I am entirely opposed to any arrangements which would in any way facilitate the ultimate adoption of this language as the Official Native Language of the Buganda in place of, or at the expense of, their own language . . .'. As the Kabaka subsequently admitted in a letter to his Saza Chiefs, the Protectorate Government had had no intention of taking such a step and his original fears had been the result of a misunderstanding by himself. However, the Kabaka was not alone in his objections: the Bishops of Uganda also protested in a written Memorandum to the Secretary of State, in which they outlined the disadvantages of Swahili and put forward a number of reasons why Luganda should be preferred as a lingua franca. At about the same time, giving evidence before the Joint Select Committee on Closer Union in East Africa, Mr S. Kulubya made the following comment. Being questioned about his belief that Swahili was being introduced in Uganda, he replied: '. . . I should say that in most cases it is being forced, instead of being introduced'. But he admitted: '. . . it has not been forced so much in Buganda, but of course we never know what will happen . . .'. In reply to a further question as to which second language he thought preferable, he was in no doubt at all, '. . . English, of course, my Lord, which is the key to everything . . .' (H.M.S.O., 1931, p. 554). From that date there was no further question of Swahili participating in Uganda's linguistic planning, though its use was continued in the Police into the fifties, a fact which was commented on tartly by the Royal Commission (H.M.S.O., 1955, p. 184). There was, however, some justification for its continued use in the northern parts of the country, where constables were likely to be in contact with people unfamiliar either with English or Luganda. It is interesting to note the support for Swahili among Nilotes in Uganda, in contrast to the opposition from them in Kenya, which does something to dispel the myth that there are linguistic reasons why Nilotes find Swahili difficult to learn. In Uganda, where the Nilotes were weak in relation to the Lake kingdoms, notably the Ganda, Swahili was both a unifying influence and a means of buttressing their position by stressing the links with Swahili speakers elsewhere. In Kenya, where the Luo were a relatively powerful group, Swahili served to diminish their position by merging them with the rest of the Bantu-speaking groups of the country. Swahili did not disappear from Uganda, however, but persisted and flourished on the football field and in various other situations where use of English or Luganda was neither desirable nor possible. As a subject for debate in the Legislative Council, it reappeared during the 1960 discussion of the annual £800 subvention to the East African Swahili Committee,[20] a subvention which seemed annually in jeopardy but which had been maintained since the thirties. Members argued eloquently, if irrelevantly, for or against it as a national language, and a similar view informed a resolution of the Uganda People's Congress in 1960 (U.P.C., 1960, para. 72), but no official action resulted.

However, a consistent policy of local language and English was pursued in education, though only in Luganda was it possible to take the language as far as the Cambridge School Certificate. Efforts were made to standardize and modernize the orthographies, and grammars and word-lists were produced in some quantity during the fifteen years before independence. A considerable portion of the attention paid to local languages was concentrated on Luganda, in which a substantial 'literature' had developed by independence; but here attempts to modernize the orthography met considerable resistance from conservatives who felt that such attempts meant essentially altering the language itself, so that though the new orthography was introduced in 1947 it made only slow progress during the next fifteen years.[21] The policy of stressing local languages and English raised some problems: it was clearly uneconomic to attempt to use all the local languages of the country, i.e. thirty or more, but any selection was liable to raise claims from those languages which were not chosen. Thus attention to Acoli provoked reactions from Lango; development of Ganda stimulated reactions from Soga and Gisu; not, in the latter case, because Gisu was held to be different from Ganda, but rather because it was similar and hence should receive similar attention:[22] production of material in Lugbara raised demands for similar study of Madi. All these movements were on a very small scale but they are worth noticing as indicative of the lines along which cleavage or fusion of regional groups might be expected to occur.

The reality of independence

Thus it was that on the assumption of independence, each country found itself with a different legacy of language planning, even though the administering authority had been the same in each case. Uganda, with the emphasis on English and local languages, has, in a sense, been forced into an increased dependence on English, though the use of local languages has also been increased particularly on the radio. There has also been sporadic interest in Swahili: for example, a seminar on mass media and linguistic communication in East Africa held at Makerere College in April 1967 recommended, among other things, that the development of English as a national language was not possible; that a strong and convincing case had been made for the status of Swahili as a national language for East Africa; and that in Uganda Swahili should be introduced as a subject into secondary schools, adult education, and mass media.[23] It must be admitted, however, that a more common attitude is that stated recently by Uganda's Acting Attorney-General, during debate of the newly promulgated Constitutional Proposals:

... official language—that need not delay us. The official language of the Government of Uganda shall be English. Now I hope that people will not spend a large expense of time on asking the Minister of Education when he is going to be teaching Swahili and Zulu; I do not know what other language! We are concerned here only with the Official Language not with teaching another language altogether, which is altogether strange. (Interruption.) Yes, if you teach Swahili, you might as well teach Gujerati. Swahili is no nearer to the language of the hon. Member than Gujerati. I want to challenge him on that. No nearer. He might as well learn what they speak in Paraguay as learn Swahili.[24]

Tanzania has made Swahili the national language and begun actively to discourage the use of English in those contexts where Swahili has proved to be an effective substitute. Kenya has extended the teaching of English but also, in certain areas, and more cautiously, that of Swahili. Increased attention is being paid to the study of local languages as a requirement for increased efficiency in the teaching of English.

It may be that Uganda's major language problems will centre on the role that her local languages can play in the development of a national culture,[25] though the political significance of language has not been lost on the supporters of the Rwenzururu movement even though they have none of the means for implementing it. Tanzania's clearly stated language policy has done much to raise the status of Swahili and to ensure its use even in remote areas where formerly it had been little used. Swahili was, for example, the official language of the 1965 elections and all candidates—including Asians and the single European—were required to argue their case in it. In the absence of a 'party-ticket' it was clearly essential that each candidate should emerge as a convincing representative, and it is a striking fact that command of Swahili could be of some importance in a context such as this where local ties might be regarded as being of paramount importance.[26] Tanzania does, however, face many problems in implementing her language policy, particularly in the provision of viable courses at all levels of the educational system.[27] There are also a number of spheres of day-to-day Government business in which Swahili cannot play its predicted role until a suitable terminology has been worked out and approved, e.g. in law,[28] health, finance, natural resources, etc. The Kenya approach is an empirical one, and it seems likely that planning will follow the emergence of situations which develop as a result of present trends. The role of Swahili as a possible language of internal communication over East Africa as a whole is somewhat problematical: one might argue that the sooner an economic or political federation becomes a reality the less likely it is that Swahili will act as the language of that federation in any official sense, if only because at the moment the only effective means of communication at that level throughout East Africa is through English. The longer such a federation takes to develop, the better chance for Swahili, since Tanzania will have consolidated her own policy and the use of Swahili as an urban language may well have gained for it more adherents.

Yet whatever solution is advocated in terms of an official policy the ultimate arbiters are people themselves. A government may do a great deal to give support and direction to popular feelings and aspirations in language matters but the difficulties of implementing an unpopular policy are greater than most present-day governments can surmount,[29] and the same problems attend the implementation of over-ambitious or unrealistic measures in support of even a popular policy. Whatever degree of public conformity is entailed, privacy permits alternative linguistic choices; and in countries as linguistically diverse as those of East Africa it may well be the patterns of private multilingualism that reveal how popular language choice is being allocated.

NOTES

1 There is a large bibliography relating to European nationalism. Useful introductions are Chadwick, 1945; Kohn, 1945; Deutsch, 1953 & 1966 —the latter work providing a good bibliography and a commentary on recent developments.

2 I use the terms 'first, second, third' in a diachronic sense, of the order in which the languages are acquired.

3 cf. the Indian situation where each of the 14 officially recognized languages is spoken by at least 10 million speakers.

4 A good general introduction to this subject is Le Page, 1964; and C.C.T.A./C.S.A., 1962. See also Maxwell, 1967.

5 More detailed discussion of the theoretical issues involved is given in Fishman, 1964.

6 Reported in *Uhuru*, 5 January 1967. A good example of state planning is given in Heyd, 1954.

7 i.e. those speaking the same first language.

8 The situation is, of course, much over-simplified. More detailed discussion is given in Obote, 1967.

9 Consider in this context the comment of an official from the Ministry of Community Development and National Culture, Tanzania: '. . . our immediate need is to build a nation with cultural homogeneity, which will ensure the preservation of our national unity' (Mushi, 1966, p. 14).

10 By Mazrui, 1966a & 1966b.

11 The situation is admirably summed up by E. R. Leach: 'For a man to speak one language rather than another is a ritual act, it is a statement about one's personal status; to speak the same language as one's neighbours expresses solidarity with those neighbours, to speak a different language from one's neighbours expresses social distance or even hostility' (Leach, 1954, p. 49).

12 Thanks are expressed to the respective editors with reference to Whiteley, 1956 & 1957 for permission to utilize material first published there.

13 Though there is little evidence of this from the newspapers of the time, other perhaps than the number and success of the papers themselves. There had been newspapers in Swahili from the end of the nineteenth century, but there is little variation from the 'parish-pump' presentation at this period and little interest in language.

14 Sukuma, Haya, and Nyakyusa were the only local languages in which newspapers were produced. In Dar es Salaam at the present time it is among households in which Haya, Chagga, or Nyakyusa are spoken as a first language that one finds the greatest concern for the use of the local language—even where the families have operational control over English and Swahili. See Whiteley, 1967.

15 Especially from the team of specialists sent out by the Nuffield Foundation (1953).

16 For the implications of the use of Swahili as a political language, see Whiteley, 1961.

17 Though from 1930 onwards Kenya contributed about £700 annually to the Inter-Territorial Language (Swahili) Committee—later the East African Swahili Committee.

18 Note the opening speech of the Governor to Legislative Council in October 1929: '. . . Government is also most anxious to increase the study of the vernaculars. That is the only road to the true understanding of African habits and feelings. Government is considering steps to encourage the learning of vernaculars by Administrative Officers and modifying the constant move from station to station which at present makes the acquisition of vernaculars thankless and difficult' (*Proceedings of the Legislative Council*, 1929).

19 In earlier literature these languages were called 'Nilo-Hamitic'. Greenberg reclassified them as 'Nilotic', and Tucker as 'Para-Nilotic'.

20 *Proceedings of Legislative Council*, Part III, 40th Session, 1960, pp. 1225–9.

21 Such situations are by no means unique to Africa: see the very detailed study of language planning in Norway in Haugen, 1966.

22 For example: '. . . Bugisu is a country with strong finances and we should have a written language to keep the records of its progress.' Correspondent in *Uganda Argus*, August 1958.

23 The conclusions as a whole were reprinted in *East Africa Journal*, May 1967.

24 *Uganda Parliamentary Debates (Hansard)*, 2nd Series, Vol. 72, 1967, p. 330.

25 It is interesting to note that Okot p'B'Tek's long poem (1966b) was originally in Acholi. The role of African languages in African literary developments was raised by Wali in *Transition* (Wali, 1963) and continued in discussions over the next few issues.

26 Though it is clear from the recent study of the elections in Tanzania in 1965 that in at least some of the areas discussed in detail, notably Rungwe (Nyakyusa) and Ugogo (Gogo), local languages were a factor of some importance (Cliffe, 1967).

27 I have set out some priorities for linguistic research in Tanzania in Whiteley, 1966. See also Whiteley, 1968.

28 The Institute of Swahili Research, University College, Dar es Salaam, is preparing a new Swahili dictionary, and the newly established National Swahili Council will also prepare specialized word-lists. The most notable achievement to date is the preparation of a legal dictionary by a small committee under the chairmanship of Prof. A. B. Weston of University College.

29 Even in as highly controlled a situation as that described in George Orwell's *1984*, it was realized that an indefinite time would elapse before the official language, Newspeak, finally and completely supplanted Oldspeak.

REFERENCES

C.C.T.A./C.S.A. 1962, *Symposium on Multilingualism*, C.C.T.A./C.S.A. Pub. No. 87.

CHADWICK, H. M. 1945, *The Nationalities of Europe and the Growth of National Ideologies*, Cambridge University Press.

CLIFFE, L. 1967, *One-Party Democracy*, E.A. Publishing House, Nairobi.

DEUTSCH, K. W. 1953, 'The Growth of Nations: Some Recurrent Patterns of Political and Social Integration', *World Politics*, 5, 2.

1966, *Nationalism and Social Communication* (2nd ed.), M.I.T. Press, Cambridge, Mass.

ELIOT, C. 1906, 'The Progress and Problems of the East African Protectorate', *Journal of the Royal Colonial Institute*, 37.

FISHMAN, J. A. 1964, 'Language Maintenance and Language Shift as a Field of Enquiry', *Linguistics*, 9.

1965, 'Who Speaks What Language to Whom and When', *La Linguistique*, 1.

HAUGEN, E. 1966, *Language Conflict and Language Planning*, Harvard University Press, Cambridge, Mass.

HEYD, U. 1954, *Language Reform in Modern Turkey*, Oriental Notes & Studies, No. 5, Jerusalem.

H.M.S.O. 1931, *Joint Select Committee on Closer Union in East Africa (Minutes of Evidence)*, H.M.S.O.

1955, *East African Royal Commission, 1953–5, Report*, Cmd. 9475.

KOHN, H. 1945, *Prophets and Peoples: Studies in Nineteenth-Century Nationalism*, Macmillan.

LESLIE, J. A. K., A survey of *Dar es Salaam*, Oxford University Press, London.

MANANI, G. M. 1966, 'Problems Facing East African Music', in *East Africa's Cultural Heritage* (Contemporary African Monographs No. 4), East African Publishing House, Nairobi.

MAXWELL, N. 1967, 'India and Language', *New Society*, 21 December.

MAZRUI, A. 1966a, 'The English Language and Political Consciousness in Colonial Africa', *The Journal of M. African Studies*, 4.

1968, 'Some Socio-Political Functions of English Literature in Africa', in *Language Problems of Developing Nations*, ed. J. A. Fishman, Wiley, New York.

MUSHI, S. 1966, 'The Role of the Ministry of Culture in National Development', in *East Africa's Cultural Heritage* (Contemporary African Monographs No. 4), East African Publishing House, Nairobi.

NUFFIELD FOUNDATION 1953, *African Education*, Crown Agents, London.

OBOTE, M. 1967, 'Language and National Identification', *E. Africa Journal*, April.

P'B'TEK, O. 1966a, 'The Future of Vernacular Literature', in *East Africa's Cultural Heritage* (Contemporary African Monographs No. 4), East African Publishing House, Nairobi.

1966b, *The Song of Lawino*, East African Publishing House, Nairobi.

SOUTHALL, A. W. and GUTKIND, P. C. W., *Townsmen in the Making*, Routledge & Kegan Paul, London.

TUCKER, A. N. 1963, 'The Linguistic Aspects of Mass Literacy Movements', in *Symposium on Popular Education*, Afrika Studiecentrum, Leiden.

UGANDA PEOPLES CONGRESS, 1960, *Policy Statement*, U.P.C., Kampala.

WALI, O. 1963, 'The Dead End of African Literature', *Transition*, 4, 10.

WHITELEY, W. H. 1956, 'The Changing Position of Swahili in East Africa', *Africa*, 26.

1957, 'Language and Politics in East Africa', *Tanganyika Notes and Records*, 47/48.

1961, 'Political Concepts and Connotations', *St. Anthony's Papers*, No. 10. Chatto & Windus.

1966, 'Priorities for Linguistic Research', in Owen, D. F. (ed.) *Research and Development in East Africa*, East African Publishing House, Nairobi.

1967, 'Loan Words in Linguistic Description', in Rauch, I. & Scott, C. T. (eds.) *Approaches in Linguistic Methodology*, University of Wisconsin Press.

1969, *Swahili: the Rise of a National Language*, Methuen.

WILSON, M. 1951, *Good Company*, Oxford University Press.

WRIGHT, M. 1965, 'Swahili Language Policy, 1890–1940', *Swahili*, 35.

TRIBAL FACTORS IN THE ESTABLISHMENT OF THE EAST AFRICAN LEGAL SYSTEMS

Eugene Cotran

As in the political field, so in the legal field, the history of modern East Africa is characterized by the development from a tribal to a national system. From a purely tribal system of laws and courts initially, there emerged during the colonial period a superimposed English system running in parallel with tribal institutions. In the latter years of the colonial period and in the subsequent period of independence, there began a movement towards integrated national systems of courts and a serious attempt to bring together the customary and the imported English laws to produce a national whole. The object of this paper is to describe this development and to examine how far it has been successful in Kenya, Uganda, and Tanzania.[1] It is necessary for this purpose to consider the problem in respect of (a) the courts, and (b) the laws.

The Pre-Colonial Period

In considering the legal and judicial systems of this period, it is important to bear in mind the complex of peoples and their cultures of the East African region. They had a wide range of ethnic and linguistic origins, political systems, economic systems, religions, etc.; and these differences were, of course, reflected in their legal and judicial systems.

(a) The courts : settlement of disputes

Without seeking to make detailed distinctions, there were,

broadly speaking, two main types of courts or systems of dispute settlement in the indigenous societies of East Africa. Sometimes both were operative in the same society. These two types may be described as arbitral 'courts' and judicial courts.

In societies without chiefs, and in the absence of centralized political authority (e.g. most of those in what is now Kenya), the settlement of disputes was principally by arbitration and negotiation within the local community. Typically the process of arrangement of a settlement was conducted by the elders or other influential men of family or kin groups, in those cases where disputes related primarily to such affairs as marriage, custody of children, inheritance, land tenure, and other similar rights and obligations. Where disputes arose between neighbours within the same community, arbitration and negotiation were conducted by formal and informal leaders of varying kinds (e.g. family elders, age-set leaders, heads of dominant lineages, etc.). The distinctive features were the absence of judges and of enforced judgments, the emphasis on conciliation, and the idea of the community (or some part of it, such as a constituent kin group) resolving its disputes through agreements negotiated by accepted leaders or influential men. Such 'courts' were not, however, limited only to chiefless societies, for they also operated sometimes within the local communities which comprised a centralized kingdom.[2]

The second general type of court—the judicial court— existed in those societies which had centralized political authority. Usually there was a hierarchy of courts reflecting the political hierarchy, with appeals going from the lower courts (e.g. those of the minor chiefs or headmen) to the higher courts (e.g. the greater chiefs). In the Buganda kingdom, for example, in the middle of the nineteenth century, the system of administering justice was of a most complex kind: there was a variety of judicial tribunals connected in a pyramidal structure, so that appeal lay from the minor chiefs through the great chiefs to the chief minister (Katikkiro), and thence to the Kabaka (Haydon, 1964). Among the Sukuma the judicial system consisted of various courts of the different grades of chiefs, although there does not appear to have been a system of appeals (Cory, 1953). The main features of this type of system were the formal courts with established judges (who were most usually political office-holders) who had the authority to summon witnesses, to award fines or punishment or compensation, and to enforce the execution of judgments.

(b) *The law*

There has been much controversy in recent years about the most suitable term by which to describe the laws of African societies. Such terms as 'customary law', 'tribal law', 'native law', 'native law and custom', 'indigenous law', and 'local law', amongst others, have been suggested. I think that for this pre-colonial period under discussion, one can legitimately speak of 'tribal law', although nowadays this term may be inaccurate and it may have objectionable connotations. It was 'tribal law' because, on the whole, each tribe had an autonomous set of laws, with little, if any, outside influence.

An analysis of the nature of 'tribal law' lies outside the scope of this paper, but it is important to emphasize three distinctive features of it in order to see to what extent these features have undergone change in the later periods. First, the law was unwritten. There were no written codes, no written record of changes that have been introduced, and no written court judgments. Second, the law (with a few reported instances of tribal legislation) was customary, in that it was intrinsic to and emerged out of the customs and practices of the people. Third, despite the variety and differences among the peoples of East Africa which has already been emphasized, there was much similarity in the actual content of the laws of these peoples.

The Colonial Period

The result of the imposition of British colonial rule on East Africa, so far as the legal and judicial system was concerned, was to produce a dual or parallel system of courts and laws. Whilst introducing a completely new system of courts and law based on the English system, the colonial power retained, so far as possible, existing tribal institutions.

(a) *The courts*

The dualism or parallelism in the courts was very marked in

East Africa, compared with other British colonial territories. On the one hand there were the British or general courts consisting usually of different grades of magistrates from which appeal lay to a High Court. These were composed of British judges, had jurisdiction over all persons in criminal and civil matters, and applied basically English law. On the other hand, there were the native courts (otherwise called native tribunals, African courts, or local courts). The British administration tried as far as possible to preserve the previous nature of these tribunals. Thus they were composed of either the traditional local chiefs or local elders who also exercised executive powers; they only had jurisdiction over Africans; and applied, subject to a few exceptions, the customary law prevailing in the area of the jurisdiction of the court. The native courts were supervised by administrative officers who had, subject to certain qualifications, appellate jurisdiction. The Administration, moreover, and not the Judicial Department, had full control over the appointment and dismissal of the court members. Advocates were not allowed to appear before these courts.

Thus the two systems of courts—British and African— developed separately, and there was no link between them at all. It was only in the 1950s, towards the end of the colonial period, that an attempt was made to produce some sort of integration between the two systems (see Reports of Judicial Advisers' Conferences, 1953 and 1956). This was principally done at the appellate level, e.g. by provision for the revision of, and appeal from, native court proceedings by the High Court, as in Uganda. In Tanganyika a Central Court of Appeal, presided over by a High Court judge, was established in 1951 to hear appeals from the local courts (i.e. African courts); and a similar Court of Review was created in Kenya in the same year, though this was to be presided over by a person holding high judicial office, and not necessarily by a High Court judge.

Another important development in the later years of the colonial period was the change in personnel of the African courts. In the first place there was an attempt to separate the executive and judicial functions of chiefs and local elders, so that gradually the personnel of African courts exercised judicial functions only. Second, programmes of training were initiated with a view to giving the personnel some basic training in court administration, recording of cases, etc.

This period also witnessed the beginnings of a process of Westernization of native court procedure. In addition to the programmes of training, African courts were issued with circulars or handbooks laying down a simplified system of practice and procedure based on English law.

Despite these reforms, however, there is justification for saying that the African courts in the major part of the colonial period remained to a large extent 'tribal courts' because they were principally composed of the local elders or chiefs of the tribe and their jurisdiction was restricted to Africans.

(b) *The law*

Dualism existed to the same extent in the administration of the law. The British or general courts were empowered to apply the English common law, doctrines of equity, and statutes of general application at a certain date, but only so far as the circumstances of the territory and its inhabitants permitted, and subject to such qualifications as local circumstances rendered necessary. In fact this latter proviso was largely ignored, and there was little, if any, attempt to accommodate the English law to suit local conditions. The African courts, on the other hand, were enjoined to apply customary law 'in so far as it is not repugnant to natural justice or morality'. In effect, customary law was left to develop separately and very little use was made by the appellate courts or the revising officers of this repugnancy provision. Furthermore, although the British courts were enjoined by legislation to be 'guided' by customary law in cases where Africans were parties, this provision was again largely ignored, and the British judges were invariably guided by the law with which they were familiar, i.e. English law.

The result of the dualistic system was that there was an almost complete isolation of African courts and customary law in the colonial era. The British administration, whilst giving full recognition to customary law, interfered little with it. Furthermore, there appears to have been a general lack of interest by the colonial governments in the problems arising from the content and application of customary law.

Thus, generally speaking, no serious attempts were made for the study of the subject, no attempts for the recording of customary law, its development, its reform or unification. Various consequences stemmed from this lack of interest.

First, there was no governmental initiative for the systematic study or recording of customary law. It is true that in all three East African countries individual researchers, mainly anthropologists, made studies of customary law, and indeed some of them made very valuable contributions to the subject; but they were not sponsored in any way by the colonial government. A possible exception to this was Tanganyika, where government sociologists were appointed to make studies of customary law in certain areas. An example of this is the valuable work undertaken by the late Mr Hans Cory, who was responsible, during the trusteeship period in Tanganyika, for the recording of the customary laws of several Tanganyika tribes (Cory, 1953; Cory & Hartnoll, 1945). But as the name of the office-holder implies, the primary interest of these government sociologists was in the sociological rather than in the legal aspects of customary law.

Another venture was the setting up of Law Panels in Kenya from 1950 onwards to record and modify customary law. Unfortunately these panels, until they were reorganized in 1960, worked very haphazardly and, because they had no guidance in recording customary law, produced little of value to a lawyer.

In Uganda, not only was there a lack of interest in customary law but government policy was actively concerned in discouraging any attempt at recording customary law in any official manner. The official view amongst both the judiciary and the administration seemed to be that one should leave customary law alone and allow it to wither away.

The second consequence that stemmed from the lack of interest of the colonial governments was that customary law remained to a large extent unwritten and was treated as a matter of fact rather than law in the courts. Third, no active attempts were made at reforming customary law, nor at seeking unification between the different customary laws or between customary law and the written law. Fourth, no attempts were made in the legislation to resolve the conflicts which arose between customary law and statutory law.

Finally, customary law was in the colonial era kept away from the province of the professional lawyer. Advocates were not allowed to appear before the African courts, with the result that they never came into contact with it. Customary law remained the domain of the anthropologist, the sociologist, and the administrative officer, but not of the professional lawyer or the legislator.

I hope I have not given the impression from what I have said of the colonial period so far that customary law remained static and unaffected. It would indeed be surprising if an alien rule lasting over half a century did not materially affect both the application and content of customary law. What is significant is that whilst in the independence period there was an active, positive attempt on the part of the governments to give serious consideration to the problems relating to customary law, most changes that occurred in the colonial era were probably a result of the policy of indirect rule and of natural development.

One of the most important changes to customary law in the colonial era was the departure from the traditional patterns of dispute-settling, i.e. the radical change which occurred gradually upon the introduction of a system of courts which, though originally based on existing institutions, tended to become more and more westernized.

'With the introduction of a local courts system set up and supervised by the colonial rulers there were radical departures from indigenous patterns. To a large extent efforts were made to use existing institutions, but it was easier to do this with peoples who had developed governmental institutions than with people who had minimal government, just as it was easier to control and influence the settled agriculturalists than the wandering pastoralists. To everybody the local courts system presented at least some unfamiliar features and to some people the whole idea was totally and incomprehensibly alien. Judicial bodies with defined jurisdiction and fixed personnel were superimposed on less clearly defined institutions and often the geographical area of jurisdiction cut across tribal and even ethnic boundaries. The personnel of the courts were by no means always elders according to native law and custom and in a number of places government-appointed chiefs, owing greater allegiance to government than to tribe exercised judicial powers. Moreover, the functions that those bodies were required to perform were not identical with those of the indigenous institutions that were being built on. Most significant of all, perhaps, was the creation of a ladder of appeals and revisions with expatriates stationed at the top of the ladder, and the provisions, in some instances, enabling the same expatriates to participate in proceedings at all levels. It was this general overlordship of the local courts by European administrators that provided the most important channel for the infusion of alien ideas into the administration of justice at the lower levels and at the same time it acted as a unifying influence. Local court-holders came to know what was expected of them and some of them may sometimes have imitated what they had seen when acting as witnesses or assessors in the superior courts' (Twining, 1963).

A striking illustration of this assimilation of English rules into the customary law through the judges of the native courts can be seen in Buganda. A glance at the customary law reports of Buganda will show how there has been a clear adoption of English legal principles in the Buganda customary law relating to contracts, torts, and crimes.

Another method by which customary law in the colonial period was affected was through the introduction of English-type laws which, though not specifically abolishing or changing customary law, made available to Africans the option of governing their legal relationships by the Western-based laws. The best example of this occurs in the laws relating to marriage, where in all three East African countries, Marriage Ordinances were introduced which, while specifically recognizing customary marriages, made available to Africans the choice of marrying monogamously under the Ordinance.

Yet another way in which customary law was affected under the colonial period was through direct legislation. I have already indicated that generally there was little interference with customary law through legislation—but there were a few exceptions. In Kenya, for example, the introduction of a system of land consolidation and registration meant that customary land law virtually ceased to apply in the registered areas.

The Independent Period

The independence of the East African countries in the early 1960s did not bring about a legal revolution. Broadly speaking, all three countries inherited the judicial and legal system of the colonial power. There was certainly no desire to revert to the pre-colonial tribal system. On the other hand, there was a desire to modify the inherited English legal institutions and to Africanize them as much as possible. How did the East African Governments set about this task, and how far have they been successful?

(a) Integration of courts

First, the East African Governments directed their attention to completing the process of integration or unification of courts which had already commenced at the end of the colonial period.

In Tanganyika the Magistrates' Courts Act, 1964,[3] substituted for the former dual system a single, three-tier hierarchy, i.e. primary courts from which appeals lie to district courts and finally to the High Court. All courts have jurisdiction over all persons irrespective of race.

In Uganda the Magistrates' Courts Act, 1964,[4] abolished African courts and substituted therefor magistrates' courts which may be presided over by a Chief Magistrate or a Grade I, Grade II or a Grade III Magistrate. Appeals from Grade II and III Magistrates lie to a Grade I Magistrate and from a Grade I and Chief Magistrate to the High Court. As with Tanganyika, all courts have jurisdiction over all persons irrespective of race.

Kenya has recently completed the process of integration of courts by the introduction of the Magistrates' Courts Act[5] which abolishes African courts and introduces a three-tier hierarchy consisting of District Magistrate's Courts of three classes, Resident Magistrates' Courts and the High Court. Appeals from Class III District Magistrates lie to Class I District Magistrates or to Resident Magistrates, and appeals from Class II and Class I District Magistrates and from Resident Magistrates lie to the High Court. Like Uganda and Tanganyika, all courts have jurisdiction over all persons.

To a large extent, this process of unification of courts has meant that the tribal factor in relation to the courts has almost disappeared in East Africa. First, all courts, as has been pointed out, have jurisdiction over all persons irrespective of race. Second, all courts can apply both the received English law and customary law. The Tanganyika Act lays down very detailed provisions relating to the circumstances in which customary law is applicable in a dispute. The effect of these is that the test for the application of customary law to a person no longer depends on his race, i.e. whether he is an African or non-African, but whether he is a member of a community which recognizes rules of customary law. The Uganda and Kenya Acts have no such detailed provisions, but make it equally clear that Magistrates' Courts may apply both customary law and the received English law. Third, the judges of the newly established courts are more and more ceasing to be local lay elders. The programmes of training begun in the colonial period have been intensified, so that the personnel of courts are becoming more and more sophisticated. It is now not uncommon to find that the local magistrate is a person from a different area, unfamiliar with the local tribal customs. Finally, the process of transferring the local courts to the judicial branch of government has been completed, so that all appointments, supervision, and dismissals are made by a Judicial Service Commission.

Although one can therefore observe a gradual removal of all tribal elements from the courts system, it is difficult to discern any 'Africanization' in the resultant process. The local courts have been developed on English lines, and their practice and procedure are being assimilated to the procedure observed by the superior, i.e. English-type, courts. In all three East African countries there are now legislative provisions under which the local courts must observe, with slight modifications, the practice and procedure of the High Courts.

(b) *Integration of laws*

An outstanding feature of the independence period is the great interest shown by East African Governments in the problems relating to customary law. Far from letting customary law develop on its own, as in the colonial period, we find the East African Governments actively engaged in the study, recording, harmonization, unification, and reform of customary law.

(i) *Criminal Law.* In 1960 the London Conference on the Future of Law in Africa, which was attended by representatives from the East African countries, recommended that the general criminal law should be written and should be uniformly applicable to persons of all communities within a territory having its own separate judicial system (Allott, 1960). This principle has in fact been incorporated into the constitutions of Kenya and Uganda, both of which provide that after a certain period no person could be convicted of a criminal offence unless that offence was defined and the penalty therefor prescribed in a written law. Similarly, Section 66 of the Tanganyika Magistrates' Courts Act provides that no person shall be charged with, tried for, or convicted of any offence contrary to customary law.

In all three countries, therefore, customary criminal law has ceased to apply as a separate system. It is interesting to see, however, the different ways in which this result was achieved in the three countries.

Tanganyika seems to have taken the easy way out by simply abolishing customary criminal law, with the result that criminal offences which existed in customary law but which were unknown in the written law (e.g. adultery, seduction of an unmarried girl) no longer apply. In other words, the present written criminal law of Tanganyika takes no account whatsoever of customary criminal law.

In Uganda (other than Buganda) there is a slight improvement on the strict Tanganyika position. This is that the offence of adultery which was regarded as criminal under many Uganda customary laws is now inserted as a new offence in the Uganda Penal Code.[6] There is no restriction in its applicability to particular persons and hence it becomes an offence for all in Uganda whether or not the offender is a person subject to customary law.

In Buganda the recently enacted Customary Offences Law,[7] is really a comprehensive penal code, which is on the lines of the Uganda and India Penal Codes but which also contains offences known only to Buganda customary law, such as offences against the Royal Family.[8]

In Kenya the Government decided in 1960 to initiate a research project for the ascertainment and recording of customary criminal offences with a view to their incorporation into the written criminal law of Kenya. This was done in collaboration with the Restatement of African Law Project, initiated by the School of African and Oriental Studies, under the directorship of Professor A. N. Allott. In June 1960 I was seconded by the School to the Government of Kenya to undertake the recording of the surviving customary offences recognized by the Kenya tribes. The work consisted of visiting every district in Kenya and recording the customary offences in a systematic fashion with the help of the Kenya Law Panels to which I referred earlier. The panels, however, were reconstituted and their members carefully selected. Having recorded the offences in each district, it was found that the offences recognized as criminal were very similar amongst the different tribes, and an attempt was made to unify the offences at provincial level. In the final analysis I found that there were some ten offences which were recognized as criminal by most of the Kenya tribes but which were not criminal by the Kenya Penal Code. In my report to the Kenya Government I made recommendations as to how these offences could be inserted into the existing criminal law of Kenya.[9]

(ii) *Civil Law*. Whereas in the field of criminal law, all the East African Governments arrived at the same result in different ways, all three governments have tackled the problem of the customary civil law in different ways.

Kenya

In Kenya the view was held that the greatest defect in the customary law lay in the fact that it remained largely unwritten; that it was not possible to initiate sound reform before such laws were fully ascertained; and that consequently the first step was to undertake a restatement or recording of the different customary laws of Kenya.

I have already described how the Kenya Project commenced with a restatement and unification of the surviving customary criminal offences. When this was completed, I was invited by the Kenya Government to continue with the recording of the customary civil law to cover the law of marriage, divorce, succession, and family relations. This again I did with the assistance of Law Panels which, however, were reconstituted on an ethnic rather than on a District basis. The civil law investigation differed from the criminal one in that there was no attempt at unifying the civil law of the various tribes. Nor was there an intention to codify the civil law in the sense of incorporating it into the written law as legislation. The restatements of each ethnic group will simply be used as guides to customary law. Arrangements for the publication of these restatements have been completed between London publishers, the Government of Kenya and the Restatement of African Law Project.

These restatements of the customary law, as has been pointed out, were made separately for each ethnic group, so that there is a restatement for Kikuyu law, Luo law, etc. The Kenya Government, however, do not propose that the process should stop at the restatement stage. In April 1967 the Government of Kenya established two Commissions,[10] one on the law of marriage and the other on the law of succession; their terms of reference are to review these subjects with the object of replacing the existing multiple systems, based on English law, Indian law, customary law, Islamic law, and Hindu law, with new codes relating to marriage and succession which will apply uniformly to all the people of Kenya. Undoubtedly the existing restatements of the different customary laws will greatly facilitate the task of the Commissions.

Tanganyika

Whereas in Kenya the first stage of reform consisted of restating the customary laws of the different ethnic groups, Tanganyika launched in 1961 a project—unique in Africa—aimed at the full-scale unification of all the customary laws of the various tribes of the country. The project was launched by President Nyerere himself, who stressed in a letter addressed to all Members of Parliament, District Secretaries of the Tanganyika African National Union and Chairmen of District Councils, that one of the main reasons for the project was 'the importance of a unified customary code of law to the building of a nation in Tanganyika'. The political significance of the undertaking was thus underlined from the very beginning.

Research began under the direction of the late Mr Hans Cory who had already made investigations into several customary laws in Tanganyika, and notably the laws of the Haya, Sukuma, and Nyamwezi tribes. The method of work was as follows: tribal representatives chosen for their expert knowledge of the customary law would meet with Mr Cory and agree on a first draft. In fact the project was started in Sukumaland and the Sukama text (already published) was used as a basis. The draft was then submitted to a national panel of experts which considered it and referred it back to the District Council for approval. Once the District Council approved the text the Minister made an Order under which the codified customary law became binding in the area.

Although the original intention was that this procedure should be followed in each area, i.e. for every ethnic group, in practice, since the Government was particularly anxious that the unification should be completed as soon as possible the project gradually changed character and consisted mainly of persuading the uninvestigated ethnic groups to accept the already unified draft without prior restatement.

Although the project was only started in 1961, the vast majority of the ethnic groups of Tanganyika (both patrilineal and matrilineal) have now accepted one unified customary law relating to Bridewealth, Marriage, Divorce, Status of Children, Guardianship, Wills and Intestate Succession.

Certain features of this unification are worth noting. First, once the Minister applied the declaration of customary law to a District, it becomes a code which binds the courts, i.e. it is not merely a guide to customary law. Second, although the principal aim was to unify the different customary laws, the unified version contains many reforms and rules unknown to any of the customary laws which it purports to unify. Third, the declarations are in Ki-Swahili, now the official language of the Tanganyika Primary Courts.

Uganda

Unlike Kenya and Tanganyika, Uganda has not embarked on any project of recording or unifying customary law. It appears that the pre-independence opposition to the recording of customary law has persisted. This policy is in fact stated in a paper submitted by the Uganda Government to the African Conference on Local Courts and Customary Law held in Dar es Salaam in 1963, which says:

> The codification of customary civil law would be a task of enormous complexity and is not envisaged. It is hoped that with the complete integration of the courts systems in Uganda, statutory civil law will in time become accepted everywhere.

Rather than make a start with ascertainment of the customary laws before embarking on reform (as Kenya has done), the Uganda Government preferred to go straight into the question of unification and reform of those aspects of the law that needed reform. Thus in January 1964 a Commission was appointed . . .

> To consider the laws and customs regulating marriage, divorce and the status of women in Uganda, bearing in mind the need to ensure that those laws and customs, while preserving existing traditions and practices as far as possible, should be consonant with justice and morality and appropriate to the position of Uganda as an independent nation and to make recommendations.

The Report of the Commission which was published in 1965 (Uganda Government, 1965) makes various recommendations principally designed to remedy the inadequacy of the protection which the law affords to a wife or widow married under customary law; e.g. that a man is only able to register one marriage, and that a widow should share a life interest to the extent of a third of her deceased husband's estate.

It appears that the Uganda Government have not taken any action on this Report. On the contrary, the recent publication of a Succession (Amendment) Bill with a guide to the proposed new law suggests that so far as succession is concerned, the Government are not following the Commission's recommendations.

Assessment of Position Today

In the preceding parts, I have attempted to describe the history of the development of the East African legal systems from a tribal to a national system. The object of this part is to assess the achievements of the East African independent Governments, especially in the light of their apparently conflicting desires:

(i) not to re-introduce any changes based on a tribal system,
(ii) to modify the inherited English system in such a way as to 'Africanize' it, but at the same time keeping it as modern and progressive as possible.

(a) *The courts*

As far as the court systems are concerned, all three Governments have chosen the path to full unification, i.e. abolishing the dual or parallel system and having one set of courts with jurisdiction over all persons irrespective of race. In this respect, the East African Governments have succeeded in establishing a court system that is in no way 'tribal'. On the other hand, as has been pointed out, they have, in the process, Anglicized the courts to such an extent, that it is difficult to find anything particularly African about the courts. The informal practice and procedure, an important characteristic of the traditional and colonial African courts, has been replaced by the rigid English process. This is rather a pity, for there is much to be said for a system of procedure which the ordinary man can understand and which is quick, simple, and flexible. In this respect it does not follow that modernization must mean Westernization, and I do feel that this is an area in the legal system where the East African Governments might well have fulfilled the Africanization policy by building upon the traditional methods of dispute-settling by arbitration.

(b) *The law*

(i) *Criminal law.* Here again, all three East African Governments have chosen to have one written criminal law applicable to all. But it is significant that all three countries have done this by either abolishing customary criminal law or incorporating very few customary offences into the existing general law, i.e. the Penal Code. The Governments have proceeded on the assumption that the existing East African Penal Codes (based on English law) are themselves adequate. This is by no means a correct assumption. Here again full Anglicization was chosen. Again, I would submit that this was a missed opportunity. If the criminal law of a country is to be a reflection on the social, economic, and moral ideas and beliefs of the community, then it would have been necessary, in the East African context, to produce a criminal law incorporating indigenous African ideas of crime, punishment, and criminal responsibility.

(ii) *Civil law*. It is in this sphere that the East African Governments were faced with the greatest dilemma, for whereas in the criminal law field customary law played little part at the time of independence, in the civil field—especially in the laws relating to family relations, marriage, divorce, succession, and land tenure—customary law still played a very large part and indeed governed the relations of about 90 per cent of the population. The dilemma was even greater because here one gets the real conflict between the desires to get away from tribal law and tribalism and, on the other hand, to Africanize and not adhere strictly to English law.

We have seen the different ways in which the East African Governments have tackled this problem. Restatement first in Kenya, and then reform or unification. Full-scale unification of the customary laws in Tanganyika. And in Uganda, first some wishful thinking that customary law is going to disappear quickly, then a commission to suggest reforms.

In effect, it is possible to criticize all these methods. Of both the Kenya and Tanganyika projects, it has been said that the *method* was faulty since Law Panels are unreliable, and that in any case it is not possible to produce abstract statements of customary law devoid of their social content (Twining, 1963). The Tanganyika unifications have been criticized on further grounds that: (a) they do not represent the law of any one tribe; (b) that this hotch-potch customary law will not satisfy

any of the Tanganyika communities; (c) that the reforms introduced are halfhearted; (d) that the restatement is very badly
drafted; (e) that since the people are dissatisfied with the new
law, they will tend to avoid the courts; and (f) that codification, i.e. legislation, tends to freeze customary law and hinders
its development (Tanner, 1966, p. 105).

The main criticisms of the Uganda Report on Marriage are:
(a) that it is no more than a slavish imitation of the Ghana
Marriage, Divorce, and Inheritance Bill, which never got on
its feet in Ghana and was finally abandoned; (b) that it
suggests reforms in ignorance of what the detailed rules of
customary law are—hence the references in the report to 'self-
acquired' property as opposed to other property, a well-known
conception in West Africa, but not in Uganda; (c) it does not
make recommendations on some of the most important and
controversial problems relating to customary law, such as the
question of bride-price, prohibited degrees, etc.

It is, of course, all too easy to criticize these projects, but one
must remember that they are all pioneering efforts formulated
and undertaken in the short spell of four or five years. They
are, of course, only the beginnings of a process of law reform
which will probably take many years—if one is to hazard a
guess, until the end of this century. This at least can be said of
the approach adopted by the East African Governments—
that they were fully conscious of the fact that any future legal
system in their countries must be based on the realities of the
situation, which is that their countries have a multiplicity of
laws which must be welded together and modernized; and that
an overnight legal revolution replacing the existing laws by
something completely novel (as happened in Ataturk's Turkey)
will lead to absurd results.

The final question is where and how will the East African
legal systems move? Will tribalism ever disappear from the
legal scene? Will people stop talking of 'Kikuyu law', or
'Ganda law', or 'Chagga law'? The answers to these questions
are inevitably linked with the political future of the East African
countries. In Kenya a few years ago, when 'regionalism'
(*majimbo*) was in vogue, the Kalenjin people were very unwilling to talk about anything except Nandi law or Masai law,
etc. I feel sure that now, with the coming together of K.A.N.U.

and K.A.D.U., and with centralization, people will undoubtedly be more willing to talk of Kenya customary law. Again in Tanganyika there is no doubt that the speed in which the customary law unification was achieved was a direct result of the favourable political atmosphere of *umoja*. On the other hand, I very much doubt whether any Muganda, with the recent political upheaval there, would be willing to talk of unification.

Assuming, however, that the shape of the East African political systems will continue to put heavy stress on unity and strong central government, it is likely that the process of unification of customary law, which has already begun, will continue even more vigorously. Quite apart from active governmental unification on the Tanganyika lines, customary laws will tend to converge by reason of the unification of courts, the more rapid mixing of populations, intertribal intercourse, and urbanization. It is also possible to predict that the process of integration between the customary and statutory law which has also begun will be intensified and extended to fields other than the personal law.

NOTES

1 Zanzibar is excluded from this survey, and thus references are to 'Tanganyika'.
2 For example, in the Nyoro kingdom of western Uganda (Beattie, 1957).
3 No. 55 of 1963. For details of the integration of courts in Tanganyika, see Cotran, 1965.
4 No. 38 of 1964. For a note on this Act, see Morris, 1965.
5 No. 17 of 1967.
6 Uganda Penal Code, section 150A. Another offence, namely 'elopement', has recently been introduced.
7 Further details about this law and the reason for its enactment are given in Morris, 1965.
8 The Uganda High Court has ruled that if the Buganda law contains any offences which are covered by the Uganda Penal Code, then such offences are *ultra vires*. This paper was written before the new constitution was introduced in Uganda, abolishing the Kingdom of Buganda.
9 Cotran, 1963. No action was taken by the Kenya Government on this Report, with the result that all customary offences lapsed in June 1966 —the date set by the Constitution for the disapplication of unwritten criminal law.
10 Detailed terms of reference of the Commissions are given in 'Notes and News', *Journal of African Law*, 11, p. 1. The Commissions submitted Reports in 1968.

EUGENE COTRAN

REFERENCES

ALLOTT, A. N. (ed.) 1960, *The Future of Law in Africa*, Butterworth.
BEATTIE, J. 1957, 'Informal Judicial Activity in Bunyoro', *Journal of African Administration*, 9, 4.
CORY, H. 1953, *Sukuma Law and Custom*, Oxford University Press.
CORY, H. & HARTNOLL, M. M. 1945, *Customary Law of the Haya*, International Afr. Institute, London.
COTRAN, E. 1963, *Report on Criminal Offences in Kenya*, Govt. Printer, Nairobi.
1965, 'Integration of Courts and Application of Customary Law in Tanganyika', *E. African Law Journal*, 1, 2.
HAYDON, E. S. 1964, *Law and Justice in Buganda*, Butterworth.
MORRIS, H. F. 1965, 'Changes in the Structure and Jurisdiction of the Courts and in the Criminal Law they Administer', *Journal of African Law*, 9.
TANNER, R. E. S. 1966, 'The Codification of Customary Law in Tanzania', *E. African Law Journal*.
TWINING, W. 1963, *Place of Customary Law in the National Legal Systems of East Africa*, University of Chicago Law School.
UGANDA GOVERNMENT 1965, *Report on Marriage, Divorce and the Status of Women in Uganda*, Govt. Printer, Entebbe.

EDUCATION AND NATIONAL IDENTITY

J. W. Tyler

Introduction

SCHOOLING helps to equip the individual with a body of knowledge and a number and variety of skills. But neither the knowledge nor the skills may be considered in isolation. The school is also a powerful socializing agent. It changes individuals and it changes them in a number of ways. It may reinforce a set of attitudes and values characteristic of a particular society and, in addition, it may place emphasis on a more restricted set of values and attitudes relating to a specific segment of the society. In these ways schooling acts as a conserving force, and both the knowledge and the skills imparted are an essential aspect of the socializing process. At the same time the transmission of a body of knowledge and skills may be associated with new aspirations which ultimately result in a pressure towards social mobility effectively assisting in changing the structure of the society and the distribution of attitudes and values within it. For example, a skill which may be acquired through schooling is a capacity for critical thought and independent judgment which may act contrary to the conserving socialization theme of schooling. Powerful as the effects of schooling may be, however, the school has no exclusive prerogative as an agent of either conservation or change. The individual is rarely separated or isolated completely from the socializing effect of kinship groups or from the impact of the total society beyond the school. The school, therefore, is not the only socializing agent or the only educational force.

Before the introduction of western-type schools, societies in East Africa socialized and educated new generations without schools in the modern, western sense, although institutionalized forms of education in several East African societies bore many of the characteristics which would identify them as schools. However, without entering here into a discussion of what is or is not a school, it may be said that western-type schools introduced an entirely new socializing factor to the societies of East Africa. Prior to their introduction, socialization and education functioned primarily to sustain knowledge, skills, attitudes, values and aspirations within a more or less exclusively tribal context. It cannot be assumed that change did not take place in the process, but the emphasis was undoubtedly culturally and socially conservative, and specific for each tribal society, despite cultural similarities which extended over considerable areas, as among the inter-lacustrine societies, for example.

The factor introduced by western-type schooling was different in two ways. First, despite the variety of origins of the providers of schooling (the missionaries, who represented most of the countries of Western Europe), the knowledge, skills, attitudes, values, and aspirations which they were ready to transmit were similar throughout East Africa. Second, the emphasis of the process the missionaries were to initiate was on change, although, paradoxically perhaps, it was essentially one designed to conserve, quite rigidly, the values they wished to impart.

What were the effects of this new educational force? A number of questions may be asked. First, during the period of missionary enterprise and the following period of colonial rule, was the influence of western-type schooling such that the socialization element in the schooling aroused interests and sentiments which created a sense of identification with groupings other than tribal ones, and if so of what kind? Second, what common interests and sentiments emerged in response to the uniform content of East African schooling? Third, what part, if any, did schooling play in the rise of nationalism after the Second World War which resulted in the emergence of three independent African States?[1] And fourth, given the fact that by the time independence was achieved an *East African* tradition of formal education had emerged and three separate educational systems had been established, to what extent has schooling been instrumental in assisting the creation of national identity during the period of transition immediately following the emergence of the three independent states?

The introduction of western-type schooling in East Africa

The period of missionary free enterprise in East Africa was a long one. From the time when Krapf started the first small school at Rabai Mpya in 1848 to the time that territorial colonial governments accepted a fully active role in education, upwards of sixty years elapsed. Kenya established an Education Department in 1911, Tanganyika in 1922, and Uganda in 1924. And it was not until 1925 that the British Government, through the Advisory Committee for Education in British Tropical Africa formed in 1923, produced the first statement of educational policy for its African dependencies.

Meanwhile, missionary enterprise was accompanied by competition between the numerous mission societies, each seeking to expand its influence and mark out a territory in which to carry out, as exclusively as possible, its works of religious conversion. Aiming to transmit their beliefs and to build a religious community, the missionaries demanded allegiance to God and, emphatically, allegiance to the particular church or denomination they represented. The school became the most important agent for achieving these aims. Each mission station had its 'Central' school. But marking out a territory was achieved through the 'Bush' schools spreading outwards from the mission stations. The number and distribution of these schools, and the number of recruits to them, of all ages, were the chief criteria of success.

The earliest schools were not accepted at once. Krapf, for example, describes how pupils at Rabai Mpya refused to attend, 'fancying that we ought to pay them for coming to school' (Krapf, 1860, p. 187). Chiefs and elders quickly perceived the disruptive potentialities of the missionaries' schools upon tribal culture in general and upon the pattern of authority in particular. But this early unpopularity may be attributed also to the fact that the missionaries' teachings were not at first perceived to be relevant to the aspirations of the individual within the tribal society in which he was already partly or completely socialized.

Indeed, the impact of the missionary invasion of East Africa was only partially the impact of the *content* of missionary teachings. The social organization of the mission societies made available a new set of statuses which were essentially statuses of achievement. Once it was recognized that schooling provided avenues to the achievement of such statuses within the mission organization (statuses, moreover, which might confer a degree of power and prestige within tribal society), recruits to the schools became more plentiful.

The degree of acceptance of the missionaries, and in particular their schools, may be correlated also with the balance between statuses of achievement and statuses of ascription within the different tribal societies. A society in which many positions of authority and prestige were achievable, it is suggested, more readily accepted schooling. Highly ascriptive societies, on the other hand, more readily rejected it.

The Baganda system may be considered one pole of the achieved/ascribed continuum with regard to the balance of statuses carrying with them prestige and authority. The traditional political system contained a hierarchy of chiefships and other positions of influence and prestige. These were not ascribed on a hereditary basis but were all open to achievement. As Apter points out: 'The struggle between the two Christian factions' (Catholics and Protestants) 'was translated quickly from a doctrinal matter, which only confused the Baganda, into a struggle for power, which they well understood.' 'This', he suggests, 'accounts in part for the relative alacrity with which the Baganda accepted one or the other religious position. To remain aloof was to become powerless' (Apter, 1961, p. 74). But status achievement, which the Baganda well understood, was possible also through schooling and within the mission system. Such achievement was readily transferable to the political system and reinforced the possibility of success in competition for office. Schooling, therefore, 'became one important point of entry into positions of power and prestige' (Apter, 1961, p. 129). So readily, in fact, was a mission education adaptable to the needs of the Ganda social and political system that allegiance to one or other of the missions became part of the social and political scene, and was soon so truly 'Ganda' that, as Low suggests, 'it was the pagans' (and therefore the unschooled) 'not the Christians who were "detribalized"' (Low, quoted by Apter, 1961, p. 131).

In contrast with the Baganda, the Masai social system, for example, was strongly ascriptive. Even where missionary contact was permitted its influence was slight. Masai were able to translate little of what the missionaries had to offer into the values of their society. The achievement opportunities offered by schooling could only be accepted by contracting out of the Masai society. Few Masai were prepared to do this, or needed to. The opportunities offered by the missions were attractive, possibly, to social misfits, but on the whole the Masai system did not produce them. Inheritance, for example, was equable, and each man had a status in the age-set system.

Throughout East Africa, then, the impact of missionaries and their schools was approximately proportional to the balance between ascription and achievement with respect to the social positions conferring influence and prestige. In societies less ascriptive than the Masai, and less achieving than the Baganda, the impact of the schools was related to the extent to which the individual saw the opportunities offered as reinforcing the achievement dimensions of status or conflicting with ascriptive dimensions.

The mission organization presented a number of new social positions essentially achievable and not ascriptive; and it should not be overlooked that becoming a pupil in school was itself a new achievable status and the first step towards an achieving society. At first that achieving society was only the mission organization itself. If the rewards of schooling could not be translated into the values of tribal society and transferred to the patterns of statuses within that society the opportunities were either rejected or accepted by breaking with tribal society. But the majority of East African societies fell in varying degrees between the two extremes exemplified by the Baganda and the Masai. In many pastoral societies, and some sedentary ones, the likelihood of a break was high, and thus the deterrent to acceptance of schooling was correspondingly great; but in many sedentary societies with an orientation to statuses of achievement the break was less marked and afforded the opportunity for integration of the characteristics of both tribal and mission society. Thus, in the majority of East African societies the degree of opportunity or deterrent varied according to the pattern of ascription and achievement statuses.

But if the highly ascriptive Masai system met the needs of its members so well that there was little incentive to accept the new opportunities offered by the missions and schooling, the same was not true of all societies with a more or less rigid ascription status system. In societies in which younger sons were unlikely to benefit in the inheritance of property, for example, or where members of junior lines were debarred from obtaining office as chief, ritual expert, or lineage head, the opportunities provided by the missions and schooling offered the chance to *some* people to break out of an ascriptive system and move into the achieving mission one.[2]

Thus the chief impact of the missionary invasion of East Africa upon the social organization of tribal society was the widespread introduction of a new pattern of essentially achievable statuses of which, as we have already noted, becoming a pupil in school was for some people, but by no means all, the first opportunity they had had to break with ascriptive status systems. Others found that there was little to be gained from breaking with the indigenous status system; while a third group, possibly the largest, found that schooling increased their chances of success within existing achievement status systems.

Despite the uniformity of knowledge, skills, attitudes, and values which the missionaries aimed to impart, chiefly through their schools, throughout East Africa, new social groupings which emerged functioned primarily in a tribal context. They did not significantly cut across tribal boundaries to unite peoples intertribally. Divisions appeared in tribal society between the converted and the unconverted, the schooled and the unschooled. Where more than one mission society established itself in a single tribal area, divisions also appeared between denominations, notably between Catholics and Protestants, and, functionally less important, between the various sects of the Protestant church. In Buganda, the divisive effects of denominational affiliation were rapidly reflected in the political organization of the Buganda state, became an integral part of Ganda social and political life, and later played an important part in party politics before and after independence, having become a factor in the political life of the whole of Uganda.

But, even in Buganda, whether a man was a Catholic, Protestant, or Muslim, he remained a Muganda. And the same was true of other tribal areas. The effects of missionary influence and schools brought about re-groupings within tribal society but provided no mechanisms for creating an identity in other than a tribal context.

With the establishment of territorial colonial government in East Africa, a new factor was introduced which significantly affected the role of schooling even before the governments accepted formal responsibility for education or developed an educational policy. The very presence of colonial administrations extended at once the range of achievable statuses beyond those already available within the missions' organizations and within tribal social systems where achievement in the schools could be translated into tribal values. This extension was both actual and potential: actual as a result of the need of the administrations for personnel with the style of achievement only mission schools could provide; and potential in that the individual's horizons were broadened by recognition of many new types of statuses which, although not within immediate reach, clearly revealed the way in which the offerings which were provided through the mission schools might ultimately enable the individual to acquire prestige, power, and material wealth comparable with the personnel of the colonial administrations.

The policy of indirect rule, however, channelled these aspirations primarily into the tribal social systems. The governments required chiefs and subordinate personnel through whom they could communicate and execute colonial policy. Schooling provided the type of individual best suited to the administrations' needs.

The mission societies early embarked on an élitist form of schooling by setting up in some areas, particularly in Uganda, special schools primarily for the sons of chiefs. Their aim in opening these schools was not, perhaps, coincident with the aims of the administrations—schooling for the families of chiefs might result in their subjects being encouraged to attend the mission schools and thus swell the number of converts—but they provided the type of education the colonial administrations sought. If, however, there were individuals anxious to acquire the knowledge and skills the administration wanted, they did so not because of any desire to carry out colonial policy. Primarily they aimed either to acquire new achievement statuses and the rewards they carried, or to enhance their chances of success in competition for existing ones. Ambivalence of attitude was, perhaps, inevitable. A degree of identification with the power-holders from whom new influence and prestige stemmed by delegation undoubtedly arose. But the policy of indirect rule and the division of authority into 'Native' and 'Colonial' effectively ensured that ultimate identity remained with the tribe and not with the administration.

Schooling and policy in the colonial period

During the early years of territorial colonial government in East Africa the British administration took little active part in schooling and had no defined educational policy. Direct involvement with education was confined to ad hoc grants to the mission societies and to the opening of a small number of Government training establishments designed to supply the semi-skilled labour needed to support technical and other services. The identification of a general education with christian education and moral training was as much a part of the values of colonial administrations as it was of the missionaries. The provision of schooling, therefore, was clearly seen to be an appropriate activity for missionaries.

In 1923, however, the British Government, in 'fuller recognition of the principle that the Controlling Power is responsible as trustee for the moral advancement of the native population', set up an Advisory Committee for education 'with the object of creating a well-defined educational policy' (A.C.E.T.A., 1925, p. 3). The policy outline by the A.C.E.T.A.[3] was accepted by Parliament in 1925, and it became the basis of educational thinking throughout the colonial period.

The second Phelps-Stokes report of the same year was highly critical of the results of missionary enterprise in education in

East Africa. In particular, the overstretching of the missions' resources in spreading schools at the expense of quality of instruction, inadequate supervision, and the absence of any properly graded system, received unfavourable comment. Of the children in school in Uganda, for example, the Commission observed that, 'The most that can be said for a majority of them is that they are under some kind of moral influence and ready to receive instruction when it can be given' (Jones, 1925, p. 152).

It is evident from the A.C.E.T.A. memorandum that note had been taken of the Phelps-Stokes criticisms.[4] Nevertheless, the Committee affirmed its support for the mission societies and welcomed the continuation of voluntary, i.e. missionary educational effort.

In considering the policy outlined by the A.C.E.T.A., what kind of societies, we may ask, did British colonial policy aim to create, and what were the functions of schooling seen to be? Was education viewed in relation to social integration as a powerful force which might be employed to diminish tribal loyalties and shift allegiance to larger social units related to the territories of Kenya, Tanganyika, Uganda, or East Africa; or was schooling seen primarily as a personal education, changing attitudes and values, from which might emerge in the due course of time, in some manner not defined, a society on the British model?

The principles and aims set down by the A.C.E.T.A. emphasized a general, personal education to be pursued in the spirit of moral development and social welfare. Education, the Committee observed, should be adapted to the mentality, aptitudes, occupations, and traditions of the various peoples; what was sound in the indigenous tradition should be conserved. True ideals of citizenship and service should be inculcated; capable and trustworthy, public-spirited leaders of the people, belonging to their own race should be raised up. Any socially integrative role that education might exert through schooling the Committee saw only in the tribal context. Schooling should be tribe-centred, and should strengthen the feeling of responsibility to the tribal community. Moreover, education thus defined, the Committee thought, would narrow the hiatus between the educated class and the rest of the community.

But it was recognized also that education must necessarily tend to weaken tribal authority and the sanctions of existing beliefs. The greatest importance therefore should be attached to religious teaching and moral instruction. The recipe was one of muscular christianity: character training through the discipline of work, field games, and social recreations; the formation of habits of industry, of truthfulness, of manliness, of readiness for social service, and of disciplined co-operation (A.C.E.T.A., 1925, pp. 4–5).

The need for a religious basis to education, linked with the support given to the continuation of voluntary effort in the provision of schooling, ensured that the mission societies, who already held a monopoly, would continue to do so. Government control of education was, in effect, to be confined to the provision of grants-in-aid and overall supervision of the voluntary effort, except in the sphere of broadly technical education, which was to be undertaken by government in conjunction with the appropriate government departments.

With the establishment of government departments wholly concerned with education, and with the guide-lines provided by the A.C.E.T.A., education in East Africa entered a new phase. The period of free enterprise and competition between the mission societies was succeeded by a period of private enterprise and competition with the support, assistance, and protection of the state.[5] In practice, government control of education did not encroach on the freedom of each society to own and manage schools, and to open new schools when and where they were able, with or without government financial aid.

The overall colonial policy of indirect rule designed to preserve tribal identities was not only reflected in the educational principles and aims pursued in East Africa but also in the pattern of administration of the educational system. Government control of education was itself an extension of the indirect rule principle, preserving the separate identities of each of the voluntary educational agencies operating in the name of the various churches.

As the educational system expanded and the numbers of schools increased, so the administrative needs of the churches' voluntary educational agencies expanded also. Education

Secretariats with a growing cadre of administrative and professional personnel became firmly established, grant-aided by Government in keeping the voluntary principle. Governments were no longer grant-aiding schools but grant-aiding several parallel educational services which owned and managed the schools. The position of the agencies became entrenched and strengthened. Competition between the agencies continued unabated, the emphasis changing from competition for territorial expansion, although this continued, to competition for grants-in-aid. Schools built in close proximity to each other, owned and managed by rival churches like rival chain-stores in a London suburb, the particular denomination often identifiable by its architecture, became a familiar part of the rural landscape.

The combined effects of the overall policy of indirect rules and an educational policy of indirect rule served to insulate schooling and the schooled from full participation in a state-wide system of which both teachers and the taught might feel a part, and through which the germs of identity with a territorial state might have emerged. Teachers were the employees of the voluntary agencies, not of the state or local authority; their aspirations and interests could find an outlet only in the tribe or in the church.

African education was further isolated by the policy of ethnic segregation of schooling. The knowledge that African schooling was essentially on the British model inevitably gave rise to feelings of uncertainty about its authenticity. In the absence of any direct knowledge of European schooling the suspicion grew that African education was an inferior article, and was intended to be so. With the eventual development of full secondary schooling leading to the Cambridge Overseas School Certificate this uncertainty remained. Anxiety arose from the fear that the teachers, who were almost exclusively Europeans, might be withholding knowledge essential to the acquisition of a high-grade certificate, or might be 'wasting time' on matters not relevant to the syllabus. The textbook came to be valued as, possibly, a greater source of security than the teacher.

But if such fears were never completely allayed, pupils were not loath to study subjects having little or no relevance to local conditions if this brought parity with the British model closer. The model of what might be ultimately achieved through the academic style of schooling, which the majority of the power-holders has evidently received, was ever visible. An academic style of education, therefore, far from being rejected as possibly of little relevance to local conditions, remained much sought after. Attempts throughout the colonial period to relate schooling to an agricultural way of life were thus notably unsuccessful and rejected as a symbol of further attempts at isolation.

But to what uses could parity through schooling be put once it was achieved? In the state system ethnic segregation existed in the majority of occupational statuses confining the schooled to subordinate and supporting roles. Statuses carrying power and prestige in the state system were the preserve of Europeans recruited and replaced from overseas. Aspirations of achievement acquired through schooling could, for the most part, find outlets only within local and tribal political structures, or within the organization of the churches. And within the voluntary agency educational system was the one achievable status, the status of teacher, which could absorb an ever-increasing number of recruits. Schooled and trained within a denominational religious system, the teacher was fed back into the voluntary agency system as an employee of the church.

Colonial educational policy supporting the policy of indirect rule was not designed therefore to change the structure of the colonial social system, but to maintain it. The very provision of formal schooling and its steady expansion made ultimate change in the social system inevitable. But planning to accommodate the pressure which would mount from the products of schooling was largely avoided. 'Africanization' of the public service, which meant in effect admission of Africans to statuses of real power in the state system, was delayed until the countries were on the very threshold of independence. Primarily, schooling was seen as a 'civilizing' influence; secondarily, it was to provide a limited number of persons with specific skills to be slotted into the colonial system in subordinate roles to maintain the status quo. The civilizing effects of schooling would somehow bring their own rewards without the need to prepare a social system to receive changing attitudes and values; only the available skills need be absorbed, and of these the skill of high academic achievement was to become an embarrassment.

The A.C.E.T.A. in 1925 saw the inevitability of the eventual growth of higher education up to and including university level, but even as the idea took root, became a possibility, and matured into a certainty, the impact of higher education on the shape of East African society as a whole was left largely to chance.

Secondary schooling, as understood in Britain, was slow to be developed in East Africa; and full secondary schooling leading to a qualification having more than local significance, even more slowly. It was not until 1935 that Makerere College presented the first six candidates for the Cambridge Overseas School Certificate examination. Five of the six were successful. Neither Kenya nor Tanganyika possessed schools offering School Certificate courses at this time, although courses of a secondary character stopping short of the School Certificate were available in four schools in Kenya, five in Tanganyika, and five in Uganda. Of these, only Tabora in Tanganyika was a Government school.

The voluntary agencies were, of course, concerned primarily with evangelization for which the schools were essential. Consequently their educational efforts continued to be devoted to reaching the greatest numbers through the primary school. With the exception of the handful of schools offering the lower levels of secondary schooling, they applied their resources in post-primary education to teacher training and seminary work, both of which directly assisted evangelization.

Apart from support of the agencies' educational efforts through an indirect rule policy, governments' educational interests were, as we have seen, highly pragmatic. Yet, Makerere College, the first school to offer a course leading to the School Certificate was a government establishment concerned primarily with vocational training. In 1938, as a result of the De La Warr Commission Report on higher education, it became partially independent and received a university-type constitution.

The impetus given to higher education by the Report also resulted in the upgrading of several of the voluntary agency secondary schools to the School Certificate level. Thus, with the exception of Tabora and Makerere College schools, the latter now separated from the higher-education functions of the College, full secondary schooling also came within the scope of the voluntary agency system.

Both the development of Makerere as the higher-education college of East Africa and the further advancement of full secondary education were delayed by the War. But even after the War the aspirations of the consumers were not met by a rapid development of full secondary education to the School Certificate level. Reflecting the colonial attitude to secondary and higher education, the Worthington Development Plan for Uganda in 1946 put forward the view that 'Academic secondary education cannot stand still, but its aim in the immediate future should be to provide no more than an adequate supply of comparatively highly educated men and women for Makerere, for teaching, and for Government service and commerce' (Worthington, 1946, p. 50). Post-primary education, it would seem, would continue to be geared to maintaining the colonial system.

The development of full secondary education, and, more important, the introduction of a qualification, the C.O.S.C., having more than local value and carrying equal weight with its counterpart for schools in Britain was possibly the most important step towards setting the East African territories on the road to self-determination. Obtaining the C.O.S.C. had the important consequence of enabling the holder to postpone dependence on the existing structure of the colonial system for occupational status on the completion of schooling. Hitherto the majority of the products of the education system could occupy only statuses within the tribal, mission, or government structures carrying comparatively low prestige in the total system. Postponement of this dependence had two vital consequences. First, progress to higher education in the newly constituted Makerere College was possible. Second, and of far-reaching significance, entry to universities overseas, particularly in Britain, became more readily possible. At first departure for higher education overseas, delayed by the War, was only a trickle, although it was to be a highly influential trickle. The acquisition of higher educational qualifications, in particular British university degrees, meant that for the first time a substantial number of Africans emerged who could claim educational parity with the best of the power-holders. Many of the power-holders, however, attempted to explain away such qualifications as providing merely a veneer, thereby underestimating the strength of the very values which colonial educational policy was designed to impart, and consequently blinding themselves to the forces being mobilized. But such attitudes only sharpened the determination of the growing élite to meet their colonial masters on equal terms. Apart from the gaining of parity through qualifications obtained overseas, their resolve was strengthened by experience of ethnically non-segregated academic life in Britain and through the many contacts made in Britain with influential people lacking sympathy with colonial social systems.

The nascent political movements which emerged in all three East African territories after the war were not formed by the direct efforts of the new, highly educated élite. But the availability of such an élite quickly transformed them into political parties with both purpose and direction. The purpose was to achieve self-determination; the direction, a growing nationalism. The mainspring of the movements was the very nature of the colonial system itself. Indirect rule reinforced tribalism; and ethnic segregation in both schooling and occupational selection after schooling denied equality of status within the total system. Higher education emphasized these characteristics, providing at the same time the personnel to match the power-holders with the type and quality of expertise needed to mobilize the forces which could change the system.

Few if any East Africans living today were born into societies without western-type schools. Schooling has yet to become universal, compulsory, or entirely free. Nevertheless, it has been a part of the expectations and aspirations of several generations of boys and an increasing number of girls. And to East Africans who have not been to school, what may be achieved through schooling, and the relative rewards for their children or grandchildren obtainable from successive levels of schooling, is clear. Schooling therefore is very much a part of the contemporary social system and the culture into which all

East Africans are born. From this standpoint the western origin of schooling is of little importance to the consumer today. Each of the new states has its own educational system which, in theory, it is free to develop in accordance with its interpretation of the country's needs. However, the colonial context in which the three educational systems developed had far-reaching consequences for the type of education tradition with which the peoples of each new state entered the post-independence period. Both providers and consumers possessed a knowledge of the major facts of the history of educational development, acquired as part of their education, which structured attitudes about the way in which their educational needs should be met. Few people in Britain today possess a comparable knowledge of the development of their own education system. The educational values thus acquired during the colonial period provided a condition of cultural inertia which resulted in considerable ambivalence about educational provision. On the one hand there was continuity between the educational values of the pre- and post-independence periods, and on the other a discontinuity in that the former consumers were, for the first time, the providers. The purposes that the present providers consider that schooling should serve are not necessarily the same as the purposes which the previous providers perceived them to be.

The chief characteristic of the East African education tradition inherited from the colonial period may be summarized thus:

1. A personal education based on religious principles and religious teaching provided predominantly in schools owned and managed by religious, voluntary agencies and staffed almost exclusively by teachers trained locally in colleges also owned and managed by the voluntary agencies, or recruited overseas on their behalf.
2. An almost complete segregation of pupils along denominational lines, progress through the system from primary to secondary being dependent to a marked degree on the availability of schools and places in them of the same denomination.
3. Ethnic separation of schooling with the schools for each

ethnic group financed and controlled as separate educational systems.

4. A predominantly academic tradition. Despite efforts by governments and churches alike to relate schooling to practical skills and to the economic development of the three countries, particularly through agriculture, the demand for an academic style of schooling strengthened rather than weakened over the years. Promotion from one level to the next was uncertain, but the academic route provided the only continuous route marked by symbols of achievement, particularly the C.O.S.C., offering ultimate parity with the model provided by power-holders in the colonial governments. Colonial education emphasized moral education, character-building, and practical skills as desirable ends in themselves. The consumers, however, sought power, prestige, and parity which only the academic route could provide.

5. Schooling was a scarce commodity, particularly at the secondary and tertiary levels. Although an established part of East African social and cultural expectations it was not, therefore, an expectation that could always be fulfilled in practice. An absence or shortage of schools and the need to raise school fees acted as controlling factors in relation to expectations. And almost everywhere the need for fees and the status of women operated selectively in favour of schooling for boys.

These characteristics of the education tradition provided the materials from which post-independence educational policies were to be shaped.

Education in transition

Colonial education policy and the speed with which the nationalist movements achieved their aims of self-determination resulted in the emergence of Tanganyika, Uganda, and Kenya as countries with education systems ill-adapted to the task of supporting viable states without continuing outside assistance, or of building nations. None of the three possessed a fully integrated state-wide education system. Each inherited a number of sub-systems catering separately for each ethnic group. In Tanganyika and Uganda, however, steps towards ethnic integration of schooling were taken before independence was actually achieved. Within the African sub-system, in particular, religious interests, operating through the ownership and management of schools by the voluntary agencies, divided the system further. Such was the dominance of the voluntary agency system that local authorities providing nondenominational schools found themselves also in the position of voluntary agencies, competing with the church voluntary agencies for grants and teachers, the latter trained for the most part in denominational colleges.

The dominant position of the voluntary agencies was also associated with a complex education administration resulting in considerable overlapping of services, both administrative and professional, provided on the one hand by the agencies and on the other by central and local governments. Teachers in the schools, employees of the voluntary agencies, were thus beset by two sets of authorities. Moreover, the overlapping of services ensured that scarce, trained personnel were not utilized to the maximum advantage of the educational system.

After independence there was the suspicion that the power of churches, particularly in education, was a perpetuation of colonial influence through ties with churches in the western world.

Indirect rule of general education through the voluntary agencies had encouraged the development of primary education at the expense of full secondary and higher education, with the result that the secondary and tertiary levels were unable to produce sufficient middle- and high-level manpower to replace expatriates in governmental, para-governmental, and commercial sectors of the economy, and, at the same time, meet the urgent needs for expansion.

In no sense, then, could the education systems of East Africa at independence be said to possess the characteristics of state systems or to be national in their orientation.

Recognition of the inadequacies of the colonial educational legacy and the need for urgent reform may be judged by the speed with which each new state took stock of its educational resources and prepared to plan for the future.

In 1961, shortly before independence, during the period of internal self-government, Tanganyika invited U.N.E.S.C.O. to provide a mission 'to plan the further development of the educational system'. The Mission, led by Professor L. J. Lewis, carried out its work between June and October 1962 and reported in January 1963. Uganda and Kenya appointed their own commissions. The Uganda Commission, under the chairmanship of Professor E. B. Castle, began work in January 1963, only three months after independence and almost exactly ten years after Uganda's last major report on African education prepared by the De Bunsen Committee in 1952/53. In December 1963, some six months after independence, Professor Simeon Ominde was invited to become chairman of the Kenya Education Commission. The Commission began work the following February and produced the first part of its report in October 1964.

In Tanganyika preparatory planning had been extensive. A draft Five-Year Plan for African Education covering the years 1957–61 prepared by the Trusteeship Government marked the end of the colonial period. In 1959 an International Bank Mission visited Tanganyika and prepared a report on the economic development of the country, education receiving particular attention; and finally, a three-year development plan based largely on the World Bank report was prepared for the first three years of independence, education again receiving special attention.

The U.N.E.S.C.O. Planning Mission was requested to prepare its report 'with regard to the educational developments contained in the three-year development plan and the goals set by the Conference of African States on the Development of Education in Africa at Addis Ababa in May 1961'.

In 1961 Uganda, like Tanganyika two years earlier, received an International Bank Mission, and it was in the light of its educational recommendations that the Castle Commission was invited to examine the educational system.

The Kenya Commission had few studies to guide it, no major report on African education having been made since the Beecher Committee recommendations of 1949.

A comparison of the terms of reference of the U.N.E.S.C.O. Planning Mission to Tanganyika and the two Commissions for Uganda and Kenya is of considerable interest.[6] All three, directly or indirectly, indicated that the content of education should be examined and revised. All three suggested that the content and structure of education should be adapted to the needs of their respective countries. These needs, however, were expressed chiefly in relation to manpower and economic development: except for the Kenya Commission. The Kenya Commission was provided with terms of reference directing attention specifically to the relationship between education and national unity: educational policies should 'appropriately express the aspirations and cultural values of an independent African country', and should 'contribute to the unity of Kenya' (Ominde, 1964, p. 2).

In its report the U.N.E.S.C.O. Mission to Tanganyika concentrated largely on the overall efficiency of the education system with special reference to planning procedure and development policy. Secondary schooling was given a high priority. Educational policy in relation to national unity was barely mentioned.

The Castle Commission Report, on the other hand, laid considerable emphasis on the quality of education and on the maintenance of moral and religious values, which it saw to be threatened. In support of this latter view it argued in favour of the retention of the voluntary agency system, a proposal later to be rejected by the Government. Parts of the Report, indeed, are reminiscent of the A.C.E.T.A. memorandum of nearly forty years earlier.

In Kenya ethnic division, education provision, and manpower development were all closely related to the problem of national unity. The level of schooling most decisively linked with the development of high-level manpower in all three countries—the secondary level—was dominated in Kenya by schools hitherto for Europeans or Asians only. No such problem faced Uganda. Uganda had never developed secondary schools for Europeans. The Asian secondary schools, in response to the colonial government's belated policy of ethnic integration in schooling had a substantial and growing intake of African pupils by the time independence was achieved, and in addition a single multi-racial secondary school had been opened in Kampala. Tanganyika had only one secondary school for

Europeans. In both Uganda and Tanganyika, most Europeans had always obtained secondary schooling for their children in either Kenya or Britain.

The problem in Kenya, however, was complicated by the presence of a number of European boarding schools with comparatively high standards and correspondingly high fees. Even after legislation in independent Kenya against ethnic exclusiveness in schooling, access to these schools by Africans tended to be limited to a small, wealthy élite, largely because of these high fees.

If the Kenya Commission's terms of reference, emphasizing the utilization of the educational system for the fostering of national unity, arose from considerations of ethnic separation in the country, the Commission interpreted its brief more widely. The Report identified three major 'divisive influences' in education—'tribe, race and religion'. Detailed proposals were set out for the revision of both the content of schooling and the structure of the system to minimize their effects. The aim was to build an integrated system 'as an instrument of the secular state' and to create strong national interests and sentiments in which ethnic, religious, and tribal identity would not be destroyed but submerged. Much of the first section of the Ominde Report was devoted to this analysis. In addition, the section concerned with secondary schooling dealt almost exclusively with the problem of integrating the European boarding schools into a state system with truly national functions.

The attention given to national unity in Part I of the Ominde Report is striking when compared with the U.N.E.S.C.O. Mission Report on Tanganyika and the Castle Commission Report on Uganda. In this respect it is perhaps of no little significance (although other factors were also relevant) that the Kenya Commission was the only one of the three to be led by an East African. The Ominde Report reflects not only the specific problems of Kenya after independence, but also a vivid awareness of the potential dangers of disunity arising from ethnic, tribal, and religious factors common in varying degrees to all the East African countries; and it emphasizes the role that education could play in overcoming the divisiveness inherited from the colonial period.

The educational policies adopted by all three states in the

immediate post-independence years were not directed towards calculated efforts to induce through the schools loyalty to the state or specific sentiments of nationhood to reinforce the wave of nationalism which speeded the achievement of independence. In 1964 President Nyerere summed up retrospectively that spirit of nationalism when he said: 'Our people wanted independence for two reasons; to establish their human dignity and self-respect; and to get an opportunity to create their own future'.[7] Though he was speaking to mainland Tanzanians, his words, nevertheless, were applicable beyond the boundaries of that country. The momentum of nationalism thus defined may have been sufficient to provide national unity in the immediate post-independence years, and to inhibit the divisive forces inherited from the colonial period. Educational policies were not framed with indoctrination through the schools in support of the state as a goal. Professor Ominde's detailed recommendations for national unity in Kenya through the education system were not of this character.

First and foremost, educational policies were framed to meet the urgent, practical needs for an increase in the production of middle- and high-level manpower so that the new states could, indeed, 'create their own future' and pave the way for economic development. The nature of the colonial legacy together with post-independence pressures, both internal and external, ensured that efforts to this end were concentrated on secondary schooling, higher education, and teacher-training. External pressures operated through international agencies, such as the World Bank and educational assistance schemes. The latter were provided by several countries, but notably by Britain and the United States. Sponsors of aid schemes wished to be assured that investment in education would make a real contribution to economic advancement and state viability. External pressures, therefore, reinforced the concentration of educational effort by the new states on the production of trained manpower. And, though the possible role of education in stimulating national unity as distinct from state viability was not neglected, inevitably it received less attention.

One of the major goals set by the Conference of African States on the Development of Education in Africa, held in Addis Ababa in 1961, had been universal primary education by 1980. All three East African states have regularly re-affirmed their support for this ultimate aim, but in practice the expansion of primary education has received a low priority compared with the secondary and tertiary levels. However, the fiascos enacted in some newly independent states where universal primary education has been attempted have been avoided. No doubt all three East African governments took careful note of these experiments.

Emphasis on manpower development, however, has not prevented attention being given to changing the structure of the educational systems in the direction of unified state systems, principally by attempting to eradicate the division of schooling along ethnic lines and to reduce the power of the churches in the administration and control of schooling. As we have seen already, the history of schooling in East Africa resulted in the power of the churches being strongest at the primary level, including teacher-training. Neither Tanzania, Uganda, nor Kenya has attempted to separate religious education from secular education (on the American model for example). Their aim has been to separate religious teaching in schools from the administrative control of schools by church educational agencies, a distinction not always appreciated either by the churches or the educational consumers who, as part of their educational tradition, have come to associate schooling and the provision of schooling with the religious bodies.

In Uganda, for example, the government in 1965 removed grants-in-aid from the voluntary agencies' administrative organizations and closed the secretariats. Apart from complications arising from the legal position of the agencies as owners of the schools, often with rights in the land on which the schools were built—complications which have yet to be fully resolved—the transfer of administration and control of the primary schools from the voluntary agencies wholly to local authorities resulted in protests from parents that the government was taking away their schools. In some areas, particularly where Catholic schools predominated, parents picketed the schools to prevent access by government education officers. Cases also occurred of strong protests by parents when teachers of one denomination were directed to teach in schools nominally of another denomination.

By no means of least importance, attention has been given to the content of education, particularly in the primary schools, where syllabuses are not tied to external examination requirements. The aim has been to provide a basic education genuinely East African in character. The design of syllabuses in History, Geography, Social Studies, and Civics began to develop towards the end of the colonial period and has greatly intensified since independence. However, the preparation of suitable textbooks and teaching materials and the training of teachers is a comparatively slow task and are not as spectacular as the opening of a number of new secondary schools. But it is at the primary level that education in East Africa is, perhaps, best able to take a truly national form. To receive full expression therefore, it must ultimately be linked with universal primary schooling.

The building of a unified state system of education may provide the essential framework within which may best operate any power that schooling has to develop national interests and sentiments. But it is easy to overestimate the contribution of formal schooling to the process of nation-building in new states. Other mechanisms may operate more powerfully than schooling to create such interests and sentiments, or, conversely, to mitigate against their formation. Identification with the charisma of a strong leader of the state, or development of a one-party political system, may act more positively and swiftly, though neither may ensure continuity. The strengthening of the state at the expense of local interests and loyalties may operate negatively. The recent dismantling of the political structure of the Buganda Kingdom in Uganda, for example, was designed to strengthen Uganda as a state. But it may yet prove to be a strong force in reaffirming *Kiganda* national identity, rather than in the encouragement of a Uganda national identity among Baganda through a rationalization of the education system.

The organization of the colonial education system emphasized tribal, religious, and ethnic affiliation and provided no strong basis from which a wider identity might grow through equality of opportunity and full participation in the total system. The development of unified state systems of education and the growth of national educational policies will not destroy group identities associated with religion, tribe, or ethnic group, but it can contribute to the formation of an identity based on the wider community through the possibility of full participation and equality of opportunity where previously, during the colonial period, such possibilities were circumscribed.

We have argued that the real breakthrough in education in East Africa came with the introduction of the Cambridge Overseas School Certificate and the possibility that it offered, for the first time, of achieving ultimate parity with the colonial power-holders. After the Second World War the products of the secondary and tertiary levels of the education systems were able to mobilize effectively a growing opposition to the colonial system in the conviction that they possessed the same knowledge and skills, if not the experience, upon which the legitimacy of the power-holders to govern was ultimately based. However, the three East African dependencies entered the self-determining phase of their history on a wave of nationalist sentiments and interests without any supporting social cohesion other than that derived from the power of the state. Moreover, the education systems they inherited were adapted to develop attitudes and values more conducive to the continuation of divisions in society along ethnic, tribal, and religious lines than to the creation of cohesive nations. Kenya, Uganda, and Tanganyika become independent, therefore, as new states, but not as nations.

On achieving independence the imperatives deriving from the colonial legacy, internal and external pressures, demanded that the education systems be utilized in the interests of rapid manpower and economic growth. To support these aims the creation of integrated state-wide systems of education, which would harness all available resources and employ them as efficiently as possible, was clearly desirable.

For reasons we have considered, an academic style of education was the most highly valued aspect of the colonial education system. For the purposes of manpower development the values of that style of education were not inappropriate and could best serve that purpose by putting the system into top-gear production.

Again, the colonial system which had placed emphasis on a personal education and not on social integration, and inadvertently provided the search for influence and prestige as the chief goals of schooling, was not an unsuitable vehicle for immediate post-independence aims.

But, with the stability of educational development at the secondary and tertiary levels in sight, and the emergence of systems adapted, if imperfectly as yet, to the needs of middle- and high-level manpower development, a new phase has begun to emerge which at present is most evident in Tanzania. The personal motive for high achievement through schooling may assist in providing the manpower requirements of new states. But in states which are dominantly agricultural (with many areas at a near-subsistence level), the continued development of high-level manpower has only served to increase the size of the privileged élite and, at the same time, to increase the distance between that élite and the rest of the population. Further educational provision has not, as the A.C.E.T.A. assumed more than forty years ago, decreased social distance. Moreover, as throughout the colonial period, it has failed to make any significant impact on the problem of increased agricultural productivity.

No doubt with these two problems very much in mind, the educational changes proposed by President Nyerere, in his statement of *Education for Self-Reliance* (1967), are aimed to halt the effects of having moved into top-gear production an educational process in which the values and goals are basically a colonial inheritance, and to attempt to harness schooling to national development rather than state development. The central aim is not a policy of indoctrination through schooling in loyalty to the state, although a National Ethic has been made explicit. It is to link the whole education system, at all levels, to activities seen to be essential to the development of the economy, primarily agricultural. The essential characteristics of President Nyerere's proposal is to provide a community basis for these activities in which everyone, including pupils at school and students at university, will participate. Such communities will depend upon self-help and be self-supporting. Community projects would be integrated with formal schooling, and performance in them would be a measure of educational success judged equally with formal examinations. The argument would seem to be that the social distance between the educated and the agricultural peasantry can be reduced by a sharing of common interests, chiefly agricultural, in the service of the local community. Direct involvement with the interests and activities of the local community would then encourage the development of a truly national identity, and, at the same time provide the foundations from which the need for agricultural expansion might be met.

The need for Tanzania, Uganda, and Kenya to become viable, politically and economically, resulted in an emphasis on the development of mechanisms to ensure the stability of the state. The movement towards one-party government and the utilization of the education system to produce high-level manpower growth may be seen primarily as serving to strengthen the state without necessarily providing a basis for the growth of national identity, which has yet to emerge strongly in East Africa.

The outcome of President Nyerere's plans for re-shaping the educational system in the interests of national unity will no doubt be followed closely by both Uganda and Kenya.

NOTES

1 Only mainland East Africa is discussed in this essay.
2 I am indebted to P. H. Gulliver for drawing my attention to some aspects of the impact of missionary education upon social misfits.
3 The full title of the Committee formed in 1923 was 'The Advisory Committee on Native Education in the British Tropical Dependencies', abbreviated here for convenience to A.C.E.T.A.
4 The A.C.E.T.A. memorandum and the second Phelps-Stokes Report appeared almost simultaneously. The secretary of the A.C.E.T.A., however, was also a member of the Commission.
5 Carter identifies three stages of educational development in East Africa: 'the period of private enterprise principally associated with the activities of the Christian Missions, the period of State-supported private enterprise, and the period of State responsibility and planning' (Carter, 1966, p. 11).
6 See U.N.E.S.C.O., 1963, pp. 4–5; Castle, 1963, p. i; Ominde, 1964, p. 2.
7 President Nyerere presenting the Five-Year Development Plan of 12 May 1964 (Annual Report of the Ministry of Education, United Republic of Tanzania, 1964).

REFERENCES

A.C.E.T.A. 1925, *Education in British Tropical Africa*, H.M.S.O., Cmd. 2374.
APTER, D. E. 1961, *The Political Kingdom in Uganda*, Princeton University Press.

CARTER, J. R. 1966, *The Legal Framework of Educational Planning and Adminis-tration in East Africa*, U.N.E.S.C.O., Paris.

DE LA WARR, EARL, 1937, *Higher Education in East Africa*, H.M.S.O., Col. 142.

JONES, T. J. 1925, *Education in East Africa* (the second 'Phelps-Stokes Report'), Edinburgh House, London.

KRAPF, J. L. 1860, *Travels, Researches and Missionary Labours Following 18 years Residence in Eastern Africa*, Trubner, London.

LOW, D. A. 1956, *Religion and Society in Buganda 1875–1900*, E.A. Institute of Social Research (E.A. Studies No. 8), Kampala.

NYERERE, J. K. 1967a, *Education for Self-Reliance*, Govt. Printer, Dar es Salaam.

1967b, *Socialism and Rural Development*, Govt. Printer, Dar es Salaam.

OMINDE, S. H. 1964, *Kenya Education Mission Report, Part I*, Govt. of Kenya, Nairobi.

1965, ditto, *Part II*.

U.N.E.S.C.O. 1961, *Final Report of the Conference of African States on the Development of Education in Africa*, Paris.

1963, *Report of the Educational Planning Mission for Tanganyika*, Paris.

WORTHINGTON, E. B. 1947, *A Development Plan for Uganda*, Govt. Printer, Entebbe.

Part Two

REGIONAL AND
CASE STUDIES

TRIBALISM AMONG THE GISU

An anthropological approach

J. S. La Fontaine

'TRIBALISM' is a word with a variety of referents, so that it is as well to start with a working definition of it before examining one particular manifestation. It has been used to characterize a clinging to traditional life as opposed to acceptance of modernity among peoples exposed to rapid cultural change. It has also been used to designate (and often deplore) nepotism in modern African states where the tie of common ethnic origins may be given precedence over other, more Western, allegiances. Again it has been used to describe the emotions of solidarity aroused by leaders who mobilize supporters by appealing to the common cultural values of their tribe. Political parties may be described as 'tribalist' when they recruit members on the basis of birth into a particular linguistic, cultural, or regional group. Underlying all these meanings is a common denominator—the solidarity derived from common membership in a tribe, as expressed in certain cherished values. The term 'tribe' has itself no clear referent; anthropologists use it in a number of different ways. As an adjective 'tribal' becomes an alternative to 'primitive' or 'preliterate' in denoting a type of society. More frequently, however, tribe is used to describe a social grouping. Depending on what value is taken as the definitive criteria, the term can be an inclusive one, designating a whole, more or less homogeneous cultural unit, such as the Ganda or the Kikuyu. Other anthropologists reserve 'tribe' for a group which is bounded by a single political structure; with this definition the Ganda are a tribe and the Kikuyu are a number of related tribes. Evans-Pritchard, who uses this term in its restricted sense when writing of the Nuer of the Sudan, uses 'congeries of tribes' to refer to the wider cultural unity of which the tribe is a section (Evans-Pritchard, 1940, p. 5). He states that the defining characteristic is that within the tribe the rule of law is recognized, whereas between tribes there is only war. Here we have a definition which incorporates the idea of a solidarity associated with membership of a group but identifies the group as a localized political community.

There are thus two types of meaning for 'tribe': one which refers to cultural homogeneity, usually symbolized by a single language, and another which denotes a group organized as a political unit. The first is closely associated with the idea of tribalism as a conservative force in a changing society. The second contains the more precise connotation of a structured group with the further implication that it is organized to protect common interests. This paper aims to show how common cultural values relate to the tribe as a political entity by acting as symbols which can be used to mobilize loyalty. I am thus concerned with the way in which two apparently different aspects of 'tribe', cultural and political, are related to one another.

I shall use the word 'tribe' in its wider rather than in its narrower sense. If we restrict the word 'tribe' to a group organized by a single political structure, in many instances the 'tribes' would be very small indeed. This is the case among the Gisu,[1] a Bantu-speaking people living on the south-western slopes of Mount Elgon, which straddles the Kenya/Uganda border. They numbered about a quarter of a million when I studied them in 1953–5, but traditionally there was no single political structure unifying them. Nevertheless, they were and are acutely aware of their 'tribal identity'; it is with this that I am concerned.

When, in 1953, I began an anthropological study of the Gisu, my first problem was to decide what the Gisu tribe was —its social limits and geographical boundaries. The line demarcating the Elgon Forest Reserve at a height of approximately 7,000 feet above sea-level provided a clear-cut boundary to the east, but other boundaries were not as clearly drawn.

To the north of the Gisu live the Sebei, speaking a language of the Nilo-Hamitic group. The Sebei also practise female circumcision which the Gisu do not. The border-line between the two societies defined in terms of language and culture is unambiguous, although the territorial boundary is blurred, because of the existence of a small mixed group of Bantu-speakers, who are intercalary between Gisu and Sebei at certain points. In addition Gisu migrants have been encroaching steadily into former Sebei territory. On the plains to the west live a number of smaller tribes, differing among themselves in language and cultural origin and distinct from the Gisu as far as border criteria are concerned. In addition, there is a tradition that a stretch of unsettled country formerly separated plainsmen from the hill-dwelling Gisu. There thus remained the boundary to the south-east, now the territorial boundary between Kenya and Uganda. The problem was to decide whether this boundary followed a traditional social distinction, or, as in other cases, formed an artificial division between sections of the same people.

The Vugusu who live on the Kenya side of the interterritorial boundary resemble the Gisu markedly in many features of their culture. The language they speak is similar to, and mutually intelligible with, the southern dialects of the Gisu language. In fact, there appears to be less difference between the southern dialects of Gisu and the Vugusu language than between southern and northern dialects of the Gisu language itself. Gisu sometimes refer to themselves and the Vugusu as one people, the people of Masaba—Masaba being their common name for Mount Elgon. This term, however, is not a reliable index of tribal identity, being used by different peoples with different referents: by the Gisu for themselves with or without the Vugusu, by the Vugusu for the Gisu, and by peoples of the southern part of the Nyanza region for the Vugusu. The term appears to have a directional meaning rather than existing as a tribal name. In social organization the Vugusu resemble the southern Gisu in many respects; and there were traditionally, and are today, many social and economic contacts between the two people. There was no clear territorial distinction comparable to the no-man's-land to the west, though it seems that the compact walled villages inhabited by the Vugusu during the nineteenth century were not found in Gisu territory. The evidence is thus conflicting: are the Gisu a separate tribe or are they part of a larger unit which includes both Gisu and Vugusu? If you ask a Gisu what makes him a Gisu, he will say: 'I have been initiated in our Gisu rituals'. Yet both the Vugusu and Sebei practise initiation including the rite of circumcision. Confronted with this problem, the hypothetical informant will say: 'Yes, but the Sebei are different; they also circumcise women, which is bararous? The distinction here is made in terms of differing cultural practices. Such a distinction cannot be made as far as the Vugusu are concerned. They do not circumcise women and their ceremonies appear to differ only slightly from those held in south Bugisu. But Gisu say that Vugusu are not Gisu because 'they have their ceremonies and we have ours'. On closer examination this remark is found to refer to the organization of the ceremonies, which are arranged independently for the two groups, although Vugusu circumcisors do work in Bugisu. Indeed, this seems to be the one clue to the limits of Gisu society—participation in a series of linked initiation ceremonies which form a sequence progressing through Gisu territory but excluding Vugusu. The timing of the ceremonies for a Gisu group is related to the progress of ceremonies in the group placed earlier in the cycle, which is not related directly to the timing of ceremonies in Vugusu. The ceremonial cycle of initiation ceremonies, held normally every two years, is thus a representation of a social unit and evokes a cultural entity, neither of which is embodied in a permanent unifying organization.

The traditional symbol of Gisu unity, such as it was, was an organization, but an organization for periodic ceremonial rather than political purposes. Politically, the Gisu consisted of a series of autonomous descent groups of which small segments were the political units. There was no overriding authority which might express or implement common policy. These groups differed from one another in dialect and details of ritual practices and often were mutually hostile. Before the introduction of Pax Britannica and the construction of roads, many Gisu had little or no contact with tribesmen in distant parts of the tribal area. Initiation ceremonies as a unifying symbol were occasional and situational, not a frame-work within which other spheres of action might be associated with this ceremonial entity. However, the cycle did define a physically bounded unit occupied by the groups participating in the ceremonies, and this was thereby identified as tribal territory. The boundaries were not fixed or immutable, since the population was expanding and moving northwards to encroach on Sebei territory, but border groups combined to prevent encroachment by others. The ceremonies then symbolized a set of people, speaking one language and sharing a common culture and territory—a tribe.

A further characteristic of the traditional tribal symbol was that it was exclusive as well as inclusive. Gisu were defined both by participation in the ceremonies and by the identification of non-participants, i.e. outsiders. It thus represented unity in opposition to non-Gisu who were outsiders by virtue of their exclusion from tribal ceremonies. Associated with this exclusion, and with the area contained by the ceremonial cycle, were cultural features which were adduced as further symbols of the division into Gisu and non-Gisu.

These cultural features, beliefs, and practices—what one may call secondary tribal symbols—were not different in kind from symbols marking the internal differentiation of the Gisu people. The different groupings and sub-groupings within the tribe were expected to, and did, possess as marks of their identity, variations of dialect and custom, particularly as regards ritual, which distinguished them from other similar groups. These differences were represented by a genealogy which charted the internal structure of the tribe as a series of related descendants from a common ancestor. Degrees of cultural and linguistic closeness, as well as geographical proximity were symbolized by closeness of putative genealogical links as far as the founding ancestors of the group were concerned. Intertribal relations might also be represented in this way. Thus, usually the ancestors of the Gisu and Vugusu peoples are represented as brothers, while the ancestors of the Sebei and another Nilo-Hamitic people known to the Gisu as Batwa[2] appear as their agnatic cousins. The form of the genealogy varies in different parts of the country according to local awareness of cultural similarities and divergences;[3] during the last century it has been extended to embrace other peoples, including Europeans, with whom the Gisu have come into contact. A constant feature of this genealogical charter is the attribution of a single ancestor to the people now known as Gisu. This ancestor is usually named as Masaba, the name given by the Gisu to Mount Elgon. This intertribal genealogy was never used as a charter for common action, as was the genealogy representing the structure of the Gisu tribe, who associate the institution of male circumcision with their founding ancestor. It may be considered rather as an extension of Gisu structural symbolism into the field of intertribal relations. The system of symbols rests on the association of language, culture (particularly ritual), and geographical location, with descent, in order to indicate separation or identity. We cannot then use any one of the four criteria as independent proofs of either but must see them as aspects of the underlying social entity, the Gisu tribe, which is mobilized only in the ceremonial cycle which is its most potent symbol.

This, then, was the traditional picture, which has been modified during the last half-century. The advent of British colonial administration in 1904–5 was preceded by a period of pacification undertaken by Ganda, acting as agents of the British. The events of the first decade of the twentieth century, which was never entirely free from outbursts of violence by the Gisu against their new overlords, heightened the tribal consciousness of the Gisu. Subsequently communications improved, and the establishment of central institutions, such as mission stations, and an administrative system which drew its personnel from all parts of Gisu territory, brought Gisu from different tribal sections into contact for the first time. In particular the mission schools were a potent force, making Gisu tribesmen out of lineage members as well as Christians out of pagans. The administrative organization provided an overall structure which eventually came to serve as a skeleton for a unit which became much more closely-knit than the loose association of autonomous units of tradition. The hierarchy of chiefships within the administration of the territory and later the hierarchy of councils established as part of the local government system, provided opportunities for leadership and power, both social and economic, that the traditional system never offered. Initially these offices were filled by Ganda; the British thus provided the Gisu with the stimulus of alien rulers, who not only appear to have despised those very cultural traits which symbolized tribal identity to the Gisu, but were prepared to proselytize their own way of life, which differed strikingly from traditional Gisu custom. An implicit comparison with the Ganda and a desire to achieve equal standing with them was an important strand in the development of Gisu tribalism.

The history of the Gisu for the first half of this century shows an increasing awareness of tribal identity and a struggle for one objective after another. I shall deal with the period up to the end of my field-work (1955). I shall not discuss in detail the different tribalistic movements or the way in which support for them was mobilized, but concentrate on the issues in order to focus on the nature of tribalism.

The first objective fought for and obtained was the replacement of Ganda chiefs by Gisu. Since by comparison with the Ganda, the Gisu appeared 'backward' and unruly to the British administration, it was not until 1934 that the last Ganda serving in the administration of Gisu territory retired, although the first Gisu chiefs were appointed in 1913. Gisu were first appointed to subordinate chiefships, senior posts being filled by Ganda. Even after 1934 Luganda remained the official language of the administration and schools. Ganda influence has thus been strong in this area and has been associated with the superior power and knowledge of the Europeans. The Ganda social system differed radically from any of those with whom Gisu had had any contact traditionally. None of the neighbouring tribes possessed the centralized and sophisticated political system which so impressed the first Europeans who came into contact with the Ganda. To the Gisu the cultural difference between themselves and the Ganda appeared as a distinction in power. Their first reaction appears to have been to adopt Ganda customs; the first chiefs assumed the white robe or *kanzu* worn by Ganda and the traditional Gisu house was gradually replaced by buildings closer to the Ganda style then current.

Reaction to Ganda rule showed first in 1925 with the founding of the Gisu Welfare Association, which aimed to protect Gisu traditions. In particular, the Association pressed for a recognition of traditional land law which, the founders felt, had been misunderstood by the administration. It is possible that Ganda interpretation of Gisu customary law had been responsible for the belief which was then current, that among the Gisu individual tenure of land did not exist. Gisu land was held to be the property of the clan, administered by a clan head or elders so that individual clan members had the status of privileged tenants. The misapprehension had resulted in the alienation, by Gisu claiming to be elders of the clan, of land owned by individuals who had abandoned it and fled to avoid tax payments or who had allowed it to lie fallow. Agitation on this point resulted finally in the appointment of a Commission to investigate traditional Gisu land tenure. The Commission was appointed in 1939, chaired by Mr C. Gayer, and a number of leaders of the Bagishu Welfare Association sat on it. Its findings were delayed[4] because of the outbreak of war, but it satisfied Gisu public opinion and embodied the main Gisu claims to a system of limited individual tenure in its findings.

Another issue shows the growing awareness by the Gisu of the value of their own culture. The educated élite established a committee to choose a common form of the Gisu language that could serve as a written language for a newspaper, Bible and prayer-book. The members of the association, which they called the Lumasaba[5] Language Committee, regretted the use of an alien language as the official medium of administration, education and religion, and were also concerned to prevent the impoverishment of the Gisu language by the neglect of Gisu words which were being replaced, in educated speech, by Ganda terms. The Committee consisted mostly of members of the Protestant church, some of them priests, who had been brought into contact through their religion and who were chosen to represent the different dialect areas of Bugisu. The main problems of orthography and vocabulary had not in fact been solved when I left the field, each member being concerned to preserve the pronunciation and special features of his own dialect. Nevertheless, it was felt to be, and clearly was, a tribalistic movement designed to give the Gisu language equal standing with better-known African languages, such as Luganda.

Another category of issue which aroused Gisu tribal feeling

was concerned with boundaries and the demarcation of administrative units. The border between Bugisu and the tribal territory to the west was the subject of considerable feeling, which was not satisfied with the adjudication of the District Commissioner, Mr Perryman, and the division, in 1923, of the former Eastern District into three—Bugisu, Bugwere, and Bukedi—the first including the Sebei together with the Gisu. From 1941 to 1954 the three areas were once more administered as one from the District Headquarters in the town of Mbale, which gradually grew in both size and importance. When a division was made again, into two areas—Bugisu and Bukedi (including Bugwere), in 1954—the bone of contention was the town itself, leaders of the African Local Governments of both Bukedi and Bugisu declaring that it fell in their traditional territory.[6]

The reasons which lay behind the boundary dispute and the claim to Mbale show an important aspect of tribalism, the protection of its territorial integrity against outsiders. Whereas this had been an aspect of former tribal structure, it had been a fragmentary defence of Gisu territory. Each lineage protected its own holding but could call on the help of its neighbours against a common enemy, i.e. non-Gisu attackers. The boundary disputes and the claim to Mbale were the first instances of tribal loyalty in action. In the latter event, the tribal case was argued by the officials of the African Local Government which had come to represent the tribe as a political entity. There was also an element in the second claim that distinguishes it from the first. It was clear that Gisu felt that their claim to Mbale was justified as much by their position in the Eastern Province as the largest and richest tribe as by traditional jurisdiction of the area on which it stood. The recognition of Mbale as a Gisu town would have given the Gisu a status symbol indicating equality with Ganda and other peoples considered by the Gisu as powerful within the State of Uganda. The Gisu wished to make Mbale their town much as independent African states wish to establish their own university, as a symbol, as much as for its own sake.

Other issues on which Gisu feeling has run high, though not always evenly throughout the whole society, have been: *for* administrative unity with the Vugusu rather than the

Sebei on the grounds of cultural and linguistic similarity; *for* the installation of a permanent head of the tribe, equivalent to the Kabaka (this has now been achieved, but not without internal dissensions); and *against* the introduction of circumcision in hospitals instead of by tribal ceremony. I shall refer to the last issue again. The first two I shall not go into detail for they show the same features that have occurred in tribalistic action in other contexts. There are two main themes which recur. First, an attempt to match cultural, linguistic, territorial and political boundaries, as in the Gisu desire to separate from Bukedi, to use Gisu as the official language, to join with the Vugusu, or to include within their borders all land where Gisu were living. In addition, tribal policy aimed at making the Gisu equal in status with other similar units within the wider society of which they were now a part: to have control of their own affairs, their own head of affairs, and their own urban centre. This aspect of tribalism could be called the struggle for power, and concerns competition with other like units. By implication it is a modern phenomena, for this is a struggle within a wider society which did not exist, for the Gisu at least, in pre-colonial times. Paradoxically, then, tribalism implies its opposite, the supertribal state.

This paradox derives from the fact that it was only in the supra-tribal state that the Gisu became aware of common interests which could be secured by joint action. The first of these, speaking historically, was the power wielded over the whole tribe, made possible by the British administrative system and held first by aliens (Ganda). Later, economic interests became important: the Gisu coffee co-operatives fostered by the British came to represent a source of tribal income, which the Gisu wished to control. (Ambitious Gisu encouraged the spread of the idea that the British Government was withholding from the Gisu growers an unfair portion of the proceeds of each year's sale.) Gisu resented the use of District finance to improve roads outside Gisu territory (i.e. in Sebei County), and wished for similar reasons to control Mbale township in order to promote Gisu interests there. Thus the fifty years of British administration in Uganda introduced into Gisu tribal life common interests and aims which had not existed formerly. In addition they created the administrative and political machinery through which the Gisu could make a bid for a share of the new power and wealth.

Historically one can say that the development of tribalism in Bugisu has passed through two stages. The first stage was that of the development of a truly tribal awareness of common cultural features and common interest, which had existed before only in a ritual context. Second, there emerges what I have called (somewhat misleadingly, because it was never clearly formulated) Gisu tribal policy. This is action by Gisu leaders on behalf of the tribe as a whole over issues which appeared to them either to threaten their new identity or seemed to deny them rights accorded to other tribes. Tribalism in Bugisu is thus the mobilization of loyalties which, in the traditional system, were latent and expressed only ritually, into a political pressure group.

What emerges clearly is that the acceptance of certain values marks off a community whose members regard themselves as mutually allied, as against strangers (the non-Gisu) who could be expected to be hostile. Gisu initiation thus defines unequivocally for any Gisu the widest group with which he can identify himself. This community can be described as 'we', as against its opposite, 'they', the non-initiate aliens. This common identification indicates the acceptance of common values and a common code of ethical norms, so that what is defined is a moral community, i.e. a category of people whose guiding values are known and accepted by all members. Allegiance to common values imposes no specific obligations between tribesmen; rather it implies a generalized loyalty which can be mobilized in particular situations as a moral sanction or to legitimize a claim for support. Thus in towns it is common to find tribal solidarity utilized in founding voluntary associations, in maintaining trading partnerships or landlord/tenant relationships. In these cases the existing structure is given additional moral force by being reinforced by acceptance of a common moral code (Cohen, 1966, p. 25).

In Bugisu itself, the tribal sentiment was mobilized by tribal leaders, whose position was made possible by the heightening of tribal consciousness, and whose actions in turn tended to increase tribalist feeling. At first it was opposition to the Ganda which made it possible for leaders to appeal to 'Gisuhood' against the alien values of their rulers. (This appeal to traditional Gisu norms existed together with, and in spite of, the very keen desire of leading Gisu to emulate the dominant Ganda people, and, later, the powerful Europeans.) The replacement of Ganda chiefs by Gisu was felt to be a tribal achievement. When later British policy aimed at transforming the upper ranks of the chiefs into a corps of mobile civil servants instead of local representatives, those Gisu who were given chiefships in areas of Bugisu remote from their home villages were forced to seek support for their authority in terms of Gisu rather than local loyalties. In later years, when nationalist parties were canvassing for support in Bugisu in the pre-independence years, they used Gisu cultural symbols to provide a link between themselves and their supporters. In a situation where the leaders were often economically and educationally distant from the bulk of the population whose support they wished to gain, common tribal values provided the only ideological basis on which an appeal might successfully be made. Indeed, the undefined solidarity invoked by tribal symbols could be, and was, translated into a moral duty to give political support.

What I have called cultural symbolism is the use of key cultural features to symbolize structural unity. Language is the commonest symbol, for it represents in its grammar and vocabulary a paradigm of a common way of life and enshrines common values. For the Gisu, male initiation was another potent symbol. The ceremonies provided the only definition of the Gisu tribe as such and they dramatize the basic values of Gisu society. They are tribal in every sense of the word. Continuing pressure from Ganda chiefs, British administrators and missionaries of all denominations, failed to bring about their decline. Gisu still declared vehemently to me in 1954 that a Gisu man born in Bugisu and living according to Gisu norms, was yet not a true Gisu if he was uncircumcised in tribal ritual. Conversely, the son of a Ganda chief who had undergone Gisu ceremonies of circumcision was said to have 'become a Gisu'. I am told that since independence and the lifting of administrative pressures to abolish the ceremonies, they are being performed with renewed enthusiasm and with addition of both new ceremonies and details which had fallen into disuse.

If one asks why initiation ceremonies, essentially concerned with the passage of individuals from boyhood to maturity, should symbolize tribal unity, then a further facet of tribal identity emerges. The nature of the transition which is accomplished by Gisu initiation ceremonies is closely associated with Gisu notions of power. Initiation qualifies a youth to enter the adult world of men, which is characterized by a competition for power. All initiated men were free to seek such power as they could wield over others; uninitiated men were debarred from so doing. Hence the ceremonies demarcated the political community by demarcating the category of individuals who were eligible to participate in the Gisu political struggle. The uninitiated and, *par excellence*, those who did not pass through the rituals because they were not Gisu, were excluded from the widest political unity, the *potential* universe of power. That the traditional structure was such that no man ever rose to a position of leadership over the whole tribe does not affect the argument. Although the tribe possessed no traditional mechanism whereby political unity might be organized, nevertheless the tribal symbols referred to a moral community with political potentiality. The creation of a tribal structure of administration during the last fifty years has given new meaning to the traditional symbols. No Gisu chief, however modern his outlook and however close his dependence on a source of power outside the tribe, could afford to ignore them. A certain sub-county chief was unable to achieve the standing and influence of his colleagues, largely, I was told, because, twenty years earlier, he had shown fear at his initiation. Moreover, circumcision in hospital, being devoid of the character of an ordeal and shorn of traditional ritual, could not qualify the new élite for a legitimate title to power. Initiation as the representation of tribal structure is still the most potent of Gisu cultural symbols.

It is worth pointing out here that language, or ceremonial, or other cultural features are *not* common to all Gisu. I have already stressed the wide variation in dialect and ritual practices within Gisu society, which serve as differentiating factors. So that the same symbols, invoked with reference to their details, may divide where their general characteristics may serve as the rallying point for tribal unity. 'Tribal culture' provides an ideology of unity rather than any real identity of interests, by symbolizing the moral community. The Gisu are not united by a common language and rituals rather they are united when opposed to non-Gisu and represent this by reference to language and culture. The cultural symbols of tribalism are thus abstractions from cultural reality, not its basic elements.

Traditionally, Gisu symbols referred to a potential political community, rather than an organized political unit. The effective political unit was a small localized segment whose relations with other neighbouring units (with distinct and often opposed interests) were represented genealogically and made manifest in ritual and dialect. The sequence of historical events which followed the arrival of the British introduced interests which concerned wider groups than the traditional unit and provided opportunities for power on a far wider scale than was possible previously. Gisu leaders, both chiefs and early 'tribalists', used traditional symbols which had tribal significance in order to acquire a following big enough to enable them to seize these opportunities. These cultural symbols enabled the widest community to join in common political, rather than ritual, action.

To return to the relation between the two definitions of tribe with which we started, and hence to the meaning of 'tribalism': it is now clear that the cultural and political definitions are interrelated. The cultural items which define the 'tribe' refer to the widest group for which common values permit common action. However, there appears to be a problem in that the symbols of community—language and custom—may, in simpler societies, refer to a wider unit than that defined by the traditional political organization. Hence they are thought of as having some prior and autonomous existence. The use of the moral bonds implied in common tribal membership in modern, urban situations encourages the view that emotional loyalty to a language and certain cultural traits is the essence of tribalism. What this essay has sought to demonstrate is that, whatever the particular cultural items relevant for any tribal sense of identity, they are selected as symbolic of a local community. That community may not always be politically cohesive, but it subscribes to a single system of political values such that, given common interests which oppose it to similar units, it may emerge as a political pressure group within the wider system which evoked those interests.

This interpretation may have some validity for our appreciation of nationalism, which appears to be similar in structure if not in scale (Mair, 1963, p. 113ff.). Nationalist movements aim at autonomy, whereas tribal movements are concerned with relative power within a wider framework. These are distinctions of policy rather than structure. Nationalism also arises in opposition to an alien ruling group, whose distinction from the nationalists may be symbolized by colour, language or religion. These symbols refer to abstractions from social reality at a far more general level than those which serve as tribal symbols, for nationalism is usually associated with a more heterogeneous group. Language may cease to be an effective symbol and abstract ideas such as 'The American Way of Life' or 'Ujamaa' serve more effectively as diacritical signs of national identity. In the early stages such symbols refer directly to the opposition between the ruling group and the nationalists; when autonomy is achieved, national unity is endangered, for the former opposition is no longer apposite. The search for national symbols after independence is a vital task for the leaders of the new African states and often opposition to and conflict with other states becomes a political necessity. It is perhaps as attempts to create permanent national symbols that we should consider the formulation of African socialism and the personality cults in these states.

In this paper, I have limited myself to a discussion of the structure of tribalism in a rural setting and have provided only the merest sketch of how tribal loyalties are or have been manipulated by political leaders in recent years. Nor have I dealt with tribalism as a feature of modern heterogeneous towns, where tribal identity is also of importance. I think, however, that an anthropological approach, such as I have used here, would reveal no fundamental inconsistencies in these areas with what I have set out here as the structure of tribalism in Bugisu.

NOTES

1 Anthropological data on the Gisu are given in La Fontaine, 1959 and 1960.

2 The Batwa, known also as Konyi or Elgon Masai, live above the forest lines on Mount Elgon.

3 Thus northern Gisu make few distinctions among the southern Gisu, while recognizing the existence of a separate tribe between themselves and the Sebei. The southerners ignore the existence of this group, but emphasize their distinctiveness from north and central Gisu on the one hand and Vugusu on the other.

4 The Report was not published until 1957 (Uganda Government, 1957), but it had been signed as correct by the Land Tenure Committee of the District Council in 1945. During my period of field research its provisions were being administered by the courts as Gisu 'customary law'.

5 Gisu refer to themselves as BaMasaba, the term 'Gisu' being strictly applicable only to the northern section of the people. Its use by the British Administration has given the term 'Gisu' official recognition as the tribal name. The use of the traditional name for the language was deliberate on the part of the Language Committee in order to indicate its relevance for the whole tribe and its concern with traditional values.

6 The dispute was finally solved, to the dissatisfaction of both parties, by making Mbale a neutral zone with its own administration.

REFERENCES

COHEN, A. 1966, 'Politics of the Kola trade', *Africa*, 36, 1.

EVANS-PRITCHARD, E. E. 1940, *The Nuer*, Clarendon Press, Oxford.

LA FONTAINE, J. S. 1959, *The Gisu of Uganda* (Ethnographic Survey of Africa), International African Institute, London.

1960, 'The Gisu', in A. I. Richards (ed.), *East African Chiefs*, Faber.

MAIR, L. P. 1963, *New Nations*, Weidenfeld & Nicolson, London.

UGANDA GOVERNMENT, 1957, *Land Tenure in Uganda*, Government Printer for Ministry of Land Tenure, Entebbe.

'TRIBALISM' IN EASTERN UGANDA

Michael Twaddle

'TRIBALISM' is a very slippery word for scholars to use when writing about the contemporary history of tropical Africa. Like 'imperialism', it frequently arouses emotions which are so violent and so contradictory that they confuse clear thinking. Yet the phenomenon persists, and must be discussed. Thus, purely as a working definition, we may accept May Edel's typification of 'tribalism' as a sense of 'ethnic loyalty and identification' in preference to 'commitment to traditional patterns of culture'[1] (Edel, 1965, p. 371), since that is the way in which the word is most commonly used in Uganda today. We may also accept her suggestion that among the stateless societies of that country 'the experiences of the recent past have acted as a catalyst for the emergence of new and wider ethnic identifications' (Edel, 1965, p. 367) as the theme for our discussion. In this essay we consider some of the ways in which this 'catalyst' seems to have shaped 'ethnic identifications' among the stateless societies of eastern Uganda since the start of this century.[2]

During four years preceding the First World War, a young Muganda writer contributed a short series of travel articles to *Ebifa mu Buganda*, the Anglican vernacular magazine, commenting on the social condition of the peoples of 'Bukedi', as the region of eastern Uganda occupied by segmentary societies was then called by both the British and the Baganda. In these articles, he divided the peoples of Bukedi into ten 'tribes' (*mawanga*) on the basis of differences in language. *Bamiro, Bateso, Bakumamu, Bakoromojo, Bambai, Bagweri, Banyuli, Basamia,* and *Badama* each seemed to speak dialects which were unintelligible to their neighbours, while as for the *Bageso* on Mount Elgon they appeared to be hardly capable of making themselves understood to one another, so numerous were their local variations in vocabulary. Each 'tribe' was also distinguishable from its neighbours by certain cultural differences. The *Bageso*, for example, were notable for their attachment to male circumcision, the *Bakoromojo* for their devotion to cattle, the *Bagweri* for the skirts worn by their women. But none of these peoples appeared to possess much administrative unity before the coming of colonial rule in Uganda; 'they did not know how to rule themselves' (Musoke, 1911–14).

Today, each of these segmentary peoples is listed as a separate 'tribe' in the official *Atlas of Uganda* (Uganda Government, 1962), though naturally under a more consciously indigenous name. Each is also largely contained within single administrative units—the Lango (*Bamiro*), Teso, Karamojong, Sebei (*Bambai*) and Gisu in special 'Districts', the Samia, Nyole (*Banyuli*), Gwere, Kumam, and Padhola (*Badama*) in separate 'Counties'. Linguistically and culturally the differences between these peoples are probably as great as they were fifty years ago, and politically each people appears to be much more conscious of its ethnic identity.

How this seems to have happened we must now consider.

The *Ebifa mu Buganda* articles already quoted provide us with a clue to one set of influences shaping 'tribalism' in eastern Uganda over the last half-century—the phenomenon of 'Baganda sub-imperialism'. For between 1899 and 1906 the greater part of the region was controlled by Ganda chiefs organized in a Bantu kingdom under Semei Kakungulu, a Ganda general who left Buganda for that purpose; and thereafter it was administered on behalf of British officials by 'Agents' who were Ganda, exploited by traders in cattle and ivory who were Ganda and evangelized by Christian and Islamic teachers who were also Ganda.[3] This expansion of Ganda influence into eastern Uganda during the first years of this century appears to have provoked ethnic feeling in the region both positively and negatively.

Positively, it seems to have provoked 'tribalism' in at least three ways. To begin with, the official classification of 'tribes' adopted by the Protectorate administration and now followed by the successor government largely derives from the division of peoples decided upon by the Ganda administrators and teachers who worked in the region before the First World War. Had British colonial administrators been more numerous and knowledgeable in Uganda at that time, the ethnic division of eastern Uganda adopted by the Protectorate administration might have been a rather different one. 'There are a large group of tribes to the north and north-east of the Busoga district, who are known in Busoga as the Bakedi, though this name is really not the name of the race, but means people who are naked, and is frequently applied by the Baganda and others to the Bakavirondo and Lango tribes', commented William Grant, Protectorate Sub-Commissioner for eastern Uganda during the early 1900s (Grant, 1902). 'The principal tribes of the Bakedi are:

1. Bamiro	8. Bagwere
2. Bazerera	9. Banyori
3. Bangola	10. Bagesho
4. Bagogonya	11. Babamia
5. Bamoyta	12. Badama
6. Bakidaea	13. Banamito
7. Bamisa	14. Balasi.'

The list bears certain resemblances with the one propagated by the Muganda writer in *Ebifa mu Buganda*, but the principle of ethnic classification adopted is a different one—political autonomy rather than linguistic distinctiveness. But William Grant had little chance to persuade his Protectorate superiors to accept the superiority of his classification on this principle since he was retired from the Uganda colonial service at the close of 1903 on the grounds of ill health: he was replaced by a succession of British officials less fluent in local vernaculars than himself and more dependent upon their Ganda collaborators for local intelligence.

These Ganda also appear to have stimulated 'tribalism' in eastern Uganda by injecting their more developed notion of 'tribe' (*eggwanga*) into the political vocabularies of the local peoples themselves. This they did as much through educational activity as by administrative control. Most of the history text-books used in primary schools throughout the region before the Second World War were composed by Ganda authors, three popular ones being *Basekabaka Be Buganda* by Apolo Kagwa (1901), *Ebisoka Okuigiriza mu Byafayo mu nsi zona* by Samusoni Bazongere and H. T. C. Weatherhead (1911) and *Geography Ensi* prepared by the White Fathers (1931). Before subjection to Ganda-orientated education of this sort, local perceptions of ethnicity appear to have been more diffused and imprecise, though exactly how diffused and imprecise remains very much a matter for further research.[4]

Third, the Ganda presence in eastern Uganda during the early colonial period seems to have stimulated 'tribalism' by providing an ostentatious 'reference group' with which the indigenous peoples of the region could compare themselves. The Gisu provide a conveniently documented example. 'There is a marked movement towards Christianity in the district', reported one European missionary regarding this people during 1919; 'the example of the Baganda who have entered the country in large numbers as administrators and teachers has great weight with the Bagisu, and a desire to "become as Baganda" was sometimes being given as the reason for asking for baptism' (C.M.S., 1919, p. 49). Further evidence of this anticipatory socialization is provided by a similar source published in the previous year (C.M.S., 1918, p. 5). 'Now there is a great demand for instruction, mostly in Luganda', commented this source. 'The influence of the Baganda is very strong and they are looked up to generally as representatives of a more advanced race; to read is to become a Muganda, a superior person. . . .' Besides that revealing remark on Bugisu, the same writer also commented that among the other segmentary areas of eastern Uganda there was also a widespread demand for Christian instruction, 'after a better status in the society of tribes'.

Negatively, Ganda sub-imperialism seems to have structured ethnic feeling throughout the region in other ways. Culturally, it appears to have provoked 'tribal' reactions of both a ritual and a religious kind. Again the Gisu provide an outstanding example: with that people the reaction seems to have taken a largely ritualistic character, a deeper attachment to male circumcision ceremonies linking local lineages on the westerly slopes of Mount Elgon, in response to frequent Baganda expressions of distaste towards those ceremonies. The trend is difficult to document precisely,[5] but it appears to have found its strongest expression in repeated demands to hold united celebrations in Mbale Township for all 'brothers-in-circumcision-age-sets' (*bamagogi*) after the 1920s. With the Nyole, on the other hand, 'tribal' reaction to Ganda cultural influence appears to have taken a more markedly religious form, a wider attachment to the spirit-cult of Nahidugya. In his chronicle-history *Ebyafayo bya Bunyole* composed during the 1930s, Eria Higenyi gave the statement, 'We have one god Nahidugya', as one of the reasons 'Why we are called Banyole', as well as providing details about the more restricted extent of that spirit-cult in Bunyole during pre-colonial times.

During the 1920s, negative reactions against Ganda influence in eastern Uganda took a more clearly political form as a result of anxieties about land. Towards the end of the First World War, several Ganda notables living near Mbale Township banded together to form the Baganda Association of Mbale in order to agitate for estates of freehold land (*mailo*) to be granted to them alongside that already given to Semei Kakungulu, their former leader. This was largely to compensate them for what they considered unduly early retirement from Protectorate service as colonial administrators in order to make way for local men. Throughout the 1920s, this Association served as a constant irritant to Protectorate officials stationed at Mbale. It also annoyed many of the 'new men' created by missionary education among the segmentary peoples occupying the surrounding areas. In 1930 a small group of young teachers, junior chiefs and separatist church leaders among the Gwere people united to form the Young Bagwere Association 'in order to stop the Baganda who had been followers of Kakungulu from persuading the Protectorate government to give them Mbale', and also 'to fight the Baganda who had been ruling us as *Gombolola* clerks, *Saza* clerks and *Saza* chiefs'.[6]

Several years before, the Bagishu Welfare Association had been formed to pursue very similar objectives among the Gisu. Its members consisted 'of different communities of Bagishu, namely Teachers, Chiefs, Clerks and peasants of different faiths', declared an early Memorial.[7] Its founder was Erisa Masaba, now Anglican Bishop of Mbale but then merely an obscure teacher of the C.M.S. connection, who modelled the society on the Kavirondo Taxpayers Welfare Association formed by Archdeacon Owen in Western Kenya during 1923. Masaba had read about Owen in the *East African Standard*, talked about him with theological students at Mukono College in Buganda, and met him personally at Butere in Nyanza while down there on a visit during 1919. 'He seemed to us', commented Masaba in an interview, 'to be doing the same thing in Kenya that we wanted to do in Bugisu—save our land.'

The anxieties creating tribal associations among the segmentary peoples of eastern Uganda during the 1920s and 1930s were thus more than merely negative reactions to Ganda sub-imperialism. They were also motivated by a concern to defend local territory against alien intruders of other kinds. Some of these other intruders were demonstrably official, but some were of the insidiously unofficial sort. Two quotations may serve as illustrations. The first comes from a letter on 'The Bagishu Land Problem' composed by a newspaper correspondent who was most concerned that Protectorate policies regarding Crown land should not interfere with traditional landholding on Mount Elgon. In Bugisu, declared this correspondent, 'there are no Kings, but only clan leaders. For centuries now the tenure of land has been and still is by clans, and then by families down to the individuals. This shows clearly that individual tenure of land existed among the Bagishu long before the British flag over Uganda. So it is that the tenure of land is closely associated in the minds of the Bagishu and is the key note of Bugishu prestige.'[8] The second quotation comes from the records of the Bagishu Welfare Association, recording the conclusions of a meeting with the local Provincial Commissioner. 'The P.C. asked why the Ass. says that the Government will give the Bugishu land to the settlers in Kenya. He was replied that because the Bagishu people are not informed when the foreigners are allowed to build shops, cotton ginneries, corn or coffee factories, etc., and Indians are allowed to cut down people's trees without the landowners getting anything.'[9]

Besides resentment against Asian traders and influences

arising from contemporary events in Kenya, these tribal associations were also pervaded by a positively Victorian attachment to 'improvement' of all kinds. The Young Bagwere Association was motivated, so one of its founders claimed, by the desire to learn 'how to teach properly' and 'how to rule ourselves properly', as well as by the wish to oust the Baganda and 'safeguard our land'. Even the desire to get rid of the Baganda was closely linked to a sense of social backwardness: as the same informant put it, 'Baganda influence was still strong and we were backward'. The Bagishu Welfare Association was equally concerned with internal reform in Bugisu. As an early constitution proclaimed, its objectives included working for 'the uplift of the Bagishu', attempting to 'develop the land handed down to us by our forefathers', agreeing to 'assist financially any member needing help', and trying to be 'faithful to our denominational faiths'.[10]

This quest for 'improvement' within a tribal context was partly denominational in inspiration. The Bagishu Welfare Association was largely an Anglican affair, despite frequent protestations by its founders to the contrary. Archdeacon Mathers of the C.M.S. Nabumali Mission was its official 'Patron' for many years, while its Bagishu membership was frequently dismissed by local Protectorate officials as simply 'Nabumali Old Boys'.[11] The Young Bagwere Association was similarly indebted to the *Abamalaki* separatist church movement in Bugwere for spiritual stimulation, two of its founding members being local leaders of that church, Sulemani Mutaise and Yokana Toto. *Abamalaki* motivation in this matter seems to have largely arisen from a sense of relative deprivation, a feeling that they were being unfairly treated by local chiefs compared with other Christian denominations. 'We were the only teachers ordered to make roads', testified Yokana Toto in an interview; 'this made us want changes'.

Besides these connections, Christian missions in eastern Uganda may also be said to have fostered 'tribalism' through their language policies, albeit seldom completely wittingly. Local languages were transformed into literary vernaculars through the efforts of these missionaries, while as a result of labours by the same evangelists Luganda also became a common dialect throughout the region. Both developments appear to have encouraged the emergence of 'new and wider ethnic identifications' in the region. For today Luganda is the language in which members of the Bugisu District Council (*Lukhobo*) address one another, while in Teso District the language of politics at this level nowadays is the standardized form of Ateso. Both linguistic developments have also stimulated the growth of ethnic feelings among the smaller peoples of the region. The ethnocentricity of the Padhola, for example, has been reinforced both by the transcription and teaching of Dhupadhola by Catholic missionaries at Nagongera, and by local resentment against the use of Luganda as the language of interviews for salaried posts in local government.[12]

The first District Council to be established in eastern Uganda during the period of British Protectorate rule was the one founded in Teso during the 1930s by F. R. Kennedy, the local District Commissioner, with the double aim of undoing the administrative consequences of Ganda sub-imperialism and implementing contemporary notions of 'Indirect Rule'. But during the 1940s similar Councils were introduced into the modern Districts of Lango, Bukedi and Bugisu for a variety of other reasons, prominent among them a desire to silence the agitation of tribal associations which had disturbed Protectorate administrators working in eastern Uganda before the Second World War.[13] British colonial officials also attempted to curb agitation of that kind by rearranging administrative boundaries to accord with local ethnic groupings. In his annual report for 1939, for example, the Provincial Commissioner of the Eastern Province declared that he had divided the Budama District of that time 'into counties roughly corresponding with the tribal distribution of the inhabitants, and that these boundaries 'were settled by a series of plebiscites among the villages along their borders' (Dauncey Tongue, 1940, p. 10).

To some extent British objectives were achieved by these means. Overt ethnic agitation did die down for a time, as 'tribalism' was institutionalized and the purposes of societies such as the Young Bagwere Association and the Bagishu Welfare Association were served by other organs. Yet ethnic rivalries continued to disturb Protectorate officials in eastern Uganda as the forties gave way to the fifties. This was due to a variety of reasons, prominent among them the continuance of differences over the tribal ownership of Mbale Township, and, more recently, the character of the independence struggle. We may take the question of Mbale first. Though little is known about 'tribalism' among urban dwellers in eastern Uganda, we do know that the location of Mbale Township along the narrow strip of land separating the westerly slopes of Mount Elgon from the easterly stretches of the Lake Kioga drainage-system has been a stimulant to ethnic rivalry between the Gwere and the Gisu for fifty years or more. Apart from the anti-Baganda agitation which started the dispute, ethnic feeling over this issue has also been exacerbated by several changes in District boundaries by the British Protectorate authorities. In the early 1920s the original Bukedi District was divided into three, forming separate Districts for Bugwere, Budama, and Bugisu, with Mbale Township acting as the administrative headquarters of Bugwere District. But in 1937 Bugwere and Bugisu were amalgamated to form a single District with Mbale as the common capital; and then in 1954 this amalgam was dissolved to form the new Districts of Bugisu and Bukedi, whilst Mbale Township became a separate 'Territory'.[14]

With the approach of independence, antipathies between Gwere and Gisu over Mbale reached a climax. As the debates of the time in the Bugisu *Lukhobo* indicate, the main reason for the increase in tension was the urgency of getting the boundary between the two ethnic areas adjusted before subjection to majority rule by other Ugandan 'tribes'. 'Some people, especially those belonging to some new political parties from Buganda, argue that we should wait for self-government before doing anything about the land because at that time the Queen will have divested herself of the control over the lands, so that we shall be in a better position to negotiate with an African Government regarding land matters', declared one *Lukhobo* committee during the 1950s. 'We would ask one of these people to stand up and give us a guarantee that we shall not receive better hearing under the present seemingly foreign Protectorate Government. It is highly doubtful that anyone can give us such a guarantee. We should not forget the fact that Bugisu is only a very small portion of the Protectorate and at the time of self-government everything will be decided by votes' (Lukhobo, 1957). By 1962, the year of independence, the dispute over Mbale had become so bitter that the Uganda government was forced to appoint a special commission of inquiry. This commission submitted a report recommending an elaborate compromise as a solution to the quarrel, Gisu acquiring nominal title of 'ownership' to Mbale but the occupants of Bukedi District retaining full rights of access and use (O'Connor, 1962). But it took several years before the Uganda government attempted to implement this solution: it was not until July 1967 that the country's Minister of Regional Administrations felt strong enough to order the Bukedi District administration to move its headquarters from Mbale to Tororo,[15] and even then there were 'teething troubles'.[16]

The Mbale dispute has affected recent political activity among the Gisu and Gwere peoples at several levels. Among many students and teachers it has taken a largely literary form. During the 1950s a number of young Gisu came together to form the Masaba Research Society in order to collect and collate local traditions of origin relating to Mbale and its ethnic environs. But increasingly this society has become a collection of straightforward antiquaries as its political intentions have been frustrated by official delays. Today its members are attempting to standardize the Lumasaba language, record old circumcision songs, and collect materials for an ambitious *History of Bugisu* to be edited by the Society's President, George Wamimbi. The Mbale dispute has also affected literary production at Makerere University College, where Gisu students publish *Mulembe*, a magazine which has urged the social improvement of Bugisu as well as propagating the Gisu view on Mbale during its first years of publication.

The independence struggle has also provoked 'tribalism' in eastern Uganda in other ways. The exigencies of electioneering before the ballot box required aspiring M.P.s to Uganda's first National Assembly to cultivate a territory for themselves, and in eastern Uganda this was necessarily a tribal one.[17] Furthermore, 'tribalism' frequently seems to have shaped campaigns for votes as well as determining the actual identities of parliamentary candidates during the first national elections in Uganda. For example, in north Bugisu, an area with which the present writer is acquainted, all the candidates for election to the Uganda National Assembly during 1962 are remembered as having employed the traditional arts of personal persuasion and generosity, which Gisu call *nganika*, in attempting to achieve success, as well as exploiting current dissatisfaction with coffee prices and the local distaste for strangers.

'National' politicians in Uganda have also found it useful to manipulate ethnic feelings in the region on occasion. On 22 November 1961, for example, the Democratic Party government in Uganda announced in parliament that the marriage of Bugisu and Sebei in one District was 'an unhappy one'. Soon afterwards a Bill was passed legalizing a divorce and elevating the 'County' of Sebei into a new 'District'—a move accompanied by the personal transfer of most Sebei politicians to the Democratic Party from the Uganda Peoples' Congress (Rothchild and Rogin, 1966, p. 412). The D.P. had its reasons for acting as a marriage broker in reverse over this matter. The Party had won a majority in the national elections of March 1961, but that majority was a very precarious one and further elections were known to be pending before the final granting of full independence to Uganda. It was therefore willing to accommodate tribal separatism providing that separatism was able to provide it with a safe parliamentary seat as well as a majority in any newly-constituted District Council. But, as it happened, the D.P. lost the Uganda national elections of April 1962; and as a consequence in 1964 the roles of Sebei politicians were reversed, most of those politicians rejoining the U.P.C. in return for a road, a hospital and several other social benefits (Wazei, 1965, pp. 7–12).

Besides the recent politics of independence and the more distant phenomenon of Ganda sub-imperialism, 'tribalism' in eastern Uganda has also been stimulated by an economic movement whose importance is clear if largely unchronicled. For underlying much ethnic feeling in the region are the differing rates of response exhibited by its peoples to the economic changes introduced by British colonialism. The disparities are most marked between the largely agricultural peoples already considered in this paper and the pastoralist Karamojong. The Karamojong have spurned most of the appurtenances of British colonialism, administrative and educational as well as economic. The reasons for this comprehensive disdain are relatively easy to identify. To begin with, the Karamojong were never subjected to that close control which Ganda chiefs exercised over the agricultural areas of eastern Uganda during the early colonial period. The Bataringaya Committee commented on Karamoja in 1961: 'It is true that the Kiganda-type of administration was eventually introduced but it was only the system that was introduced and not the drill and discipline that goes with it, which Kakungulu and the other Baganda agents inculcated into the other tribes [of eastern Uganda]' (Bataringaya, 1961, p. 7). Nor were the Karamojong offered very much by other colonial administrators which seemed to afford much advantage or opportunity in the harsh physical environment of their relatively remote country. Evangelization by Europeans did not begin until the 1930s, and then only in a limited way. The paucity of external influences and the poverty of their country have allowed the Karamojong to resist changes. 'Karimojong adhere tenaciously to a scheme of pastoral values', comments a social anthropologist. Their 'pattern of behaviour towards Government is . . . less open conflict than simple disregard of its existence wherever possible, coupled with quiet breach of its policy where it conflicts with their own' (Dyson-Hudson, 1966, pp. 237–9). With the Karamojong, it appears that 'tribalism' is synonymous both with a sense of 'ethnic loyalty and identification' and with 'commitment to traditional patterns of culture'.

But even among the largely agricultural peoples of eastern Uganda, considerable 'tribal' disparities have grown up as a result of differing rates of response to Western economic influences. These differences are impossible to quantify precisely in our present state of ignorance about colonial economics, but they are clear enough in general terms for even the most superficial observer to notice. The Gisu, for example, are clearly the most productive suppliers of coffee to Government coffers in eastern Uganda, while their neighbours the Teso have become equally impressive cultivators of cattle and cotton for the cash market. With both these peoples, cultivating such cash crops appears to have become closely connected with their 'tribal' identities.[18]

With the Gisu, cultivating cash crops has also had the effect of creating another sub-imperialism in eastern Uganda. During the last fifty years, many Gisu have moved from densely populated sub-counties on the Bugisu periphery with Sebei into Sebei itself. In Sebei, these Gisu migrants prospered to such an extent that by the year of independence in Uganda they were producing about two-thirds of the coffee crop marketed in Sebei, though comprising barely one-third of the population in that area, as well as owning proportionally more cattle than the Sebei people themselves. As a Gisu student recently admitted in an undergraduate essay at Makerere: 'The Bagisu as a whole did not like the presence of Baganda in Bugisu as rulers and the Sebei easily saw a similar situation in their area with the Bagisu. As one of them put it to me: 'If you complained about Buganda "imperialism" in Bugisu, then we are also right in our efforts to get rid of "Bugisu domination" in Sebei' (Nangobi-Gubi, 1967).

Yet here a problem arises. Economic developments such as these are just as likely to fragment 'tribalism' as to consolidate it. Bugisu may provide our main example since that area has figured so much in this essay. In Bugisu the care of coffee may have provided the local people with an ostentatious trademark distinguishing them from other 'tribes' in eastern Uganda; but it has also sharpened local particularisms among them, as even a most cursory acquaintance with the recent history of the Bugisu Co-operative Union will reveal.[19]
    What can be argued about economic developments can also be said of the other forces considered in this essay. Bugisu, again, may serve as our main example. As regards administration, British Protectorate rule may have given Gisu a wider sense of their tribal identity as 'Bagisu' by providing them with a District administration and modern roads; but by making the 'County' the main unit of local government on the Buganda model, and by aligning the major roads in the District accordingly, it has also deepened the divisions between peoples coming from the northern, central, and southern parts of Bugisu. As regards religion, missionary evangelism may have stimulated the tribal associations of the 1920s and 1930s, but it has also divided Bugisu into religious factions which frequently coincide with lineage divisions. As regards language, missionary

evangelism may also have equipped Gisu with a common lingua franca in Luganda, but even that contribution must be seen as a source of disunity as well as of unity. As a missionary observer commented in 1918, the 'preference for Luganda' in Bugisu was 'a prejudice which is strengthened by the mutual jealousy of the clans, all the Lugesu literature being in the dialect of the Nabumali clan' (C.M.S., 1918, p. 5).

Similar tendencies towards tribal fragmentation as well as consolidation may be detected among the other acephalous agricultural societies of eastern Uganda. In 1958, for example, the proceedings of the Teso District Council were disrupted by factional differences between Iseera and Ngoratok, differences partly attributable to resentment against the predominance in Teso politics of school graduates from the Ngora missions (Uganda Government, 1958b). In Bugwere ten years before, there was open opposition to an African census for a very similar reason: envy of the political success of the chiefly products of the Budaka mission schools combined with a sense of relative deprivation among disgruntled sub-clans in Bugwere. This opposition was articulated in a pamphlet entitled *Lwaki Abakedi Obutabalibwa* ('Why the Bakedi were not counted properly'), addressed to the District Commissioner at Mbale in 1948. The principal signatories to this pamphlet were Sulemani Mutaise and Yokana Toto, two leaders of the Abamalaki separatist church in Bugwere, at the time and two of the founders of the Young Bagwere Association nearly two decades before.

Thus, upon examination, our 'catalyst' turns into a paradox. During the last seventy years 'tribalism' may have expanded on several peripheries among the segmentary peoples of eastern Uganda, but meanwhile the phenomenon seems to have disintegrated at the centre. Politically its gifts are therefore ambiguous.

NOTES

1 Edel's choice of a definition is, however, less clear-cut than mine.
2 This omits Busoga from the discussion, but includes part of Lango and also the pastoralists of Karamoja. The unfootnoted material analysed in this paper was collected informally between 1962 and 1964 whilst I was working under the 'Teachers for East Africa' scheme, and more

rigorously during the last five months of 1965 in the course of research into political change in eastern Uganda between 1900 and 1939. I gratefully acknowledge an award of a State Studentship by the Department of Education and Science which enabled me to undertake that research.

3 On this expansion, see Roberts, 1962, pp. 435–50, and Twaddle, 1967.
4 For a preliminary discussion, see Twaddle, 1967.
5 A revelation of its outline is given in Mayegu, 1960.
6 *Gombolola* is the vernacular name for 'sub-county', and *saza* that for 'county'.
7 Mbale District Archives: B.W.A. to D.C., Mbale, 11 April 1939.
8 *Uganda Herald*, 1 March 1939 (letter from 'A Mugishu').
9 Mbale District Archives, 17 October 1938 ('What the Hon. the P.C. Eastern Province talked with the officers of the Bagishu Welfare Association').
10 Mbale District Archives, 1938b (Calendar containing constitution of the B.W.A.: file 4/0/37).
11 Mbale District Archives, 1938.
12 See Burke, 1964, chapter 6. At the 1959 Census in Uganda, Teso numbered 524,716, Gisu 329,257, and Padhola 101,451.
13 The Bukedi District Council is discussed in Burke, 1964.
14 A summary of these changes is given in O'Connor, 1962, Appendix iii.
15 *Uganda Argus*, 5 July 1967 ('Tororo to be Bukedi H.Q.').
16 *Uganda Argus*, 19 July 1967 ('Talks on Bukedi H.Q. transfer').
17 Only one African M.P. in Uganda represented a constituency outside the ethnic area of his birth at the beginning of 1966. Ironically enough, that was Daudi Ocheng, Secretary-General of the Kabaka Yekka party in Buganda.
18 On the Gisu compare Roscoe, 1924 with La Fontaine, 1959. On the Teso see Lawrance, 1957.
19 See Uganda Government, 1958a, Ehrlich, 1963 and Wotaluka, 1967.

REFERENCES

Bataringaya 1961, *Report of the Karamoja Security Committee 1961*. Government Printer, Entebbe.
Burke, F. G. 1964, *Local Government and Politics in Uganda*, Syracuse University Press.
C.M.S. 1918, *Uganda Notes*, 19 (Kampala, C.M.S.).
1919, *Proceedings of the Church Missionary Society 1918–19*, C.M.S., London.
Dauncey Tongue, E. 1940, *Report of the Provincial Commissioner, Eastern Province, 1939*, Government Printer, Entebbe.
Dyson-Hudson, N. 1966, *Karimojong Politics*, Clarendon Press, Oxford.
Edel, M. 1965, 'African Tribalism: Some Reflections on Uganda', *Political Science Quarterly*, 80.
Ehrlich, C. 1963, 'Some Social and Economic Implications of Paternalism', *Journal of African History*, 4.

GRANT, W. 1902, 'Uganda Intelligence Report, January 1902' (Appendix D, encl. Jackson to London, 3 Feburary 1902), *Public Record Office*, FO/2/804.

LA FONTAINE, J. 1959, *The Gisu of Uganda*, International African Institute, London.

LAWRANCE, J. C. D. 1957, *The Iteso*, Oxford University Press.

LUKHOBO, 1957, *Report of the Land Tenure Proposals Committee*, Bugisu District (mimeo).

MAYEGU, A. 1960, 'The Tribal Circumcision Periods', unpublished MS. in possession of author.

MUSOKE, P. K. 1911–14, *Ebifa ma Buganda*, Budo, King's College ('Bukedi', February 1911, pp. 6–8; 'Miro, Bukedi', February 1912, pp. 11–14; 'Lango Nabieso', November 1912, pp. 18–20; 'Samia, Bukedi', May 1914, pp. 84-6).

NANGODI-GUBI, G. 1967, 'The Sebei Separatist Movement', unpublished MS. in possession of author.

O'CONNOR. 1962, *Report of the Commission appointed to review the Boundary between Bugisu and Bukedi*, Government Printer, Entebbe.

ROBERTS, A. D. 1962, 'The Sub-Imperialism of the Baganda', *Journal of African History*, 3.

ROSCOE, J. 1924, *The Bagesu*, Cambridge University Press.

ROTHCHILD, D. & ROGIN, M. 1966, 'Uganda', in G. M. Carter, *National Unity and Regionalism in Eight African States*, Ithaca, N.Y.

TWADDLE, M. 1967, *Politics in Bukedi, 1900–1939*, unpublished Ph.D. thesis, University of London.

UGANDA GOVERNMENT, 1958a, *Report of the Commission of Enquiry into the Affairs of the Bugisu Co-operative Union Limited*, Government Printer, Entebbe.

1958b, *Report of the Commission of Enquiry into the Management of the Teso District Council*, Government Printer, Entebbe.

1962, *Atlas of Uganda*, Lands & Surveys Department, Entebbe.

WAZEI, M. 1965, 'Background to Sebei News', *Mulembe* (March).

WOTALUKA, L. M. 1967, 'The B.C.U. Since October 1966', *Mulembe* (September).

THE CHAGGA

Kathleen M. Stahl

TANZANIA remains one of the least tribally torn places
in Africa, yet paradoxically its Government is bent on
detribalizing the people in the interests of unity and of
building the nation on the pattern of African socialism and a
classless society. Local loyalties, local vested interests, bourgeois
love of hearth and home, are discouraged. That part of tribalism which clings to one area is taboo. To survive now, one
has to think in terms of Tanzania as a whole and be prepared
to move anywhere.

It may well be that this is not a policy against tribalism so
much as a policy of general political security prompted by the
needs of the central Government to unite the country.

At the same time the country's rulers sometimes talk about
the pre-European tribal past, idealizing it as a time of perfect
democracy in which everyone helped everyone else, in order
to ground the evolving African socialism of today on this old
tribal heritage.

So the term 'tribalism' is bandied about. In the case of
idealizing old tribal days there is a need to appraise the true
picture. In the case of today's policies one may wonder how
far modern African governments, though they may have ban-
ished this concept from their thinking, are in fact causing people
self-consciously to think more tribally than before by the very
thoroughness of their detribalization measures, under whatever names these go. A comparable case was the policy of multi-
racialism introduced as a political measure by the colonial
power in the 1950s. This had the effect, not of uniting Africans,
Asians and Europeans as its innovators intended, but of making

Africans cohesive, aware of themselves and their power as never before. It seems at least possible that this may be so in the matter of detribalization, particularly since it has been found easier to break up the old pattern than to replace it with the new one. As one notable example: in 1962 the Government of independent Tanganyika abolished hereditary chiefship throughout the country, and took pleasure at the ease with which this operation was accomplished and the readiness with which ex-chiefs accepted posts away from their old chiefdoms. By 1967 this mood had been succeeded by one of sober reflection which saw the creation of a new, reorientated society as a long process which might take a generation. By 1967, too, it was acknowledged in retrospect that the view advanced at the time in the highest circles of Government, that the institution of chiefship should not be abolished but be gradually allowed to wither away, might well have been considered more seriously.

In the local context, when one talks today of Chagga tribalism it really amounts to local patriotism and local pride. When things are going well these feelings are an incentive to modern achievements and expand easily into the larger loyalty to Tanzania as a whole. When things go badly, when people feel themselves threatened or blocked from any clear way ahead, they withdraw into themselves, taking refuge in the traditional past.

There are two sides to the Chagga and have been throughout their history. They are outward-looking people. They go out to trade, seize every new opportunity, adapt innovations, absorb newcomers, grasp the economic and educational ladders to success and, for those whose particular chiefdom has been oppressed, as an escape from the living past on Kilimanjaro. During the British colonial period 1916–61, they were to be found all over Tanganyika as an élite of clerks and teachers. Since independence in December 1961, with its widening opportunities of professional posts, they have played a full part. At home in the nineteenth century one hereditary chief after another welcomed the Swahili traders and the early European travellers; so in the twentieth century they welcomed people from all over Africa and Europe and parts of Asia to see their fine coffee co-operative, the Kilimanjaro Native Co-operative Union (K.N.C.U.), and their Chagga Council.

The Chagga are inward-looking too. They always like to go back home. What is more, they have homes to go back to— more than their neighbours down in the surrounding plain. A Chagga house, whether a traditional round thatched bee-hive hut or a rectangular concrete bungalow, stands in its own plot of rich, well-watered land, usually marked off by a hedge; and round the homestead grow bananas and coffee, flanked by yams, tomatoes, onions and a bit of everything else. For those to whom they return, those who live on the mountain, involvement in the past is strong. The history of one's own particular chiefdom, sometimes even of one's own *mtaa* or parish, is still the thing that matters; and old intrigues and feuds live on, influencing the way one aligns oneself on modern political issues. When in 1962 the Government of independent Tanganyika abolished hereditary chiefship, the immediate reaction of the Chagga to this break in their history varied from chiefdom to chiefdom. Their differing attitudes could be superficially explained as being dependent upon the extent to which each particular ruling chief happened to be acceptable; but the true motivation went much farther back, hedgehopping from one great issue of the past to another, sometimes for as much as a hundred years.

Strong local feeling has been helped by long settlement on that particular compact spot. By any standard in the world, Kilimanjaro has wonderful soil and a sparkling climate, and it has produced a dynamic people. Perhaps more precious, the mountian stands as an unassailable natural fortress within which one can, in times of trouble, withdraw. Again, unlike their neighbours down in the plain, the Chagga have a tremendous sense of place. In fact it might be said that a sense of place was the first thing they had in their genesis as a people, and it will be the last that can be taken away from them.

Looking back, one can see the heyday of Chagga local pride and awareness as one rounded period from 1952 to 1960, under the rule of their popularly elected *Mangi Mkuu*, or Paramount Chief, Thomas Marealle. The *Mangi Mkuu* was elected supreme over the sixteen hereditary chiefs of individual chiefdoms on the mountain, and over the three divisional chiefs (the latter being a recent British creation), and was made chairman of an enlarged, more representative Chagga Council.

Mangi Mkuu was expressly elected to symbolize the unity of the Chagga tribe and to represent it in all dealings with Government, which was then the British colonial administration of Tanganyika. Before 1952 British paternalism shaped events on Kilimanjaro and after 1960 T.A.N.U. shaped them, both these being outside influences; in the middle period, 1952–60, the Chagga themselves shaped their own destiny.

It was not the first time that they had had a sense of unity and identity. In pre-European times, in the nineteenth century, the story is one of the upward rise of Kibosho chiefdom, culminating in the reign of Mangi Sina (*c.* 1870–97) as the unchallenged, most powerful ruler on Kilimanjaro. After Sina's death some of this feeling endured, though it suffered many setbacks. It endured because from 1886 onwards the incoming German administration, and then later the British, kept hereditary chiefship as the basic territorial pattern. The main thing which complicated their tribal outlook during the colonial period was the fact that first the Germans and then the British built up, not the greatest power on the mountain, Kibosho, but two hitherto obscure chiefdoms: the Germans built up Marangu, the British built up Machame.

This required the greatest reorientation in people's minds, for it involved the making of political myths and the distortion of their past to serve modern political ends. Yet it might be held that the Chagga went on feeling united by their true past history. On the surface they accepted the myths and were ready, for reasons of their own security, to repeat them. Below the surface, recognized by all from one end of the mountain to the other, the true past lived on in their minds. They tenaciously held on to their heritage. If you asked in the 1960s, in one part of the mountain or another, why people voted as they did in territorial or local elections, you would be given a perfectly rational explanation in terms of the current situation; but if you went deeper you would find that the real reasons went far back into the past. Any political issue on Kilimanjaro still starts up these sounding-gongs in the memory.

So perhaps the *Mangi Mkuu* over-emphasized the fragmentation of the Chagga before his reign began in 1952. He was concerned to present himself as the great unifier of the people. He came from the chiefly family of Marangu, the small chiefdom which had been built up by the Germans in the 1890s; and he took the style Chief Thomas Marealle II, claiming that his grandfather had been the first Paramount Chief of all the Chagga. That he, an able man in the modern way and an essentially popular leader, should feel the need to make such chiefly claims is a fair indication of the blend of old and new in Chagga life.

Looking at the period 1952–60, the period of the Paramount Chieftaincy, one may first ask how it came about. It was achieved through a party organization, the first of its kind on Kilimanjaro, created and established right across the mountain. It was the work of two Chagga commoners, Mr Joseph Merinyo and Mr Petro Njau. They formed the Kilimanjaro Union and the Chagga Citizens' Union, which later were amalgamated to form the Kilimanjaro Chagga Citizens' Union (K.C.C.U.). The K.C.C.U. established links with neighbouring peoples, the Meru, the Arusha, and the Shambala. On Kilimanjaro the K.C.C.U. wanted a Paramount Chief created, and they wanted this post to be filled by Mr Thomas Marealle, then working for the Tanganyika Broadcasting Corporation in Dar es Salaam. They succeeded against the wishes of the paternal British colonial administration and against that administration's trusted agent, the shrewdest and most capable chief, Chief Abdiel Shangali of Machame.

The immediate cause was popular ill-feeling against the local constitution of 1946, on the ground that it had been imposed by the British administration without proper consultation, and had elevated Chief Abdiel by giving him control of half the mountain.

Older causes of dissatisfaction went back to the beginning of the 1930s. There were three main ones. First, in 1931, the K.N.C.U., the great Chagga coffee co-operative, was formed out of an earlier planting association. During the 1930s the K.N.C.U. established primary societies in all the chiefdoms on the mountain and embarked on its great annual general meetings of members, so that from the 1930s onwards the Chagga received through the co-operative their grounding in democratic processes and became used to doing things for themselves. This training in the economic field had repercussions on their attitude to political matters. In fact from 1931 onwards the two lines of activity are interwoven. By 1946 it was natural that the Chagga should want the same say in their political affairs as they already had over their coffee. Second, in the 1930s too, feeling was aroused against Chief Abdiel through what was thought to be an ambivalent attitude towards the introduction of compulsory co-operative marketing for all Chagga coffee. At first he had seemed against it and then had switched to being in favour of it, as the right hand of Government in this matter. To this were added other sources of opposition to Chief Abdiel as the years went by, a main one being simply that he had been a dominating figure for so long and had become identified with the British administration. Third, in 1934 the British administration itself took the initiative in suggesting to the Chagga chiefs that it would be desirable for the Chagga to have a Paramount Chief, provided they were willing to pay for him. The British administration thought in terms of Chief Abdiel for this post; however the Chiefs, the only people consulted, clearly favoured Chief Petro Marealle of Marangu, uncle of the future *Mangi Mkuu*. The administration therefore withdrew the whole idea, and the plan was put into cold storage.

It had the effect, however, of sowing on the mountain the idea of creating a Paramount Chief, which was to bear fruit in 1952. Thus, when after 1946 the Chagga sought modern reforms, they still thought in terms of yet another Chief. Perhaps they would have done so anyway, so involved were they in their chiefly past and living as they did in the narrow world of the Tanganyika of those days, with its lack of public opinion and lack of central Government policy about any clear way ahead. The Paramount Chieftaincy idea provided them with the vehicle for winning the mountain politically against the established order.

The Chagga felt that they had won a victory in 1952. In the field of local government they had seized the initiative. They were, however, saddled with a clumsy constitution. With their new Paramount Chief at the head of local government, they had no need for the three divisional chiefs created in 1946, yet the British administration tenaciously clung to the continuance of these posts. The *Mangi Mkuu* himself was both daily administrative head in the Chagga Council and the permanent chairman of that council. The latter function raised difficulty as time passed.

The first five years of the new régime, 1952–7, were years of solid achievement helped by an extraordinary spirit of buoyancy on the mountain and by economic prosperity. The Chagga felt proud of what they were accomplishing, and their zest and pride were reflected in many new songs. One popular song ran:

> Many days we covered ourselves in our blankets and kept quiet
> Now settle down and don't roam around
> There's dawn in Chaggaland.
>
> Remember home you who are far away
> And come back home
> Let's join our leaders and see how we can go forward
> It's dawn in Chaggaland.
>
> Let's try hard, now don't sleep again
> We are going forward
> Our old people were wandering around
> Because our country went to ruin
> For many days we covered ourselves in our blankets and kept
> quiet
> Now think again and don't wander around
> It's dawn in Chaggaland.

Coffee prices rose to an all-time peak in the years 1953–6. In 1953, the best year of all, the price of coffee reached £591 per ton. This compared with an all-time low of less than £30 in the late 1930s and with £308 in 1965.

The coffee cess levied by the Chagga Council swelled local revenues, which were spent on new schools, roads, hospitals and dispensaries all over the mountain. Peasant farmers drew good proceeds from the coffee co-operative, which they devoted to housing and better living standards. Moshi, at the foot of the mountain, rapidly grew into a prosperous town. Expenditure on education was striking: primary and middle schools were built, of most pleasing design, to meet the insatiable Chagga demand for educational facilities. The whole aspect was bright. The Chagga were still outward-looking; in the groping search for unity in the Tanganyika of that time they were the spearhead. Other peoples, elsewhere in the country, toyed with the idea of getting a Paramount Chief of their own who,

as in the case of the Chagga, might show the way ahead.
From 1952–7 Paramount Chieftaincy in Chaggaland and
the new national movement, T.A.N.U., flowed together.
T.A.N.U. only came into existence in 1954, two years after the
new Chagga régime began, and through the years until 1957
Chagga aims were like a microcosm of national aims and
Chagga achievements provided tangible evidence of the aspirations of the national movement in the rest of Tanganyika.

The two individual leaders, Chief Thomas Marealle and Mr
Julius K. Nyerere, were in harmony. In 1956 the Governor,
Sir Edward Twining, created the United Tanganyika Party
(U.T.P.) from the unofficial members of the Legislative Coun-
cil in order to promote multi-racialism as a national policy
against the aim of T.A.N.U. for a democratic African state.
Both leaders reacted in the same way in their different spheres.
In Dar es Salaam, Mr Nyerere attacked the Governor's action
with devastating logic in a long memorandum.[1] In Moshi,
the *Mangi Mkuu* and his councillors were visited in the Chagga
Council by the two organizers of the embryonic party, Mr
Ivor Bayldon and Mr Brian Willis, who were conducting a
roving campaign in Tanganyika to enlist support for U.T.P.
The Chagga, alone of all the people visited on that journey,
dared to speak out in no uncertain terms: they made it quite
clear to their visitors that the Chagga people would not be
prepared to accept the aims of U.T.P., nor were they supporting U.T.P. in any way. They asked how they could be expected
to believe in the ostensible aims of U.T.P., when in practice
multi-racial policies in other parts of Africa were completely
at variance; and they supported their arguments with many
quotations and references, which incidentally provide an
indication of their interest in the outside world.[2]

The climax in the harmony between Nyerere and Marealle
came in 1957, when they went to the United Nations and spoke
together on the need in Tanganyika for gradual progress to
becoming an African state. It must be remembered that during
these years up to 1957, Nyerere was, as he styled himself, 'a
political agitator'; while Marealle, as *Mangi Mkuu*, was an
established figure, a great chief of a modern kind, one of the
best-known and publicized people in East Africa.

Was *Mangi Mkuu* a 'stooge' of colonialism, a tool of the British administration? Rumour was spread by certain interests in Tanganyika at that time that this was the case, and these old rumours are believed, for example in Bukoba, to this day. At the same time it was also said of the Chagga in a denigrating way, that they were only businessmen and were upstarts without any history. These smears have been perpetuated, and in 1967 you could still hear it said, as a point against the Chagga, that they were the darlings of colonialism.

The truth is quite different. *Mangi Mkuu* was never such a puppet; quite the reverse. He was subjected to considerable pressures. On the one hand the British administration made much of him outwardly, speaking of him as King Tom and, when they had foreign visitors to whom it was desirable to show some progress in Tanganyika, sending them always to Moshi to see what the Chagga had done. On the other hand the Governor personally chose the District Commissioners who successively served in Moshi and, with one brief exception, they were antipathetic to *Mangi Mkuu*. There was little trust between *Mangi Mkuu* and the officer serving as District Commissioner. This was particularly tragic in the early years when *Mangi Mkuu* was liberal-minded, confident, open to suggestion. Had there been mutual trust, his actions in later years when he was under attack on the mountain might have taken a different turn. Nyerere, on the other hand, had been spared this ambiguity, for the British administration were quite simply against him. Later, as Prime Minister, he was to suffer it as a most wearing experience.

The years 1958–60 saw the break between *Mangi Mkuu*'s régime and T.A.N.U., ending with T.A.N.U. in power on Kilimanjaro as elsewhere in Tanganyika, and *Mangi Mkuu*, deposed by a public referendum held in February 1960, reduced to the status of a private citizen living in Moshi town. By 1958 the national movement, T.A.N.U., under Nyerere's wise leadership, had irresistibly swept across Tanganyika; backed by a strong organization, it was the Government in all but name. In December 1959 Nyerere's five years of manoeuvring for political power ended victoriously with the announcement in Legislative Council by the new Governor, Sir Richard Turnbull, of a timetable for Tanganyika's independence as an

African state. One might have expected that the most progressive local government in the country, that of the Chagga, would have continued to support the national movement now that its aims were becoming realities, and that *Mangi Mkuu* would have played a leading part. The opposite was the case. Local rivalries determined the issue. And it was the Chagga critics of *Mangi Mkuu* who ranged themselves behind T.A.N.U. Significantly enough, Kilimanjaro was the last place in Tanganyika to be won by T.A.N.U., and the price of victory was the downfall of *Mangi Mkuu*.

Mangi Mkuu's downfall was due to two main reasons.

First, he lost support among educated people. When Chagga students at Makerere University College criticized him in their college magazine, he publicly humbled them when they came home, in an old tribal way which they never forgave. He placed his faith in Mr Petro Njau, the elderly astute party organizer who had put him in, but Njau now had only very dubious old tribal solutions to offer. From 1958 Njau set himself the task of enlisting the support of the old conservatives, the clan elders, though he knew very little about clans himself and became confused in his searches on the mountain to collect and enumerate them. This was a spurious return to the tribal past. But *Mangi Mkuu* believed and trusted implicitly in him, and in the exaggerated accounts of his popularity which Njau reported. It became fatally clear during 1958 that he would never give up Njau.

Second, *Mangi Mkuu* crossed swords with T.A.N.U. on his home ground of Kilimanjaro. This is a complicated matter to explain. He still supported the national aims of T.A.N.U. for Tanganyika. He continued to support Nyerere personally as the national leader long after he had begun to deal summarily with local T.A.N.U. critics at home, perhaps because these critics did not need to be taken seriously, since they were insignificant unrepresentative people. When in 1957–8 the British administration were belatedly trying to organize a Council of Chiefs in Tanganyika as a delaying action against T.A.N.U., *Mangi Mkuu* wrote to the Governor asking that Nyerere himself should be invited to address the Chiefs. The request was refused. It was not until 1959, when he was fighting for his political life, that *Mangi Mkuu* cut across Nyerere personally and cut across the national movement as such. In January 1959, by which time he was sharply on the defensive at home, *Mangi Mkuu* criticized Nyerere's visit to Moshi to hold an open-air T.A.N.U. meeting in the town. A few months later he circularized the chiefs on the mountain, threatening to sack them if they supported T.A.N.U.

In the local field of Chagga politics, however, the break came earlier. It is interesting to note that it did not come from T.A.N.U. branches as such which, though they had started in 1955 on the mountain, had made little headway among the people. It came from Machame, from the chiefly rival whom *Mangi Mkuu* had supplanted in 1951. Chief Abdiel Shangali threw the weight of his authority behind his son-in-law, Mr Solomon Eliufoo, and this was the decisive factor.

Mr Eliufoo, a commoner from one of the oldest clans in Machame, and a Lutheran-trained teacher, was abroad in the United States and Great Britain from 1953–6. In 1957 he returned as a teacher and joined the T.A.N.U. branch in Machame. In 1958 he entered politics: he became a nominated member of the Chagga Council, being nominated by Hai divisional council of which his father-in-law, Chief Abdiel, was chairman. That same year also he was elected as a Member of Legislative Council in Dar es Salaam on the T.A.N.U. ticket. From 1958 onwards he was engaged in central politics, becoming Minister of Health from 1959 to 1960, and in 1962 Minister of Education, a post which he still held in 1967. At the local level, Kilimanjaro, he organized and led the opposition to *Mangi Mkuu*, forming a new party for this purpose called the Chagga Democratic Party. This party aimed to democratize local government, and it called for the resignation or abdication of the *Mangi Mkuu*. The important point to remember is that from 1957 Mr Eliufoo was a T.A.N.U. man and that he enjoyed the support of Chief Abdiel. Hence by 1959 he had been instrumental in calling forth a much more formidable opposition to *Mangi Mkuu*, which had the effect of bringing *Mangi Mkuu* himself out against T.A.N.U.

Towards the end of 1959 the opposition of the Chagga Democratic Party forced a deadlock in the Chagga Council. A vote was taken in the Council as to whether a referendum should be held on Kilimanjaro to decide whether the Chagga wanted the Paramount Chief for life, or a periodically elected president. The vote was carried by a narrow majority. In February 1960 the referendum was held and resulted in the choice of a periodic president. This was followed by the election of the president, Mr Eliufoo himself. He was installed in Moshi as President of the Chagga by the new Chief Minister of Tanganyika, Mr Julius Nyerere, in December. Little more than a year later, in February 1962, the new president left Moshi to go to Dar es Salaam as Minister of Education and for a few months, until the post of president was abolished by central government, *Mangi Mkuu*'s uncle, Chief Petro Marealle, was acting president.

In retrospect, the post of President of the Chagga seems like a stopgap, a way of tiding over the situation, of easing out *Mangi Mkuu* and preparing the way for the step which immediately followed. This was the establishment of a democratically elected Chagga Council, with councillors choosing a chairman from among their own number.

The Chagga were rudely brought down to earth in 1960, with their own great local impetus to progress in discredit. And yet, with only a little alteration in timing, it might have been quite different, and they might so easily have had their local renaissance not against, but as part of T.A.N.U. Their misfortune was that they acted so soon, three years before T.A.N.U. was created. Similarly, had Thomas Marealle not become Paramount Chief, it is likely that he would have become one of the early T.A.N.U. workers in Dar es Salaam, but again he left his broadcasting job in the capital two years before Nyerere returned there from Edinburgh University.

If the 1950s are the decade of Chagga local pride, the 1960s are the decade of their readjustment to their place in the new Tanzania. There were several reasons why readjustment during the years following 1960 was not an easy process. First, through their own local achievements they had already anticipated many territorial measures of the new central Government: for example, the increase in schools, adult literacy classes and training facilities, the extension of co-operatives and agricultural schemes, the introduction of women's clubs and youth clubs, all kinds of development which were greeted as an exciting novelty in less-developed parts of Tanzania, were already established features on Kilimanjaro. Second, the Chagga, unlike many other people in Tanzania, had had no need to call on T.A.N.U. to help them out of their difficulties during the 1950s, so that here also the sympathetic link was missing.

Third, their best men had gone into the movement to obtain a Paramount Chief, with the result that in the new T.A.N.U. establishment on the mountain the quality of local supporters remained a problem. Fourth, in 1962 hereditary chiefships were abolished, but by 1967 nothing had yet replaced this ancient focus in Chagga life. The new situation was that seven divisional executive officers on the mountain, all Chagga, were required to cover the former area chiefdoms, each being responsible for a division containing two or more areas. As part of the territorial policy of posting officers away from their homes, lest they come to be regarded like chiefs instead of employees of the district councils, great pains were taken to ensure that each divisional executive officer did not live in his own division. They visited each area once or twice weekly, and departed after office hours. At the same time, the leading local government posts down in Moshi town had been awarded to people from less-developed parts of Tanzania, and this inevitably meant a drop in the standard of personnel and of the handling of local matters. The Chagga pondered two questions. Who was there in charge who understood their problems? Who was there now on the mountain to whom they could go in times of trouble? It was not the loss of their chiefs so much as the lack of any replacement which had given rise to perplexity. They had stepped off the river bank and had not yet found a footing on the other side.

Fifth, by the mid-1960s Chagga farmers were feeling discouraged by the burden of new taxes and levies on their coffee crop imposed by central Government. These left them with greatly reduced incomes to meet their regular commitments, to pay school fees, medical expenses, and family maintenance. They were only saved by their food crops, bananas and maize, from finding themselves really badly-off.

Sixth, they were bourgeois people and the values, outlook and standards of a bourgeoisie were an anomaly in the classless society which the central Government aimed to create.

Looking at the position of the Chagga in 1967 in Tanzania as a whole, those of them who had left the mountain were flourishing in the new system and were playing their full part in leading posts in Dar es Salaam and other centres. The prominence of the Chagga in such posts was an irritant to other peoples. Another irritant was that the Chagga continued to win a disproportionate number of the secondary-school places in the country.

At home on the mountain, the hearts and minds of the people were not yet fully behind the new system: they felt bewildered. During the previous seven years, since 1960, Kilimanjaro had deteriorated. Negatively, the Government of independent Tanzania had succeeded there. Positively, its victory had still to be won.

NOTES

1 Julius K. Nyerere, President of T.A.N.U., T.A.N.U. Territorial Headquarters, Dar es Salaam, to all officers of T.A.N.U.: reference 65/56/65 of 22 February 1956.

2 These arguments are summarized in a letter in the Chagga council records ('United Tanganyika Party Statement in the Northern Province') from the Information Officer, Chagga Council, to the Editor, *Tanganyika Standard*, 28 March 1956.

THE CONSERVATIVE COMMITMENT
IN NORTHERN TANZANIA

The Arusha and Masai

P. H. Gulliver

O NE most important dimension of the 'tribal factor' in modern East Africa is the continued commitment of territorially-defined groups of people to their distinctive, more-or-less coherent systems of social institutions, values and attitudes: to a culture, in the anthropological sense, or more generally to a 'way of life'. Both the degree of commitment and the extent of cultural distinctiveness vary a great deal from people to people, and both may depend on the kind of emphasis given in particular contexts. But a number of fundamental questions are raised in this connection. For example, what does it mean to be a member of a particular ethnic community, or tribe? Why do members of such a community seek to maintain their social and cultural identity? Why have some communities been more committed, in effect, to their culture, and why have they been less willing to accept innovation or to become involved in the wider, modern society? The detailed answers to these kinds of question obviously depend on the ethnic community that is considered. On the one hand it is necessary to examine the nature of the particular socio-cultural system in its ecological and historical contexts; and on the other hand, account must be taken of the modern opportunities and compulsions impinging on it. This takes us to the grassroots of one significant aspect of 'tribe' in East Africa, though of course it is not the only aspect. Particularism engendered by the conservative commitment, in whatever degree, cannot be ignored, although the tendency sometimes to attribute to it an almost mystical character and to regard it as *sui generis* is scarcely helpful. There are good reasons of an historical, economic, political, and organizational kind which are the real sources of commitment. That is, there are important interests, rights, and privileges to be safeguarded, and there is a concomitant desire to preserve established ethical standards, values, and attitudes.

In this essay I consider two people of northern Tanzania— the Arusha and the Masai—who in different contexts, and for somewhat different reasons, have demonstrated a notable commitment to their own particularistic institutions and values. These two peoples are not assumed to be typical in their social reactions of other East African peoples—not even of the more conservative peoples. They do afford, however, examples of all those cases (and perhaps of all cases in some degree) where adherence to the ethnic community, to tradition, and to a particularistic socio-cultural system, has so far remained strong. Neither of these two peoples are influential or significant at the national level in Tanzania. They are too small in size and too poor economically to carry much weight; and they themselves take little interest in national policies and politics. Their effects on national unity, in politics, or in the administration of the new state are negative rather than positive, as they represent the particularism of local, ethnic interests and loyalties.

The Arusha

Not all the tribes of East Africa are long-established groups whose culture and tradition have emerged out of a distant, largely unknown past. As a settled and recognizable group, the Arusha community was founded in about 1830 when a few small groups of Masai-speaking people came to settle on the lower edge of the forested, south-western slopes of Mt Meru.[1] These settlers were refugees from Masai internecine wars of the early nineteenth century. They established a new sedentary agricultural community. With excellent natural conditions— fertile soils, plentiful and reliable rainfall, a fairly cool climate, a long growing season and opportunities for irrigation, the new community prospered and began to increase in size. It was gradually augmented by new immigrants: first, by refugees and captives from the neighbouring people, the Meru, who lived on the south-eastern slopes of the same mountain and who were largely subjugated by the Arusha; and then by Chagga refugees from the dynastic wars endemic to the slopes of Kilimanjaro, some fifty miles away to the east.[2] The growing community expanded up and across the mountain slopes, cutting into the virgin forest. Arusha began serving as mercenaries for Chagga chiefs after about 1860 (Stahl, 1964), and in the late 1880s they began to be strong enough, and confident enough, to challenge the surrounding pastoral Masai. This development was short-lived, for it was summarily stopped by the new German forces which decisively defeated the Arusha in two pitched battles at the end of the century.

The German colonial administration halted the upward expansion of the Arusha on the mountain slopes (then at about 5,500 feet altitude) by the imposition of a forest reserve. Much of the then unoccupied land to the south and west, immediately below Arusha settlement, was alienated for European farmers. The British continued this policy after 1918. But the Arusha population continued to grow rapidly; and by the 1930s, in order to obtain farm land, people were compelled to begin to colonize the former Masai lands in the peripheral plains, off the mountain slopes and below and beyond the alienated lands.

The modern town of Arusha was established on the south-western edge of the area of traditional settlement. It has become a major commercial and communications centre (with a railhead from Mombasa and Tanga), providing for important regional governmental requirements and for the growing needs of non-African farmers. It has later become a centre for the big-game tourist industry and for manufacturing enterprises. Non-African farmers (largely European, but some Asian) developed new agricultural enterprise in the commercial cultivation of coffee, maize, beans, wheat, and sisal. Services of all kinds, and marketing and retail facilities, grew to meet the demand arising out of this economic development.

The Arusha themselves took no part in all this. It was, of course, a European-inspired development, mainly for European interests. But the Arusha appeared to want no share in it: they did not even offer themselves for the new employment engendered by this economic development, and employers had to recruit their African workers from farther afield. Yet there is little or no evidence that the Arusha were actively discouraged from participating by the Administration or by the farming and commercial interests. The tiny number of Arusha who adhered to the Christian missions, received some modern education, and accepted new agricultural aims and methods, did so only by cutting themselves off from their own society and forfeiting opportunities in the traditional system. Their well-favoured, fertile land could reliably produce a wide variety of profitable crops, and now the markets, services, and communications were immediately to hand. But as the 1930s and 1940s passed, the Arusha disposed of little more of their farm produce than was essential for minimal income needs to pay taxes and for men to buy the simplest clothing. The people remained, by more or less conscious choice, little above subsistence level, tenacious of their own institutions and values.

The population continued to grow rapidly, however—at an annual rate of increase of about 2·6 per cent after the Second World War. Land shortage became acute. The amount of cultivable land in the peripheral plains is severely restricted because of inadequate rainfall and with no possibility of irrigation. By the early 1950s, Arusha colonization in the plains, and with it the limited opportunities for expansion, were virtually ended. Meanwhile population density on the fertile mountain slopes had continued to rise—to about 1,000 people per square mile in 1957. In a few mountain areas it had reached almost 1,500 people to the square mile. These conditions began to force the Arusha to adapt themselves to ineluctable necessity in order to continue their farming livelihood. They began in the 1950s what they had resisted for half a century: to grow cash crops and to grow them for the market income they could yield. The main possibility lay in coffee, for which the natural conditions and Arusha intensive, small-scale farming methods are well suited. In addition, some Arusha have taken to growing onions for the East African market (particularly for Nairobi and Mombasa), vegetables, fruit, and bananas for local markets, and seed beans, wheat, and pyrethrum for foreign markets. I emphasize the primacy of very severe land shortage as the cause of the eventual beginning of the change that had been long resisted. By the end of the 1950s there was a clear correlation between the density of population and the degree of involvement in the cash-crop, market economy. Areas with the highest density were almost entirely under coffee; areas with only some 900 people to the square mile still tended to rely on smaller coffee plots among fields of subsistence crops. The men first to change to the cultivation of cash crops were those whose land holdings were so limited that persistence with a primarily subsistence agriculture became impossible. In particular, this meant the men who had inherited or acquired only small farms; in general, it meant the men who lived in the areas where population pressure built up earliest.[3]

Necessarily—wholly by compulsion, as they saw it—the Arusha began to be inextricably involved in the modern cash economy. This radical change brought with it the beginnings of the acceptance of change in other spheres of social life. Money income from crops began to be used not only to purchase essential food but also to obtain other available consumer goods. With involvement in the market economy came some recognition of the value of understanding and manipulating its mechanisms, and the utilization of new skills and new behaviour patterns. The turning-point was passed in the middle and late 1950s (Gulliver, 1962, p. 444ff.). Yet the degree of receptivity and adaptability continued to be restrained, for the Arusha are neither happily nor whole-heartedly committed to change. For example, they have resisted the Christian missions in their midst for over half a century, and still in 1967 no more than one in ten had accepted conversion (Flatt, 1967). Enthusiasm for schooling remains comparatively weak. Although population density has continued to rise (being over 2,000 people to the square mile in some areas on the mountain slopes by 1967), Arusha still comprise less than 10 per cent of the large local labour force on estates and farms, and in the rapidly expanding manufacturing and service industries in the town. The Tanzanian Government has sought to prevent the women from wearing their traditional leather clothing, and the younger men from adorning themselves with red ochre and wearing only loose cotton cloaks. Spear-carrying had to be made illegal. In 1967 Arusha were arrested because of their defiance of Government orders in these matters. Traditional-style houses and homesteads remain the common norm. There was considerable passive resistance to the political propaganda of T.A.N.U. before independence, and still interest in and support for the national government policies is somewhat temperate.

In all this, the Arusha have to a considerable extent retained their particularistic xenophobia towards the outside world. Indeed they have been much inclined to lay all the blame on outsiders for the sad necessity of change—on the government and its officials (whether colonial or independent), on immigrants (African, Asian, European), and on the commercial interests symbolized by the town of Arusha. There is apprehension of the outside world and what it can force upon them. It is generally believed that the need remains to unite in common opposition and defence in order to preserve Arusha interests and Arusha institutions and values.

What are these institutions and values? And what has it meant to be an Arusha? First, by birth a person belongs to a patrilineage founded by one of the original pioneer-settlers some 130 years previously. This lineage is a recognized segment of a named sub-clan, and thus fits into an established hierarchy of (in ascending order) sub-clan, clan-section, clan, and moiety of the whole tribe. Through this any Arusha has a readily-determined, ascribed relationship with every other Arusha, and this defines certain expectations and obligations of mutual support and political and ritual interaction.[4] Automatically all non-Arusha are excluded from this system of all-embracing categories, and they are therefore excluded from the social action organized through the system.

Second, an Arusha adult male is invariably an initiated man (through the rituals of circumcision) and therefore a member of a corporate age-set within a tribe-wide, integrated system of age-sets. Thus in an alternative and quite different way, every man is ascriptively linked in a coherent pattern to every other man; and again, non-Arusha are excluded. Furthermore, this age-based system prescribes a man's general role at successive stages of his life, and it involves him directly in vital co-operative, political, judicial, and religious activities. Almost no social activity of importance to the Arusha occurs outside the frameworks of these two systems.

Third, each homestead head, and through him all of his dependants, have inalienable claim to use and pass on inherited rights in agricultural land within Arusha country. As the Arusha see it (though this is scarcely the true modern legal position), non-Arusha can hold land rights merely on sufferance, whilst Arusha themselves are the only legitimate right-holders. These rights, which are highly individualized, are prescribed by peculiarly Arusha custom and are guaranteed by the community as a whole. Arusha conceive of themselves as farmers, each man on his own farm, following traditionally-established agricultural practices in what are considered to be distinctively characteristic styles (even if, to the outside observer, these styles are in fact shared by other African farming communities).

Fourth, in addition to the two universal and ascribed systems of relationships, each Arusha has an individual network of interpersonal relations, based on cognatic and affinal kinship and on neighbourhood, which extends into many parts of their country. Therefore every man (and so his wife and children) can relate himself both by descent category and by formal age prescription to every other man; and often he can personalize the double linkage through his individual network: as a personal kinsman, a kinsman's kinsman, a neighbour's kinsman, or a kinsman's neighbour.

Fifth, for an Arusha there is a concentration of interests, rights, obligations, and social interaction at many levels within the recognized boundaries of the tribal society: a bounded human group of some 100,000 people in a specific land area. These interests, rights and obligations are sustained and controlled through the sub-systems already mentioned, and through a particular, highly-valued pattern of practices, customs, beliefs and values concerning the whole of social life, from making a livelihood to communication with the ancestors, from birth to death.

There are, of course, and always have been many inconsistencies, conflicts, tensions and structural cleavages among the Arusha in their society. They do not inhabit Utopia. The people are aware of many of these: for example, the often violent antagonism between members of age-sets adjacent to each other in the total system; or the conflict of interests and loyalties from membership of an age-set as against membership of a lineage. Arusha consider these as peculiar to themselves and to their social system, and therefore as factors of distinctiveness from non-Arusha. To a very large extent the people are quite correct in conceiving the totality of their own sets of social relations and the pattern of their culture as marking them off from all other peoples. Many or most of their cultural features and organization are by no means peculiar to the Arusha in fact, for they have many traits in common with the Masai in particular, and also with the Meru and Chagga. But the specific patterning of the whole, and the entailment of rights and relations upon other Arusha to the exclusion of non-Arusha, provide in their totality the framework, the conditions, and the opportunities of a social life peculiar to them alone. With all this are linked many distinctive features of dress, deportment, gesture, speech, and learned motor actions of a highly specific kind.

What have been the sources of the markedly conservative commitment among the Arusha? This commitment was breached, as I have briefly indicated, only by the sheer, acute pressure of population on the land, and not because the people came to recognize the value to them of external opportunities. My summary explanation concentrates on three interrelated factors, of which the first is dominant and crucial to the other two.

First, the Arusha have, I believe, always seen themselves as the inhabitants of a fertile and pleasant mountain island in a surrounding sea of arid, inhospitable plains. They have seen their island threatened by forces from the outside world—a hostile world in their estimation. Their livelihood is assured, and their aspirations realizable, only on their island. At first they expanded rapidly and successfully, and with increasing aggressiveness towards the outside world. This phase was sharply and violently cut short by German colonial power. Successive European administrations prevented further Arusha expansion up into the mountain forests, and land immediately below traditional Arusha settlements was taken for allocation to alien farmers. The Arusha were hemmed in between government forest reserve and alienated lands (including the modern town). When rising population pressure compelled territorial expansion off the mountain slopes, Arusha were forced to leap-frog beyond that alienated land to areas obviously poorer for their agriculture: where they could not grow their staple bananas nor obtain reliable yields of other crops. Both the town and the alien farmers took liberally of the mountain water-supplies, leaving the colonized plains in severe shortage. Even the supplies of the mountain-dwellers were seriously interfered with at some points, to the advantage of the non-Arusha. Later the town boundaries were extended for residential and com-mercial expansions, at the further expense of neighbouring Arusha. Modern tarmac road construction and electricity supply pylons also interfered with Arusha land rights; and again for no direct benefit that the people could understand.[5] The Arusha have come to feel not only restricted by outsiders but positively open to invasion by them. They have been and continue to be aware of the danger of losing land and the eco-nomic livelihood it provides and represents; and they are apprehensive about their water-supplies. In brief, they have seen their legitimate rights, interests and livelihoods continu-ously threatened and sometimes actively damaged or denied; and this has occurred at the same time (since the start of the colonial age and into the independence era) when inexorably the population has increased rapidly and the growing demand for agricultural land has resulted in smaller and smaller farms for Arusha families.

This, I believe, has been the crucial source of Arusha com-mitment to tradition and of their unwillingness to accept modernization. In the face of the threat (sometimes its actual implementation) to their interests and livelihoods, it has seemed essential to them to emphasize their common plight among themselves, so as to unite against it and its non-Arusha per-petrators. And this has been achieved—not, of course, as a fully conscious reaction—through the appeal to and emphasis on adherence to their traditional culture, to the Arusha way of life. This resort in communal self-defence has acquired its own momentum, so that Arusha institutions, standards, and values, have come to be defended for their own sake as well as for the xenophobic unity they represent.

This brings us to the second source of Arusha conservatism in the midst of radical opportunities, but one that is largely dependent on the first. The traditional social system of the Arusha is characterized and dominated by roles, statuses and relationships, which are designated by birth, age and place of residence. The major social units, groups, and categories are based on this essential prescription. Status acquired by individual achievement is both possible and approved, up to a point; but achievement is limited within the prescribed framework, and a man's interests and rights, and his opportunities for co-operation, are bound up in it. The key to success for a man is to perform as well as he can the roles set for him, and to make full use of what they offer him. Opportunities and possibilities from outside—economic, political, educational, religious, etc.—are of minimal advantage in improving or protecting a man's status. One cannot readily acquire higher status, more prestige, greater security of co-operation and assistance, by seeking to tap outside wealth, power, or influence, or by appeal to alien values. Indeed, resort to them carries the real danger that a man may be cut off from the system, since he chooses to use means and pursue interests not contained within it nor consistent with it.

I am inclined to think that such an ascriptive social system is inherently less amenable to change: it may require quite fundamental and general innovation, almost to the point of replacement, rather than gradual adaptation to a new socio-economic environment, in order to get any change at all. But that raises issues beyond the immediate concern of this essay. What is significant in the Arusha case is that this particular social system and its associated values came to represent unity and hoped-for security against the threats from the outside world. By maintaining it as fully as possible, and emphasizing its ascriptiveness, and all its symbols and their expressiveness, the Arusha found common cause in their struggle against external threat to practical interests, chiefly their land. To resist change meant to resist the outsider (African, Asian, and European) with different standards and interests who sought to impose his will. Thus Arusha traditional culture (institutions, values, etc.) not only provides for the common cause of unity and self-defence: it also clearly distinguishes Arusha from all other peoples, from non-Arusha, who are seen as source and agents of the threats to Arusha interests. For an individual to give way, to accept new outside ideas and practices, was essential disloyalty to his fellows and subject to personal obloquy and the withdrawal of support and approval.

This links with a third source of Arusha conservatism: the firm, overt link with the surrounding pastoral Masai. Earlier economic links are now less important, but many Arusha have kinship connections with Masai which are both prestigeful and economically useful. More important, the Arusha have continued to be linked with the Masai both organizationally and ritually, particularly through the common age institutions which play a vital and fundamental part in the social and individual lives of both peoples. The timing of major rituals and of critical phases of passage of men from one grade to another are determined by the Masai and merely followed by the Arusha. The peak of ritual leadership lies among the Masai. Many, though not all, basic social institutions, and many accepted values and attitudes (always excepting Arusha adherence to agriculture) are not only held in common with the Masai, but have been conceived as being inherently Masai-inspired. The Masai have been explicitly and unquestioningly accepted as the true source of proper standards and values. Masai have been the élite and the reference-group; whilst Arusha have seen themselves as necessarily cultural dependants. But the Masai, in the arid natural environment, often remote from modern influences and opportunities, have remained notably conservative (as discussed later), and as the dominant reference-group they have therefore acted as a brake on any Arusha desires for change. Arusha have invariably explained their commitment to tradition in this way; and although in part this is doubtless a convenient ideology, it does at least explain something of the refusal to take advantage of modern opportunities. It also helps to explain chauvinistic hostility by the Arusha towards both Europeans and other Africans.

It is most significant therefore that, when change eventually became no longer avoidable, it became necessary to break away from this traditional subordination to the still-convervative Masai. This revolution began in the 1950s; and by the late 1950s and early 1960s it was being frequently argued, even by middle-aged men, and especially by younger ones, that the Masai were an inferior offshoot of the Arusha, and that the Masai had a degenerate form of the proper (i.e. Arusha) tradition and culture. It was held that the Arusha had been the leaders and were now the careful innovators in the face of Masai rusticism. Arusha take great pleasure in spreading stories of Masai ignorance, uncouthness and credulity, in ridiculing them, and in scoring minor triumphs over them. It would seem that the Arusha had to free themselves of their moral dependence on and cultural subservience to the conservative Masai, to assert their own power of self-determination in adapting to the inevitabilities of social change. I am here oversimplifying a good deal, for brevity. The process was not straightforward and there were many reservations and much ambivalence. For instance, despite threats to exercise autonomy, the Arusha spokesmen continued to accept Masai leadership in 1959 at the time of the major age-set transfer rituals. And, as I have already noted, Arusha willingness to change has continued to be less than enthusiastic. But essentially the moral *volte-face* did occur, and over a fairly short period of time coincident with the urgent need for innovation. It was a symbolic act representing the beginning of the acceptance of the inevitability of change.

In brief, the marked and persistent commitment to tradition among the Arusha has been primarily a reaction to real threats against their rights and interests, and against those—the outsiders, non-Arusha—who cause the menace. The Arusha perceive and in effect use tribal identity and self-consciousness as a defensive mechanism; and thus they express and maintain the positive values to themselves of their own traditional culture.

The Masai

In the context of this book, a principal interest in the Masai is that they are often held to be the classic case of an East African people who are strongly committed to their particular cultural tradition. They have combined an ostensible refusal to accept change with the appearance of an attitude of implicit superiority towards other peoples.

The Masai also provide an especially clear example of an African people who are markedly different from their neighbours. They are purely pastoralists of a semi-nomadic kind, and by East African standards they are very wealthy in cattle. They positively reject agriculture, despising both the activity and the peoples who practise it. On the whole their country is arid and poorer in natural resources than that of most of their sedentary, agricultural neighbours. Apart from the Arusha (who are but one of many neighbours, and rather unimportant to many Masai), these pastoralists have an economic, social, and cultural system significantly unlike that of other peoples of the region with whom they have contact. There is a good deal of both traditional and modern antagonism between the Masai and these others. And (again excepting the Arusha) they are visually clearly identifiable by distinctive dress, decorations, deportment, and general demeanour. They often appear, and are commonly alleged to be, of different physical stock.

The pastoral Masai have what might be called a very loosely organized, confederative social system, operative among a widely and thinly dispersed, mobile population. It is important to emphasize that they all acknowledge a common pattern of institutions, values and attitudes, and that they adhere to a common ritual system. More particularly, the Kisongo Masai —the largest single group in Tanzania, some 35,000 people scattered over many thousands of square miles—operate within a coherent hierarchy of social units, and they recognize the overall mystical leadership of a single ritual expert (*olaiboni*).

Being a Masai means, first, for a man, initiation by circumcision and, therefore, permanent membership of an age-set in close association with his coevals. His age-set is placed in a hierarchy of sets by order of age seniority. In this hierarchy every set and each member of a set has a specified status ascription; and through the system each man is linked with every other man, as an equal, or as a senior or junior of a certain degree. Pairs of alternative age-sets, and thus their members individually, are particularly allied in political and ritual activities. A man's general role at consecutive phases of his life, his status, and his expectations of and obligations to other men, are all significantly prescribed in the total Masai age-based, social organization. This organization is the dominant feature in the political, legal, military, and religious life of these people. It underlies most forms of co-operation. It provides the basis for leadership and influence, for group loyalties and units of social action, and for the allocation of social tasks, obligations, and privileges. Indeed, it is difficult to overemphasize the social significance of their age organization for the Masai, and it is most important to appreciate its critical role in demarcating the Masai from other peoples.[6]

Second, each Masai family with its herds belongs to a semipermanent herding group or camp; and a number of these make up a localized community, controlling grazing and water within its area. Membership of such a community is not fixed, but on the whole it changes only slowly over a period of years. The local community is the order of lowest level in a hierarchy of territorial units. The highest order in this system (sometimes referred to in the literature as the 'tribe') is most simply defined as the unit of people recognizing a common ritual expert and periodically performing together the major rituals of Masai life. The 'tribe' (in this restricted sense of the term) is an autonomous unit, and several of them, each named, comprise the total Masai people of Tanzania and Kenya. The social group at each territorial level, up to and including the 'tribe', has its own operative segment of the age-sets in the age organization. Thus, at each level, pastoral rights and interests are secured and controlled, public affairs (political, judicial, religious) are dealt with, and leadership is identified.

Third, a Masai man is a cattle-owner and herder, almost entirely dependent on his herds for livelihood. The Masai are wealthy cattle people: before the 1960–1 drought and famine they possessed an average of about thirteen cattle for each human being, and most men also have some goats and sheep. Few neighbours of the Masai possess more than one or two cattle per family, and none are more than marginally dependent on livestock. To the Masai, in clear contrast, cattle and cattle husbandry lie at the roots of their social and individual lives. Masai food is the milk, blood and meat of their animals. Older men and women may eat some cereal foods obtained in trade from outside; but younger men (*ilmurran:* members of the junior age-sets) should not eat farm produce, and on the whole they do not. The Masai have a myth purporting to show that all cattle should properly belong to them, the herdsmen, whilst other (inferior) peoples must make do with farming and hunting. Cattle are, however, not important only for economic livelihood, for they are deeply involved in the marital, legal, political and religious activities and values of the people.

Although the Masai have a patrilineal moiety, clan and sub-clan hierarchy something like that of the Arusha already described, it is by no means so well-structured and is of rather little significance in relating Masai together in an operative, interactional sense. Kinship and descent scarcely distinguish them from other peoples: on the other hand, the cultural pattern of family and kinship relations, and of modes of behaviour and expectation, beliefs and values, are conceived of as peculiarly Masai, as different from and superior to those of their neighbours. In general the Masai express and demonstrate a marked conviction of their inherent superiority over all other peoples, African or not. Other peoples are, for them, not merely different and outside the Masai social system: they are essentially inferior. This assumption is primarily held in respect of the surrounding agricultural peoples, but it applies with only lesser force even to their pastoral neighbours also.

Despite their seemingly implacable attitudes and this evaluation of others, the Masai have for several generations recruited and accepted non-Masai into their communities. Women have been taken in marriage from both Bantu-speaking (e.g. Kikuyu, Chagga) and Nilotic neighbours; and alien children, sought as herdsboys, have stayed on to become Masai. Non-Masai immigrants have even been tolerated, and later accepted, so long as these had both the means (i.e. cattle) and the proved desire to live as Masai. The alleged physical distinctiveness of the Masai is likely to be somewhat illusory, being principally the result of deportment, dress and diet.

The interesting question here is: Why and how have the Masai been able to remain so different from other East Africans, so unchanging and so committed to tradition? It is fair to say that this is what the Masai have done so far during the twentieth century. The full explanation would require a most

complex analysis, and would no doubt still leave imponder-
ables. Only a brief examination is attempted here.

The crucial factor seems to lie in the fact that the Masai of
Tanzania, like many other East African pastoralists, live in
fairly or very poor country. Although rainfall (the vital consideration in such country) is on the whole rather higher in
most of Masailand than in the pastoral regions of, say, northern
Kenya, the reliability is very low. Rainfall is adequate over
the whole country no more than once in six or seven years.
Pastures are fair, but agriculture is scarcely possible except in
scattered areas of favoured land. The pastures are interspersed
with infertile stretches and tsetse-ridden thicket, whilst water-
supplies are scattered. The Masai have been able to make a
fairly successful pastoral livelihood, though always under the
threat of devastating drought about once a generation or less.
But the outside world—African farmers and, more recently,
European colonialists and Western-educated administrators and
politicians—has had remarkably little to offer to the Masai
which is of direct and immediate advantage to them. It was
far less difficult for the Western, or Western-trained, administrator to see what could be done in favourable agricultural
regions—cash crops, marketing, education, technical skills,
transport and communications, etc.—even if it was not always
put into effect very vigorously or successfully. But the same
administrators seem to have had little to offer to the Masai
(and other African pastoralists) other than general exhortations
and, often, despair tinged with romantic illusion.

The Masai have developed a social system, a pastoral régime,
a family and territorial organization, which are fairly closely
geared to the limitations of their rather severe environment.
In that environment there is relatively little scope for experiment with new possibilities. Change is fraught with potential
disaster: even in the better years a man has to husband his
livestock well in preparation for the inevitable threat of bad
years to follow. Changes from the established and proven
régime are, or certainly seem to be, likely to endanger the constant struggle against poor, unreliable natural resources. An
African farmer can, on the whole, experiment with new crops
or new methods on one part of his farm (or on a new piece of
land) whilst sustaining his subsistence production and without

critically endangering his livelihood. Most agricultural change began in that way, cautiously but fairly safely. A herdsman has less margin of safety to play with, and experiments with change can adversely affect his herds if they fail. Mere exhortation to improve the quality of livestock, or to reduce herd sizes and thus reduce pressure on available pastures, for example, seem in Masai eyes (and to a considerable degree rightly) to be a potential threat to the main aim of building up the largest possible herd against the next bad year, which will come inexorably. Cattle of better economic quality (milk- and beef-producing) may well be less resistant to drought and famine. This is not necessarily true, of course, but it may be so, and Masai have been unwilling to court disaster in seeking to find out. Furthermore, the quality improvement of livestock in order to gain economic profit in the modern market economy seems to offer little advantage to the Masai in the terms of their own social and cultural system. Certainly such novel, and unsought, opportunities seem much inferior in their attractiveness to the need and advantage of maintaining a viable herd over the years which can best meet the threat of natural disaster. Similarly, attempts to persuade Masai to adopt new methods of pasture usage and control seem to them to threaten the necessary possibility of mobility which is built into their social system and which is important in affording flexibility in periods of drought.

It has, of course, been inherently difficult to establish Government services in the wild extensiveness of Masailand, among this mobile population which cannot readily be anchored to modern roads or to centres of administrative and educational operations. Costs of maintenance are high, and the social and economic returns tend to be both low and slow. More populous, better-favoured areas (i.e. of sedentary farmers) have received higher priority in the allocation of limited finances, materials and men. There the demand is more positive, the opportunities and possibilities are more readily perceived, and the results are likely to be more quickly seen and to be greater. Moreover, the political pressures have been, and will continue to be, stronger among the agricultural and urban populations actively seeking development.

In brief, then, conservative pastoralists such as the Masai

have been offered rather little of real advantage, or that can be seen to be of advantage by the people themselves. Nor have they raised much demand for anything, except to be left alone. They are unwilling to experiment with change which is not immediately and obviously advantageous, but which, to the contrary, seems to threaten an already hazardous social ecology. The economic incentives of the outside world appear to offer little opportunity in terms of their own culture. On the other hand, the Masai have been quite willing to accept innovations which promise direct utility without increasing risk: for example, new artificial water-supplies affording access to under-used pastures, cattle medicines, or the use of bus services for individual travelling.[7]

Much of what the outside world immediately experiences of Masai conservatism—dress, decorations, deportment, aloofness—is really only the external symbolism of a strong self-defensiveness protecting vital interests. Continued expression of superiority and antagonism to other peoples, and to alternative forms of economic and political organization, are all parts of this essential defensiveness. The case has been examined most summarily here, but it suggests quite positive reasons for the continued conservative commitment by the Masai. There is no need to resort to semi-mystical explanation of the intrinsic durability of Masai culture, let alone to suggest (as sometimes has occurred) that there is something inherent in the 'Masai personality' which produces conservatism. The Masai, like other East African pastoralists, are concerned to protect their own interests, which always tend to be at hazard in their harsh environment. They have seen few possibilities of change which are of secure advantage, and which do not threaten those interests. To enter the modern world, dominated by sedentary farming and urban peoples and their interests, requires immense, radical change and seems, to the Masai, to threaten not only 'a way of life' but the very basis of social and economic existence. Therefore they are not prepared to give up their particularistic commitment, except with the very greatest caution and reluctance. The Masai are in principle little different from other East African peoples in seeking to preserve and develop their interests, and to follow ways which seem to offer the possibility of success in that. In the circumstances, for the Masai, conservatism appears to be preferable; but for other peoples, in other circumstances, new opportunities appear to offer direct and realizable advantage.

Conclusion

The marked commitment of both the Arusha and the Masai involves, first, the defence of vital common interests which seem to be threatened from the outside; and, second, the positive and largely conscious effort to maintain both social and individual identity. This commitment operates in the context of a strong and alien outside power (the modern state), and against the involvement in a strange, wider social order. The possibilities and advantages of change are, for the Masai, both limited and seemingly incalculable. Opportunities for innovation have not been clearly perceived or understood by either people; rather they have appeared to be threats. The Masai remain still before the threshold of major change: the Arusha eventually began to accept the inevitability of change only under the extreme pressures of the most acute land-shortage. Both peoples have retreated within themselves, chauvinistically expressing superiority in self-defence.

These two peoples are not, of course, the only East Africans who continue to maintain a conservative commitment to their indigenous systems. In many other cases the same sort of factors are operative: defence of threatened interests, the absence of advantageous innovation or the failure to perceive what the advantages might be, and the involvement in a coherent system of institutions, interrelations, and values, which tend to set them apart from others and to turn them in upon themselves. These are not necessarily exhaustive of the forces of 'tradition', and they are invariably affected by the nature of external contacts during this century. Nevertheless they do, I think, afford explanation of some of the roots of tribal commitment, and of the persistence of the tribal factor, of persisting tradition, in contemporary East Africa.

NOTES

1 The approximate dating is made by reference to age-set chronology: cf. Fosbrooke, 1956.

2 Sample surveys suggest that as many as two-thirds of modern Arusha are descended in the male line from such immigrants (Gulliver, 1963, p. 12).

3 These areas on the mountain slopes were those from which, for several reasons, there had been the fewest emigrants during the period of the colonization of the peripheral plains.

4 See Gulliver, 1963, p. 111. Meru, Chagga, and other nineteenth-century immigrants were incorporated into Arusha lineages by fictional kinship, so that their modern descendents are fully involved in the total system.

5 The process continues with the earmarking of a further area of one-and-three-quarter square miles of Arusha-occupied land to meet the need for urban expansion consequent on Arusha town becoming the base for the new East African Community in 1967.

6 There is, as yet, no really good account available of the Masai age organization or of the social system: the most useful is Fosbrooke, 1948. But Jacobs, 1965, is preferable if it can be consulted.

7 In Kenya, as compared with Tanzania, many Masai seem to be poised on the verge of accepting major innovations in their pastoral and economic organization. Although, in the past, many policies and schemes of successive Kenya governments have been failures, a great deal has been learned as a result. It appears that modern range-type and co-operative schemes may soon be put into operation, with the assistance of international agency funds and specialized personnel. No less importantly, it appears that the Masai themselves welcome these projects as being within the realm of feasibility and advantage. In Tanzania, on the other hand, it may be that frontal attacks on certain external items of Masai culture (e.g. dress and decorations—symbols of their conservative commitment) may only convince the people once again of the threat to their lives by unreasonable outsiders.

REFERENCES

FLATT, D. C. 1967, 'Changing Religious Institutions Among the Ilarusa and the Relevance of the Gospel', unpub. MS., Chicago.

FOSBROOKE, H. A. 1948, 'An Administrative Survey of the Masai Social System', *Tanganyika Notes & Records*, 26.

1956, 'The Masai Age-Group System as a Guide to Tribal Chronology', *African Studies*, 15, 4.

GULLIVER, P. H. 1962, 'The Evolution of Arusha Trade', in Bohannan, P. & Dalton, G. (eds.), *Markets in Africa*, Northwestern University Press, Evanston.

1963, *Social Control in an African Society*, Routledge & Kegan Paul (Boston University Press).

JACOBS, A. H. 1965, 'The Traditional Political Organization of the Pastoral Masai', Oxford University, D.Phil. thesis.

STAHL, K. 1964, *History of the Chagga Peoples of Kilimanjaro*, Mouton, The Hague.

SONGS OF
THE RWENZURURU REBELLION

The Konzo Revolt against the Toro
in Western Uganda

Kirsten Alnaes

THE Konzo (Bakonjo) are a minority tribe in Toro District, Western Uganda. Together with the neighbouring Amba, they have been administered by the Toro Kingdom since the British introduced indirect rule in the area by the Toro Agreement of 1900.

In 1962, when the new Toro Agreement was being prepared, the Konzo and Amba submitted a claim for equal status with the Toro within the Agreement. This was refused by the Toro government, and subsequently the Konzo and Amba broke out in open revolt. Simultaneously they submitted a claim to the Uganda Central Government that their area should be declared a separate District, to be named Rwenzururu. This claim has not been granted, although it is still being pressed.

I will here describe how the songs which were composed in connection with the revolt reflect the attitudes of the Konzo in the different phases of the revolt. I will argue that the rebel songs serve as an idiom through which the rebel leadership and their followers express their attitudes and feelings towards the rebellion and their own position in it. By analysing the songs in order of composition, and juxtaposing them with the corresponding phase in the revolt, one gets a doubly-evidenced picture of the line of development of the revolt. My argument is dependent on the exact dating of the songs, and I have, as far as possible, established the dates as correct. The songs on which I base my analysis were composed during the period from a couple of years before the outbreak until 1967. Some of the songs were sung to me by a group of Konzo schoolboys in Kampala in 1964, some were sung by the composers, but the bulk were recorded during a visit to the area in 1967. My analysis is based on information from Konzo both in the area and outside.[1]

Analysis of the rebel songs shows that in the course of its short existence the Rwenzururu rebel movement has gone through a series of phases. At the outset, the Konzo were powerless in the face of their overlords. In this state of subjection, they could only *dream* of ultimate justice which they would achieve in heaven, a dream which is a reflection of modern, christian ideas. The second phase of the revolt was 'reformist', as the Konzo and Amba demanded *equality* with the Toro within the existing Toro administrative system. This demand was turned down, and the revolt entered its third phase. The Konzo and Amba seceded from the Toro Kingdom and demanded control over their own area. This was also refused, and the revolt entered a phase which I would call *'the crisis of action'*. Until then, all aggression had been canalized into non-violent activities; now, however, it turned into a violent rebellion. Violence and bloodshed did not bring the Rwenzururians nearer to their goal, and after a time the rebels withdrew up into the mountains or down into the Semliki forest. In the course of this phase of *withdrawal*, the Konzo returned to their *dream* about ultimate justice which one day will be achieved. This time, however, they abandoned their christian dream and turned to the traditional dream of the promised kingdom which had been promised at the end of the nineteenth century.

Although the Rwenzururu revolt has been a joint action by the Konzo and the Amba, I will here refer mainly to the Konzo part of it, since all the songs I analyse are Konzo, and most of my informants were Konzo.

The rebellion

The Konzo live in the foothills of the Ruwenzori Mountains and on the plains to the south. On the western slopes they share an administrative county with the Amba; on the southern slopes Konzo comprise the majority of the inhabitants; and in the east they are a minority in mainly Toro counties. In 1959 there were in the Toro kingdom 103,868 Konzo and 32,866 Amba—a total of 136,734 as against 183,492 Toro. Counties and sub-counties, the administrative units of the kingdom, are each headed by a chief and his council, and sections of a sub-county have lesser chiefs. All county chiefs were Toro until the early 1960s, when an Amba was appointed county chief in Bwamba county. Over the years there have been a few Konzo and Amba sub-county chiefs, but as late as 1963 there were only six of these in a total of thirty-eight sub-counties in the whole kingdom.[2]

The Toro language has been used in all matters at county and sub-county levels—in courts and councils, and also in schools and churches. Toro predominated among the Toro kingdom's officials, the majority of teachers were Toro, and the medical service was almost exclusively staffed by Toro. Thus there were few opportunities for Konzo and Amba in the local administration, and they resented the fact that they had little say in the running of their own affairs. Just prior to the rebellion, they saw all Toro actions in the light of their own inferior position. They felt that the Toro treated them in a high-handed and arrogant fashion. Toro teachers were suspected of teaching Konzo pupils badly so as deliberately to keep them from being educated; and Toro chiefs were said to exploit their positions by forcing the Konzo traditional elders to allocate land which was most suitable for coffee-growing to Toro immigrants. From the time the British arrived in the area, the Konzo looked to them for protection. In the late 1950s I often heard them say: 'We are safe here as long as the British are here. When they go, the Toro will cut our throats'. Significantly, the rebellion broke out in 1962, only a couple of months before the British were to leave.

There had been an early attempt, in 1919, by the Konzo to rise against the Toro. Both this rising and the present one were allegedly prophesied by a medium in the late 1890s. During field-work in 1958–60 I never heard the earlier rising mentioned at all; but in 1967, the story of the 1919 rising and the two heroes, Tibamwenda and Nyamutswa, who were

hanged in 1921, were mentioned very frequently. After the
effects of the first rising had subsided, there was no direct
opposition to Toro overlordship until the early 1960s.
The forerunner of the later rebellion was 'The Bakonjo Life
History Research Rwenzori', formed in the early 1950s.
Isaya Mukirane, a young schoolteacher, was the most important figure in the foundation and later development of this
history society. Another figure was Samwiri Bukombe, a very
influential man at that time. He had been sub-county chief in
Bwamba from 1931–42, and had become one of the wealthi-
est men in the area. After his retirement, Bukombe began to
write down Konzo history in the Toro language. The young
men around Mukirane were teachers, clerks, and farmers,
with a certain amount of schooling. Most of them belonged
to the Church Missionary Society. Despite their relatively
superior education they turned to the older generation for
advice, and appointed three men as advisers. One of these was
Bukombe. It is of importance that some supporters and advisers of the older generation, including Bukombe, were
influential men who had no possibility of achieving senior
positions in the persisting, indigenous, political organization.

After about a year Mukirane established branches of the
society in all parts of the Konzo country, and he formed his
'Special Committee Bakonjo Life History Research Rwenzori' with himself as the chairman, and the central office in
Bwamba. Every branch of the history society had its representatives on this Special Committee. At the end of 1956
an additional branch was formed in the adjacent area of the
Congo.

Despite the very obvious Konzo nationalist tendencies of
the history society, the most fervent members of it were at the
same time most anxious to appear like the Toro. Many had
adopted Toro as their language, saying that they had forgotten
their own language since they could much more adequately
express themselves in Toro. They ignored circumcision because
they wanted to be like Toro who, unlike the Konzo, have
never practised it. They wanted to emphasize, by adopting
Toro customs, that a Konzo could be just as good as a Toro.
There was also much emphasis in the society on modern,
Western values. As far as we could gather at the time, the

general Konzo attitude to Mukirane and the history society varied. The younger people sympathized with him. The older members of the society showed some opposition to him, while others were either indifferent or seemed to regard him and his society suspiciously.

At the 1961 elections to the Toro Parliament, the Konzo and Amba got twenty-one seats. Among those elected were Mukirane and two Amba, Y. Kawamara and P. Mupalya. The parliament appointed a Constitutional Committee to draft the new Toro Agreement, but no Konzo or Amba representatives were included in this. After protests, Mukirane and Kawamara were appointed to the Committee. The Konzo and Amba representatives in the parliament then submitted a memorandum to the Toro king and government asking for the inclusion of the names Bakonjo and Baamba in the new Agreement alongside the name, Batoro—for they desired to be acknowledged as equals with the Toro and to get their own chiefs. This demand was refused. The Konzo and Amba representatives then prepared a petition to the Governor of Uganda, demanding a separate District, Rwenzururu.

The Toro government did not change its attitude to these demands. At the meeting of the parliament on 13 March 1962, when the report was read on negotiations with the central government, seventeen out of the twenty-one Konzo and Amba representatives staged a walk-out. Shortly after, Mukirane, Kawamara and Mupalya were arrested and charged with insulting the Toro king. They were sentenced to eight months' imprisonment, but were released on bail in July pending their appeal to the Uganda High Court, and ordered to remain in the vicinity of Kampala meanwhile. They were joined there by a group of Konzo and Amba, many of whom were previous members of the Toro parliament. Together they prepared a memorandum in which they outlined their grievances and explained their demand for a separate district. This was presented to the Uganda Minister of Regional Affairs on 31 August 1962.

Mukirane stayed in Kampala until October, when he suddenly returned home. In November, when he was called for the appeal case, he refused to attend. He thus became an 'outlaw' and remained in the Ruwenzori Mountains until he died in August 1966. The other two men lost their appeal and served the remaining four months' imprisonment.

In August 1962 the first wave of violence swept the area. The first incidents of violence were directed against Toro chiefs. After about three weeks the violence subsided. The Uganda Government appointed a Commission of Inquiry which submitted its report on 10 October 1962. As long as the Commission was at work, the area was relatively quiet; but violence broke out again in November. A state of emergency was declared in the Konzo and Amba country in February 1963. Under the emergency regulations the Uganda Government took over direct administration there. Government Agents replaced Toro chiefs, and Special Force units of the Uganda Police and companies of the Uganda Rifles were stationed there. Despite these measures there was an average of thirty-five to forty incidents of violence per month between Konzo and Amba on the one hand and Toro on the other. The rebels did not recognize the Agents, regarding them as working indirectly for the Toro. Thus they attacked and victimized the Agents just as they attacked the Toro and those of their own people whom they suspected of supporting the Toro. Toro immigrants were forced to leave Konzo and Amba country.

During the period between the main outbreaks of violence in 1962 and 1964, Mukirane consolidated his position. His headquarters were in the southern mountains, from where he made frequent visits to the Congo side of the border. He established the Rwenzururu Kingdom Government with himself as king, surrounded by a council of ministers. His kingdom was divided into administrative units on the Toro pattern, but with Konzo names. The Rwenzururu chiefs had the same duties as Toro chiefs. Mukirane set up his own army and police, and organized schools in the mountains. He tried to get his earlier colleagues to join him: some of them came and stayed, others were unwilling to work under the conditions he could offer. Those who refused had to leave the area for fear of reprisals. The traditional Konzo system appears to have operated in conjunction with the Rwenzururu administration. Rwenzururu leaders often used the houses of traditional elders for their meetings. This might indicate that Mukirane needed the elders and their influence; but possibly the elders expected that they might expose themselves to violence if they antagonized the rebel leadership.

When Mukirane established his kingdom, some of his followers forsook him, stayed in the lowlands, and continued to press for a separate district by submitting memoranda to the Uganda Government. Some informants said that the splinter-group disagreed with Mukirane on the necessity of violence. Others had accused him of going beyond their original aims in establishing a kingdom in the mountains: they had joined him to fight for a separate district, not for a kingdom.

On 8 February 1964 some of the early leaders, including Kawamara and Mupalya, were detained by the Uganda Government. In June 1964 there was another wave of violence.[3] Most of this occurred on the eastern side of the mountain where Toro settlement bordered Konzo country. Elsewhere in Konzo country there were scarcely any Toro left. People whom the rebels accused of collaboration with Toro were attacked, and some were killed. When the violence temporarily subsided Konzo villagers remained open to attack from three sides: from the Toro, who struck very violently; from members of the police and army, who behaved with great brutality in their hunt for rebels; and from the rebels themselves, who 'punished' people who did not appear to support the rebellion.

Since 1964 there has been no major outburst of violence, and tension in the area has gradually subsided. The State of Emergency was terminated at the beginning of 1965, but the Uganda Government continued to administer the area. In the middle of 1965 the detained leaders were released and came back home.

In 1967 the situation was that the Konzo rebels and their followers had withdrawn to the mountains, where they lived in what might be called a 'stagnant rebellion'. This they could do fairly undisturbed since their terrain offers them excellent natural protection. The administrative system established by Mukirane continued to operate: the chiefs collected taxes, and courts and schools worked. Supplies of food and consumer goods were brought to the mountains by the women going to the lowlands markets. Since Rwenzururians paid no taxes to the Uganda Government, the able-bodied men dared not come to the lower areas for fear of arrest by the police. Government institutions, such as dispensaries, were generally boycotted and only the more serious cases were taken for medical treatment. People on the lower parts of the mountain were in a difficult position. They were within reach both of Government and Rwenzururu forces. As long as they gave the rebel leadership no reason to think they were actively co-operating with the Government they were left alone. But a Konzo who took a Government job went in fear of reprisals. Loyal Rwenzururu supporters tried to avoid paying taxes to the Government, but some people have chosen to pay taxes to both sides in order to be left in peace.

Near the headquarters of Government administration lived people who had made themselves unpopular with the rebels and who dared not move into rebel country. Many of these, regarded as 'stooges' or 'traitors', were people who had taken work for the Government or the Toro. This was not clear-cut, however. Some people in Government posts could move freely in the mountains; others, though they had never worked directly for the Government or the Toro, were suspected of betraying the rebel cause. Many of Mukirane's early followers and members of the history society were now in Government posts.

To the majority of Konzo the word Rwenzururu symbolized freedom from the Toro. Most Konzo were convinced that any co-operation with Toro would eventually lead to subjugation. The Konzo rebel leadership stood for continued non-co-operation, and they were not willing to compromise. Thus they could still count on the general support of the majority of Konzo, although opinion varied about the inner politics of Rwenzururu.

Analysis of the rebel songs

First, I will refer to the role of songs among the Konzo in general. There are two main types of songs: those sung in an institutional context—for instance, being part of a ritual. These I refer to as 'traditional songs'. They, or at least their main themes, are known by most Konzo, and they are learnt as part of general upbringing. Second, there are songs composed as a response to a particular event. I refer to these as 'popular songs'. They usually spread as 'hits'; everyone sings them for a while and then they disappear again. The composer is not usually known. These popular songs can be regarded as part of a news-service in that they give information about new events. They may also be regarded as a means of maintaining common values in that they indicate the common attitude to the events in question.

The structure of traditional and popular songs is roughly the same. Both types utilize play on words, and both are open to free improvisation. They use the same stylistic devices, such as the repetition of a name or phrase. There is no limit to the length of a song: that is entirely up to the singer and his inspiration.

The rebel songs diverge in certain respects from this common pattern. In style they are nearer to European songs or modern East African songs than to ordinary Konzo songs. Many of them are composed to the tune of a hymn or a similar type of song. In a song in European style, the text is usually fixed. Here the element of improvisation comes in through an additional verse which may be composed on the spur of the moment to suit the situation. There is little play on words. That is to say, these songs have adopted a new style, similar to that in other areas of Africa which deals with problems of party politics, wage labour, unemployment, etc. The Konzo rebellion was initiated by young men of the Konzo-educated élite who put an emphasis on modern values. They therefore seem to have chosen a form of expression which corresponds with their own outlook, rather than the traditional style of their own society.

At one point the Rwenzururu administration decided to establish committees which were to be attached to the administrative centres and whose duty it was to compose songs. I was told that 'when the administration has made a decision, they take their decision to their committee which then turns the message into a song'. Thus the Rwenzururu leadership deliberately utilizes songs for propaganda and to spread information. Most of the rebel songs are sung by the younger generation, the schoolchildren and young educated people; but they are known by most Konzo.

The first song to be analysed is one which took its theme from the biblical parable of Lazarus and the rich man.

Lazarus and the Rich Man

1 Long ago there was a rich man
He dressed in beautiful clothes
He was never short of food
He always had good meals.
Reward.
Reward came to Lazarus
He was taken from earth to heaven.
Reward.

2 At his door there was a man
His name was Lazarus
He slept outside
He had many sores.
Reward.
Reward came to Lazarus
He was taken from earth to heaven.
Reward.

3 The poor man ate the crumbs
Which fell from the master's table
The dogs licked
The sores of Lazarus
Reward.
Reward came to Lazarus
He was taken from earth to heaven.
Reward.

4 After a few days
The poor man Lazarus died
He was taken to the land
The land of Abraham.
Reward.
Reward came to Lazarus
He was taken from earth to heaven.
Reward

5 The wealthy man died
He was thrown on the fire of hell
When he lifted his eyes
He saw Lazarus.
In the land of heaven
Lazarus is in a state of grace.
Sorrow.

The rich man's sorrow was
That wealth has no profit.
Sorrow.

6 Lazarus said to him:
There are many obstacles in the land
You cannot come to me
Nor can I come to you.
Sorrow.
The rich man's sorrow was
That wealth has no profit.
Sorrow.

The song gained popularity in the Konzo area in the early 1960s, before the outbreak of rebellion. Although it may not have been meant as a political song, I regard it as significant in expressing the Konzo feeling about their position at that time. The singer introduced it to me: 'The song is about the rich man who lived long ago. It is about the sufferings of Lazarus. The rich man mistreated him.'

As noted earlier, the Konzo resented their inferior position *vis-à-vis* the Toro; but, like Lazarus in the song, they felt powerless in the face of Toro overrule. They were not thinking in terms of active opposition; they merely lamented their fate. In this state of passive, powerless inferiority, the only hope for justice appears to be in the life hereafter. In the song this is clearly expressed in the refrain: 'Reward came to Lazarus. He was taken from earth to heaven'; and later: 'The rich man's sorrow was that wealth has no profit'. In heaven the roles are reversed. Lazarus has obtained reward after his sufferings at the rich man's door. The rich man has lost what gave him power, namely his wealth. He is now forced to look at Lazarus in a state of bliss which he will never be able to obtain for himself. He can only look at Lazarus 'In the land of heaven'. Lazarus, on the other hand, feels power for the first time when he tells the rich man: 'There are many obstacles in the land/ You cannot come to me/Nor can I come to you.'

A song which appeared at about the same time was *Love makes the Burden Light*. Here we find similar expressions of hope for ultimate justice and peace. The hereafter is now symbolized by the coming of the saviour, Jesus. I will quote only the first verse in full:

KIRSTEN ALNAES

On the day when Jesus comes
Light will appear in the sky
All those who do not know him are going to cry
Love makes the burden light.
/Refrain:/Love makes the burden light
Love makes the burden light
Jesus' death restored our life
Love makes the burden light.

The other verses deal with other aspects of the coming of the saviour. The last verse promises sorrow for many people in the country:

On the day when Jesus comes
Sorrow will come to the land
All those who do not know him are going to cry.

The song was composed in 1960 and I heard it shortly after it had first appeared. The 'sorrow in the land' and 'all those who do not know him' referred indirectly to the Toro who were going to cry when salvation had been obtained by the Konzo. As in the song about Lazarus and the rich man, the roles are reversed after the saviour has come. The song was still sung in 1967, and the singers explained it to me like this: 'The Toro made us suffer. But then we said: "On the day when we rejoice, the Toro will cry here". This was while they were still troubling us.'

Similar feelings of hopeless lack of power are expressed in the Rwenzururu National Anthem.

Rwenzururu National Anthem

1 Our Rwenzururu, our Rwenzururu
Our Rwenzururu, the land we cry for
Where are you now?
When we think of how you were
Tears flow.

2 Our language, our language
Our language from long hence
Where has it gone?
Now it has turned into Torro
Omwatsi has become *amakuru*.[4]

254

The song dates from before the outbreak of rebellion and is a lament over the country which was lost. The anthem does not mention the possibility of regaining their country; instead, the Konzo can only let the tears flow. In the second verse the Konzo also lament their language, for which the Toro had substituted their own. The 'loss' of their language was one of the main grievances of the Konzo before the rebellion. Similarly, the regaining of the Konzo language is one of the most cherished results of the rebellion in the minds of many of the people.

The following is one of the first songs to appear after the Konzo and Amba had walked out of the Toro Parliament and had adopted a more militant and less resigned attitude.

When the Time Came

1 When the time came
The Europeans told us:
'There are going to be direct elections
You must elect those whom you trust.'

2 When it was time for election
The Toro prime minister rose
He said: 'Elect people of action
It is of no use to elect people
Who are going to sleep all the time.'

3 When it was time for election
The Konzo elected Isaya
The Amba elected Kawamara and Mupalya
They became their representatives.

4 When Parliament came in session
The representatives suggested:
'Since we are not mentioned in the 1900 Agreement
Let us make a new agreement today.'

5 But the Toro refused it
The Amba and Konzo opposed them:
'Today you refused to incorporate us in the constitution
We are therefore going to break away from you.'

6 The representatives staged a walk-out
They told the news to the people
'The Toro have refused to incorporate us in the agreement
We have therefore broken away.'

7 People encouraged them: 'You go ahead
They will give us our Rwenzururu
We cannot continue to be oppressed
We have no say when we are among the Toro.'

This song is an account of the events leading up to the walk-out from the Toro Parliament and the decision to secede from the Toro kingdom. It describes the preparations for the elections to the Toro Parliament, and how the three men who were elected emerged as leaders of the secessionist movement. In the fifth verse the representatives are quoted as saying, when they walk out of Parliament, 'We are therefore going to break away from you', using a form of the verb which refers to the near future. In the sixth verse, however, when the leaders tell the news to the people, they say, 'We have therefore broken away', using the perfect tense of the verb. This may indicate that the composer wishes to emphasize that it is the leaders who took the decision, and that the people followed them. Thus the importance of strong leadership and of the people's support are emphasized in those verses. It is likely that this song was deliberately put into circulation in order to inform and influence the Konzo at a crucial stage of the rebellion.

The next song, *Konzo, Stay No Longer Motionless*, contains the first indications that the Konzo attitude towards their position is beginning to change.[5]

Konzo, Stay No Longer Motionless

Konzo, be no longer uncertain
/Refrain:/ *Ipapa na leo kolengo*[6]
Konzo, be no longer uncertain
Uganda is led by Obote
Tanganyika is led by Kawawa
And Kenya is led by Kenyatta
Rwenzururu is led by Isaya
Friends, we are in danger
Friends, what is destroying us?
Thus spoke Isaya before he left us:
'Here I am, elect me for the task
I will bring you work on the land.'

Work which he spoke of before he left
Work which will bring us Rwenzururu
Friends, we are in danger
Friends, what is destroying us?
Konzo, we are in danger
Friends, be no longer uncertain.

The reference to Kawawa's premiership in Tanganyika and to the fact that Mukirane had left (i.e. for the mountains) indicate that the song was composed in the latter part of 1962. The song is in a style which is common in other parts of East Africa. Although I was told that the title of the song was *Konzo, Stay No Longer Motionless (Bakonzo, muleke ihanda)*, in fact the first line, as I heard it, is slightly different: 'Konzo, be no longer uncertain' (*Bakonzo, muleke iganya*). An informant explained that *eriganya* is 'to be uncertain, confused'. When children do something against their father's will and the father asks who did it, all children will defend themselves by denying their offence. *Erihanda* is to 'deny out of fear, to be inactive out of fear'. Thus the first line of the song, as well as the title, exhort Konzo to get out of their confused, passive condition and to act. They are assured that Isaya leads them, just as the three East African countries are led by their statesmen. Nevertheless, the song expresses a gnawing feeling of insecurity: 'Friends, we are in danger. Friends, what is destroying us?' The song seems to indicate a certain ambivalence which became apparent after the Konzo had adopted their new policy of activist opposition. On the one hand they were afraid to give up the relative safety which their inactivity had afforded them, but on the other hand they saw the necessity for action and fight.

At the beginning of 1963 the two Amba leaders, Kawamara and Mupalya, were released from prison and came back to the area, where they stayed until they were placed into detention. They were given a great welcome, for the Amba and Konzo seem to have drawn the conclusion that they had come back after signing an agreement with the Uganda Government to the effect that Rwenzururu was to become a separate district. One of the songs composed at this time was:

All of us Here

1 All of us here
Friends, we are filled with joy
Because of the visitors who have come
And I, I am delighted.
/Refrain :/Our joy is great
It is our companions who have arrived.

2 You Toro, I cannot imagine
Where you will be going
You will soon be overcome by shame
Rwenzururu has now come to us.
/Refrain/

3 You, who opposed Rwenzururu
You will soon be overcome by shame
Rwenzururu which we cried for
We have now obtained.
/Refrain/

4 Friends, we are going to rejoice
We will sing about our joy
All of us here.
Friends, let us clap our hands
We will all rejoice
We have achieved Rwenzururu.
/Refrain/

5 Friends, let us clap our hands
Rwenzururu which we admire
Friends, it has come to us
Friends, we will welcome it.
/Refrain/

The singers introduced the song to me: 'Now we will sing a song which was sung to welcome Kawamara and Mupalya when the Government had cheated them, saying they had been given Rwenzururu'. It is a praise-song for the two returning leaders, and it reflects the exuberance of the people at the thought of their newly obtained freedom. This song immediately became a 'hit', and was sung at political meetings throughout the Konzo part of Bwamba county. Note that the attitude towards the Toro is one of reproach rather than aggression. There seems to be no feeling of revenge or wish for retaliation on the part of the Konzo: the Toro are merely to be overcome by shame.

A similar note of optimistic cheerfulness appears in the following song which appeared at about the same time.

Our Lovely Rwenzururu

1 Our lovely Rwenzururu
Friends, it is our country
We cried for it when the Toro rejoiced.
/Refrain/
But on the day when we call it our own
Truly we will sing cha cha cha.[7]

2 The Toro came and raided our country
They extracted poll tax from us
But Nyamutswa did not agree to this.
But on the day when we call it our own
Truly we will sing cha cha cha

3 The Toro caught Nyamutswa
They also got Tibamwenda
They dug a grave where they both were put.
But on the day when we will call it our own
Truly we will sing cha cha cha.

4 Then our man, Isaya, appeared
He reminded us of our past
He began by writing books, and today we
                    will have free elections.
But on the day when we call it our own
Truly we will sing cha cha cha.

This song was still popular in 1967, and I heard several versions of it. The versions which I recorded were identical; the only difference was that the verse about the coming of Isaya appeared in only one of them. This may be accounted for by the fact that after Mukirane's death people did not sing about him at all. One informant put it like this: 'When Isaya died, our hearts became filled with grief. We sat down, we could do nothing else. While he was alive, we sang to praise him; but after his death we could only cry because now when he is dead we may be taken over by the Toro again'.

The song, *Our Lovely Rwenzururu*, mentions the leaders of both the first and second revolts. The two early leaders were killed, but Isaya is described in such a way that one would believe he was going to carry the rebellion through. The song is only one of many which are concerned with the first rebellion. I was told that many of the present songs about the two heroes of the past are based on old, traditional epics about the event. It is interesting to note that the Konzo have only recently begun to recollect this first revolt. This is perhaps a way in which they justify the present state of rebellion. They identify themselves with the heroes, only with the difference that they are going to accomplish what the earlier rebels had failed to achieve.

In *Our Lovely Rwenzururu* there is no bitterness. The lines about the Toro raids and the death of the two early rebels are told in a direct, almost dry manner. And the Konzo's cheerful hope of independence recurs in every refrain, which is repeated twice, and which therefore permeates and colours the whole song with its optimism.

A song which dates roughly from the same time makes a point of showing the equality of Rwenzururu with the kingdoms of Uganda.

A Song About the Leaders of Uganda
(Abwolikyonga)

/Refrain:/Konzo/Amba—Rwenzururu[8]
The Kabaka is the leader of the Ganda
Kyabazinga is the leader of the Soga
The Nyoro have their king
The Konzo have an old man
I alone have an old man
The Ankole have a king
We all have Obote
All of you must help me.

Another version runs as follows:

There are Many Tribes in Uganda
(Version by Stephen Bwambale & chorus)

There are many tribes in Uganda
/Refrain:/Konzo/Amba are saying[8]
There are the Ganda, their leader is the Kabaka

260

Father of the people is the leader of the Soga
The Nyoro have their king, mama
The Nyankole have their king
The Toro have their king
The Nyoro have a good king
Rwenzururu has an old man
Rwenzururu has an old man
Uganda is beautiful, mama.

The song was composed by a young school-teacher and musician, Mr Abwolikyonga, who was a member of the Bakonjo Life History Research Rwenzori, and took part in the drafting of the early letters to the Central Government about a separate district. Later he left Mukirane on the question of the necessity of violence, and was therefore regarded as a collaborator by the rebel leadership.

This song also became very popular over large parts of the Konzo area. I heard it sung by the schoolboys in Kampala as well as by the composer himself. It is composed in the same modern East African style which I mentioned earlier. The two versions I heard do not differ very much. They are both mainly a catalogue of the traditional kings of Uganda and their countries, and both refer to the leader of Rwenzururu with the honorary title 'old man' (*omusiakulu*), without mentioning his name. There are, however, a few differences which might be significant. The composer called it 'A Song about the Leaders in Uganda'. In his version there is no mention of tribes, only kingdoms and their leaders, and he equals Rwenzururu with these kingdoms because Rwenzururu has an 'old man'. In other words, he wants to emphasize the equality of the Konzo with a kingdom, which is another way of claiming equality with the Toro. Furthermore, in the composer's version, he stresses the unity of Uganda by saying that 'We all have Obote'. This emphasis on equality with the Toro and on the unity of Uganda reflects the more moderate attitude among the Konzo.

The schoolboys introduced the song slightly differently from the composer. They said: 'This is a song which tells us that there are many tribes in Uganda'. And the first line of their version says just this. The schoolboys did not sing the line about being united under Obote; instead they refer to the beauty of Uganda. This may be significant. Both versions were sung to me in 1964. The composer had retained the earlier attitude of non-violent reform aiming at equality, while the schoolboys regarded themselves as supporters of Mukirane. One feature of Mukirane's approach was to turn against the Central Government and their agents in the area. Thus the version which the schoolboys sang may reflect a rejection of the more moderate attitude of the original song.

The years 1963 and 1964 were tense and troubled for the Konzo villagers. They constantly feared attacks by Police and Army, and by the Toro and also reprisals from some of their own people. If people expected raids they fled into the bush and left their homes unattended. Gardens and fields were destroyed and food was scarce. One song, by Obwolikyonga, which especially concerns itself with this side of the rebellion is:

The Country is Ruined

1 The country is ruined
  Everything is spoilt
  My dear, we have to go and hide.

2 They caught my father's younger brother
  His young wife had hidden in the bush
  His younger brother has taken refuge
  My dear, we have to go and hide.

3 When you hide, you leave everything behind
  You only bring the radio
  The goats are left without care
  My dear, we have to go and hide.

This song was composed at the end of 1963. It is a lament for the country which is ruined because of the disturbances. The second verse describes how 'they' have caught father's brother and how members of the family have to seek refuge in the bush. The third verse shows how one has to leave everything behind when one has to flee. The goats are left behind without care; the only thing one can manage to take is the radio. It is worth noting that the song does not indicate who the attackers are. Mr Abwolikyonga told me that he composed the song because he was deeply depressed about the sufferings which innocent people had to endure. The villagers are helplessly exposed to attacks and suffer heavy losses. The song is a description of the fate of the Konzo non-combatants, a fate they share with civilians in any war.

The new outburst of violence which occurred in 1964 created a feeling of despair in many Konzo. One song which was composed at the time reflects this utter despondency.

The Year 1964

1 The year of 1964
Brought us disaster
The disaster overwhelmed us and destroyed our people.

2 There are many Konzo
Who died for Rwenzururu
But the first of them all was Watsurawa.

3 All of us here
Are also going to die
There is not a single man who is not going to die.

The death toll in 1964 was very high. Watsurawa, who is mentioned in the song, was shot during the riot on 31 August 1962 in Busaro market in Bwamba. Many Konzo maintain that the original intention had not been to kill, but to make trouble, and that Watsurawa's death released strong, pent-up feelings which led to the use of violence and resulted in suffering and heavy losses. In the eyes of the composer, all Konzo are going to share Watsurawa's fate.

However, at the same time as this song was composed, two militant songs appear. The songs originated on a spur in Bwamba county where people are well known for their musical abilities, and were in the process of spreading when I heard them in 1964. In these two songs there is no mention of a reward in the life hereafter; moreover, it is no longer a question of obtaining equality with the Toro—i.e. equality within the existing system. The rebels demand their own country, and they are fighting to obtain it here on earth.

A Song to Honour Isaya

1 Let us honour Isaya
The leader of Rwenzururu
He who claims Rwenzururu
Our country which was lost
Isaya deserves our gratitude.

2 Long ago the Toro
Mistreated us
But now we have the power
To show them our contempt
Leader Isaya deserves our gratitude.

3 Amba and Konzo
Praise Isaya
The hero of Rwenzururu
Rwenzururu which we admire
Truly Isaya has the power.

4 Honour is to Isaya
He who claims our country
Let us show Isaya our gratitude.

In the first verse, Mukirane is praised as the one who took the
initiative to restore Rwenzururu. Then the composer describes
how the Konzo had been mistreated by the Toro, 'but now
we have the power to show them our contempt'. Isaya Mukirane gets the credit for reclaiming Rwenzururu for the Konzo,
and he is attributed as a powerful leader. The unity of Rwenzururu is strongly emphasized. Although the Konzo have
regarded themselves as one people, they were never strongly
united politically. It is significant that one of the first things
Mukirane did after taking over the leadership of the Bakonjo
Life History Research Rwenzori was to extend the history
society to all parts of Konzo country. This is likely to have been
a conscious attempt to create amongst the Konzo a sense of
political unity which he considered an element essential to the
later opposition against the Toro.

The song introduces new concepts which may indicate a
new phase in Konzo nationalism. Words like 'power' and
'contempt' in relation to the Toro have not been mentioned
earlier. That these words are introduced in this song is an
indication that the Konzo rebels have completely shed their

earlier, moderate claim for acceptance as equals. The Konzo rebels want to assert their own identity. They have moved far beyond the claim for equality; they want to stress that they are *better* than the enemy, that they have power to treat him as he used to treat them. The roles are reversed again, but this time on earth (cf. *Lazarus and the Rich Man*). Power is attributed both to Mukirane and to the Konzo as a people (see verses 4 and 2), but it is clear from the context that the Konzo owe this newly-found 'power' to Mukirane. It is interesting to note that in the Konzo text Mukirane is referred to as *omwami*, a word which is commonly used for chief or leader in many parts of Uganda, and not the traditional Konzo term *omusiakulu*, by which he was referred to earlier. One must bear in mind that although rebellion is a recent phenomenon in Konzo society, it is a common phenomenon in contemporary Africa. The Konzo rebels have shown that they want to be associated with other African peoples in their struggle for freedom. They also demonstrated this in their emphasis on modern values in the history society, and by the style they chose for their songs. It is therefore in accordance with their way of thinking to call the leader by a term which is much used outside their own territory.

The next rebel song I discuss summarizes the attitude to the Toro at the time. It also gives a vivid picture of the situation in the Konzo area.

The Konzo Fought Like Men

1 We can prove that the Konzo fought like men
They put down their spears, they threw stones.
/Refrain:/To kill, to kill, to kill, to kill, to kill the Toro.

2 A Konzo, try to fight him, he is a man of strength
He truly fought the herons, he does not know fear.
/Refrain:/To kill, to kill, to kill, to kill, to kill the herons.

3 In the county of Busongora the Konzo fought
They killed a heron there.
/Refrain:/Many, many people were killed with guns.

4 In our county Bwamba the Konzo fought
They beat the herons who again killed us.
/Refrain:/Many, many people were killed with guns.

265

KIRSTEN ALNAES

5 We can prove that the Toro fought like women
They called the herons in to kill the Konzo.
/Refrain:/Many, many people were killed with guns.

6 Konzo, stay no longer motionless, Rwenzururu is yours
Give the name to Konzo and Amba, stay no longer still.
/Refrain:/Many, many people were killed with guns.

The title of the song, *The Konzo Fought Like Men*, reflects the
militant attitude which pervades the song. In the first verse it
is stated that 'We can prove that the Konzo fought like men',
and their intention is 'To kill . . . the Toro'. But the Toro are
no longer the only enemy. The second verse recounts how the
Konzo are also fighting the herons—a nickname for the emergency forces—with the intention of killing them. The third
and fourth verses refer to fights with the emergency forces.
It is an uneven fight, however. One member of the emergency
forces is mentioned as having been killed by the Konzo, while
'Many, many people were killed with guns' on the Konzo side.
In the fifth verse the Toro are described as effeminate weaklings
who cannot fight their own battle, but had to call in the
emergency forces to do it for them. The last verse begins with
the incitement to action which was used in the song, *Konzo,
Stay No Longer Motionless*. The Konzo are assured that 'Rwenzururu is yours/Give the name to the Konzo and Amba', but
the refrain still goes, 'Many, many people were killed with guns'.

The attitude expressed in this song is a far cry from the
Konzo self-identification with the poor man who got his reward
in heaven, and from the feeling of anxiety expressed in the
lines: 'Friends, we are in danger/Friends, what is destroying
us?' The Konzo rebels are now engaged in open fight with the
Toro and those who fight the Toro's battle. As in the previous
song it is emphasized that the Konzo are much *better* than the
Toro. The Toro are described as weaklings, while the strength
of the Konzo is repeatedly stressed. It should be noted that
the incitement to *kill* the enemy has not appeared in any of the
previous songs. The Konzo rebels seem to have developed an
attitude which is the reverse of the attitude they had at the
outset of the rebellion. They emphasize their strength and
their bravery. One may say that the song is an incitement to
fight; the rebels have come down to earth and the only way

266

in which they may obtain their freedom is to fight for it, not ask for it. This militancy and determination is also reflected in more recent songs. The song, *There is Power in our Mountains*, emphasizes that the Konzo now rule themselves. I only briefly outline the theme here. The Konzo have established their own country. They thank God for the help he gave by bestowing upon them the power to chase the Toro out of their territory. Everybody has contributed, 'The fathers and the mothers, all of us we have/Power in our mountains'.

The attitude that the Konzo will continue to rule their country and that they are not going to be persuaded into co-operation with the Toro again, is described in one of the latest songs which was very popular in Bwamba in the middle of 1967.

We have taken the Power from the Toro

And even if they drop a bomb
/Refrain:/We have taken the power from the Toro.

Even if they call in the Police force
We have taken the power from the Toro.

They may bring in the K.A.R. on us, but
We have taken the power from the Toro.

If the Toro should dare to come
We have taken the power from the Toro.

They may bring in the Russians, but
We have taken the power from the Toro.

Let them bring a cannon to shoot
We have taken the power from the Toro.

Should they use their bullets on us
We have taken the power from the Toro.

This song is, unlike most of the rebel songs, in the traditional Konzo style. The versions I heard did not differ much, however, despite the singer having a much wider scope for improvisations. According to the song, the Konzo have accomplished their task, they have 'taken the power from the Toro'. However, their independence is illusory in the eyes of the outside world, and the song somehow admits this: They envisage the outside world bringing bombs, cannons, bullets, Army and Police to wrest away from them their newly found independence. But they are going to withstand this. There is no compromise, they will never give the Toro back the power over them. Instead they withdraw into their mountains, holding out against a hostile world.

In connection with this last stage of the rebellion, I would like to look more closely at Mukeri's prophecy. He described the two rebellions and, according to oral tradition, he said in this connection:

> A kingdom by the name 'Whom do I ask?' is going to come. But this will only happen after people have suffered heavy losses and many have died. Only one pregnant womb will be left. From that will appear first two, then three, then five people, all from this one womb. After them others will come and there will again be many people in the country.

One informant, commenting on this, said: 'We who live today, we see how the situation is and we say to ourselves: What Mukeri foretold has come true. The only thing we are waiting for is the coming of the promised kingdom of "Whom do I ask?" '

At the earlier stages of the rebellion I heard no mention of Mukeri's prophecy, neither was the first rebellion talked about as far as I could gather. At present, however, when the Konzo continue to hold out against outside pressure, this oral tradition is vivid in their minds. Although the forerunner for the rebel movement was a history society, the general emphasis on oral tradition among the Konzo seems only to have appeared latterly. I suggest that this is the result of the present (1967) 'unresolved', stage of the rebellion. The Konzo are no longer able to visualize any means by which they can bring about their real independence from the Toro. In this state of stagnation the Konzo turn back to their initial condition—a hope for the promised kingdom—but this time with independence partly achieved and with a strong determination not to compromise.

Conclusion

My analysis of the Rwenzururu rebel songs has revealed two things. On the one hand it shows the role of songs in a movement of this kind; on the other hand, that the songs can assist an analysis of the development of a rebel movement.

I have argued that the rebel songs express attitudes and feelings which Toro oppression, and the Konzo revolt against it, have created. The bulk of the rebel songs are composed for the Rwenzururu administration by special committees; thus one might assume that the songs reflect the leadership's attitudes as they develop and change in the course of the rebellion. By putting the songs into circulation, the leaders may persuade their followers to accept their own point of view. I would argue that the songs which spread most rapidly—the 'hits'—correspond most closely with the feelings and attitudes prevailing in the society at the time.

However, the rebel songs are not only expressions of one attitude existing only in one phase of the rebellion. Songs from different phases are still remembered and sung. This may suggest that they reflect many shades of opinion and many currents of feeling existing at the same time. I also believe that the songs serve as an emotional outlet for individual Konzo. The many and different rebel songs may reflect the often conflicting sentiments and opinions which one individual may harbour at a time when the situation demands many and frequent sacrifices of him.

Second, it is clear from this account of the Rwenzururu rebellion and my analysis of the rebel songs that the Konzo 'spirit of revolt' has gone through phases similar to those found in other parts of Africa. In the present rebellion, the first signs of Konzo nationalist feeling came with the founding of the Bakonjo Life History Research Rwenzori. This history society was mainly led by young, educated Konzo who coupled the collection of Konzo oral tradition with an emphasis on modern values and Konzo unity. It was a vehicle of Konzo cultural nationalism and a forerunner of the rebel movement. At that time the dominant sentiment was still one of hopelessness and powerless inferiority in the face of Toro domination. This was expressed in several songs, among them the one taking its theme from the parable of Lazarus. That song suggests that justice can only be expected in the life hereafter. We find similar feelings of impotence *vis-à-vis* overwhelming and superior powers which cannot be overcome during life on earth, in religious separatist movements in other African societies. For instance, in one of the parables of the South African Shembe movement:

There were ten virgins. And five of them were White and five of them were Black. . . . All of them came to the gate [of heaven]. But the five white virgins received the same answer as the rich man received [in the parable of Lazarus and the rich man]: 'because the Whites rule on earth, the Blacks do so in Heaven'. (Sundkler, 1964, p. 291).

This mood of resignation was followed by a phase of demanding better conditions here on earth. The Konzo demanded equality within the existing administrative system. After this demand had been rejected, Konzo rebel attitudes developed rapidly through a first incitement to action, which was mixed with fear and anxiety, to a mood of open aggression against the oppressor with the intent of destroying him. Finally, the rebellion came to a standstill; but the Konzo maintained their determination not to compromise, for they have taken power out of the hands of the Toro and seek to keep it.

Van Velsen has argued, with reference to Rhodesian nationalism, that

the history of African nationalism in different countries generally starts with a movement which may be called 'reformist'. It voices a demand for a fair share of educational attainments and aims at eliminating social and economic colour-bars. In other words, it simply accepts the existing structure but it wants a 'slice of the cake', so to say, but certainly not the whole cake. . . . The stubborn refusal of the rulers to concede to the demand for the removal of social and economic colour-bars has led African leaders to switch their attention from social and economic demands to political agitation (Van Velsen, 1964, pp. 141–2).

We have seen how the Rwenzururu movement also goes through phases which Van Velsen described.

During the last phase of the revolt the Konzo have withdrawn to the mountains, determined to reject co-operation with the Toro, and at the same time turning to the promised kingdom of earlier prophecy. Similarly, in the last days of the Mau Mau fighting in Kenya, the forest fighters turned to a hope of divine help. Barnett writes: 'with forest conditions steadily deteriorating and rational means of military success gone, greater and greater stress was laid on the hoped-for intervention of Ngai. Thus, Kahinga Wachanga states in this period that

> . . . we prayed continually that Ngai would intervene on our behalf and repeated over and over again the old saying: 'Justice must first be sought with gentle hands and only then by force; when both fail it remains only to pray Ngai's assistance.' The prayers we were saying went like this: 'We pray you, Ngai, please rid us of our enemies. You are our defender, we have no other . . . The whole of Kenya is full of tears shed by those who wonder when their freedom will arrive' (Barnett & Njama, 1966, p. 491).

The last phase in the Mau Mau rebellion shows trends which are also found in the latest phase of the Rwenzururu rebellion.

The development of the Rwenzururu rebellion from resignation, through open rebellion, to withdrawal and resignation expressed in more traditional terms, may have comparative value as a pattern of change in liberation movements which have not succeeded.

NOTES

1 Axel Sommerfelt and I did field-research among the Konzo, mainly in Bwamba county, in 1958–60. In 1964 and 1967 I returned for further research. The whole of my field-work was sponsored by the Norwegian Research Council for Science and the Humanities.

2 Uganda Government, 1962, p. 8.

3 There were 266 incidents in the first 24 days of June: from a statement by the Minister of Internal Affairs in the National Assembly, quoted in *Uganda Argus*, 27 June 1964.

4 The Konzo word for 'news' is *omwatsi*; the Toro word is *amakuru*. The usual Konzo greeting includes the phrase, 'What news?' The line in the National Anthem refers to the Konzo adoption of the Toro word in their greeting.

5 Here and in the following, I use 'the Konzo' as a term referring to the Konzo as a people, but recognizing that there are likely to be many shades of opinion among the Konzo during the whole time of the rebellion. A song does not necessarily reflect the attitude of every Konzo.

6 The singers could not translate the refrain, which they believed to be in Swahili. Each line of the song is followed by this same refrain.

7 The refrain is repeated twice after each verse.

8 The refrain is repeated after each line.

271

REFERENCES

BARNETT, D. L. & NJAMA, K. 1966, *Mau Mau from Within*, MacGibbon & Kee, London.

SUNDKLER, B. 1961, *Bantu Prophets*, Oxford University Press.

UGANDA GOVERNMENT, 1962, *Report of the Commission of Enquiry into the Recent Disturbances Amongst the Baamba and Bakonjo People of Toro*, Government Printer, Entebbe.

VAN VELSEN, J. 1964, 'Trends in African Nationalism in Southern Rhodesia', *Kroniek van Afrika*, June.

TRIBE AS FACT AND FICTION
IN AN EAST AFRICAN CITY

David J. Parkin

A NUMBER of the most prominent, sociological studies of African towns have stressed the need to analyse urban activities without presupposing that there must be tribal factors at work.[1] The significance of tribal factors, if there be any, emerges through observation of specific situations or of interconnected situations over time. Results of this approach suggest that a simple arbitrary distinction can be made between two levels or spheres of urban organization: that of urban domestic life, which, following Maine's classical definition, involves more relationships of status, and that of political, economic, and trade associations, involving more relationships of contract. Straddling these two are relationships of informal and free association, which, for brevity, I call friendships. In this essay I intend to examine briefly these three spheres of urban relationships[2] in order to see the varying significance of the concept of 'tribe' and the different ways in which 'tribe' is used as a discriminatory term. Let me first explain what I mean by these three spheres.

Urban domestic life refers to kinship relations, household composition, and marriage. Few urban workers in East Africa were born in town, even though many exhibit high involvement with urban life; and it is in interpersonal relations at this level of organization that tribal factors, or ethnocentric preferences, are most constantly evident. The preference for endogamy among certain tribespeople in Kampala reflects the strength of rural home expectations: some tribespeople allow more choice of spouse than others. The concept of tribe is here used objectively by people to distinguish groups into which a person may or may not marry. It has extended reference for distinguishing categories of kin and affines and appropriate obligations.

The extent to which ethnocentric preferences continue to operate at the level of politico-economic organization varies much more. The theme of urban sociology in the Copperbelt of pre-independence Zambia has been aptly summarized in the phrase 'trade unions transcend tribes'.[3] But recent evidence shows that in certain circumstances 'tribalism' may become more marked where an ethnic group's political and economic rights are in jeopardy.[4] I suggest that it is useful to consider another aspect of 'tribalism', namely the extent to which the concept of tribe is used as a 'blame-pinning' device.[5] Here it is used subjectively and inconsistently by both leaders and ordinary people who are not necessarily in face-to-face relationships. Choice of whom to blame for economic and other problems is affected by the social distance of accuser and accused.

By contrast, friends and neighbours see much more of each other. Both neighbourhoods and friendship networks are indices of socio-economic status differentiation. The physical structure of a neighbourhood and whether it encourages or discourages multi-tribal residence, and the tribal composition of a group of friends, not only define a person's status but also influence certain of his public decisions. Such decisions may include whether or not the person will join others in pinning blame for economic and other disorders on a particular tribal category, or on a particular individual by virtue of his tribe. Choice of whom to blame is influenced by concern at the effect on personal relationships and status.

Politico-economic organization

Political and economic changes immediately before and after Uganda's independence in 1962 modified the use of 'tribe' as a discriminatory term in Kampala-Mengo.

Kampala city is the capital of Uganda but adjoins Mengo municipality, capital of the until recently quasi-autonomous kingdom of Buganda.[6] The Ganda, who constitute 62·5 per cent of Mengo's nearly all-African population,[7] mostly prefer to live and work in Mengo, where they are able to hire, own and let land, grow crops and continue to fall under the jurisdiction of a modified form of Ganda chiefship.[8] Most of the migrants who are socially, politically, and culturally akin to Ganda, such as Nyoro, Toro, Soga, Haya, and Rwanda, also live in Mengo. While there is a substantial minority of Mengo residents who commute to Kampala city to work, most are involved in a relatively self-sufficient economic system of retail selling, beer-brewing, water-carrying, and local crafts.[9]

People who work in the city are members of what one conventionally understands by an industrial labour force. They include clerks, trained or experienced artisans, machine operators, drivers, service-men, gangers, as well as unskilled labourers, sweepers, and office messengers. Very approximately, Ganda account for 31·5 per cent of this labour force, which totalled 27,878 in 1961. Most of them live in Mengo, not Kampala city. The Luo, who came from Kenya, mostly in the fifties, constitute 11·5 per cent of this labour force. Though they are much less numerous in Kampala-Mengo as a whole, making up only 7·2 per cent as against the Ganda, 48·8 per cent,[10] as residents in Kampala city they are nearly as numerous as Ganda, being 14·3 per cent of city's resident African population against the Ganda 18·8 per cent.

The Luo preference for residence in the city has a number of origins. While the Ganda are indisputedly masters in their home territory of Mengo, they have for some years competed with Luo for dominance over employment opportunities and organizations in the city. It is popularly said that until recently the Ganda, with alternative economic outlets in lucrative rural cash-cropping, did not especially care to work in the city, which was left to be run by Luo. While this is crudely inaccurate in its details and ignores the parts played by such important and large groups as the Acholi and Kenya Luhya, it summarizes a situation in which Ganda and Luo were the key tribal groups, with Luo dominance in the city being challenged by Ganda immediately before and after independence.

A single instance of this was the complete and rather dramatic transfer of power in 1962 from a majority of Luo to a majority of Ganda in the executive of the Uganda National Union of Clerical, Commercial and Technical Employees, which was based in Kampala. In a free election many Luo workers voted for Ganda and this helped oust fellow Luo from office. Luo urban leaders, not just in trade unions but generally, encouraged such actions. With independence due in October 1962, and fearing government action against their expatriate yet dominant status, especially in labour relations, they wished to be accommodated anew as law-abiding, passive urban workers. Ganda/Luo patterns of mild hostility had been evident in Kampala-Mengo for many years. In the late fifties, tentative proposals for 'friendly meetings' were made by Luo and Ganda organizations or sponsors, sometimes being advertised in the national press. These were never more than well-meant attempts, usually by persons concerned with social welfare, to bring people from these dominant groups together. They were symbolic, rather expressive of the ambivalent and oscillating avoidance and joking relationships experienced by individual Luo and Ganda. In the housing estates of Kampala East, for instance, where Luo are dominant, it often occurred at tenants' association meetings and elsewhere that Ganda would jocularly and publicly fling accusations of 'invasion' at Luo local leaders, while these Luo would retort in light vein that Ganda in Kampala-Mengo should remember the alleged Nilotic origins of their kings and not discriminate against Luo, who, as Nilotes themselves, must be related to them. It was also a popular if bitter joke among Luo at Uganda's independence to refer to the government's new policy on employment as 'Bugandanization' rather than the official 'Ugandanization'.

But while Ganda/Luo hostility was popularly spoken of as a tribal division, it was sometimes situationally part of a wider cleavage between Uganda and Kenya workers, which was more openly expressed after independence (October 1962). Anxiety rose considerably as jobs in Kampala became scarce, with the city's labour force declining from 36,635 in 1958 to 27,878 in 1961.

Kenyans, mostly Luo and Luhya, had been dominant in Uganda trade unions in the years before independence. The new independent government, consisting of northern Ugandans as well as Ganda and Bantu southerners, attempted to alter this situation in a number of ways. It is said to have distributed circulars to employers urging them to recruit only

Ugandans in future. It demanded that Kenyans relinquish their hold on trade unions and accused them of leading unwarranted strikes. Finally, in July 1963, it announced the disfranchisement of Kenyans, together with all other non-citizens in Uganda, for all ward and constituency elections. Kenyans had been outstandingly prominent in previous urban elections. These measures consolidated a number of Kenya leaders in Kampala. Forgetting tribal differences, they protested through such organizations as the Uganda Kenya African Union against what they regarded as discrimination.

Thus, before independence national political decisions and power lay with a colonial administration and the major schism among the African population in Kampala was expressed both popularly and by ethnic leaders as between Ganda and Luo, the two dominant tribes. After independence ideological exhortations were for 'non-tribalism', and political power indeed became dispersed fairly evenly among Uganda's tribespeople, initially at least. The schism then became expressed as between Uganda and Kenya workers, regardless of tribe, in competition for a dwindling supply of jobs.

All-Kenya organizations in the city, and in the nearby town of Jinja, did for a short while protest against alleged discrimination. But then Kenya tribal associations in Kampala, notably the large and important ones of Luo and of Luhya, began stressing even more than in the past that they were a-political bodies, concerned only with the welfare of their tribes' migrants. There were re-shufflings of officers, in which those regarded as 'too political' were ejected.

Eventually all Kenya leaders in Kampala dispensed with protest and urged their people to accept passively their expatriate status. There was little else they could do and this passive acceptance was expediency as much as anything else. The number of Kenyans employed in Kampala did not drop drastically in the years after independence as many had fearfully predicted. But Kenyans continued to be sensitive about their expatriate status, and many expressed a desire to work in Kenya should employment become available there.

There seem to be three conclusions to be drawn from these few details. First, before independence economic opposition with the African urban population was expressed as a tribal cleavage of Ganda and Luo.[11] Second, after independence economic opposition was expressed in non-tribal terms. National differences had now become significant and the new government had to attempt, or be seen to attempt, to protect its own citizens from expatriate dominance in employment. Current nationalist and Pan-Africanist ideologies exhorted policies of 'non-tribalism' and so discouraged blame-pinning on specific tribespeople: strikes were blamed on Kenyans, not simply on Luo or Luhya. Third, obviously ethnocentric bodies like tribal associations, such as those of Luo and Luhya, informally redefined their aims and constitution and claimed that they were a-political. They hoped that, by nominally withdrawing from Ugandan politics, they and the people they represented would be blamed less for strikes, job-monopolizing, and political interference. This measure makes sense when it is noted that leaders in these tribal associations were often also trade union or political leaders, or had positions of economic importance in the town as professionals, traders, or high-status workers. They stood to lose most by any discriminatory actions taken against them by the Uganda government. Acquiescence was more expedient than protest.

None of this is to suggest that the real situation or conflict was changed, nor that tribal factors became irrelevant after independence. The important point, however, is that the *modes of expressing* economic opposition changed in accordance with a transfer of political power to one of the economically opposed categories.

In situations of urban economic and political conflict, blame-pinning in tribal terms is a convenient labelling system embodying usually only part of the truth. But there are areas of social life at the small group level in which the labels denote the real situation. The rural social structure of each tribespeople has a bearing not so much on the urban administrative structure, which is more directly determined by the availability or scarcity of jobs and their monopolization by certain tribes or other groups, as on the urban domestic life of each tribespeople.

Urban domestic life

For purposes of clarity and detail, I persist in analysing Ganda and Luo in the context of Kampala, though this inevitably over-simplifies.

The Luo at home are not hierarchically organized but have highly corporate, local agnatic-descent groups. Individual rights to land, cattle and property are vested in these descent groups. The lowest level 'courts' or 'moots' consist of the elders of such descent groups or related clusters of them. Though these 'traditional moots' cannot exert coercive sanctions, they may be asked to mediate land, inheritance, or marriage disputes and, unless appeal is made to the rather more expensive government courts, customarily influence what reconciliation the disputants may be prepared to accept. To a great extent, 'brothers' (primarily close agnates but ideologically extending to include other kin and affines of the same generation) rely upon mutual support in preserving economic and marriage rights, even though they may sometimes be divided on less important internal domestic issues. This relative unity of brothers persists to some extent in town: ideally brothers should lodge together and help each other financially and in other ways, and when these ideal obligations are shirked, as they often are under conditions of urban social mobility, there is considerable condemnation by the home people and some relatives in the same town.

The place of women in this complex of kinship and authority factors is especially important. At home Luo transfer a valuable bridewealth of cattle and money to the wife's family. Close agnates stand to gain from the bridewealth transferred at their sisters' marriages: it provides bridewealth for their own marriages and replenishes heritable homestead property. Since bridewealth is recoverable by the groom's family in the event of a bride or wife's elopement with another man, desertion or barrenness, brothers and fathers are keen that their sisters and daughters should maintain conjugal harmony and stay with their husbands. Before marriage they watch over the activities of these girls, exercising restraints on any tendencies to promiscuity, which is popularly associated with infertility and which may therefore lower their bridewealth value. After producing children a wife becomes fully incorporated in her husband's family while her ties with her own are considerably weakened.

The relevance for all this for urban life is that at the appropriate stages of a Luo woman's fecund life-cycle there are either male kin or husband and affines with a common interest in maintaining the stability of her marriage. An errant wife may be forcibly sent back to her husband's rural home. Wives whose fidelity is not in question nevertheless experience very little independent choice of action. Husband's permission must be sought before they visit friends and relatives or engage in certain other activities. Moreover, for some Luo, many of these constraints are either proclaimed or effectively exercised not only by the full Luo tribal association, the Kampala Luo Union, but also by smaller formal associations representing subtribes, clans and local descent groups of varying sizes. These associations deal with an additional number of situations arising from exigencies of urban life: repatriating the corpses of deceased Luo males, helping the destitute, or litigants at local courts, providing recreation, giving advice, attempting to settle disputes between 'brothers' and others. These situations are all what might by extension be included under the rubric of urban domestic life. They are certainly concerned only with small groups, households, or even dyads of persons, and not with wide-scale protest or protection movements relating to employment opportunities. Thus the position of women, and to some extent the tribal associations among Luo in Kampala, relate to the operation of tribal factors, notably the overall consequences of a system of highly corporate patrilineal descent groups.

The situation of Ganda in Kampala may be analysed similarly. Comparison of Ganda with Luo is rendered less convincing by the fact of Ganda proximity to Kampala and their dominance in Kampala-Mengo. However, repeating again that in Kampala city proper, and especially in Kampala East, Ganda dominance has been shared with Luo, there is some basis for assuming that the situations of Luo and Ganda in urban domestic life are analytically comparable.

The development of a powerful kingdom among the Ganda offered considerable social mobility which was later encouraged by an individual land-tenure system and cash crop economy in colonial times. It inevitably weakened the practical and ideological benefits of descent group membership. Nowadays there are few large extended families or descent groups. Brothers aspire to the purchase of individual plots of land in order to grow coffee or cotton and often settle distantly from each other. Intermediary and upper-level chiefships are much sought after. Land may be bought after or during a successful urban career. Land and property are not normally jointly inherited by brothers. One or more are likely to be favoured quite definitely in preference to others. Women may inherit, own, and transmit land and property. The bridewealth paid to a woman's family is not normally recoverable and does not entitle the husband to his wife's children if they are not begotten by him, as it does among Luo. It is often little more than a token transaction, sometimes exceeded in value by large wedding expenses, all payable by the groom.

None of these factors encourage the strong economic and ideological ties of the kind uniting Luo brothers. Nor do they require brothers to scrutinize the activities of their unmarried sisters; and, indeed, Ganda women, and those from other kingdoms of the Great Lakes, are found in all major East African towns. There is no consistent organizational procedure for repatriating unfaithful wives or 'promiscuous' unmarried women as among Luo, though spasmodic and so far unsuccessful attempts have been made. In town, Ganda brothers and sisters are permitted a high degree of individual choice in marriage, residence, and friends and favoured relatives.

The incidence of urban intertribal cohabitation and marriage among Ganda is much higher than among Luo, who usually return from town to home to arrange a marriage with a suitable Luo girl. Luo townsmen rarely marry any other than a Luo girl and usually marry in the customary manner. A very small number of Luo in Kampala, however, do live with Ganda or Toro or Nyoro mistresses or lovers, though these unions almost never attain the position of a 'permanent' marriage. Certainly in marriage preferences Luo are extremely ethnocentric compared with Ganda. Apart from the very few cases in Kampala of Luo cohabiting with Ganda women, these two tribespeople do not intermarry. The same applies to certain other tribespeople in Kampala who are similarly differentiated.[12]

Taking the rate of tribal endogamy as a measure, it surely is permissible to distinguish tribal and ethnic categories. Two main ethnic categories or 'supertribes'—that is, people who are linguistically, culturally, and geographically close—may be distinguished in Kampala.

Ganda, Toro, Nyoro, Haya and others are one, and Luo, Acholi, Lango, Alur, and Padhola are the other. Intertribal marriage and cohabitation *within* these supertribes is possible, though in fact practised much more in the former than the latter. The incidence of intertribal marriage even within a super-tribe may be regarded as an index of the strength of obligations and sanctions within the urban domestic field. Those who resist intertribal marriage or cohabitation in town, even with people who are linguistically and culturally akin to them, tend to have more formal, or stricter brother-brother, brother-sister, and parent-child relationships: they are told, or at least advised, with whom they should marry, lodge or be friends. Such people tend also to value more highly descent-group membership, fictitious or actual, and may manipulate this principle for certain urban activities. The Luo and others fall in this category. The Ganda and others fall in the contrasting category among whom there is much more permissiveness within family relationships or in what I call urban domestic life.

The contrasts between Luo and Ganda in urban domestic life and their reluctance to intermarry are not entirely disso-ciated from certain economic relations. I recorded a number of cases in which it seemed profitable for one or more Ganda and Luo to co-operate in establishing a small business, say a shop or service, or in merging already successful enterprises. One or both parties recognized the possible advantage of such a move, sometimes by jocular though revealing statements, and sometimes seriously, with a few direct approaches being made. But I recorded no cases where co-operation of this kind ensued. An obvious factor impeding such economic integration was the tendency for certain businesses to cater for people of a single tribe or tribal cluster occupying a specific region and perhaps sharing a similar diet, so that, for instance, food supply and town-to-home taxi services were most efficiently ethnocentric. But this factor could not apply to those businesses, such as tailoring, shoemaking, general stores, beer bars, and many others, which were not tied to an ethnic clientele. Citizenship differences certainly discourage partnerships. Some Luo, as Kenyans, saw a possible merger with Ganda partners as a means of protecting their economic interests in an alien town and nation. But none to my knowledge translated this ideal into reality—possibly because the Ganda they approached resisted the merger but certainly also because none had confidence in overcoming the difficulties of what they called 'the differences in our customs'. Since similar 'difficulties' were expressed by Ganda in the face of apparent economic advantage, it is worthwhile investigating what was meant by differences of custom.

When closely questioned on this nebulous expression, these small-scale businessmen would point to the differences in residence patterns, local authority relations, marriage and inheritance. Luo would ask 'How can I live away from my father as the Ganda do?', referring in summary to the strong agnatic ties of Luo which determine patrilocal as against the increasing tendency among Ganda to neolocal residence. They would say, 'I or my children could never marry a Ganda woman who would run away from her husband'. They would cite the difference in inheritance rights, contrasting the preferential Ganda with the egalitarian Luo system. Ganda would make similar distinctions, though less frequently, and tended to draw on what they saw as differences in personality or character as reasons for not merging.

Objectively it must be conceded that few of these so-called differences of custom would in fact be barriers to successful mergers of some urban businesses mentioned. There is no reason why a merged business could not flourish in town, with each of the two partners dealing independently of each other with such problems as the marriage of his children, the inheritance of his part of the business, and his own eventual residence. But the businesses I refer to are often family or kin-based enterprises, sometimes run by 'brothers', real or classificatory, sometimes by in-laws, and sometimes by a man and his wife. They are often run by men and women who cannot obtain more lucrative urban wage employment, and so are necessarily small-scale, though a few develop into markedly more profitable concerns. They are at the grass roots of the urban commercial structure, occupying a position below the larger private Asian, European, government, and the few African enterprises. Again, they are an extension of urban domestic life and the conceptual framework within which they operate is governed by ethnocentric expectations and preferences. It may be speculated that when a business becomes larger and has its administration transferred from family or kin group to a committee, council or board of persons who are not recruited along kinship lines even though they may be of the same tribe, the possibilities of an intertribal merger of such contrasting tribes as Luo and Ganda are enhanced, and that the difficulties likely to be cited will be to do with citizenship or nationhood rather than tribe.

I have been dealing so far with some of the conceptual frameworks within which people express the various divisions and alliances of categories around them. I have suggested that we may utilize a useful though arbitrary and overlapping distinction between urban politico-economic organization and domestic life. At the latter level there is the greatest congruence between 'reality' and persons' statements that tribal factors are determinants of social relations. The rural social structure is an important criterion of integration at this level. In urban politico-economic organization the competition for control over employment opportunities may or may not be expressed in terms of tribal conflict. The rural social structure is much less consistently relevant. Before independence, Ganda in Kampala saw themselves in competition with Luo. After independence, with an alteration of the power structure, the same competition was expressed as Ugandans versus Kenyans. Still later, in 1966, when the unity of Ugandans as against Kenyans seemed established, the unity in Uganda cracked and the problem of a privileged and powerful kingdom, Buganda, coexisting in one state with less privileged peoples in the north was stripped of constitutional wrappings. Northern Ugandans had finally and successfully taken their stand on the national position of the Ganda and other southern kingdoms, and seemed to have emerged as a new power, both politically and in urban employment. Ordinary people living in Kampala often referred to the conflict as being between Ganda and 'Acholi'; whereas the government and city élite, for reasons of prudence as well as accuracy, stated publicly that it was a necessary revision of the quasi-autonomy of the southern kingdoms and was not a fight between tribes. The tribal and non-tribal modes of explanation were thus used, respectively, by people at the lower and upper halves of the social ladder. This is no more than a very general impression, but one is tempted to speculate that, assuming no further political upheaval, the official view will percolate to a larger proportion of the ordinary workers, especially the better-off and secure, who see advantage in associating their attitudes with the establishment. Those who persist in the tribal explanation may typify the disillusioned or unemployed, or unsuccessful in general.

If this suggestion is correct, then use or non-use of tribal explanations for political and economic oppositions will be a subjective attribute of urban status and class differences. Ethnocentric preferences within the urban domestic field will continue to reflect much more the 'real' situation and difficulties and will have much less to do with delineating class and status: only among the nation's very top people are mixed marriages of Ganda/Luo kind encountered, and then not frequently.

Friends and neighbours

Sociologically distinct from and yet interconnected with the urban domestic and politico-economic fields are the relations of neighbours and friends. Friends and neighbours provide relationships of escape from the custom-hallowed demands of kin. They also provide more ambitious townsmen with useful economic and political contacts in what often appears as an unremitting struggle for status. They thus 'bridge' the urban domestic and politico-economic fields.

It is difficult to ignore one's neighbours, or at least their opinions, and some sort of relationship, whether of conflict or co-operation, tends to develop. Neighbours, like friends, may be of any tribe. Much depends on the area of residence, a point to which I shall return. Neighbours may become friends, as may workplace associates. The sheer necessity to interact together on a factory floor or in an office, and the common-sense view that this is best done amicably, help to break down what prejudices may exist between men and women of different tribes. Similarly, the social stigma against neighbours ignoring one another forces at least some relations on them, and of these some are likely to develop into friendships. That these may turn to relationships of hostility is a possibly quality of any friendship and does not deny the positive nature of these ties. Most African urban areas present a varied pattern of such relationships.

While there is usually more choice open to the individual in formulating relationships in town than in country, there are limiting factors. As an axiom one could say that most new urban migrants prefer as friends people from their home areas, who share a common language, culture, and customs. But the factors of neighbourhood and workplace just mentioned may oblige them to have at least some friends, and enemies, from different tribes.

P. C. Gutkind refers to the existence of localities of migrants in Kampala-Mengo in which the residents are nearly all of one tribe, often with an elected headman or 'leader'.[13] I personally know of Toro, Ankole, Haya, Luo, and Lugbara areas of this type, almost all in Mengo municipality. While the residents of these 'urban villages' are involved with the life of Kampala-Mengo, either because they work as wage-earners or are in some other way dependent for their livelihood there, their social and domestic life is clearly much determined by the ethnic 'community' which they constitute. Some of these communities are much more ethnocentric than others. Thus, members of the Ankole community living in some twenty-five traditional huts at the foot of Mbuya Hill all know each other and sanction each other's behaviour. They are young men without wives, except for the 'leader', who has worked in Kampala for at least ten years and has his wife with him. He, too, lives in a traditional Ankole hut and, like the younger men, he works in the public sector as a labourer. The young men have come for the express purpose of earning enough cash for bridewealth. Few have stayed more than two years in Kampala and their average length of residence is only eighteen months. They spend very little on food and almost nothing on recreation. Indeed, apart from essential visits to kin in other parts of Kampala, they venture no further in the city than required by the journey to work and back. Their recreation consists for the most part in drinking traditional beer and smoking in traditional manner in groups around their huts at night or weekends. Theirs is perhaps the closest one can get to a physical transportation of Ankole social life to Kampala-Mengo. Even the city council labour gangs in which they work are mostly made up of Ankole, or a related people, the Ciga. In these circumstances there is little pressure on these men to associate with other tribespeople. For eighteen months or two years they are committed to the role of urban worker, but they are not by preference attached to the role of townsman:[14] they do not consort with prostitutes, which costs money and which in any case would invoke the anger of the other men, who see such acts as disruptive of the common aims for which they have come to Kampala; they do not join voluntary associations which, as well as costing money, necessitate interaction with a category of townspeople who are of much longer urban residence and much more highly involved in the city's activities, and who do not wish to return home as soon as possible; and in general they do not go out of their way to seek new friendships in other parts of Kampala, in contexts other than those of their urban village. For them their neighbourhood is tailored to suit their parsimonious needs. They pay a very small rent to the Ganda owner of the plot and are left in privacy. They do not interact with other Ankole in Kampala, least of all those involved in the city, who would tend, anyway, to have skilled or clerical occupations. They are at once an ethnic, local, and status group.

Two contrasting types of Kampala 'ethnic villages' are those of the Luo and Haya. One Haya settlement in Kampala East, just inside the city boundary, is known as Kwaziba, literally 'at the place of the Ziba', an alternative name for the Haya. The Haya are renowned throughout East Africa as providing the largest numbers of prostitutes in towns. Kwaziba is an area dominated by such women, who live and provide their services in small huts, scattered around a number of stalls, half of them run by men, selling finery, such as cloth and beads and various bric-à-brac. Only a few of the women have children, and none have 'husbands' living with them or ever apparent. Most of these women have been in Kampala many years, some as many as twenty. A number have moved through various towns in East Africa, such as Jinja, Nairobi, Mombasa, and even Dar es Salaam, staying at each for varying periods. They do maintain close links with their homes, however, and it must not be thought that they are stigmatized very much for their activities by home kin. They send money home to help parents, siblings, or their own children left in the care of relatives. They themselves expect eventually to settle down at home, in their own house and living a relatively independent retirement. But while they are in town they are clearly very highly involved in urban life. The more successful of them branch out into other small businesses, such as stall-holding or other forms of trade. Their neighbourhood is essentially their workplace, where they provide their services and receive their clientele. As such Kwaziba inevitably attracts many forms of lower-status recreation such as drinking groups, dancing and drumming teams, and clusters of men playing the board game common throughout much of Africa. The Haya women are not part of the conventional Kampala labour force. They do not work in factories or offices. Yet they are both committed and attached to their roles as townswomen and differ extremely from the Ankole in these respects. The nature of their work and of the area in which they live obliges them to establish ties with people of all tribes, both women in professions similar to their own and men. At the same time they stress ties within their own ethnic group in order to keep open the contacts which play an important part in their remarkable migrations to and from towns in East Africa.

The Luo 'village' of Kisumu Kidogo in the settlement of Kibuli also contrasts with the Ankole 'village' in the degree of involvement in city life by its residents. The Luo headman of the area has been in this suburb of Kampala some twenty years; and while there is also a strong minority core of low-status Luo who have also lived there for a considerable number of years, the majority aspire to more 'respectable' places of residence, commonly on one of the housing estates in the city. For many Luo their Kampala careers begin with residence in Kisumu Kidogo, lodging with a 'brother' or friend, getting a job, again with the help of a relative or friend, and finally moving to their own rented room or house, either in another suburb or, by preference, on a housing estate.

The Luo, as well as being among the more numerous of the migrant tribespeople, also have jobs ranging from the most to the least skilled. The ethnocentric pressures of life in Kisumu Kidogo thus apply only to those who cannot afford to move out, the relatively unskilled, and those lodging with relatives and still searching for employment. Unlike the low-status Ankole, Luo, both low- and high-status, have not come for a short period for no other purpose than to accumulate enough in savings for bridewealth. Luo bridewealth either as cash or converted into cattle is certainly high and most new migrants will be expected to save for all or much of their own bridewealth. But, unlike the Ankole, their social horizons are broader and urban employment is seen as a lifelong occupation. It is the Luo who have provided much of the leadership and impetus for trade union movements and voluntary associations throughout East African towns. Like Haya women, they are highly involved in a complex network of migration, in their case linking individuals, associations, and even clan groupings in many towns.

In a suburb like Kisumu Kidogo, the residential turnover of a majority of Luo, their coming and going, helps advertise the urban status system, in which the prestige of a good, rented house in a 'better' area, new furniture, a radio, and even a car is much sought after. The better-off Luo are within reach of these prestige acquisitions, and there are always those not so well off who nevertheless make the attempt. Almost paradoxically, while the Luo are among the most ethnocentric and conservative in marriage, kinship, and household obligations— that is, in urban domestic life—they are perhaps the most open to new ideas and relationships. This receptivity to innovation is complemented by an eagerness to establish friendships with neighbours and workplace associates, and, incidentally, sociologists.[15] It is small wonder that, while the members of the Ankole 'village' rarely make the attempt to broaden their network of urban friendships, the Luo of Kisumu Kidogo are often impatient to move out of the area. They wish to loosen ties with the relatives and 'old people' who, while being the initial providers of accommodation, food, and even jobs, now perhaps restrict the successful young migrant's attempts to enter the urban prestige and status system by constantly advising against 'extravagance', reminding him of home obligations, and expecting occasional financial aid themselves.

The outward-looking Luo are really products of the total Kampala Luo community. This community, as explained, is both large and widely scattered in terms of skills. It is an ethnic community, which has within it marked status, almost class, differences. The poorer members of the community are ill-equipped to enter the status system and live congregated together in the cheaper areas, leading a life of limited aspirations such as their budgets allow them. They are not parsimonious by choice, as are the poor Ankole, and have considerably longer urban residence; yet the recreational life they lead is similar in being with the same people living near them. This close-knit recreational network of fellow Luo in Kisumu Kidogo is by definition ethnocentric, and through mutual moral and material support has the latent function of discouraging men from becoming too closely absorbed in the lives of other urban tribespeople.

An essential difference between the Ankole and Luo close-knit networks of poor men is that the Ankole have a very clear idea of their common aims: they are working in town for a limited period for the sole purpose of acquiring cash for bride-wealth; the residential and recreational restrictions are voluntarily submitted to and it is a manifest function of the 'leader' and young men to correct deviant members of the network. The poor Luo do not choose to be restricted in this way, but have little alternative and are by no means clear as to what their aims are in Kampala, individual or collective. The unmarried have bridewealth in mind, but beyond this are not sure, while the married (sometimes men who have lived and worked in Kampala for years with only a small amount of savings to show for this) see urban employment as little more than a preferred alternative to working the land at home, though originally they may have had grander and more positive ambitions. Some of these poorer Luo move out of the area, not to a 'better' place of residence, but to multi-tribal 'villages' of similar socio-economic status, such as Kisenyi or Mulago.[16] Though their economic level is unaltered, they are at least drawn more strongly into relationships with other tribespeople and in this way become more highly involved in the social life of Kampala. Those who have quarrelled may make this movement, as may those who simply wish to escape the ethnocentric expectations already mentioned. But the movement, while promising a more varied social life, does cut off certain immediate sources of comfort and aid and so is not to be made lightly.

These Kampala ethnic 'villages' of Haya, Ankole, and Luo, are just three examples of a relationship in Kampala between type of occupation or occupational scatter, residential area, and ethnic community. The Haya 'village' is also workplace and an essential node in the extensive network of Haya women in many East African towns. The Luo village is, like its residents, a mere fraction of a much larger and more diverse Kampala Luo community, which has internal status differences and is highly mobile. The Ankole village is extremely self-contained, admittedly relying for its existence on wage employment yet remaining aloof from other social contact in the city. It reflects the general socio-economic status of most Ankole workers in Kampala, who fall in the unskilled category.

More generally the settlements represent three types which can be found elsewhere in Kampala and probably also in other African towns. The Ankole ethnic village consists of low-status, low-income target and temporary urban workers; the Haya of a professionally segregated group; and the Luo of long-term, committed and involved urban workers.

These types of ethnic 'villages' developed outside the immediate jurisdiction or planning area of the city. Thus most are situated in the Ganda capital of Mengo municipality, which had until recent years very little planning policy. Only a few occur inside the Kampala city boundaries, in areas which are among the last to be scheduled for planned development. Spontaneous suburbs of this type are not necessarily ethnic or dominated by one tribe. Indeed, the majority in Kampala-Mengo have mixed tribal populations. Given the availability of land, it is merely suggested that certain lower-status categories of a single tribespeople may be grouped together in this way for purposes of mutual support and recreation, or for the pursuit of common economic interests.

With the special exception of the Ganda, who aspire to a house of their own in Mengo, the higher-status townsmen rent houses in the city, the bulk of them on housing estates or home-purchase areas, run either by the city council or by public services like the railways and police. In the city housing estates of Kampala East, practically all the tenants (mostly non-Ganda) regard residence there as more prestigeful as well as more comfortable than in suburbs of the type described above. A majority in earlier years had moved from such suburbs. For those who came from ethnic 'villages' of the Kisumu Kidogo type, a close-knit network of fellow-tribesmen was substituted by a looser-knit network, including a larger proportion of neighbour-friends and friends made at workplace, both of other tribes.

The estates are thus multi-tribal neighbourhoods, in which the individual and his family have no choice in deciding who will be their neighbour.[17] Houses are allocated according to a waiting list and what parity exists between neighbours of adjacent houses is of a socio-economic kind, since house rents vary according to size and quality and houses are only awarded to applicants if these are considered able to pay the rent. Clerks live next door to clerks and also to skilled and perhaps semi-skilled artisans. Labourers and sweepers live next door to one another. People of both high and low status are thus made even more aware of their ranks in the occupational scale by their place of residence as well as such other attributes as dress, personal possessions, and whether they go to bars and drink 'European' bottled beer or sit at home in small groups drinking traditional kinds of beer. With modifications, these tenants are not dissimilar in these status attributes from tenants described in various British communities, especially housing estates.[18] They differ in the complexity of their varying ethnic or tribal origins. Not even Liverpool, Cardiff, or parts of London can match the babble of tongues occurring in a single housing estate of about 1,500 adults in Kampala East. Nor indeed in Britain are there urban areas where almost 100 per cent of its population expect to retire in the country, to an exclusively ethnic way of life, after urban employment. Yet both are highly involved in urban life, perhaps the closest parallel being between the majority of urban migrants in Kampala and the Irish in Britain, who are obliged to play both alien urban and home (usually) rural social systems simultaneously.

In short, the housing estates bring home much more clearly than elsewhere that prestige rewards emanating from status differences are more important than tribal membership for assessing day-to-day relationships of neighbours and friends. This non-tribal basis of free association is reflected in the composition of certain voluntary associations on the estates, in their struggles for leadership and in their rivalries. It is not at all uncommon in the tenants' association for, as an example, a Luo and his following of six men, none of them Luo, to be in conflict and dispute over an issue with another Luo and his five followers, only two of them Luo. And at the dyadic level it is not uncommon for two English-speaking clerks of different tribes to establish a firm friendship, going together to beer bars or the cinema, sharing possessions, girl-friends, and even accommodation. Admittedly the social distance between individual tribespeople is a factor influencing the incidence of intertribal friendships, but once the friendship is firmly established tribal membership ceases to have much relevance. The striking exception to this is in the urban domestic field, not so much in reference to accommodation as to marriage. Thus, in one example, a Toro suggested that his Acholi friend should marry his sister. While the Acholi was prepared to court her and even live with her as his urban mistress, he could not bring himself to persuade his parents and other home people to accept her and, in the face of their opposition, had to break with her. The Toro/Acholi example is structurally parallel to Ganda/Luo and other cases, where there are the same sets of conflicting custom encouraging ethnic endogamy.

In summary, a first point which emerges is that there seems to be a higher incidence of ethnocentric interaction and expectations among friends and neighbours at the lower levels of the socio-economic scale than at the higher levels. Limited budgets restrict recreational scope and prolong the usefulness of home companions as sources of aid and comfort. Higher-status people inevitably move more easily into the urban prestige system. They tend also to move much more in the direction of official exhortations in acting and associating on a non-tribal basis, not always consciously. The type of residence available to them, especially housing estates, may be an important means enabling them to act in this way.

Second, this parallels what I said earlier that, except for those personally and immediately involved, more high-status people will assume the official non-tribal explanation of a political or economic division. They have social and economic stakes in maintaining good relations with their many workplace and neighbour-friends and prefer a neutral explanation to one in which the tribes of some of their friends and colleagues may be involved. A larger number of lower-status people have more ethnocentrically-based recreational activities, friends and neighbours. Again, the type or residence available to them and their degree of involvement in urban life are important mitigating factors. Among themselves at the small-group level they feel they need be less guarded about using tribal explanations, though even they would hardly make their opinions publicly known. The more deprived people of lower status may indeed get compensatory emotional satisfaction in describing a conflict in tribal terms, to judge by the vehemence of some explanations I have been given of the attempted Ugandanization of employment in Kampala following independence.

Third, the urban domestic field of relations appears relatively unaffected by status and residence differences on the most important issues, especially those concerning marriage and the position of women. With few exceptions, Luo of high status still find it hard to marry any other than Luo, or allow their daughters and sisters to do so. The incidence of Ganda intertribal marriage and cohabitation is comparatively high, regardless of status and area of residence.

This is all very much an ideal system of norms operating in the 'normal' periods between political crises. It is in a sense turned upside down during political crises themselves. At such times high-status men, including leaders, may urge tribal solidarity in an endeavour to preserve the political and economic support on which their positions depend directly or indirectly. Whether they express this solidarity in tribal or national terms depends on the political advantage or disadvantage from either usage at the time. Before independence Luo and Ganda leaders openly attacked each other and their people, each fearing the dominance of the other. After independence, they operated as and in conjunction with other national leaders of different tribes and expressed their opposition in a national idiom.

Tribe is, as Mitchell established, a 'category of interaction'.[19] In this sense it operates quite clearly in enabling an extension of rural social structure into urban domestic life. In this sense, too, it provides an obvious common ground for friendships and commercial relationships to develop. But friendships are also formed at workplace and through neighbourhood and are limited or modified by differences of income and degree of personal compatibility. The extent to which there continues to be ethnocentrism or tribal 'in-talk' and the accompanying tribal prejudice depends largely on the composition of a person's circle of friends. A tribally-mixed circle obviously inhibits such talk, while the single group does not. This leads to the second sense of tribe—namely, as a concept used by townsmen for describing urban divisions and casting blame. As such it is frequently emotive and mythical, and therefore highly flexible, enabling various people to have different explanations of the same issue. As well as being a category of interaction, therefore, tribe has sociological significance as a many-sided explanatory concept of urban cosmology.

NOTES

1 cf. Mitchell, 1965.
2 Mitchell (1965) would probably classify these as categorical, structural, and egocentric relations.
3 Mayer, 1961, p. xiv.
4 Cohen, 1966. Parkin, 1969.
5 Douglas, 1967, p. 73. The parallel is a loose one but perhaps worth making: while national political leaders frequently blame 'tribalism' for economic and other shortcomings, in rural areas the prevalence of witchcraft is often blamed for personal and social difficulties.
6 My data on Kampala refer to the situation before the exile of the former Kabaka of Buganda. My Kampala field research ended in March 1964, but I use the present tense.
7 At the Uganda population census of 1959 the African population of Mengo was 52,673. Asians, Europeans and others numbered 7,660.
8 Gutkind, 1963: there it is stressed that there is not merely an extension of traditional chiefship in this area.
9 Southall & Gutkind, 1957.
10 The total African population of Kampala-Mengo at the 1959 census was 76,729. There were 26,800 Asians and 3,539 Europeans. The residential

proportions of these latter racial groups were much higher in Kampala than in Mengo.

11 By contrast, in the Zambian Copperbelt before independence different tribespeople closed their ranks in common economic and political opposition to the ruling European minority. See Epstein, 1958.

12 See Parkin, 1966, and Southall, 1960.

13 Gutkind, 1962.

14 The distinction between role-commitment and role-attachment is made by Goffman (1961) and quoted by Frankenberg, 1966, p. 242.

15 See Southall & Gutkind, 1957, p. 216.

16 The two areas studied in Southall and Gutkind, 1957.

17 cf. Epstein, 1961, p. 43.

18 See Frankenberg, 1966, chapter 8.

19 Mitchell, 1956.

REFERENCES

COHEN, A. C. 1966, 'Politics of the Kola Trade', *Africa*, 36, 1.

DOUGLAS, M. 1967, 'Witch Beliefs in Central Africa', *Africa*, 37, 1.

EPSTEIN, A. L. 1958, *Politics in an African Urban Community*, Manchester University Press.

1961, 'The Network and Urban Social Organization', *Rhodes-Livingstone Journal*, 29.

FRANKENBERG, R. 1966, *Communities in Britain*, Penguin.

GOFFMAN, E. 1962, 'Encounters', *Two Studies in the Sociology of Interaction*, Charles E. Merrill Books, Chicago.

GUTKIND, P. C. 1962, 'Accommodation and Conflict in an African Peri-Urban Area', *Anthropologia*, N.S. 4, 2.

1963, *The Royal Capital of Buganda*, Mouton, The Hague.

MAYER, P. 1961, *Townsmen or Tribesmen*, Oxford University Press, Cape Town.

MITCHELL, J. C. 1956, *The Kalela Dance*, Rhodes-Livingstone Paper No. 27.

1965, 'Theoretical Orientations in African Urban Studies', in *The Social Anthropology of Complex Societies* (A.S.A. Monographs No. 4), Tavistock.

PARKIN, D. J. 1966, 'Types of Urban African Marriage in Kampala', *Africa*, 36, 3.

1969, *Neighbours and Nationals in an African City Ward*, Routledge & Kegan Paul, London.

SOUTHALL, A. W. 1960, 'On Chastity in Africa', *Uganda Journal*, 24.

SOUTHALL, A. W. & GUTKIND, P. C. 1957, *Townsmen in the Making* (E. African Studies No. 9), E. Afr. Institute of Social Research, Kampala.

THE TRIBAL FACTOR IN AN
EAST AFRICAN TRADE UNION

R. D. Grillo

THIS paper[1] considers the extent to which identification with, and allegiance to, the social groups normally referred to as tribes affect the behaviour of Africans in an urban and industrial institution, viz. a trade union. It is concerned with the workers in one industry only, the Railways, and with the members of one Union, the Railway African Union (Uganda), with special reference to those employed at Kampala. In a chapter on the Railway Union in a recent book (Scott, 1966, chapter 6) the author, a political scientist, commenting on several recurrent conflicts over the Union leadership, suggests that in them tribalism, or rather rivalry between two tribal groups, played a considerable part. This paper examines that contention in the light of my own data, which refers to certain episodes that occurred at Kampala in 1963–5.

In order to clarify the material presented in this case study it will be necessary to provide a brief outline of the social framework within which it is set.

The organizational framework of the East African Railways and Harbours

The East African Railways and Harbours (hereinafter the E.A.R.H.) is an interterritorial body within the East African Common Services Organization. It is a public service, operating extensive goods and passenger rail, road, and lake traffic in Kenya, Uganda, and Tanzania, as well as the coastal ports.

It is an important employer of many different categories of workers.

The E.A.R.H. is organized in 'departments' and 'districts' with the H.Q. of the whole body at Nairobi. Within the district the primary organizational unit is the 'depot' at which workers of one or more departments may be stationed. There are seven departments broken down into 'sections' and 'subsections', each having a distinct function and sphere of competence. In Uganda, which is treated as a single district, the local H.Q. and most important depot is at Kampala, where the following departments and sections are represented: the General Manager's Department, with Sections devoted to Welfare, Industrial Relations and Public Relations: the Engineering Department whose Sections include the Inspectorate of Works, the Health Inspectorate, an Office and the Permanent Way Inspectorate: the Mechanical Engineering

TABLE I

The African labour force of the E.A.R.H. depot at Kampala (June 1965): departmental and sectional distribution

Department	Section	Number	% Kenyan	% Ankole
General Manager's	ALL	29	34·5	0·0
Engineering	Office	41	36·5	5·0
Engineering	Health	81	30·0	39·5
Engineering	Works	279	30·0	2·0
Commercial and Operating	Office	42	26·0	2·0
Commercial and Operating	Station	115	31·0	16·5
Commercial and Operating	Yard	93	33·0	2·0
Commercial and Operating	Goods Shed	327	39·0	2·0
Mechanical Engineering	Office	11	55·0	0·0
Mechanical Engineering	Loco Shed	217	69·0	0·5
Mechanical Engineering	CxR*	49	71·0	2·0
TOTAL		1,284†	41·2	5·5

* Carriage and Waggon Examiners.
† This total excludes c. 300 workers in the Permanent Way Inspectorate.
Source: E.A.R.H. Departmental returns to Uganda Labour Enumeration, 1965.

Department, including Office, Locomotive Shed and Carriage and Waggon Examiners: and the Commercial and Operating Department with Station, Goods Shed, Marshalling Yard and Office. As may be seen from Table I (p. 298), the numbers employed in each section vary considerably.

Departments, Sections, and Subsections are hierarchically-ordered units each in the charge of an office-holder with competence only within his own unit. The Departmental Section at each Depot has a fixed number of posts which form part of the Department Establishment. Every railwayman is assigned to one of these posts, which have their own sphere of competence and which are graded in accordance with the E.A.R.H. system described below. In his post a railwayman is placed in a number of structural relationships with other workers. In

TABLE II

The Grading System of the E.A.R.H., with salary scaled in force in 1964/5

(a)	(b)	(c)	(d)	(e)	(f)	(g)
				Total Nos		
		Salary range,	*Class*	*employed,*	*Africans*	*Africans*
Groups	*Grades*	*£ per annum*	*of house*	*all races, April 1965*	*April 1965 %*	*Oct. 1962 %*
Superscale	6c–1	1650–3650	1	136	16·2	0·8
A	III–I	900–1524	2	120	16·7	4·0
	Cadet	762–828	2	27	89·0	76·8
B	Executive	1200–1500	2	53	0·0	0·0
	III–I	786–1110	3	2,070	45·5	13·4
	V–IV	510–766	4			
	VI	402–474	4	3,983	74·2	39·1
	VII		5			
	VIII	294–366	5			
	IX	222–270	5	7,369	99·3	99·0
	X		6			
	XI	150–186	6			
C	NC1	105–180	6	c. 28,000	100·0	100·0
	NC2		7			
	NC3		7			

Source: E.A.R.H. Administration.

other words, each employee has a role-set deriving from a status within the Railway framework. That the behaviour of railwaymen both at work and outside the work context is regulated to a large extent by that status is of considerable importance for this paper.

The Grading System comprises four main groups (Super-scale, Group A, Group B, and Group C) each divided into a number of grades, in turn subdivided into salary points.[2] A new recruit to the E.A.R.H. may enter at one of several different levels and in the course of his career move up from grade to grade as he is promoted from post to post. The chances for promotion are not equal for all workers. In the past, posts above Group B Grade IX were largely occupied by Europeans and Asians. Since 1962, however, there has been a vast increase in the numbers of Africans in the higher grades, and the promotion rate among those in the lower and middle ranges of Group B, especially among clerical staff, has been exceptionally high, as may be seen by comparing the percentages given in Table II (p. 299, columns (f) and (g)).

Besides determining his basic salary, a railwayman's grade also determines the kind of house he lives in. The E.A.R.H. has traditionally provided free housing for its employees which is, for the most part, situated on special estates. There are seven house classifications, and the relationship between grade and class may be seen in Table II, column (d). On the estates the classes tend to be spatially separated. At Kampala the main E.A.R.H. estate is at Nsambya, adjacent to the depot.

A social profile of the labour force

The E.A.R.H. employs over 40,000 workers of all races, though in recent years the number of Europeans and Asians has fallen sharply. At Kampala there are stationed approximately 1,300 workers, of whom over half live at Nsambya. A sample survey of African railwaymen on the Estate in 1965 revealed the following salient characteristics: The mean age, about 38 years, was high for an African urban area. 75 per cent of all married men had one wife or more with them in town, and 85 per cent of those with children had one child or more with them. The mean length of service with the E.A.R.H. was about thirteen years, with nearly 20 per cent having served for twenty years or more. Two-thirds had had no job other than with the E.A.R.H.; of the rest, most had worked for a short time in only one other occupation before settling down with the Railways. Railwaymen are not short-term migrant workers. They intend to work with the E.A.R.H. until reaching the retirement age of 55, when most propose to return to their rural areas of origin.

Railwaymen in Kampala form a relatively close-knit and isolated community, but one which has many internal divisions. Each railwayman belongs to a number of different groups (departmental section, grade, occupation and so on) which at the same time unite and divide different parts of the community. Moreover, each person has allegiances determined by factors

TABLE III

African labour force of the E.A.R.H. depot at Kampala, June 1965: area of origin

District in Uganda	% of total labour force	Other countries	% of total labour force
Mengo	8·6	Congo	0·5
Masaka	1·2	Rwanda/Burundi	1·8
Mubende	1·9	Kenya	41·2
Busoga	4·7	Tanzania	2·7
Bugisu	1·3	Sudan	5·5
Bukedi	7·6		
Teso	1·2		
Acholi	3·2	Total labour force	1284
Lango	0·8		
Karamoja	0·3		
W. Nile	3·7		
Madi	1·5		
Bunyoro	4·7		
Toro	0·8		
Ankole	5·5		
Kigezi	1·4		
Total, Uganda	48·4		

Source as for Table I.

301

outside the Railway framework. Any African railwayman is actually or potentially a member of many groups which exist separately from the Railway context and which both take him outside the community and affect his behaviour within it. Two of these deserve special attention.

National and tribal divisions

In respect of national and tribal origins the Kampala Depot labour force is highly heterogeneous, as may be seen from Table III (p. 301) and the first column of Table IV (p. 307).

In the Nsambya sample of '61, men from seven different countries and twenty different tribes were represented. Two general features are, however, important. First, the number of railwaymen born in Kenya is almost as great as the number of those born in Uganda. For historical reasons the E.A.R.H. in Kenya and Uganda has always been Kenyan-dominated. Second, among the Kenyans two groups stand out: Luo and Luhya, of the neighbouring Nyanza and Western Provinces respectively. Almost all Kenyans at the Kampala Depot are from these two tribes, and in the E.A.R.H. labour force in Kenya itself these two groups account for almost half the total. Moreover, an examination of the Kenya figures over the period 1945–62 shows that the proportion of the E.A.R.H. labour force formed by these two tribes varies only slightly. Thus they comprised 47·8 per cent in 1945, 48·5 per cent in 1954, 47·2 per cent in 1958, and 47·7 per cent in 1962. In fact, if the figures are taken department by department, section by section and depot by depot, there emerges a pattern wherein these tribes consistently predominate in some sections and depots but not in others. A similar pattern emerges in the Uganda figures. Thus in 1965 Kenyans formed 41·2 per cent of the Kampala Depot labour force but 71 per cent of the Carriage and Waggon Examining Section (see Table I). Of that same section they formed in 1956 73 per cent, and in 1960 72 per cent. In the case of another group, the Ankole of Uganda, it can be seen in Table I that the proportion they form of most sections is insignificant, except for the Station and the Health Inspectorate. Throughout the 'fifties and 'sixties the Ankole constituted a far higher proportion of these two sections than they did of the depot as a whole. Analysis of all the available evidence leads to the conclusion that, with certain important exceptions, there is a persistent association between certain tribes and particular departmental sections and subsections.[3]

There are a number of possible explanations for this, including the relative proportion of each tribe in the population, the geographical distribution of sections and depots, and very low turnover and transfer rates, all of which may be ruled out. Neither is there any validity in references to alleged differences of physical aptitude for various jobs as has been suggested by Walter Elkan (Elkan, 1960, pp. 86 and 102). My own intensive data would suggest a partial explanation as follows:

Recruitment into the E.A.R.H., at any rate at the lowest levels, often depends on the work-seeker obtaining inside information that a vacancy exists, and gaining inside support from someone who can speak up on his behalf with the relevant official. Almost everyone at work has relatives or friends from 'back home' who are seeking employment, and strong obligations exist to find them a job. The extent to which railwaymen fulfil such obligations may be seen in the fact that in the Nsambya sample 40 per cent of respondents had a 'relative' working at the depot, whilst 10 per cent had a sibling working in the E.A.R.H. outside Kampala. These relationships are, of course, ignored by labour enumerations which report simply the total numbers from a certain area or tribe.

It has been necessary to go into this point in detail since this association between tribe and occupation or industry has been noted before and has led to the suggestion that it indicates the existence of tribal 'closed shops' (cf. Elkan, 1960, p. 88). Statistically the association certainly exists, but it would be wrong to induce from it a causal relationship. In recruitment preferential treatment is given to a kinsman or neighbour from home, and the fact that a work-seeker is of one's own tribe is not, of itself, a sufficient reason for finding him a job. Yet this raises the key question: Under what circumstances *might* it be a sufficient reason for doing anything for him?

In discussing the meaning and function of tribalism a number of writers have distinguished two quite separate aspects. Mitchell (1956, p. 30) for example talks of 'tribal structure' and 'tribalism'. Southall (1961, p. 35) refers to 'rural' and 'urban' tribalism. A. L. Epstein formulates the position thus: 'The concept of "tribalism" has two distinct points of reference. On the one hand, its application is intra-tribal and refers to the persistence of, or continued attachment to, tribal custom. On the other, it refers to the persistence of loyalties and values, which stem from a particular form of social organization, and which operate today within a social system much wider than that of the tribe. . . . It is in the second sense that I speak of "tribalism" on the Copperbelt' (Epstein, 1958, p. 231). For my part I accept this distinction, at least as a heuristic device. This paper is concerned with tribalism in that second sense.

Operating with a similar distinction, Mitchell has shown that tribal groupings on the Zambian Copperbelt form the basis of a system of classification, a kind of social map, and that this in turn 'provides a mechanism whereby social relationships with strangers may be organized in what of necessity must be a fluid social situation' [Mitchell, 1956, pp. 30–1). The study of tribalism as a system of classification is of interest in itself, but what concerns me here is the implication that the existence of these categories somehow affects behaviour: that a person, as a tribesman, has a role-set which organizes his relationships with members of his own and other tribes. This paper will explore how these relationships are expressed, and how they affect the behaviour of railwaymen towards each other.

It should be noted at the outset, however, that each railwayman has several statuses in a number of different frameworks —e.g. the Railways, kinship, education, religion, and so on. The question, therefore, becomes: What is the part played by the status of tribesman in the constellation of statuses with which a railwayman operates? As already stated, this question will be examined in the context of the struggle for trade union leadership, since here, superficially at least, tribalism seemed to be important. For this purpose it is necessary, first, to describe the organization of the trade union concerned.

The organization of the Railway African Union (Uganda)

Although the E.A.R.H. is an interterritorial body there is no single trade union incorporating all railwaymen. In the recent past there were as many as eight unions, with each racial group in each country having its own association. This paper is concerned with one of these—the Railway African Union (Uganda) or R.A.U.(U.).

R.A.U.(U.) members come from among all full-time African railwaymen in Uganda and only from among railwaymen. It is an industrial union comprising all occupational groups and grades. Its organizational structure follows the traditional Western pattern. At each depot where there is a sufficient number, the members are organized as a 'branch' which elects its own officials. Each year the branches send delegates to the Annual Conference, the supreme governing body, which overviews the year's progress, discusses policy resolutions, and elects the National Executive. It also appoints the President, who, at the time of field-work, was a permanent paid official and not a working railwayman. The membership fee of 2s. per month is deducted from salaries by the E.A.R.H. and paid direct to the Union. There is no closed shop. Total membership in 1964-5 was about 3,000, of whom nearly a third were at Kampala.

The Kampala Branch is organized as follows: Each year all members at the depot elect six branch officers: chairman, secretary, treasurer, and their assistants. In addition each section of each department elects one or more representatives who, together with the officers, form the Branch Committee. Representatives usually number ten. It is significant that the R.A.U.(U.) uses the Railway framework as the basis for its own organization.

Very briefly, the place of the Union in industrial relations is as follows: Management-worker relations in the E.A.R.H. are governed by the Industrial Relations Machinery Agreement of 1962, in which the unions were given a distinct constitutional function.[4] The machinery consists of a hierarchy of elected Staff Committees and Councils which discuss such disputes as may from time to time arise. Whilst the Territorial (national) and Interterritorial Councils play an important part in Management-Union negotiations on the large issues of rates of pay and promotion for Africans, the Departmental Staff Committees at the depot level have, in practice, very little to do. When disputes arise affecting the workers at one depot only—say over a section supervisor—the matter is usually taken up directly by the Union, and the official machinery by-passed. In one area of industrial relations the Unions play no part at all. In the E.A.R.H. the work process is controlled by the complex 'staff regulations', and failure on the part of a railwayman to comply with these may constitute a punishable offence. Power to charge a railwayman with such an offence lies in the hands of section heads, though the offence may be brought to their attention by the subsection supervisors.

Who are the trade unionists?

In 1964 out of a total of 4,000 eligible persons the R.A.U.(U.) had a membership of approximately 3,000 or 75 per cent. Of these about 500 were in Group B and 2,500 in Group C. Since there were about 1,000 African Group B staff in Uganda, it will be seen that 50 per cent of that group were in the Union, whilst of Group C about 80 per cent were members. The Nsambya survey revealed a similar pattern. Thus the bulk of rank-and-file members were lower-paid workers in unskilled or semi-skilled occupations; the better-paid, better-educated clerical and supervisory workers being, proportionately, under-represented. Interestingly, a high proportion of *skilled workers* in Group B were Union members.

Turning to two other aspects that concern us—country and tribe—data from the Nsambya sample presented in Table IV show that rather more Kenyans than Ugandans were Union members and, associated in part with this, that Luo and Acholi formed a greater proportion of the Union membership than they did of the sample as a whole. However, the relationship between tribe and Union membership may be affected by the intervening variables of grade or occupation. Thus although all Acholi in the sample were in the Union, they were all in fact unskilled workers in Group C; but Luo clerical workers were not noticeably more prone to join the Union than those from other tribes.

A rather different pattern is shown among those who formed the leadership of the Union. Here I confine myself to the Kampala Branch in 1963–5. By 'leaders' are meant those who held or competed for office, or who sat as section repre-

TABLE IV

Tribal and national affiliation and Union membership among a sample of African railwaymen

Tribe	% in sample	As % of Union members	% of group who are Union members
Luo	23·0	28·0	64·0
Luhya/Samia	23·0	22·0	54·0
Ganda/Soga	14·8	9·0	33·0
Acholi*	9·8	19·0	100·0
All others†	29·5	22·0	41·0
TOTAL (N = 61)	100·1	100·0	54·1

Nation	% in sample	As % of Union members	% of group who are Union members
Kenya	41·0	47·0	60·0
Uganda	44·3	37·5	48·0
All others	14·7	15·5	56·0
TOTAL (N = 61)	100·0	100·0	54·1

sentatives on the Branch Committee. During the relevant period 35 persons were concerned, of whom no less than 31 were in Group B. Moreover, most of these came from a narrow range of grades within Group B, 23 being in Grades IX or VIII.[5] The vast majority of these leaders were clerical workers, and I estimate that of all clerical workers in Grades IX and VIII employed at the depot, some 50 per cent were, at any one time, engaged in Union leadership.

There is, therefore, a sharp contrast between the leadership and the rank and file. It is no surprise to find that Union leadership is normally in the hands of relatively well-paid, well-educated clerical staff. This pattern has been noted before in the East African context and further afield, and not only in

* Includes Acholi from Sudan.
† 18 tribes.

connection with unions. It is clearly of some interest that non-clerical workers have allowed the Union to be controlled by a group which forms a small minority of the labour force, though the reasons for this are beyond the scope of this paper. It may be added that the majority of Union leaders were in precisely those grades from which, at the time, the chances for promotion were greatest. For most leaders participation in Union affairs was a temporary matter. Once promotion to Grade VI and above had been achieved, they dropped their Union interests. Often the Union was seen as a channel through which promotion could be won, since key leaders were frequently sent abroad for training which they eventually used to obtain posts in 'industrial relations'.

Was the leadership dominated by any one tribal or national group? The actual figures[6] might lead to the conclusion that Luhya/Samia and Ganda were over-represented amongst the leaders, whilst Luo were under-represented. Certain difficulties of interpretation, however, make it impossible to draw a firm conclusion from these figures. In order to ascertain the possible significance of the tribal factor, it is necessary, therefore, to turn to an alternative source of information and consider certain events in the history of the Kampala Branch of the R.A.U.(U.) in 1963-5.

Conflict over leadership in the R.A.U.(U.)

During the course of my field-work there were two 'splits' (the local term) in the R.A.U.(U.), mostly affecting the workers at the Kampala depot. These were not the first (nor the last) leadership crises to have occurred in the Union, nor was the R.A.U.(U.) the only Union which experienced such conflicts. This paper discusses the earlier and more important of the two 'splits' on which I have detailed information and concerns the activities of what I shall term the 'splinter-group faction'.

In the middle of 1963, a new Branch Committee was elected at the Kampala Depot in accordance with the constitution. Following their election, certain members of the committee, led by the chairman, began voicing criticisms of the way in which the president of the Union was handling its affairs. At the 1963 Annual Conference, held in December, the committee proposed a resolution to the effect that the office of president should be held by a working railwayman, and that of general secretary should be a permanent post with authority only to carry out the decisions of Conference and the National Executive. The resolution was rejected, to the evident dissatisfaction of the Branch Committee, some of whose officers at once called a series of public meetings at which serious allegations were made against the president. Furthermore, they closed the branch office, a corrugated hut on the Nsambya Estate, and urged all their supporters to resign from the Union. Over 200 people, about a quarter of the branch membership, answered their call and resigned. The National Executive responded by obtaining permission to reopen the office by force, and disbanded the committee. Fresh elections were held, and a new committee took office in March 1964. The disbanded committee claimed it would start a new union, though this did not happen. The repercussions of the split continued throughout 1964 until, in early 1965, a new faction containing some survivors of the splinter group founded the 'Railway Workers Union'. That, however, is another story.

Most of these events took place on and around Nsambya, where most of the participants lived. Meetings, public and private, were held in homes on the estate or at the nearby Railway African Club. The affair was conducted with considerable rhetorical, and occasionally physical, violence. It affected a large number of people. Several hundred railwaymen were forced to show their allegiance to one faction or the other. The analysis will try to show the composition of the factions, how allegiances were determined, and the extent to which the crisis was concerned with relationships between those in conflicting positions within the structural framework. Three aspects are important here: the issues, the people, and the process.

The sources of information on the issues involved are the statements, public and private, made by the leaders and the followers of each faction. Although there was considerable confusion as to what were the main issues, there was general agreement on a number of interconnected themes. The first of these concerned the position of the president. The mildest of the objections to the president was that as he was no longer a working railwayman he was out of touch with his members' problems. In addition it was felt that a person who was not a railwayman should not have power to direct policy, as the president had (hence the resolution to Conference). Furthermore, it was said that the president of the R.A.U.(U.), who was also president of the Uganda Trades Union Congress, a frequent delegate to conferences overseas, and a Uganda M.P., was trying to do too much and consequently neglecting railwaymen's interests. There were also other, more serious allegations, strenuously denied by the president and his supporters. The tenor of these may be judged from the following extract from a printed handbill issued by the president at the height of the troubles. The original spelling is retained. The document addresses the members:

'Please do not be deceived. Your Union has for several years been run on constitution and this will continue. No Union money is wasted or used for personal convenience as has been alleged that I am using your money to build a six Story House. How can my sensible members believe such open deceit or lies. Your money is looked after by a Treasurer who works in conjunction with the Secretary and Trustee. Without any of these three, not a single cent can be paid out. These office bearers are constitutionally elected. No union money is being spent on individual scholarships.'

Such allegations as are refuted by the President in this document were widely held to be true; and a belief in their veracity could be considered plausible grounds for attempting his removal from office. The issue became, therefore, the well-being of the Union. The same could be said of the second theme, that of tribalism. It was alleged that the Union was dominated by members of the president's own tribe, Luhya/Samia, that his relatives were employed as officials of the Union, and that he gave preference to his own tribesmen in the allocation of scholarships to study abroad. To this it was countered that the splinter group was Luo trying to gain control of the Union for their own tribe. Note that no one admitted that their own faction was tribally based. Accusations of tribalism, always condemnatory, related to the opponent's faction. Accusations such as these were associated with a third theme, a political one.

The argument between the two factions was often couched in political jargon current at the time, with words such as 'neo-colonialist' and 'imperialist' being used with some abandon. Since, however, the splinter group, and later the Railway Workers Union, objected to the relationship between the president and the Western-oriented International Confederation of Free Trades Unions, the possibility of an ideological difference between the two factions should be considered. Although there was at that time a real difference of opinion as to whether the Trade Union movement of an independent African country should associate with organizations unambiguously aligned in world terms, that dispute can, I believe, be discounted as a serious factor in this split. Two other political aspects are worth mention. First, the period of resignations from the branch followed shortly after the Zanzibar revolution and the East African Army mutinies, a coincidence which led some people to suggest, without foundation, that all three events were connected with an attempt by a prominent Luo politician to gain power throughout East Africa. Second, the president's faction was sometimes referred to as 'K.A.D.U.', i.e. the Kenya African Democratic Union, the party at that time forming the Opposition in Kenya. Since members of the Luhya tribe were commonly associated with K.A.D.U., both these political issues may be seen as expressions of the tribal factor.

It is clear that accusations of tribalism played some part in these events. Scott lays considerable emphasis on this. Referring to earlier crises in 1959, he says: 'Continuing resistance to [the president's] leadership came from members of the Luo tribe. . . . On three occasions, the Luo tried to assert themselves without success. On each occasion, a *basically tribal rivalry* could be concealed beneath more legitimate complaints about the union leadership' (Scott, 1966, p. 64; my emphases). Although a superficial assessment of the data so far presented might lead to the same conclusion, it should be tested in the light of further evidence.

Two factions have been mentioned as though they were groups whose personnel was quite distinct. That this was not necessarily the case will be shown through an analysis of their actual composition, considering first the leaders and then the supporters.

The date at which the composition of the two factions is examined is of some importance, and hence for the moment I consider only the situation as it was when the resignations finally occurred, i.e. in March 1964. The leadership in both factions was in the hands of two small, regularly interacting, groups, the members of each of which are listed in Table V. The lists include all those generally agreed to have been among the leaders, most of whom were, in March 1964, past, present or future members of a Union committee.

There were two features common to both leadership groups.

TABLE V

Leaders of president's faction and splinter-group faction compared

'Name'	Tribe	Grade	Occupation	Department
PRESIDENT'S FACTION				
A	Luhya/Samia	—	President, R.A.U.(U.)	—
B	Soga	B VIII	Clerk	Commercial and Operating
C	Luhya/Samia	B IX	Clerk	Mechanical Engineering
D	Luhya/Samia	B VIII	Clerk	Commercial and Operating
E	Luhya/Samia	B VIII	Clerk	Commercial and Operating
F	Toro	B IX	Clerk	Engineering
G	Toro	B X	Clerk	Engineering
H	Luhya/Samia	B IX	Artisan	Mechanical Engineering
I	Luhya/Samia	C	Storeman	Mechanical Engineering
SPLINTER-GROUP FACTION				
J	Luo	B V	Clerk	Commercial and Operating
K	Nubi	B IX	Clerk	Engineering
L	Lango	B IX	Clerk	Commercial and Operating
M	Ganda	B IX	Clerk	Commercial and Operating
N	Luo	B IX	Junior Supervisor	Commercial and Operating
O	Luo	B VIII	Clerk	Commercial and Operating
P	Luo	B IX	Clerk	Commercial and Operating
Q	Luo	B VIII	Clerk	Engineering
ALLEGIANCE DOUBTFUL				
R	Dhola	B VI	Clerk	Commercial and Operating
S	Ganda	B V	Clerk	Commercial and Operating

First, almost all were members of Group B, thirteen out of eighteen (omitting the president) being in Grades IX or VIII. Second, almost all were clerical workers. Neither faction apparently represented an occupation or grade interest. The split was not between Group B and Group C, nor between clerks and artisans or unskilled workers. This is not irrelevant, as there was a quite separate, though unsuccessful, move by footplate staff to found an 'Enginemen's Association'. Both factions were led by those most closely concerned with promotion in the E.A.R.H. and leadership in the community as a whole. There were, nevertheless, two possible distinctions between the factions. First, and this may or may not be important, the splinter-group leadership came largely from the Commercial and Operating Department, whilst that of the president's faction included some workers from Mechanical Engineering. Second, the president's faction contained six out of nine Luhya/Samia but no Luo, whilst the splinter group consisted of five out of eight Luo with no Luhya/Samia. Apparently, therefore, the conflict involved Luo against Luhya/Samia.

This was the position in March 1964. But earlier, at the time of the branch elections in 1963, the Luo against Luhya/Samia distinction was not clear. Then, two Luo competed against each other for the chairmanship, whilst the election for the post of secretary involved two Luhya. Moreover, there were other people, to whom reference is made later, whose position was decidedly ambivalent.

Concerning the supporters of the two factions, evidence from my own observations is clearly insufficient to give an overall picture. Examination of the only numerical data available, the list of names of those who resigned, reveals the following information: The proportion of Group C among the resignees was no greater than their proportion of Union membership, which supports the conclusion that the splinter group did not represent a grade interest. The same applies to occupation. There was, however, a departmental difference. Thus, only 12 persons resigned from Mechanical Engineering, whilst 120 resigned from Commercial and Operating and 80 from Engineering. (Proportional differences can be gauged from the figures in Table I.) Why were there so few resignations from Mechanical Engineering, where, it can be shown, the percentage of staff in the Union was not less than in the other departments, and where, above all, so many Luo worked? Third, whilst large numbers of Luo resigned, they were not in the majority, nor were the resignees predominantly Nilotic. Many of those who left the Union were from interlacustrine Bantu tribes, such as the Ankole and Ganda. Although few Luhya/Samia resigned, can the above facts be explained simply in terms of the tribal rivalry between them and the Luo? In order to clarify the issue, let us see what actually happened in some of the situations created by the split.

For this paper it has been necessary to select a few instances from the many on which I have information. First, let us consider how the affair affected certain staff in the Commercial and Operating Department. During 1963 it seems that some of those who later formed the leadership in the splinter-group faction were gaining prominence in the department by gradually winning places on the Departmental Staff Committee. In January 1963 a certain Luo Group C Headman was appointed by the then Station Master, an Asian, to represent the section on the committee. After he had held office for a short time he was criticized by other station staff on the grounds that he was illiterate and unable to oppose the management. The opposition was led by Messrs P. and N. of the splinter group, themselves both Luo.[7] In the election for the vacancy created by the agitation, P. was elected. Among his keenest supporters were the staff of the Carriage Cleaning Subsection of which N. was the supervisor. Apart from the Luo N., all workers in that subsection were Ankole by tribe. Soon after this the Departmental Staff Committee member for the yard, another 'illiterate', was under attack, and in the subsequent election Mr O., another Luo, won the place. From the lists of resignees it is clear that the splinter group enjoyed strong support among workers at the station and at the yard, though many were not Luo.

In the Parcels Office Subsection of the station almost all the staff (about twenty in number) were Luo. At the end of 1963 a number of workers in the subsection set up an entirely unofficial and self-appointed committee which claimed to represent the interests of Group C staff in the Parcels Office, and which briefed the station representative (Mr P.) on the Departmental Staff Committee. The self-styled chairman of the Parcels Office Committee, a Luo Group C man, a close associate of P.'s, was the local organizer, as it were, for the splinter group. Only three members of the Parcels Office failed to resign when the time came. One was a Luo who thought that if he resigned he would be sacked. The second was a Luhya, a relative of a leader of the president's faction, who, whilst he did not resign, actively supported the splinter group within the subsection and held the post of secretary on the unofficial Parcels Office Committee. The third was another Luo who thought the Union was doing a good job. This person, whom I call Francis, was unusual in other ways. Although only a Group C man, he was educated up to Cambridge School Certificate Standard and always felt himself an outsider in the subsection. The others resented what they thought were his intellectual pretensions—he was an amateur artist. Great pressure to resign was put on him in private by, among others, the unofficial chairman, who was in fact his father's brother's son. The latter phrased the pressure in unambiguously tribal terms. He did not use the idiom of kinship, partly, I think, because there was some ill-feeling between the two branches of the family. The matter came to a head (in June 1964) when Francis was asked by the new chairman of the Kampala Branch Committee to take up the Union's reserved seat on the Departmental Staff Committee. At first he accepted willingly because, he said, one thing might lead to another and he might get a scholarship abroad. Then his fellow workers at the Station, both Luo and non-Luo, began to make his life intolerable. He countered their abuse by threatening to report them to the Union president who would then have them transferred to a remote up-country depot, but later he succumbed to their pressure and resigned.

That reference could be made to tribal affiliation when bringing pressure to bear on individuals to support one faction or the other is obviously important. For some this created impossibly difficult situations. The welfare officer at the time of the split was a Luhya. Among his duties was that of supervising the Railway African Club. On one occasion the splinter-group faction proposed to call a public meeting at the club.

When the president's faction heard of this they called on the welfare officer as a Luhya to deny their opponents use of the club. If he failed to do this he would be called 'pro-Luo'; if he did this he would be called 'pro-Luhya'. He himself was trying to steer a neutral course as his office in the E.A.R.H. demanded—to be known as 'pro' any group would damage his chances of promotion. In fact he adhered strictly to the letter of the regulations and, since the splinter group had not booked the club in advance, denied them entry. He immediately balanced this in his own eyes by performing an important service for the Luo family on the estate who had lost a relative. The incident of the club had a number of repercussions. The Luo owner of a popular Nsambya bar was overheard expressing sympathy for the welfare officer's action on the grounds that the latter had acted in accordance with the regulations. He was promptly subjected to a boycott by the splinter-group leaders, who urged their supporters to do likewise. At the same time the president's faction were also boycotting his bar because, it was alleged, he had been told by the chairman of the splinter group to poison their beer.

There were also those whose allegiances were ambiguous. At the time of the December 1963 Conference, it was said that Messrs R. and S. were elected on to the National Executive with the support of the splinter group in order to curb the president's power. They were then alleged to have been 'bought' by him, and certainly throughout 1964 supported him in the Union. At the end of that year certain people in the president's faction claimed that R. and S. had been 'bought' by the group who later formed the Railway Workers Union, and R. was ousted from his position on the National Executive by Mr C.

Mr Q, a Luo, was another waverer. In 1962 he had been the Union's general secretary. In 1963 he was sent abroad on a scholarship, but on his return was ousted from his post by R., at that time an alleged member of the splinter group. Shortly afterwards Q himself joined the splinter group. Towards the end of 1964, after the splinter group broke up, he was seen to be trying to come to terms with the president's faction and was in fact promised a post at the next election. When that failed to materialize he returned again to opposition and emerged in 1965 on the committee of the Railway Workers Union.

This brief account of some of the available material should enable us to consider the problem posed earlier. Clearly tribalism played some part in the events described, but I do not feel that the data will bear the interpretation that the conflict was grounded in a 'basically tribal rivalry'. Such an hypothesis does not account for all the facts. I will try to outline one that might.

Tribalism and the struggle for power

Competition for office in the R.A.U.(U.) concerns only a small section of the community who are, characteristically, well-educated clerical workers from a narrow range of grades in the middle echelons of the E.A.R.H. hierarchy, where they are also competing against each other for self-advancement through promotion. This same group provides leadership in many other urban associations, from tribal societies to sports clubs. The R.A.U.(U.) is but one of many institutions through which the social aspirations of this group are expressed. Possession of office in the Union gives prestige, power and influence and can, moreover, be used as a basis for a move into yet more important areas of the society, into politics on the one hand, or into management on the other. The suggestion that behind their manoeuvrings lies a 'basically tribal rivalry' implies that those who compete for office do so, in part at any rate, from some notion of group interest, the group being the tribe. Yet it seems to me that it is not axiomatic that a desire to bring advantages to a certain sector of the community such as a tribe plays a fundamental part in the motivation of those who compete for office in the R.A.U.(U.). This point may be illustrated by a brief reference to the second split, that involving the Railway Workers Union. As with the splinter-group affair, mutual accusations of tribal and ideological differences abounded. The reality emerged when the self-styled president of the Railway Workers Union finally abandoned his organization and rejoined the R.A.U.(U.). His statement to a press conference was reported as follows: 'Mr — said yesterday that he had been deceived by some leaders of a political organization that he would be granted a scholarship and money if

he broke away from his former Union and formed another. ...
"I have received none of the big gifts I was promised and now
I have decided to rejoin my former union," he said' (*Uganda
Argus*, 6 May 1965).

Although those seeking office in the Union may have little
sense of tribal interest, tribalism may be one of the weapons
used in the struggle for power. Competitors for office must have
ways and means of organizing supporters—to vote or demonstrate—and of generating enthusiasm for their cause. They
are unlikely to rely on appeals on ideological grounds, since
ideological differences are minimal, and ideology does not of
itself command allegiance. Each person, however, has statuses
in various groups, and he may use these to gather support.
Some of the groups are, for those concerned with winning
power in the Union, irrelevant. Occupation and grade do not
provide frames of reference which clearly distinguish one
competitor from another. There are, however, other possible
lines of differentiation which derive from the E.A.R.H. framework, especially the departmental structure. Since each sub-
unit of a department has a specific organizational function, its
members are united by a common work interest. This sectional
and subsectional *esprit de corps* may be expressed through the
giving of farewell parties (Swahili: *chai ya kwaheri*) for those
about to be transferred and the collection of a fund for the
family of a deceased workmate. Close association at work
leads to frequent interaction outside work. Both the Union
in its Branch Committees and the management in its Staff
Committees recognize the importance of these special interests
by having representatives elected on a sectional basis. Almost
all Union leaders came to prominence first in their own sections, and used them as a basis for an advance into departmental or depot-wide 'politics'. Since, however, no section is strong
enough to dominate a depot-wide election nor has enough
representatives to form a majority on a committee, section
leaders are forced into coalitions. The junior supervisor in the
Carriage Cleaning Subsection commanded a block of some 20
votes, which he used to support the splinter group and thus
win himself a place on that faction's 'ticket'. Whilst 'his'
Ankole supported the splinter group, those in another subsection supported the president's faction. The coalitions are

necessarily fluid. For example, in this split Loco Shed workers, including Luo, supported the president's faction, but when the Railway Workers Union was founded they appear to have changed their allegiance.

Besides the section, there are other channels through which a person can seek support, including his tribe or, when large numbers of the same tribe are present, internal divisions of the tribe. There is little or no evidence that the role of tribesman entails an obligation to support other members of the tribe unconditionally in political contexts of the kind described here. No union leader had a legitimate claim on his fellow tribesmen. Even among those tribes with a traditional centralized authority (for example, the Ganda)—where, that is, there exists an authoritative institution which can clearly define the group interest and designate its representatives—it is not impossible to resist that authority. In the case of tribes with traditionally non-centralized systems (such as Luo and Luhya) there may nowadays be institutions (for example, the Luo Union) from which might emanate directives on the group interest. Yet the authority of the Luo Union, or of those who hold office in it at any one time, is by no means unchallengeable. It should be noted that never once did any of the possible sources of legitimate authority within the tribes show the slightest interest in the Union conflict. This would not matter in the least if tribal sentiment were strong enough. I suggest that it is not; or rather, that there is a wide range of opinion as to whether there exists, or indeed should exist, a tribal political interest best advanced by giving support to one tribesman rather than another.

Since no one is bound to support an appeal based on tribal affiliation, leaders may apply pressure through persuasion, promises or threats. Whilst there can be no official sanctions against a Luo or Luhya who fails to give his support, if enough people are convinced it is necessary, then the individual's life can be made extremely uncomfortable. For this and similar purposes those most closely involved in the struggle for power may gather a group of unemployed men to act as their 'youth wing'. In addition, so it was alleged, witchcraft and sorcery might be used. Tribal pressure must, however, be used with caution, since no one tribe is strong enough to dominate a depot-wide election or conflict. An appeal to one's own tribe can be a double-edged weapon. Moreover, since the notion of tribalism is under political attack in East Africa, it is not possible to make a public, corporate appeal for tribal support. Indeed, people emerge in public as critics of their opponents' tribalism, though this in the end may achieve the same result. There is some evidence that each faction deliberately set out to use accusations of tribalism to smear the other side. Generally tribal pressure is applied as privately and as quietly as possible. Sometimes, as has been shown, pressure may come from two or more opposing directions. Those who are squeezed in this way have to make the best arrangements they can.

Each railwayman has membership in numerous groups, none of which is he obliged to support in a 'political' context, and none of which is, by itself, strong enough to overwhelm all others. Political leaders must, therefore, build up support through persuasion, pressure, and alliances. The system has something in common with that of the Swat Pathans, among whom 'group commitments may be assumed and shed at will' (Barth, 1959, p. 2). That is, a railwayman has a certain freedom of choice as to whom he supports. As with the Pathans, this freedom is limited by the social framework, both for the leaders and the rank and file, all of whom try to maximize their interests bearing in mind the possible repercussions.

In this situation the tribal factor may play an important part as one, but only one, of the weapons that leaders use in the struggle for power. What is basic here is not 'tribal rivalry' so much as a system in which competition is fundamentally important and which provides a multiplicity of sources from which the competitors can draw support.

NOTES

1 Successive drafts of this paper were presented to seminars of anthropologists at London and Cambridge. Mr D. Marsland of Brunel University made several illuminating comments on an early version, and Professor Gulliver's detailed criticisms were invaluable in preparing the final draft.
2 The nomenclature of the grading system used here is that which was in force before the Harres Commission changes introduced in September 1963. The salary scales are post-Harres.
3 I should like to correct an impression given by Elkan who says that 'in

Uganda nearly all railway workers are Luo or Acholi' (Elkan, 1960, p. 64). In 1955, the period to which Elkan must be referring, there were, out of a total of 5,061 African railwaymen in the whole of Uganda, 750 born in Acholi District and 1,076 Kenyans. Assuming that Luo formed as many as 70 per cent of all Kenyans, and assuming also that all Sudan-born workers (102) were Acholi by tribe, we arrive at a total of 1,620 persons who might be Luo or Acholi. This represents 32·4 per cent of the labour force. (Source for figures: E.A.R.H. departmental returns to Uganda Labour Enumeration, 1955.)

4 At the Interterritorial and Territorial Councils the staff side is represented entirely by Union officials. Departmental or Local Staff Committees are composed of representatives elected by the workers in each section, though under certain circumstances seats are reserved for a Union nominee.

5 The actual numbers were: Group C, 4; Group B Grade XI, 1; Grade X, 3; Grade IX, 11; Grade VIII, 12; Grade VII, 3; and Grade V, 1.

6 Actual figures: Luhya/Samia, 9; Ganda, 5; Luo, 4; Soga, 3; Toro, 3; and one each of Nubi, Teso, Dhola, Lango, Ankole, Gisu, Chagga, Taita, Nyoro, one Tanzanian, one half-caste.

7 The initials 'N', 'O', etc., used here and in the rest of the narrative refer to the leaders named in Table V.

REFERENCES

BARTH, F. 1959, *Political Leadership among the Swat Pathans*, Athlone Press, London.

ELKAN, W. 1960, *Migrants and Proletarians*, Oxford University Press.

EPSTEIN, A. L. 1958, *Politics in an Urban African Community*, Manchester University Press.

MITCHELL, J. C. 1956, *The Kalela Dance*, Manchester University Press (Rhodes-Livingstone Paper No. 23).

SCOTT, R. 1966, *The Development of Trade Unions in Uganda*, E.A. Publishing House, Nairobi.

SOUTHALL, A. 1961, *Social Change in Modern Africa*, Oxford University Press.

BUGANDA AND TRIBALISM

H. F. Morris

The meaning of tribalism

THE final phase of British colonialism in Africa witnessed the overthrow of many reputations, not least that of a considerable portion of the English vocabulary. It would be most interesting to pursue the question of the influence of vocabulary on nationalism and *vice versa*, and to explore the origins of the distaste for certain words—words often innocuous enough in their dictionary meaning and for which alternatives may be hard to find without recourse to laborious circumlocutions—and, in particular, to know how far this distaste originally stemmed from the African people themselves and how far from their colonial rulers in their final stage of morbid self-examination and self-accusation. This, however, is not the place for such an exercise; but we are concerned with the present state of one of these ill-fated words—tribalism.

In the early days of European administration in Africa, the word 'tribe' was found to be a convenient term to apply to people to whom, though they might possess a common political organization, language and sense of identity, it was, nevertheless, felt to be inappropriate, either on account of size, development of political or social institutions, or other reasons, to apply the word 'nation'. So too the adjective 'tribal' was in general used normally with the unexceptionable meaning of 'indigenous', and the phrase 'tribal institutions' was seldom far from the lips of the advocates of 'indirect rule', and by tribal they meant here no more than 'autochthonous', a word, incidentally, whose popularity has waxed in recent years as that of tribal has waned. In these senses the words 'tribe' and 'tribal' were purely descriptive, but, in the last few decades of the colonial régime, 'tribal' was increasingly applied with a pejorative implication: a 'tribal' outlook was a limited and atavistic one, parochial and backward-looking, unresponsive to the lure of the ballot-box and the other panaceas of the twentieth century. Then, during the final lap of colonial rule, 'tribalism' came to be applied in a special and even more derogatory sense, as being a divisive force inimical to the emergence on independence of a strong centralized government, controlled by politicians professing a radical 'progressive' outlook and operating within frontiers inherited from the colonial régime, which often paid little heed to ethnic considerations. Now what is the significance of these words, 'tribe', 'tribal', and 'tribalism', in each of the three stages of their semantic metamorphosis, in relation to Buganda.

An historical survey of Buganda 'nationalism' during the twentieth century

As is well known, in 1890, when Lugard first concluded a treaty on behalf of the Imperial British East Africa Company with the Kabaka Mwanga of Buganda, that kingdom was, and indeed had been for at least a century, a well-organized state with a strong centralized government, throughout which a hierarchy of chiefs appointed by the Kabaka maintained order, dispensed justice and collected tribute—a state whose organization has suggested comparisons with Norman and Angevin England. The following decade, culminating in the Agreement of 1900 between the Kabaka and the Crown, witnessed a fundamental revolution. By 1900, the Kabaka Mwanga had been dethroned and replaced by a minor. Subject to the overriding control of the Protectorate Government, power lay exclusively in the hands of the notables who had won the religious wars and, as a result, composed the Native Government and the Lukiiko, now institutionalized and bearing little resemblance, save in name, to the Kabaka's Council of 1890. The clan heads, who had retained some influence until now, were reduced almost to insignificance deriving no benefit, unless they also happened to be chiefs, from the revolutionary land settlement which introduced a form of freehold (*mailo*):

here the beneficiaries were to be found in the dominant class which controlled the Lukiiko.

Secure in its relationship with the colonial power as a result of the Agreement, the new régime was in the first two decades of the century a reformist and innovating force within the kingdom. Laws were introduced reflecting the Christian, and in many ways the progressive and anti-traditionalist, outlook of the new élite. Meanwhile, as the Protectorate Government extended the area of its administration throughout the Protectorate into areas north and east of Buganda, Baganda 'agents' were used by that Government to bring 'enlightenment' and the Buganda form of administration to these people.

Buganda may appear to be an outstanding example of an African people accommodating themselves to the new colonial régime at the outset. Yet, once the honeymoon period was over, few native governments in Africa in the first half of this century can have pursued, so successfully and singlemindedly, a policy of opposition to the measures of the protecting power. Measures were resisted whenever, in Baganda opinion, they would result in interference in the internal administration of the kingdom, or would undermine her national institutions or her position as a native state, standing in a special relationship with the Crown and in a dominating position in the Protectorate as a whole. The period from about 1920 to 1953 was one of persistent friction between the Protectorate and the Buganda Governments. Reference may be made here to two issues on which the latter pursued a consistently hostile attitude towards colonial policy in what it believed to be the interests of Buganda sovereignty. These were the questions of the Legislative Council, and of closer union between the East African territories. The establishment in 1920 of a Legislative Council for Uganda aroused in Buganda alarm and suspicion: here was a body which was responsible for the Protectorate as a whole, and it appeared to the Buganda Government that it constituted both a threat to Buganda's special position and a rival to the authority of the Lukiiko. This hostility to the Legislative Council did not abate when Africans were later brought into its membership. A protracted battle to avoid the obligation to select members for the Council was waged by the Lukiiko—a battle which extended through the deportation crisis of 1953 to the immediate pre-independence years. A major part was played by Buganda in securing the abandonment, at any rate for the time being, of a policy of closer union between the East African territories with the ultimate goal of federation, which was the subject of so many reports and committees in the 1920s and 1930s. If the idea of a Legislative Council representing the interests of Uganda as a whole was distasteful to the Baganda, how much more so was that of an organization on an East African basis which would represent the interests not only of the powerful European settlers of Kenya, but also of a multitude of other African peoples among whom Buganda's voice would be negligible.

By 1953, the year in which the Governor, Sir Andrew Cohen, deported the Kabaka Mutesa II, the Buganda authorities were beginning to be seriously alarmed as to the future intentions of the protecting power and of the new political parties which were just beginning to make an impact. For the first time the prospect of independence in the foreseeable, and indeed near, future was being seriously considered. With the emphasis which the Governor was laying on the future development of Uganda as a unitary state, and his evident desire to work towards independence in alliance with political parties on a Uganda-wide basis, Buganda began to fear for her survival as a semi-autonomous state. Political parties had been formed in the past, but they had been virtually confined to Buganda and had been concerned with Buganda issues. In 1952, however, the first truly Uganda political party, the Uganda National Congress, had come into being and, though still largely Baganda in composition, its aim was clearly to make a Protectorate-wide appeal. Furthermore, the post-war years had seen a hastening of the process whereby the cultural and economic gap between Buganda and the rest of the country was remorselessly closing. Agricultural prosperity and the growth of industry in the east and the all-pervading results of a couple of generations of education in the trans-Nile provinces had all but destroyed Buganda's commanding position in the Protectorate as a whole. It was clear to the Kabaka and his Government that a positive stand against the growing forces of encroachment upon Buganda's national identity and internal sovereignty had to be made. The resurrection of the old East African federation scare provided an excellent pretext. Fully supported by the Lukiiko, the Kabaka first demanded assurances on the federation issue, and then coupled this with more drastic demands: that responsibility for Buganda's affairs should be transferred from the Colonial to the Foreign Office, and that preparations should be made for the independence of *Buganda* within a short and stated space of time. Moreover, he indicated his unwillingness to co-operate further in the compromise which had been devised whereby he nominated Buganda's representatives in the Legislative Council. As is well known, the result was the Kabaka's deportation and his elevation in the eyes of his subjects to the status of a martyr for the Buganda national cause. The Kabaka returned to his kingdom in 1955 amid the tumultuous rejoicing of his people. Though theoretically a constitutional monarch under the new Agreement of 1955, the Kabaka, supported by the devotion of the vast bulk of his subjects, now wielded far greater personal power than he or his father had ever done before.

The new Buganda Government, usually described as 'traditionalist', though 'ultra-nationalistic' in the Buganda sense would probably be more accurate, had everything its own way. Secure in its support from the Kabaka, and with the Lukiiko and chieftaincy purged of all who were not wholehearted supporters of the post-restoration régime, it had little to fear from the Protectorate Government whose powers of control had been drastically curtailed by the 1955 Agreement. Although the Governor still retained powers of veto, such as those over draft Buganda laws and the annual estimates, and could himself give formal advice, the Resident and his staff were thenceforth impotent to influence the internal administration of the kingdom. The Buganda Government, furthermore, pursued a policy of passive non-co-operation towards the ministries of the Central Government throughout the period 1955 to 1962.

The first major issue on which battle was joined with the Central Government was once again the question of Buganda's members of the Legislative Council. Under the 1955 Agreement, Buganda had to be represented in the Council. The Lukiiko, however, determined that no elections should be held in Buganda for the Council of 1958. It then fought a protracted legal battle on the issue that this refusal to elect members was not in breach of the Agreement; and the final decision of the Privy Council on this point (adverse to Buganda) was not given till 1960, by which time Uganda was about to have fresh elections for a new Legislative Council. In 1958, the Lukiiko pursued the offensive with a resolution calling for the termination of the Buganda Agreement and the restoration to the Kabaka of the powers thereby surrendered to the Crown; and it refused to co-operate with the Wild Committee set up to recommend on the form of elections for the Legislative Council of 1961 as a prelude to the granting of Uganda's independence. 1959 saw the boycott disturbances in Buganda which, directed against the Indian trading community, evidenced a xenophobic aspect of Buganda nationalist feeling: they were successful in virtually driving the Indian shop-keeper out of the rural trading centres of Buganda. Having successfully resisted pressure from the Protectorate Government to have elections in Buganda for the Legislative Council of 1958–60, though failing to establish their legal right to have done so, the Buganda authorities adopted a rather different line of resistance towards the elections for the 1961 Council. Though elections took place in Buganda, it was made clear to the Baganda that to register as an elector was tantamount to disloyalty to the Kabaka. As a result, despite all efforts of the Protectorate Government, less than 4 per cent of those entitled to do so, registered. Meanwhile, negotiations dragged on over the Lukiiko's demand for the termination of the Agreement, and a 'Plan' was drawn up by the Lukiiko for an independent Buganda within the Commonwealth and as a member of the United Nations. When, however, it became clear that the Secretary of State would not give way, a uni-lateral declaration of independence was made on 1 January 1961. Although this was a mere gesture and no effort was made to make the declaration a reality, nevertheless, with the moral victory secured by the virtually united stand made by the Baganda against registration for the elections, the Buganda Government was in a strong position at the outset of the vital final eighteen months of colonial rule. Even if it could not secure its full aim of separate independence for the kingdom (if indeed this was ever seriously considered as attainable), at least it could obtain a degree of autonomy far greater than the colonial power had ever contemplated.

The Central Government was controlled by the Democratic Party under the premiership of Benedicto Kiwanuka, himself a Muganda. It had come to power as the result of the 1961 election, and during its tenure of office internal self-government was granted in March 1962. It owed its majority in the Legislative Council, however, to the twenty D.P. representatives of rural Buganda constituencies in which only a derisory proportion of Baganda had voted. To this Government the Buganda authorities showed an implacable hostility far more intense and bitter than that which had been shown towards the former colonial régime. In its relations with the radical opposition party in the Legislative Council, the Uganda Peoples Congress, the Buganda authorities were more open to reconciliation; whilst the Congress had, during the 1961 election, adopted a far more circumspect policy towards the Buganda Government than had its rival, the Democratic Party. At first sight it would appear strange that the Buganda 'nationalists' or traditionists should have been more favourably disposed towards a party whose radical, socialist and pan-African platform must have been far more unacceptable to them than that of the comparatively conservative Democratic Party. There were, however, various reasons for the attitude of the Buganda authorities. One of these was the close association between the Democratic Party and the Roman Catholic Church, an association which repelled the members of the Protestant ascendancy in Buganda, which had, since the outcome of the religious wars of the 1890s, been dominant in the Government and administrative hierarchy of the kingdom.

The Munster Commission carried out investigations during the early months of 1961 with a view primarily to resolving the problem of the constitutional relationship between the kingdoms and the districts and the Central Government of Uganda on independence. It recommended that the existing powers of Buganda should be considerably increased, and that she should enjoy a federal position under the independence constitution; that the other three kingdoms should stand in a semi-federal position; and that, as far as the rest of the country was concerned, the government should be a unitary one. Buganda reserved her position as to whether or not she accepted the Munster recommendations, and her attitude was still uncertain when the Constitutional Conference met in September 1961. One of the recommendations of the Conference was that Buganda might, if it wished, opt for indirect elections, through the Lukiiko, of members of the Uganda National Assembly. To this Kiwanuka objected strongly; and it was at this point that an alliance was openly formed between Buganda and the Uganda Peoples Congress. An interim constitution based on the Munster recommendations was then agreed upon.

Before the Constitutional Conference in September, a new movement had been formed—the Kabaka Yekka—which was in fact, though not in name, a Buganda national political party. An understanding was reached with the Uganda Peoples Congress that the latter would not oppose Kabaka Yekka candidates in the election of members of the Lukiiko to be held in March 1962. The result of this election was an overwhelming victory for Kabaka Yekka, after which the Lukiiko opted for indirect elections to the National Assembly. In April a general election was held elsewhere in Uganda resulting in the defeat of Kiwanuka's government. The Lukiiko then selected the National Assembly members for Buganda from among its Kabaka Yekka majority and a coalition government of Uganda Peoples Congress and Kabaka Yekka came to power in Uganda.

The Constitutional Conference of June 1962 drew up a new independence constitution which differed from its predecessor principally in that it gave federal, rather than semi-federal, status to the western kingdoms and Busoga. Yet the constitutions of these other kingdoms gave them far more restricted powers than those enjoyed by Buganda. As far as the latter was concerned, she entered the independence era in October 1962 with a constitution which gave her a far greater degree of internal autonomy than any but the most extreme Buganda 'nationalists' could have believed attainable a couple of years earlier. Yet, in the last resort, Buganda would inevitably be the weaker party in any struggle with the central power, for the latter had exclusive control over the armed forces—a fact which events were to make tragically clear to the Baganda a few years later.

The alliance between Buganda, through the Kabaka Yekka, and the Uganda Peoples Congress was from the start an uneasy one. The election of the Kabaka as the first President of Uganda on the first anniversary of independence temporarily allayed Buganda's distrust of the future. The first real crisis of confidence between Buganda and the Central Government came when the latter insisted on honouring an undertaking enshrined in the Independence Constitution that a referendum would be held in two of the 'lost counties'. These so-called 'lost counties' had been part of the nineteenth-century kingdom of Bunyoro, but had, after the Omukama's rebellion in 1894, which the Baganda had helped to suppress, been handed over to Buganda. The Banyoro inhabitants of the area had never become reconciled to Buganda rule and the colonial power had belatedly tried to rectify its earlier injustice by appointing a commission of inquiry in 1962. As a result of the commission's recommendations, it had been stated in the Constitution that a referendum in the area must take place. The referendum was held and, as a result, the two counties were transferred to Bunyoro in January 1965.

In August 1964 the alliance between the Kabaka Yekka and the Uganda Peoples Congress had been formally terminated, and a year later it was decided to disband Kabaka Yekka. The Buganda authorities felt that the kingdom's interests could be better served by working through the Uganda Peoples Congress and in building up the Bantu anti-Obote elements in the party. By this time, feeling among the other Bantu people, particularly in the western kingdoms, was becoming increasingly suspicious of the always large, and now apparently growing, influence of the Nilotic elements from the north in the U.P.C. Government. Forgetting their old jealousy of Buganda, whose privileged position both during the Protectorate period and under the 1962 Constitution they had resented, they seemed ready to make common cause with Buganda in view of what they believed to be the threat of domination by Nilotic politicians. In particular, the westerners resented and feared the army with so large a Nilotic element in its composition, concerning the activities of which in Toro and Ankole disturbing reports were current. The hopes of the Bantu tended to centre around Ibingira, a Muhima cabinet minister from Ankole, and matters came to a head early in 1966. Whether or not the President, Ibingira, and his colleagues were preparing to act against the Prime Minister, Obote, the latter forestalled them. In February the President was removed from his office (though he still remained Kabaka of Buganda), Ibingira and his immediate supporters were arrested, and the Constitution was overthrown.

In April 1966, a new Constitution was promulgated which (together with a later amendment in July) reduced Buganda to the same constitutional status as that of the other kingdoms. The latter also lost certain of their powers, the power of appointment of chiefs and other members of the local civil service being transferred to the Central Government's Public Service Commission. In May, after the Buganda Government had delivered threats which they were hardly in a position to enforce, the Kabaka's palace was shelled and there was considerable loss of life as the army adopted the traditional early colonial role of 'pacification' in rural Buganda. Direct rule by the Central Government came into force, operating through commissioners in charge of the districts into which Buganda was now divided. With her Kabaka in exile and the kingdom treated virtually as a conquered country, Buganda might well ironically compare her fate to that of Bunyoro seventy years earlier: then Bunyoro had paid the price of intransigence to the colonial régime whilst Buganda had reaped the rewards of co-operation. In September 1967 a fresh Constitution was brought into force: the last remnants of federalism were swept away; the institution of kingship was abolished; and, as for Buganda, the very word no longer appears in the Constitution.[1]

The significance of 'tribalism' in a Buganda context

Can we from this brief review of Buganda's history during this century see any pointers to the answer to the first question —what is the significance of the words 'tribe' and 'tribalism' when used in their purely descriptive sense, free from any

[1] Save in Art. 102, where it is stated that reference in existing laws to the kingdom of Buganda shall be construed as references to the districts of East Mengo, Masaka, Mubende and West Mengo; these districts form four of the eighteen into which Uganda is divided by Art. 71.

pejorative implications? It will have been noticed that, in using the terms Buganda 'nationalism' and Buganda 'nationalists', inverted commas have been added. Not to use them would give rise to the charge of question-begging until the question whether there is such a thing as Buganda nationalism, rather than Buganda tribalism, has been answered. It is, however, submitted that, as far as Buganda is concerned, nationalism and tribalism are one and the same thing, the two words being interchangeable in this context. The Buganda tribe appears to have the main attributes of a nation. On the other hand, a Uganda nation hardly exists even today, except in the sense in which eighteenth-century diplomatists spoke of the Turkish nation to embrace Greeks and Serbs, that is to say, to mean all people owing allegiance to a common sovereign, the Sultan. Buganda had been for centuries a sovereign state before she accepted by treaty the protection of the British Crown. Her institutions, adapted to modern conditions, remained intact till 1966. Throughout the kingdom there is a common language and during this century there has been a growing body of Luganda literature. But above all, there has been the sense of a common identity and loyalty and a sense of pride in being Baganda. This, no doubt, all amounts to tribal feeling; but it equally well amounts to national feeling and nationalism in the European sense. As far as size and wealth goes, Buganda would not appear insignificant when compared with some of the Versailles succession states, such as Latvia and Esthonia, or even with the Irish Republic. Yet the creation of these states on the principle of nationalism and self-determination was heralded as laudable and progressive by the very bodies of political opinion in England who are ready to condemn Buganda nationalism, or its desire for self-determination, as tribal and reactionary.

Yet, although a Muganda's loyalty has been first and foremost to his own people, his Kabaka and his national institutions, this does not mean that he has (or had before the recent tragic events), no feeling of loyalty towards Uganda as a whole. Perhaps it would not be fanciful to draw a parallel between the average Muganda in this respect and the average Englishman in respect of the British Commonwealth. Interest in, and knowledge of, the Commonwealth naturally varies according to the general education and degree of information which the man concerned possesses. At one end of the scale, Englishmen may be almost ignorant of its existence, or at any rate of its identity. The average Englishman, however, is conscious of, and mildly interested in, this supernational structure. He may well, moreover, be proud of the special part which Britain has, as the result of history, played in its development. Nevertheless, he does not accept that he should automatically owe a sense of loyalty to it. Furthermore, among a large section of the community doubts are growing, rightly or wrongly, as to whether Britain, as a result of membership of such an organization whose members do not necessarily share her outlook or standards, good or bad, may not be in danger of being coerced into courses of action which might not conform to her standards of what is right, or which might not be to her national advantage. Among these people attachment to the organization is, at best, lukewarm. Be this as it may, in the final analysis, if a clear-cut choice had to be made between conflicting interests of the Commonwealth and of Britain, the vast majority of the inhabitants of this country would unhesitatingly choose the latter.

So too the Baganda have a dual tie of interest in, and affection for, Buganda and Uganda. That for Uganda has been most strongly felt among the better-educated and thus better-informed, but all have felt some sense of pride in the new nation-state, which Buganda had, in the past, done so much to create. But the degrees of loyalty felt towards the two have been of a very different quality. That towards Uganda as a whole has been largely an intellectual one, lacking emotional roots. It would, indeed, be hard for a Muganda to feel any deep sense of brotherhood and identity with, for example, the Nilotic peoples of the north whose indigenous language and culture differ from theirs as much as those of a Frenchman do from those of a Hungarian. The Muganda's devotion to Buganda, on the other hand, is that of the ardent nationalist the world over—a deep passionate love of his country, its culture, and its traditional institutions. So long as the Baganda were satisfied that the Uganda Government was pursuing policies which coincided with the interests of Buganda, they were prepared to give it their loyalty. When, however, the interests of the two clashed, then only a small minority of Baganda have been prepared to opt for Uganda. To this minority, comprising many of Buganda's intellectual élite, the recent events must have produced an especial crisis of allegiance. They have seen the forces of Uganda nationalism bring destruction to their homeland and have seen the overthrow of its institutions. Where in their hearts does their loyalty now lie?

The next question is how far the term 'tribalism' with the pejorative implications of backward-looking attitudes of mind, of retreat from the realities of twentieth-century conditions, is applicable to Buganda nationalism. Now, the nationalism of all peoples who have had to struggle to achieve, or preserve, their national identity tends to contain a large element of nostalgia for the past. History, both factual and legendary, is what nationalism feeds on—the cruelties of the people's oppressors and the glories of the golden age before the oppressors came. Ireland is a typical example of this, where the nationalist movement drew so much of its inspiration and strength from the memories of the persecutions and the myths of the golden age of saints and scholars.

The Buganda authorities, in their highly successful efforts during the decade from 1955 onwards to preserve intact their existing institutions and practices (referred to as 'traditional' even though, in fact, they often dated from no further back than the beginning of the present century), particularly in the fields of administration and justice, had, moreover, a more positive objective than the mere wish to conserve. If forces hostile to the preservation of Buganda's national identity and political security were to be permitted to insinuate into Buganda new institutions and practices, these might then be used as a means to undermine Buganda's position, and so a barrier against change from outside had to be created. An example of this is to be seen in the refusal of the Buganda Government to co-operate with the Protectorate Government in the reform of the Buganda court system, or to abolish the special jurisdiction of the clan heads, which lay outside the purview of any court of law. This refusal stemmed, no doubt, not so much from a desire to protect the existing system from change, as from reluctance to transfer any powers held by purely Buganda bodies to an extra-Buganda authority, such as the High Court, and from fear lest, once transferred, such powers might be used to undermine the Buganda régime. So, too, opposition to direct elections to the National Assembly was founded on the belief that indirectly-elected members would be more under the Buganda Government's control and less likely to transfer their allegiance from Buganda's cause. Indeed, as has already been mentioned, in the early years of the century, before Buganda had come to look on the Protectorate Government's policies as a threat to her national identity, the Buganda Government had shown itself eager, indeed almost ruthless, in the cause of reform, and even since 1955 that Government showed itself ready to undertake measures of internal reform where these did not appear as a possible threat to her national interests.

Yet, when all this has been said, one is still left with the feeling that there has been a desire to retain much of what may be loosely termed as traditional, even when this has been hard to reconcile with Western ideas of individual liberty, because this has been part of the pattern of life which the Baganda nationalists cherish. An example of this can be seen in the Customary Offences Law of 1964. Though this did not go so far as the proposed Law in the neighbouring kingdom of Toro, which would have made it a criminal offence 'to cough, sneeze or gurgle during a royal meal', it certainly contained sections dealing with 'insulting the dignity of the Kabaka' which seem somewhat incongruous in a modern state. So, too, chiefs have possessed powers, in fact if not in law, which may be described either as 'paternalistic' or 'oppressive' according to political temperament. Undoubtedly, the state of society to which the Baganda nationalists have looked has been one which would retain far more of the institutions, values and attitudes of mind and methods of administration which have been inherited from the past than would be acceptable in the typical post-independence African country. If this, however, is what the Baganda as a whole really want, it is hard to see why they should be denied it.

The answer to the third and last question, whether the term 'tribalism' in the sense of a force hostile to the growth of the national unity of the post-independence state, is applicable to Buganda, is clearly 'yes'. In such circumstances the Central Government could pursue one of three broad courses of policy. It could permit the growth of separatism and acquiesce in probable fragmentation; it could suppress, with bloodshed if necessary, the forces of local nationalism; or it could devise a constitutional compromise which recognized a reasonable degree of autonomy for those of the component parts of the state which so wished, acceptable locally and yet workable nationally. This is what the 1962 Constitution endeavoured to achieve. It would then have remained for the Central Government to wait for time to redress the balance between the two conflicting loyalties, aiding by its patience and tolerance the growth of the national, at the expense of the local, loyalty, as people came to see from the Government's policies that their true interests lay in the national unit. Such may seem the counsel of perfection, but other nations have succeeded in similar tasks, though the period involved may have amounted to centuries. In Uganda, however, neither side had, apparently, sufficient determination or sufficient trust in the other's good faith to make the compromise work; and wherever the blame may ultimately lie, the choice was made, after a brief period of three and a half years, to reject the third course in favour of the second.

NATIONALISM AND
PARTICULARISM IN SOMALIA

I. M. Lewis

As is well known, the conflict over Somali self-determination in the Horn of Africa derives directly from the fact that, due to the accidents of colonial history, the Somali nation overflows its present boundaries and reaches into French Somaliland,[1] eastern Ethiopia, and northern Kenya. The consequence is that perhaps a third of the total nation of four million are at present living under what they consider alien rule, and tend to look nostalgically towards the Somali Republic as their natural home. The conflicting positions of the parties in the resultant campaign for the detachment of the Somali areas of Kenya and Ethiopia to join the Republic need not be discussed in detail here. Kenya and Ethiopia are naturally as loath to concede these Somali demands as the Somali Republic is anxious to press them.

Yet underlying this alliance of convenience in the face of a common threat, there is a more basic imperative which drives Ethiopia and Kenya into one camp and Somalia into another. It is true that from the point of view of history, Ethiopia and Kenya could scarcely seem more dissimilar. After all, from this perspective Kenya is as a new-born babe compared with Ethiopia. The origins of Ethiopian sovereignty lie buried in fourth-century Axum; the country possesses an indigenous nationalizing core culture, that of the politically dominant Christian Amharas; and to an extent which seems almost miraculous to other African nationalists it survived the colonial partition almost entirely unscathed. This is certainly a unique legacy. But from the point of view of its underlying political

339

structure, Ethiopia lies close to Kenya at one end of a scale of national integration whose other limit is defined by the Somali Republic. Here, of course, I refer to the fact that both Kenya and Ethiopia are essentially arbitrary artificial creations, patchworks of different tribes and ethnic groups, possessing little overall cohesion and national patriotism except that conferred by strongly centralized government and a necessarily passionate attachment to the frontiers which, more than anything else, define their very existence. Even if there were no Somali presence within their boundaries, and no Somali problem, they would still have to assert their territoriality since this is the primary element of their identity, the basis of their as yet fragile nationalism. Somalia presents a stark contrast. Somalis do not have to be taught that they owe loyalty to their state. For this is founded in a partial transformation into modern statehood of an existing and historically long-standing traditional cultural nationalism. Their problem is to complete this process, to make the whole nation one state[2] and not, as in Ethiopia and Kenya and almost everywhere else in Africa, to make the state a nation.

This lack of territoriality in the Somali case exists in my view in its own right, and consistent as it is with the facts of Somali dispersion into Ethiopia and Kenya, and with the traditional nomadic bias of their society, reinforces their campaign for unification. This distinction between the Somali Republic on the one hand and Ethiopia and Kenya on the other, which lies at the basis of the Somali dispute, also gives the Republic itself a unique character. For here we see that kind of micronationalism, usually known as tribalism[3] (which almost everywhere else is a source of disunity and conflict), made the basis of statehood, and indeed the basic premise on which the Somali Republic is founded, consisting as it does of two ethnically homogeneous former colonies (British Somaliland and ex-Italian Somalia). This raises the question, if the Republic has already as its birthright that degree of national integration which every other African state aspires to attain, how does this affect its internal political structure? And, further, does its internal political life then necessarily differ quite radically from that of other African states which are less well-endowed in this respect? In pursuing these questions in what follows

I begin with a brief outline of the traditional Somali political system, and then move on to what in anthropological parlance might be called an extended case-history reviewing the interplay between the main political elements prior to and consequent on the formation of the Republic.

Cultural unity and social division among the Somali

Prior to their colonization by Britain, France, Italy, and Ethiopia at the end of last century, the Somali people formed a single cultural and linguistic unit,[4] but not a single political entity. Although a few Muslim sultanates existed from the tenth century along the coast and sometimes inland, in the main Somali political life, based on a segmentary patrilineal system, flowed on with little interruption. With the additional device of a form of political contract, binding members of a given lineage to pay and receive damages for injury and death in concert, kinship groups could achieve a degree of political cohesion which at its maximum extent might embrace as many as (but no more than) thirty, or forty thousand spearmen. And such extended unity was always rare and ephemeral because it was not underpinned by any permanent administrative organization, and because it was exercised in an overwhelmingly nomadic environment where the flux of men and livestock in the perpetual search for water and pasture strongly militated against the formation of large, stable political units. For the purposes of grazing, territory was open to all comers and no individual or group could assert prescriptive rights over it. Concordant with this was the extreme democracy of the traditional pattern of decision-making, in which, at every order of grouping, every adult man participated; and no instituted offices of chieftaincy with real power were recognized. In these circumstances traditional Somali nationalism was less a political force than a cultural phenomenon.[5]

Yet their sense of identity as a distinct people, reinforced by their long attachment to Islam, had always potential political value. And the same principles of affiliation which at lower levels of grouping were applied to mobilize lineage against lineage, also existed at national level in the form of a single all-embracing national pedigree. This national genealogy brings together all the main and subsidiary lineage divisions, and ultimately every Somali individual, as the descendants of two collateral ancestors: Somali and Sab.[6] The principal groups descended from Somali are the Dir, Isaq, Hawiye, and Darod; while Sab is the progenitor of the Digil and Rahanwin. These last two groups are in fact great lineage confederations and contain representatives of almost every other major Somali lineage. They are largely cultivators and live in the fertile belt of land between the Shebelle and Juba rivers in southern central Somalia.[7]

The Darod are both the largest and the most widely-scattered group. They live as nomads in north-east and central Somalia, in the Haud and Ogaden under Ethiopian jurisdiction, in the extreme south of Somalia, and ultimately spill over into Northern Kenya where they make up the largest element in this 250,000-strong Somali community. This wide-ranging distribution gives the Darod the most direct stake in Pan-Somali unification, a consideration out of which hostile governments have often sought to make political capital.[8] The Dir, Isaq, and Hawiye occupy respectively the north-west, north-central, and southern-central parts of the Republic, with also a small Dir community on the southern coast. Like the Darod, they are all mainly camel-nomads, though some Dir and Isaq in the north, and some Hawiye in the south practise cultivation. These three groups are more closely related to each other than any of them is to the Darod, despite their geographical dispersal, and a more direct link between the northern regions (the former British Protectorate) and the southern regions (the former Italian Somalia) is provided by the occurrence of Dir communities in each region. Thus these three groups on the one hand, and the Darod on the other, are so distributed that they provide kinship ties bridging the regional divisions between what were formerly the British Protectorate and Italian Somalia.

Since these large lineage-groups, which are today highly significant foci of political allegiance, are all ultimately related, it will be obvious that Somali politics, even at the national level, have a familistic character. It is thus no idle boast when Somali nationalists claim that they are all one family; although, like other families, a much-divided one. Moreover, the struggle for power between homologous, and in genealogical terms, related groups, which was traditionally founded in fierce competition for control of sparse grazing and water resources, was carried out within the medium of a common culture, with a shared framework of values and assumptions, and in terms of a political game whose rules were known and accepted by all. All concerned shared a common ethnic identity and an acute sense of being Somali which was by no means untinged with feelings of superiority towards their neighbours outside the fold. Unlike the situation almost everywhere else in Africa, consequently, the advent of colonial rule did not lead to the growth of an entirely new sense of national awareness. Quite the contrary occurred: this existing explicit nationalism, which many of the early colonial officials found unbearably assertive, was curtailed and confined on a regional basis by the new colonial frontiers. And in the new colonial territories into which the Somali nation was divided, the establishment of foreign administration brought new objectives and goals, new prizes, to be competed for by the various constituent segments of the nation. Thus in the British Protectorate, almost from its inception, the Isaq played a dominant role in commerce and politics, whereas the Dir and Darod communities to the west and east of the Isaq remained well outside the main flow of events. This followed from the fact that the principal early commercial centres and ports lay in Isaq territory, and this trend was reinforced in the later political history of the Protectorate by the widespread Isaq resistance to the proto-nationalist rebellion led by the fiery Darod Shaikh Muhammad 'Abdille Hassan in the period 1900–20.[9]

Further south in Somalia, again initially largely because of their location within the primary sphere of early Italian colonial activity, the Hawiye were for long nearer to the political centre and more co-operative towards the Italians than the ebullient Darod nomads of the north-east. Indeed, the fact that Mogadishu, the capital, was essentially a Hawiye settlement gave this group a permanent political advantage. Equally, although somewhat later in the history of the colony, the Digil and Rahanwin became quite closely associated with the foreign authorities through their involvement in the settler banana plantations which were created on their land, and for which they supplied most of the labour force. Their influence, it is true, tended to be weakened by the disparagement to which, as cultivators, they were traditionally subjected by the proud and ethnically 'pure' Somali nomads. For this evaluation was readily adopted by their Italian masters, especially in the fascist period.

Finally, although the overwhelmingly nomadic Darod, occupying the most arid regions of the colony, remained for long outside the mainstream of government activity, from the 1930s onwards they began to assume a prominent position as *askaris* in the colonial police.[10] Their influence was augmented by the large numbers which they contributed to the Italian armies which invaded Ethiopia in 1936. The Italian collapse and the establishment of British Military Rule in Somalia in 1942 found them again ready to play an important position in the militia. Darod recruits provided the backbone of the hastily assembled but surprisingly effective Somalia Gendarmerie formed at this time, coinciding with the birth of modern Somali national politics. The Somali Youth League, the present government party of the Republic, which was established as a club in 1943 with strong Darod support, was almost immediately spread rapidly and widely through the country; and here the Gendarmerie played an important role. Its lasting influence here can be seen quite directly in the fact that a substantial proportion of those who have since become leading political figures, from the rank of Minister down, served in this force.

In this formative period, when the question of the future status of Somalia and the other ex-Italian colonies was being heatedly debated by the four major powers, and later by the United Nations, it was predictably the Darod-dominated S.Y.L. which most adamantly opposed the return of the Italians and campaigned most strongly for independence and unity. With this opposition, the local Italian community found it fairly easy to encourage rival organizations, involving mainly Hawiye and Digil and Rahanwin elements, which were less uncompromisingly resistant to the idea of continued Italian authority and generally less radical in their aspirations. And when the Italians were in fact returned as Trusteeship administrators in 1950, although with only ten years' mandate under

United Nations authority, it was again the Darod-dominated S.Y.L. with whom they had to wrestle and eventually placate.[11]

Throughout this period of the development of nationalistic Somali political organizations it is important to reiterate that what was happening was not the creation of a new idea, inspired by foreign models, but the transformation of old ideas and loyalties into a modern idiom. To unite politically to press for independence and self-government, it was not necessary for Somalis to invoke the concept of African identity, or solidarity, which was essential to those early African nationalists seeking to summon support for a nationhood transcending tribalism. All that was required was the direct and traditionally grounded appeal to Somali self-determination. This fact, consistent as it is with Somali ethnic attitudes, has tended to isolate Somali nationalism from African nationalism elsewhere, and has not helped the Somali Republic in its foreign relations.

The end of the colonial era

That in brief is the particularistic background of clan divisions within a common culture which the two regions brought with them when they came to form the Republic in 1960. Now we must review the two distinct colonial legacies with which they were endowed. As far as the British north was concerned, development in this long-neglected 'cinderella of empire' began effectively only in the mid-1950s. By 1960, when elections were held for the Protectorate's newly expanded legislative council (first established in 1957), the party political field was dominated by two local organizations: the Isaq-based Somaliland National League (founded c. 1935), and the Dir- and Darod-supported United Somali Party. At this time of nationalist pan-Somali fervour, these two parties were allied and formed a joint government (holding 32 of the available 33 seats in the legislature) under the leadership of the S.N.L. leader as Prime Minister.[12]

By this time the Protectorate's administration had been almost completely 'Somalized', further modest developments in educational and health services had been achieved, and the hides and skins trade, the mainstay of the country's economy, was earning £1¼ million annually. Imports, however, cost almost twice as much, and the Protectorate's budget—now running at a mere £1½ million—was heavily dependent on British aid. It was with this slender endowment, and no more than a handful of university graduates, that the territory was suddenly thrust into independence on 26 June 1960, after a few weeks of frantic last-minute scramble. With this minimal preparation, the Protectorate's élite regarded, with mixed feelings, the impending union with Somalia for which they had been striving. Despite their traditional arrogant pride which, if anything, British rule had sharpened, they could not but view their country, both in terms of size (c. 750,000 inhabitants) and development, as the junior partner in the forthcoming match.

Everything that had happened in Somalia, since its establishment in 1950 as a United Nations Trusteeship with ten years to run before its independence, seemed to confirm this evaluation. Whereas in the Protectorate it was only after 1955 that progress towards independence became a clear goal, in Somalia from their return in 1950 the Italians were committed to preparing the country for self-government.[13] Here everything was done on a lavish and much-heralded scale. By 1956 all the districts and provinces of the territory were under the direct control of Somali officials, and the first national elections had been held for the newly-established legislative assembly. Here the strongly-based S.Y.L. romped home to secure forty-three of the available sixty 'open' seats,[14] leaving the opposition, Hizbia Digil Mirifle (representing much of the voting strength of the Digil and Rahanwin cultivators), holding thirteen seats as the only major party based directly on lineage affiliation.

In the first Somali government formed after these elections, the Darod hegemony within the S.Y.L. received a severe jolt. The Prime Minister, appointed by the Italian authorities, was Hawiye, and he selected a cabinet which favoured Hawiye rather than Darod affiliation. This led to dissension within the ranks of the party, and prompted the strong Darod faction within it to adopt a more radical stance on the issues of Somali unification and independence than the Prime Minister's own immediate supporters. This encouraged the Hawiye wing within the League to seek allies amongst the Digil and Rahanwin to buttress growing Darod disaffection; and this new drive for allies amongst these southern cultivators was aided by the latter's heterogeneous clan composition. Particularly amongst those elements of the Digil and Rahanwin who were of northern nomadic origin (Darod and Hawiye, etc.), and who were relatively recent client recruits, there was growing pressure for the assertion of traditional clan identity. These fissiparous tendencies threatening the solidarity of the Digil and Rahanwin were further strengthened by new legislation introduced in 1959 officially abolishing the traditional status of adopted client.

Thus in the greatly-enlarged new cabinet formed by the Hawiye Prime Minister after the 1959 elections,[15] two former leading officials of the H.D.M.S. were included as ministers, and the remaining ministries were distributed fairly evenly among the other major clan groups. In this attempt to create a government founded on the principle of clan balance, the difficulty was of course to find ministries for all those who had contributed to the S.Y.L.'s highly successful campaign. The Darod were, if anything, again under-represented, and their most radical faction remained dissatisfied and highly critical of the Prime Minister and his policies. For a short time indeed their leaders were expelled from the party. Their position, however, was soon to change very radically in the new political circumstances created by the union of Somalia with British Somaliland.

The unified republic, 1960–7

When the two territories formally joined together on 1 July 1960, as the northern and southern regions of the Republic, the two parliaments met together at Mogadishu to form a new national assembly of 123 members (33 from the north; 90 from the south).[16] The southern assembly president was elected provisional President of the Republic, his place as assembly leader being filled by a northerner; and the more difficult business of deciding who was to lead the new coalition government formed from the ruling northern and southern parties began in earnest. In this new political situation where the most direct lineage link between the two territories was through the Darod, the leaders of the radical Darod faction within the S.Y.L. were thrust to the forefront, and one of these men who had recently returned from Rome with a degree in political science[17] was selected as the most appropriate Prime Minister for the new State. The balance of power within the government now swung away from the Hawiye. The former Hawiye premier became Foreign Minister; and the northern S.N.L. leader and ex-premier became Minister of Defence. All these arrangements took place under a constitution which had been prepared in the south prior to independence and which included provisions for further unification. This constitution was, however, only provisional, and had still to be finally ratified by a national referendum which would enable the north to express its views.

In the meantime, the coalition government (S.Y.L., S.N.L.-U.S.P.) had to face the immediate problem of giving substance to the formal act of union and to address its energies to integrating the separate British and Italian colonial traditions to which it had fallen heir. By 1964, although the language question continued to pose difficulties, integration in most other aspects of government had been almost completely achieved.[18] By this time the provincial and district administrative services, the police, the national army, and the fiscal, accounting, and legal systems had been satisfactorily integrated with the aid, in many cases, of United Nations' advisers. This quite rapid accommodation between the two colonial legacies was certainly facilitated by Somalia's earlier experience of British rule in the period 1941–50.

Notwithstanding this, however, the integration process was by no means entirely without incident. Significantly it was almost invariably in relation to the north that difficulties arose. That the northern region should have provided the main focus of dissension is not surprising. Although the coalition government of fourteen ministers, formed at independence, included four northerners, a proportion not discordant with the relative strengths of the two regional populations, and although senior northern officials rapidly came to hold a larger number of top administrative appointments than their numbers warranted, the north had sacrificed more than the south. Mogadishu had considerably improved its commercial and political position as capital of the Republic: but Hargeisa, the old northern region capital, had been cut down to a mere provincial headquarters and was declining in prosperity with the drift of business and trade towards the south.

The euphoria with which the north had celebrated independence consequently soon gave place to a mood of widespread resentment and disillusionment. This was most evident in the case of those of the political and administrative élite who had pressed for immediate unification, despite their misgivings over their apparent lack of preparation in comparison with the south. These British-trained northerners were now rubbing shoulders, both locally and in the south, with their Italian-trained counterparts, whom they quickly came to regard, not always without justification, as less well-trained and equipped than they were themselves.

The political parties, which had become acutely sensitive to these pressures but had not yet adjusted to them, were now in a state of flux: and in the spring of 1963 a new party, the Somali National Congress, made its appearance under the joint leadership of the former northern (Isaq) chief minister who had resigned from the coalition government, and a prominent ex-S.Y.L. leader (Hawiye). This marked the final rupture of the uneasy triple alliance of S.Y.L., S.N.L. (Isaq) and U.S.P. (Northern Darod and Dir), and left three main parties in the field: the government S.Y.L., and the new S.N.C. and Somali Democratic Party in opposition. This latter party, which claimed the most radical position, had been formed a year earlier and sought to amalgamate dissident elements of the old S.N.L., U.S.P., and H.D.M.S.[19]

These developments helped to clear the air and brought many of the currents of north-south antagonism more directly into the party political arena. The S.Y.L., still under Darod leadership, had temporarily lost support in the Isaq north to its opponents, the S.N.C. and S.D.U. These trends were strengthened in the municipal elections held at the end of 1963 when the S.Y.L. won 665 of the available 904 seats (74 per cent), the S.N.C. 105, and the S.D.U. most of the remainder. In the national assembly elections which followed in March 1964, by which time the Republic was at war with Ethiopia, the S.Y.L. gained 69 of the 123 seats, the S.N.C. 22, and the S.D.U. 15. The H.D.M.S., campaigning effectively only in their own local inter-riverine area, won 9 seats, and smaller parties took the remaining eight. Subsequent shifts of party loyalty by deputies anxious to participate in the spoils of office further strengthened the S.Y.L. bloc in the assembly.[20]

Although at various times during this turbulent period of adjustment between north and south it had seemed likely that a separatist northern party might be formed, this had not in fact happened: rather, northern and southern dissidents tended to join forces in opposing the S.Y.L. government. In fact although the economically depressed north was still very much a potential breeding-ground for discontent, many enterprising northerners had now become deeply involved in the politics and commerce of the south. Some indeed had even found it sufficiently useful, despite their Anglophone contempt for the language, to pick up Italian, although it was becoming increasingly obvious that in the long run English would be the main foreign language.[21] All this, I think, points to a growing acceptance by both north and south of the unified Republic as a basic fact of life, an unshakeable entity within which to operate to best advantage. This, at any rate, is how I interpret the position in 1964 when the pressure of external opposition to the Republic from Ethiopia and Kenya had also no doubt helped to strengthen local loyalties in this direction. Consistent with this, the new government formed after the 1964 elections not only discouraged any further clear-cut, north-south rivalry by its inclusion of a generous proportion of northerners, but it also divided the radical Darod wing of the S.Y.L. There was intense competition for the office of premier which, though eventually won by a leading member of this group, led to the displacement of the former Darod Prime Minister. This led to a split, partly on a basis of rival lineage affiliation within the Darod, and partly on a basis of personalities and conflicting ambitions. A critical factor was the backing given by the Hawiye President of the Republic to the new premier against his opponent.

This dissension amongst its Darod leaders severely embarrassed the government and jeopardized its stability, leading to a series of cabinet changes and eventually, in the summer of 1966, to its actual resignation and reappointment. Strife within the party strongly affected the position of the government, despite the fact that the premier had now himself assumed the role of party secretary-general in an effort to bring its independent-minded members to heel. Here, however, we need to take note of the fact that the normal procedure within the assembly is for votes to be cast in secret. This greatly reduces the effectiveness of party discipline and, when it comes to the vote, encourages deputies to pursue their own private interests, however venial, and however enthusiastically they may have subscribed to policies discussed beforehand in the party caucus. Governments in Somalia are very much at the mercy of the members of the assembly who are wide open to every form of pressure and whose views on policy clearly often fluctuate very rapidly according to their evaluation of the situation in terms of their own best advantage.[22]

Political events in 1967 afford an interesting test of the validity of the picture we have drawn of the main competing elements and their relations. The presidential elections which were held in the summer of 1967 were contested by two candidates, the Hawiye incumbent (President Adan Abdulle Isman), and the former Darod premier, Dr Abdirashid Ali Shirmarke who had been displaced in 1964. The first candidate was supported by the existing premier, whom in turn he had championed through thick and thin, and to whom he is related by marriage. Clearly both these men who were in office were in a strong position.

However, the rival presidential candidate had considerable support in the party, especially from all those antagonized by the premier, and had recently, apparently, entered into an alliance with Muhammad Haji Ibrahim Igal, former prime minister of British Somaliland and an ex-leader of the S.N.C., which he had recently left to join the S.Y.L. According to informed opinion prior to the election, both these men had joined forces on the understanding that if the first became president he would call upon the second to form a government. And this is precisely what happened; the new Prime Minister formed a typical Somali government containing representatives of all the main clan groups from both north and south. For the first time a northerner had become premier and had, moreover, formed at least for the time being a successful alliance between the Isaq and those Darod clansmen who supported the new President but opposed the old prime minister.

The result which carried forward the north-south coalition also continued the Darod split. It of course left a very wide field open for manoeuvre to all the other major lineage power-blocks. From what I have said before it would seem that such an arrangement was favoured by the maintenance of a strong sense of overall unity. Could it survive without it?

Circumstances which may provide the answer are in train at the time of writing (November 1967). Immediately after forming his government the new Prime Minister launched into a series of energetic moves designed to promote better relations with Ethiopia and Kenya, and as he hoped, to a more accommodating approach on the part of these two states to the outstanding problem of the status of Somalis in northern Kenya and eastern Ethiopia. Ethiopia quickly responded and the two states agreed to stop hostile propaganda and to pursue discussions on that sector of the Pan-Somali issue. Similarly at the Arusha conference in October 1967, Kenya and Somalia agreed to restore normal diplomatic relations and to seek a peaceful solution of their differences over the N.F.D. The so-called *shifta* war had stopped, at least for the time being.

The new Somali government announced that these provisional agreements involved the acceptance by both Ethiopia and Kenya that there was an issue to settle, and that there was no question of the Republic renouncing its claim for Somali self-determination in these areas. In fact, the Kenya-Somali memorandum signed by both parties provided for the establishment of a working committee consisting of Somalia, Kenya and Zambia to find a means of settling both the 'minor' and 'major' differences between the two states. Both Ethiopia and Kenya, however, seem not surprisingly to have tended to interpret this as a Somali capitulation, and the government's enemies at home had now a unique opportunity of attacking it. This in fact is what occurred. Demonstrations in Mogadishu accused the Prime Minister of a 'sell-out', and this immediately brought cries of support for the beleaguered government from the Isaq north. The S.Y.L., whose headquarters were temporarily closed in November by the government, seems again to have fallen into disarray with the displaced Darod ex-premier making political capital out of the situation.

It is impossible to forecast what will now happen, but one

important factor in the present government's favour is that the ex-premier has scant hope of resuming his position. It would be quite unacceptable to Somali opinion for both the premiership and presidency to be held by Darod incumbents, and unless the President changes sides it seems likely that the rift in Darod ranks will continue, much to the political advantage of the Isaq and Hawiye. At the same time, working in the opposite direction will be the tendency for all the major lineage groups to close their ranks in a situation of diminished external pressure.

Integration and particularism

In the foregoing record of political events the main political groupings whose manoeuvres we have had to follow are the largest distinct lineage blocks within the nation—the Darod, Dir, Hawiye, etc. Even these, as we have seen, have by no means necessarily always unfailing solidarity, since component segments may in some circumstances judge it advantageous to strike temporary alliances across these fundamental divisions within the system. Here we have to remember that in national politics, the most abiding interest of each major local voting block is to place a kinsman in a 'chair' (as they expressively put it) in the national assembly. Under what political party banner this is achieved is of secondary importance, for even if it turns out that a member is returned on a minority party ticket, he can always change his party allegiance once he is home and dry. Moreover, these splits between closely-related kinship segments may be appealed to and manipulated by ambitious politicians jockeying for power, and inflamed by personal enmities and disagreements between their representatives in the assembly. Equally, local disputes between kinship segments in the rural areas, in the traditional political system which flows on with unchecked vitality, will inevitably have a feed-back effect on the alignments of their elected representatives in the assembly. Sometimes local lineage disputes at constituency level may run counter to the alignments pursued by their parliamentary representatives, acting on some such other principle as personal interest, pecuniary pressure, or the intrinsic merits of a particular policy. Such a situation cannot long endure without the deputies concerned losing the confidence of their constituents and being under heavy pressure to change their position. This is what occurred at a higher level of grouping in relation to the northern Isaq in the first two years of independence.

The importance of kinship ties thus remains quite fundamental in contemporary Somali politics: national party politics is not something separate and distinct from local traditional politics but rather a direct extension of it, and kinship retains its all-pervasive status as the basic, though not the sole, principle of unity and division. Every Somali is acutely aware of this, and every Somali government had pledged itself to eradicate this compelling determinant of behaviour which so readily leads to the preferment of individuals and of policies often in defiance of their intrinsic merits, which threatens general administrative and governmental efficiency, and which in sum seems to negate modern bureaucratic procedures. Although the ties involved are technically those of lineage, this is universally referred to by Somalis as the 'problem of tribalism'. And, from the point of view of many of its effects which are identical to those of true 'tribalism' elsewhere, this evaluation is entirely justified.

Once this is conceded, as it must be, is the problem posed by tribalism in its special local form identical with that in every other African state? Perhaps it will be easier to consider this question if we pose it in the form: do lineage divisions jeopardize the cohesion and security of the Somali state in precisely the same way, and to the same extent, that tribalism is supposed generally to do elsewhere?

To answer this question we must first recall the effects of unification between the two halves of the Republic, bearing in mind that what underlies the formation of the state is the common national culture shared by all its members. As we have seen, the creation of the Republic immediately altered the political circumstances of the various lineage-blocks, enlarging their sphere of political interaction and greatly increasing their possibilities of manoeuvre. The north-south sub-cultural distinction also introduced a new factor, and one which, like new embryonic élitist loyalties, is not precisely conterminous with lineage identity. To the extent that the Isaq are northerners this reinforces their sense of lineage identity and exclusiveness; but the category 'northerner' also includes the overlapping Dir and Darod communities with feet in both regions of the Republic. Further, despite their long tradition of local separatism, a wider basis for potential alliance between these and the Hawiye in opposition to the Darod exists in the widened arena of national politics through their common genealogical connection with a putative ancestor named Irir. 'Iririst' tendencies towards Dir-Isaq-Hawiye alliance, which to some extent underlie actual political alignments involving some of these communities, are an important factor and clearly further offset the stark dichotomy between north and south.

As we have seen, the net effect of these various bases of alignment is less to split the Republic into rigid divisions than to provide a set of overlapping ties which, if they tend to exert a paralysing influence on bureaucracy, also seem to contribute to overall stability. These considerations apply equally to every field of public as well as of private activity, and are by no means merely restricted to the formal sphere of party politics. Thus, although the army and police were until recently commanded by generals of different lineage groups, and strongly competitive in relation to their share of the national budget and of foreign aid, the composition of each force in terms of the lineage affiliation of its members mirrors that of the nation as a whole; and it is very difficult to conceive of a situation in which either organization could be successfully pitted against the other in concerted hostility.

So far, then, I have been arguing that although lineage ties are decisive they are also integrative, and their potential in this direction is increased by the fact that they are not the only bonds which provide a basis for common interests. Other African states have a more diversified economic structure, with both new and traditional class divisions to provide foci of solidarity to some extent independently of tribal attachments: i.e. similar overlapping ties exist which help to maintain national unity and to counteract the directly divisive effects of tribal identity. Thus here I do not think that the Republic's situation differs radically from that of other African states where the divisive character of tribalism has probably often been exaggerated.[23] If anything, indeed, it might be argued that in the Somali case these lineage ties which permeate the whole state, and whose compulsive quality has been little if at all affected by economic change, are more deeply rooted and more pervasive in their effects than tribalism elsewhere.

This brings us back to the factor which does clearly distinguish the Republic from its neighbours: the presence of a homogeneous common culture embodying the notion of Somali identity. Thus the lineage divisions we have been discussing, however pervasive and evocative their appeal, operate within a well-established framework of national unity which is something more than the mere genealogical sum of its parts. For although these lineage divisions can be fitted into an all-embracing national pedigree, Somali culture exists independently over and above this as an established fact with its own loyalties and imperatives. Thus even when the members of these divisions see themselves as autonomous units pursuing their own sectional interests, they cannot escape the fact that they are also Somali, and that the way in which they order their behaviour is dictated by the moral assumptions and institutional procedures which are part and parcel of Somali identity. Ultimately the effect is that the overall Somali political system is highly stable, however unstable and ephemeral the arrangements of its component parts.

As far as the character of modern political procedure is concerned, one of the most significant consequences of this, I believe, is the contribution which it makes to the maintenance of multi-party democracy. Here I follow J. S. Mill[24] in seeing the presence of this common cultural solvent as the precondition permitting the free interplay of competing party political interests in a manner which does not call into question the cohesion or security of the state as a whole. Thus, as we have seen, there is abundant evidence of party and governmental instability, but not of the instability of the state. From its inception to the present time this has not, so far as I am aware, ever really been at hazard; and repeated party and governmental crises have had very little discernible effect on the country as a whole. In this connection it is also probably significant that in contrast to what has happened elsewhere, the Somali constitution has so far not been changed in any significant respect since the foundation of the Republic.[25] In suggesting that this common cultural heritage favours the maintenance of parliamentary democracy we have to remember of course that it does so also in a more direct way, in that the traditional pattern of decision-making, which like so much else is carried directly into the modern political theatre, is of a highly democratic character. It is presumably this rather than anything else which gives the concept of democracy as a political ideal the considerable evocative appeal which it has for Somali politicians.

These factors also, I believe, discourage the highly centralized autocracy which other African governments, like their colonial predecessors, find so necessary for the maintenance of state security and cohesion. Equally they render unnecessary, if they do not actively discourage, the cult of personality which has become so marked a feature of contemporary African political life. National identity is independent of the many politicians who strive for power, and the incumbents of the offices of prime minister and president do not need to create personal myths of omnipotence to legitimize their authority or to compensate for a lack of effective national patriotism. This, of course, is not to say that the possibility of such a charismatic leadership emerging is automatically ruled out.

If the emprisonment of particularistic divisions within a universally-accepted culture has these effects, encouraging, or at least not preventing, loose government and the tolerance of political opposition, other factors operate in the reverse direction. The very homogeneity of the society, and the absence of any widely-based and strongly-felt doctrinal differences in religion or politics, limit the range of possible grounds for the mobilization of political parties. The north-south division could, it is true, be employed for this purpose, and although it may still have a potential in this direction it has not been so used since the dissolution of the old S.N.L. and U.S.P. parties in 1963. The most natural basis of party formation would of course be that of lineage, but in practice this is limited by the need to organize a party with a sufficiently national following to have a chance of winning the elections. Conceivably, the Darod could realistically attempt this, and so could an 'Iririst' Dir-Isaq-Hawiye alliance. But once having won the elections no such narrowly-based government could hope to survive without recourse to drastic measures which would almost certainly promote a revolution. Once the principle of multi-lineage government is established, as we have seen it now clearly is, the government party must contain a nationally representative proportion of all the major lineage groups, and so almost inevitably must the other parties. But if, as will be remembered, each local constituency lineage is the group which really seeks representation through its elected member, then clearly a multi-lineage party is in reality a coalition of opposed lineage interests, with plenty of scope for internal dissension and conflict. The commitment of these lineage representatives to particular parties is thus usually slight, and the pressure to join whichever party wins an election is strong. Thus while at the last elections (1964) the S.Y.L. actually gained only 69 of the available 123 seats, their present strength in the national assembly is 105. This, of course, does not necessarily mean that a large number of deputies have gradually become converted to a new political philosophy: what it means is that they have seen, as also have their constituents, the practical advantages of being within rather than outside the government party. Moreover, such changes in party alignment do not by any means necessarily commit the government's new recruits to always voting with it in the assembly. Because of the secret voting procedure, members may, within rather ill-defined limits, enjoy the advantages of attachment to the government without paying it unswerving loyalty.

Thus we see here a number of factors which tend to work against multi-partyism and to favour a monopolistic single party system. And if we based our characterization on the situation after a government is strongly entrenched in office this would be our conclusion. But it would be inadequate. As soon as new elections are held, the pendulum swings in the opposite direction: lineage particularisms, which despite their partial ventilation within the corpus of the government party have nevertheless been excessively stifled, now reassert themselves, and typically a rash of new and often highly ephemeral parties appears to contest the elections.[26] At this point in the cycle, the principle of multi-party democracy could not be more strongly endorsed. Those opposition parties which are in permanent existence provide the essential continuity between one election and the next. I see this as a sort of compromise which enables people to hedge their bets and provide for all contingencies.

I have said enough, I think, to show that the special circumstances of the Somali Republic do give this state a unique character which is not replicated in other African states, which lack an equivalent degree of cultural nationalism. Somalia has, from its inception, possessed that sense of nationhood which others aspire to achieve. This is one aspect of the remarkable continuity between the traditional and the modern political system. This, however, is not an unmixed blessing. For although it permits a greater degree of internal political tolerance than is yet possible elsewhere, it also carries with it the firmly rooted divisive particularism of lineage rivalries. And the strength and vitality of these lineage divisions in a sense represents the price which is paid for a ready-made nationhood. From this perspective, it might be argued that those other new states which in creating a unifying national culture have to start from scratch have in the long run a better chance, or at least a stronger motive, to free themselves from the shackles of tribal particularism. If this is a correct diagnosis, its evaluation must depend upon the extent to which tribalism has in fact everywhere, and inevitably, the deleterious effects usually attributed to it.

SOMALI CABINETS: 1956–67
(Ministers only)

	Pre-unification: Somalia only		Post-unification: Somali Republic		
	1956	1959	1960	1966	1967
Darod	2	3	6*	6†	6*
Hawiye	3	4	4	3	4
Digil & Rahanwin	0	1	2	3	3
Dir	1	1	0	1‡	1‡
Isaq	0	0	2‡	3‡	4‡

* including two northerners
† including one northerner
‡ all northerners

NOTES

1 Following the March 1967 referendum, which reinforced the tie with France, it is now styled 'French Territory of the Afars and Issas'. The latter are one of the major local Somali clans, the former are a kindred Cushitic people who now dominate the political life of the territory (Lewis, 1967c).

2 cf. Namier (1952, p. 43): 'a nation which bases its unity on language cannot easily renounce groups of co-nationals intermingled with those of the neighbouring nation'.

3 I am asserting here that what are commonly distinguished as 'tribalism' and 'nationalism' seem to me to differ only in scale. I do not know of any discussion which succeeds in effectively distinguishing between them except in these terms.

4 There was and is, however, considerable dialectical differentiation between the northern nomadic and the southern cultivating Somali.

5 A fuller account of the traditional political system is given in Lewis, 1961.

6 The name 'Somali' appears to have been extended to the joint Somali-Sab community in much the same way as 'English' has come to represent all the inhabitants of Britain.

7 On Sab social structure, see Lewis, 1969b.

8 Before the recent cessation of the propaganda war between the two states, Radio Addis Ababa broadcasts specifically attacked the 'Mijerteyn' government of the Republic. This is an exaggerated reference to the political prominence of this particular Darod clan of north-east Somalia.

9 Not all the Isaq all the time opposed the Shaikh, of course (Lewis, 1965, pp. 63–91).

10 The northern Darod region was attached to the rest of the colony initially as a protectorate, and it was only after strenuous military operations in 1925 that this area was brought firmly under central control (Lewis, 1965, pp. 99–100).

11 Fuller details are given in Lewis, 1965, pp. 116–40.

12 The detailed political history of this period (1950–60) is given in Lewis, 1965, pp. 148–55.

13 An excellent discussion of Somalia's economy prior to unification is given by Karp, 1960.

14 Ten seats were at this stage reserved for the ethnic minorities: four each were allocated to the Italian and Arab communities, and one each to the Indian and Pakistani communities.

15 The League won 83 of the available 90 seats in particularly advantageous circumstances (Lewis, 1965, pp. 159–60).

16 Since the replacement of Adan Abdulle Osman as President in 1967 by Dr Abdirashidi Ali Shirmarke, the former has (following the constitution) become a life-member of the assembly, which now totals 124 members.

17 Dr Abdirashidi Ali Shirmarke, the new premier, had played an important role in the early history of the S.Y.L., and it was merely his academic distinction which gave him the edge over other Darod leaders within S.Y.L. at this time.

18 Fuller details are given in Lewis, 1967a.
19 This party was based on the former Greater Somali League, formed in 1958 as a breakaway radical fragment of the S.Y.L.
20 Thus in August 1966 the S.Y.L. deputies numbered 78. By July 1967 they numbered 105.
21 The trend in favour of English is so strong that even Arabic seems in danger of being eclipsed.
22 Deputies also enjoy considerable legal immunity. No penal proceedings can be taken against a member except with the express consent of the Assembly.
23 A fuller discussion is given in Lewis, 1969a.
24 Mill, 1861, pp. 291–2.
25 So far as I know, the only constitutional change since independence (1960) has been the prohibition of proselytization of religions other than Islam.
26 At the last election (1964) 18 parties fielded 973 candidates for the 123 seats in the Assembly. There were 141 lists of candidates divided among the parties; 21 seats were contested by a single candidate.

REFERENCES

CASTAGNO, H. 1964, 'Somali Republic', in Coleman, J. S. & Rosberg, C. G. (eds.), *Political Parties and National Integration in Tropical Africa*, California University Press, Los Angeles.

DRYSDALE, J. S. 1964, *The Somali Dispute*, Pall Mall Press, London.

HESS, R. L. 1966, *Italian Colonialism in Somalia*, Chicago University Press.

KARP, M. 1960, *The Economics of Trusteeship in Somalia*, Boston University Press.

LEWIS, I. M. 1955, *Peoples of the Horn of Africa*, International African Institute, London.

1961, *A Pastoral Democracy*, Oxford University Press.

1965, *The Modern History of Somaliland*, Weidenfeld & Nicolson.

1967a, 'Integration in the Somali Republic', in Hazlewood, A. (ed.), *African Integration and Disintegration*, O.U.P.

1967b, 'Recent Developments in the Somali Dispute', *African Affairs*, 66.

1967c, 'The Referendum in French Somaliland', *The World Today* (July).

1969a, 'Nationalism, Tribalism and Urbanism in Contemporary Africa', *Proceedings of the East African Academy*.

1969b, 'From Nomadism to Cultivation: the Expansion of Political Solidarity in Southern Somalia', in Douglas, M. & Kaberry, P. (eds), *Man in Africa*, Tavistock.

MILL, J. S. 1861, *Considerations on Representative Government*, Blackwell.

NAMIER, L. B. 1952, *Avenues of History*, Hamish Hamilton.

NOTES ON CONTRIBUTORS

KIRSTEN ALNAES. Doctoral research student of the University of Oslo; formerly research associate of University College, Dar es Salaam. She has carried out field research in western Uganda, 1958–60, 1964, and 1967.

W. J. ARGYLE. Lecturer in Social Anthropology, Queen Mary College, University of London; formerly Research Officer, Rhodes-Livingstone Institute, and Lecturer in Anthropology at Rhodes University and University of Natal. He carried out field research in Northern Rhodesia, 1957–60, and is the author of *The Fon of Dahomey* (1966).

GEORGE BENNETT. Senior Lecturer in Commonwealth History and Fellow of Linacre College, Oxford. He has made numerous visits to East and West Africa to collect material on African history and politics. He is the author (with C. G. Rosberg) of *The Kenyatta Election* (1961), and of *Kenya: a Political History, the Colonial Period* (1963), and of numerous articles in journals and symposia.

EUGENE COTRAN. Lecturer in African Law, School of Oriental and African Studies, University of London; of Lincoln's Inn, Barrister-at-law; formerly Customary Law Commissioner, Kenya, and Member and Secretary of Kenya Commissions on the Laws of Marriage and Divorce and the Laws of Succession. He is author of *Report on Customary Criminal Offences in Kenya*, Part II of *Judicial and Legal Systems in Africa* (ed. A. N. Allott), and *Restatement of African Law*, vols. 1 & 2, and articles in African and legal journals.

R. D. GRILLO. Assistant Lecturer in Social Anthropology, Queen's University, Belfast. He carried out field research in East Africa (mainly in Kampala), 1964–5.

P. H. GULLIVER. Professor of African Anthropology, School of Oriental and African Studies, University of London; formerly Research Sociologist, Government of Tanganyika, and Associate

Professor of Anthropology, African Studies Programme, Boston University. He carried out field research in various parts of East Africa, 1948–58, and has made a number of shorter visits since. He is author of *Survey of the Turkana* (1951), *The Family Herds* (1955), *Labour Migration in a Rural Economy* (1955), *Land Tenure and Social Change among the Nyakyusa* (1958), *Social Control in an African Society* (1963), and edited (with R. F. Gray) *The Family Estate in Africa* (1964), and author of numerous articles in journals and symposia.

J. S. LA FONTAINE. Reader in Anthropology, London School of Economics, University of London; formerly *Chargée de Cours*, Lovanium University, and Lecturer in Social Anthropology, Birkbeck College, University of London. She carried out field research in eastern Uganda, 1953–5, and in Kinshasha, Congo, 1962–3. She is author of *The Gisu of Uganda* (1959), and numerous articles on the Gisu in journals and symposia.

I. M. LEWIS. Reader and tutor in Anthropology, University College, London; formerly Lecturer in African Studies, University College of Rhodesia & Nyasaland, and Lecturer in Social Anthropology. University of Glasgow. He carried out field research in Somalia, 1955–7 and for shorter periods in 1962, 1964, 1966. He is author of *A Pastoral Democracy* (1961), *Marriage and the Family in Northern Somaliland* (1962), *Swahili Poetry* (with B. W. Andrzejewski, 1964), *The Modern History of Somaliland* (1966), and edited *Islam in Tropical Africa* (1966); he has contributed articles to journals and symposia.

T. J. MBOYA. Minister of Economic Planning and Development, Government of Kenya; formerly General Secretary of the Kenya Federation of Labour, and the first African Minister of Labour in Kenya. Author of *Freedom and After* (1963) and numerous articles and speeches concerning labour problems and organization, and economic and political development.

H. F. MORRIS. Reader in African Law, School of Oriental and African Studies, University of London. Formerly in the Colonial Administrative Service, Uganda. He is author of *A History of Ankole* (1964), *The Heroic Recitations of the Bahima of Ankole* (1964), and (with J. S. Read) *Uganda: the Development of its Laws and Constitutions* (1966).

DAVID J. PARKIN. Lecturer in Anthropology with special reference to Africa, School of Oriental and African Studies, University of London. He carried out field research in Kampala, 1962–4, and in Kenya, 1966–7, 1968–9. He is author of *Neighbours and Nationals in an African City Ward* (1969), and several articles.

KATHLEEN M. STAHL. Senior Associate Member of St. Antony's College, Oxford. She has carried out field and library research in African affairs since 1944. She is author of *The Metropolitan Organization of British Colonial Trade* (1951), *British and Soviet Colonial Systems* (1951), *Tanganyika, Sail in the Wilderness* (1961), and *History of the Chagga People of Kilimanjaro* (1964).

MICHAEL TWADDLE. Lecturer in History, Makerere University College (on secondment from School of Oriental and African Studies, London); formerly Research Fellow of the Institute of Commonwealth Studies, University of London. He carried out field research in eastern Uganda, 1962–4, and has published articles on African history.

J. W. TYLER. Research Fellow and Lecturer in the Sociology of Education Overseas, Institute of Education, University of Bristol; formerly Research Fellow of the East African Institute of Social Research, and Education Officer, Uganda. He carried out field research in north-western Tanganyika, 1950–2, and has made a number of visits to East Africa in the last few years in order to collect material on educational matters.

W. H. WHITELEY. Professor of Bantu Languages, School of Oriental and African Studies, University of London; formerly Government Sociologist, Government of Tanganyika, Research Fellow of the East African Institute of Social Research, and Professor of Linguistics at University College, Dar es Salaam. He carried out field research in various parts of East Africa, 1949–58, 1961–2, 1968–9, and has worked on the Coast intermittently during the period 1952–67. He is author of specialist studies of several East African languages, of *Swahili, the Rise of a National Language* (1969), and of many articles on Swahili, linguistic and sociolinguistic topics in journals and symposia.

INDEX

DATE DUE